FOURTH EDITION

Linda Julian . Patricia Kelvin . Scott Leonard
Laurel Black . Cynthia Myers . Edgar V. Roberts

STRATEGIES AND RESOURCES FOR TEACHING WRITING
with the
SIMON &
SCHUSTER
HANDBOOK
for WRITERS

Lynn Quitman Troyka

PRENTICE HALL, *Upper Saddle River, New Jersey 07458*

© 1996 by PRENTICE-HALL, INC.
Simon and Schuster/A Viacom Company
Upper Saddle River, New Jersey 07458

10 9 8 7 6 5 4 3 2 1

ISBN 0-13-455411-6
Printed in the United States of America

CONTENTS

■ PART THREE – HELP FOR WRITING INSTRUCTORS: USING PORTFOLIOS FOR LEARNING AND ASSESSMENT   151

■ PART FOUR – ESL WRITERS IN THE COMPOSITION CLASS   187

■ PART FIVE – READING & WRITING ABOUT LITERATURE: A PRIMER FOR STUDENTS   225

■ PART SIX – WORKPLACE WRITING: TEACHING WRITING SKILLS TO WILLING LEARNERS   281

■ Answer Key to the Simon & Schuster Handbook for Writers, 4/e 319

PART ONE

Strategies for Teaching Writing

Linda Julian
Furman University

PART ONE
CHAPTER ONE

Great Expectations

The scene is a familiar one.

"Why'd ya give me a *D* on this paper? I did everything you told me to. I fixed all the things you marked wrong on my rough draft. I proofread it," the student argues, slouched in a chair across from the teacher's desk, waving the heavily red-marked essay to punctuate these assertions. Suddenly, straightening the torso and looking the teacher squarely in the eye, the student delivers the *coup de grace*: "I thought you liked my writing. You're just like all the rest!"

The look of betrayal, the raised voice, the defeated posture add force to the indictment. The teacher, overcome with a split-second vision of sins of omission and commission, attempts to salvage whatever goodwill is possible, but on a subconscious level the teacher likely admits that that student's statement contains some truth. The bitterest pill to swallow, however, is the hard truth that yet another student has been alienated from the process of learning to write, perhaps irretrievably so.

Many of our students, of course, fortunately have had teachers who made the process of writing exciting, and their interest continues into our courses. Our responsibility to these students is to sustain this excitement and help them refine their skills. Unfortunately, though, we still lose some students who have been scarred by earlier classroom experiences and who are being further alienated by some of our practices, often without our full realization. But we teachers have much more power to combat these negative experiences with writing—and negative attitudes toward writing—than many of us may realize. Engendering a positive attitude about writing can make learning it an intellectual adventure rather than a dead-end road, and this positive attitude can make teaching writing more pleasurable for us teachers as well. The most important lesson we can teach is not the grammar, structure, or tone of writing but a positive attitude towards writing that makes possible a dynamic piece of prose.

This positive attitude informs the *Simon & Schuster Handbook for Writers* by Lynn Quitman Troyka. This supplement, *Strategies and Resources for Teaching Writing*, is meant to aid teachers of writing—both new teachers and experienced teachers—in using Troyka's handbook effectively to suit the needs of their students. I offer practical suggestions for using the text in a variety of ways to accommodate different kinds of academic calendars. Like the Troyka text, this supplement is grounded in the theory that writing is a process that can be enjoyed and taught successfully.

Teaching writing is neither an arcane science nor a hit-or-miss operation but a manageable and stimulating venture that requires careful planning, a somewhat flexible spirit, and intellectual energy. As teachers, we know that learning to write well is the most important need that most students have. At the same time we realize that students today often see writing as an amorphous, vague skill impossible to master, and they often view teachers of writing as arbitrary beings who are impossible to please. Motivated by a need to succeed in college, apathetic students of writing enter into a tug of war with us over the grades we assign their writing, paying little attention to the process itself or the important potential embodied in their work. For them, Composition 101 is more of what they've had—and they don't want it. But Composition 101 doesn't have to be this way for them. We can make it a stimulating, creative, enjoyable course that will teach them skills useful for their entire lives.

We can begin this transformation of attitude by accentuating the positive. In both written and oral comments to the students, we need to emphasize what the students have done well in a given assignment. Certainly, we have a duty to tell them what is ineffective in a paper and what they must do to improve a piece of writing; but if we write only negative comments, we will engender or strengthen negative attitudes towards writing. (See Chapter 5 in this supplement for a discussion of evaluation.) If we communicate to the students our recognition of each student's unique abilities as a writer and our understanding that all writers, no matter how weak or ineffective, can improve, our words will fall on the ears of more willing listeners. If we communicate positive expectations, we will have more positive results.

One important key to success in teaching writing is realizing that we cannot march an entire class in lock step through a syllabus each term. In some other disciplines the nature of the material being taught warrants a more rigid syllabus, but an inflexible syllabus in a composition course is a death knell to growth and excitement. This realization does not mean we should have no syllabus or that we should have a hit-or-miss plan for the term. On the contrary, it means that we must be adept at constantly amending and revising our syllabus to accommodate the various levels of writers we have in a given class. Those teachers who have a syllabus planned by their department must look for ways to tailor it to the needs of the students and to flesh it out with energetic assignments.

Developing this ability to plan the course but not to over-plan it (addressed in more detail in Chapters 2 and 4 of this supplement) is one step in communicating to students our awareness of their uniqueness and the potential that it brings to the classroom. It also communicates to the students that they are partners in the writing class, not objects to be talked at. In fact, we should involve students in planning the class periodically, perhaps one day every couple of weeks. We must allow students to see the possibility that their contributions to the class will result in assignments that grow out of their own work.

And we should involve students in evaluating each other's work and in collaborating on projects that will strengthen the skills of each individual. Recent research has shown the great value of peer evaluation in teaching writing (discussed in more detail in Chapter 6 in this supplement) and the benefits to students of collaborative learning (discussed in the *Collaborative Writing* section of this supplement).

Another important key to success in teaching writing is developing ways to help students see why writing is important. Certainly, we all think that we promote this awareness in our first-day-of-class speeches about the value of the course and in our interaction with these novice writers throughout the term. Often, though, we are miscommunicating. Students quickly dismiss as empty platitudes our most sincere reasons for learning to write— unless we show how those reasons relate directly to their own immediate needs and experiences (see Chapter 2 in this supplement).

We obviously want students to know that well-educated people observe conventions in writing. We can set up discussions and assignments that show students that learning to write is much more than learning rules. We can show them the intellectual energy that writing can produce. We can show them that writing is a means to knowing, that it is a tool for discovering connections between the external world and the internal self.

Discovering these connections is especially difficult for students whose native language is not English or students whose language is nonstandard. We must be sensitive and diligent in helping these students acquire new skills with language. Many composition teachers have had little or no training in teaching English as a second language (TESL) and therefore are particularly frustrated when confronted with students who must struggle to express even basic ideas in Standard Written English. But we *can* help these students overcome their fear and frustration. Our positive attitude and our excitement about writing will go a long way toward dismantling language barriers and setting these students at ease (see Chapters 41–43 in Troyka for help in teaching ESL students).

Another important goal is to help our students become more critical readers of other writers' work. Students become more excited about the writing process as they comprehend the communal nature of writing. We can help these novice writers understand the value of their audience, and we can show them the important contribution they make to society as responsive, critical readers.

One path to this understanding of audience is the use of well-planned and well-supervised peer critiques. Recent research has shown the gains to be made if we increase students' understanding of audience, and it has supported the effectiveness of peer critiquing as one method for showing students the value of the audience.

Helping our students evaluate what they read also makes them better writers. Critical reading, which Troyka emphasizes effectively in Chapter 5 of the handbook, requires students' attention to nuances of structure and ideas in such a way that these readers pay more attention to similar nuances—and their effects—in their own writing. Critical reading stimulates students to develop subtler topics than they likely would otherwise. And, critical reading makes students aware of the power of language.

Teaching writing effectively means emphasizing what students are doing well. It means exciting them about the possibilities—and being excited about them ourselves. As we are helping our students develop more confidence in their abilities, we must have more confidence in our own skills and professionalism. With that professionalism in mind, I hope that this supplement will stimulate some new insight, sense of purpose, and sources for energy and enthusiasm as we teach and our students learn.

SUGGESTED READING

Anson, Chris M., and Hildy Miller. "Journals in Composition: An Update." "A Progress Report from the CCCC Committee on Professional Standards." *College Composition and Communication* 42 (Oct. 1991) 330–44.

Berlin, James. *Writing Instruction in American Colleges 1900–1985.* Carbondale, IL: Southern Illinois University Press, 1987.

Booth, Wayne C., and Marshall W. Gregory. *The Harper and Row Rhetoric: Writing as Thinking; Thinking as Writing.* New York: Harper and Row, 1987.

Bowden, Darsie. "The Limits of Containment: Text-as-Container in Composition Studies." *College Composition and Communication* 44 (Oct. 1993): 364–79.

Bridges, Charles W., ed. *Training the New Teacher of College Composition.* Urbana, IL: National Council of Teachers of English, 1986.

Bullock, Richard, and John Trimbur, eds. *The Politics of Writing Instruction: Postsecondary.* Portsmouth, NH: Boynton/Cook, 1991.

Catach, Nina. "New Linguistic Approaches to a Theory of Writing." *Georgetown University Roundtable on Languages and Linguistics* (1986): 161–74.

Elbow, Peter. "Reflections on Academic Discourse: How It Relates to Freshmen and Colleagues." *College English* 53 (Feb. 1991): 135–55.

———. "The War Between Reading and Writing—And How to End It." *Rhetoric Review* 12, no. 1 (Fall 1993): 5–24.

Flower, Linda. "The Construction of Purpose in Writing and Reading." *College English* 50 (Sept. 1988): 528–50.

France, Alan A. "Assigning Places: The Function of Introductory Composition as a Cultural Discourse." *College English* 55, no. 6 (Oct. 1993): 593–609.

Gambell, T. J. "Education Professors' Perceptions of and Attitudes Toward Student Writing." *Canadian Journal of Education* 12 (Fall l987): 495–510.

Hairston, Maxine. "Some Speculations About the Future of Writing Programs." *Writing Program Administration* 11, no. 3 (Spring 1988): 9–16.

———. "Diversity, Ideology, and Teaching Writing." *College Composition and Communication* 43, no. 2 (May 1992): 179–93.

Hillocks, George. *Research on Written Composition: New Directions for Teaching.* Urbana, Ill.: National Council of Teachers of English, 1986.

Hirsch, E. D. *The Philosophy of Composition.* Chicago: University of Chicago Press, 1977.

Horner, Bruce. "Resisting Traditions in Composing Composition." *Journal of Advanced Composition.* 14, no. 2 (Fall 1994): 495–519.

Horner, Winifred. *Historical Rhetoric: An Annotated Bibliography of Selected Sources in English.* Boston: Hall, 1982.

Howatt, A.P.R. *A History of English Language Teaching.* Oxford: Oxford University Press, 1984.

Kennedy, George. *Classical Rhetoric and Its Christian and Secular Tradition from Ancient to Modern Times.* Chapel Hill: University of North Carolina Press, 1980.

Kinneavy, James L. *A Theory of Discourse.* 1971. Reprint. New York: Norton, 1980.

Kirsch, Gesa, and Patricia A. Sullivan, eds. *Methods and Methodology in Composition Research.* Carbondale, IL: Southern Illinois University Press, 1992.

Laurence, Patricia. "The Vanishing Site of Mina Shaughnessy's 'Error and Expectations.'" *Journal of Basic Writing* 12, no. 2 (Fall 1993): 18–28.

Lawton, David L. "Composition Courses for College Freshmen Are Ineffective; They Should Be Abolished." *Chronicle of Higher Education* 35 (21 Sept. 1988): 332–34.

Lindemann, Erika. *A Rhetoric for Writing Teachers.* 3rd. ed. New York: Oxford University Press, 1995.

McClelland, Ben, and Timothy R. Donovan. *Research and Scholarship in Composition.* New York: Modern Language Association, 1985.

Miller, Richard E. "Composing English Studies: Towards a Social History of the Discipline." *College Composition and Communication* 45, no. 2 (May 1994): 164–79.

Moore, Sandy, and Michael Kleine. "Toward an Ethics of Teaching Writing in a Hazardous Context—The Unversity." *Journal of Advanced Composition* 12, no. 2 (Fall 1992): 383–94.

Newkirk, Thomas, ed. *Nuts and Bolts: A Practical Guide to Teaching College Composition.* Portsmouth, NH: Boynton/Cook, 1993.

Norton, L. S. "Essay Writing: What Really Counts?" *Higher Education* 20 (Dec. 1990): 411–42.

Nystrand, Martin, et al. "Where Did Composition Studies Come From? An Intellectual History." *Written Communication* 10, no. 3 (July 1993): 267–333.

Odell, Lee, ed. *Theory and Practice in the Teaching of Writing: Rethinking the Discipline.* Carbondale: Southern Illinois Press, 1993.

Parker, Robert P. "Theories of Writing Instruction: Having Them, Using Them, Changing Them." *English Education* 20 (Feb. 1988): 18–40.

Phillips, Donna Burns, et al. "'College Composition and Communication': Chronicaling a Discipline's Genesis." *College Composition and Communication* 44, no. 4 (Dec. 1993): 443–65.

Ritchie, J. S. "Beginning Writers: Diverse Voices and Individual Identity." *College Composition and Communication* 40 (May 1989): 152–74.

Runciman, Lex. "Fun?" *College English* 53 (Feb. 1991): 156–63.

Saks, A. L., and Richard L. Larson. "Annotated Bibliography of Research in the Teaching of English." *Research in the Teaching of English* 28, no. 2 (May 1994): 208–23.

Schultz, Lucille M. "Elaborating on Our History: A Look at Mid-19th Century First Books of Composition." *College Composition and Communication* 45, no. 1 (Feb. 1994): 10–30.

Sommers, Nancy I. "The Need for Theory in Composition Research." *College Composition and Communication* 30 (Feb. 1979): 46–49.

Spellmeyer, K. "A Common Ground: the Essay in the Academy." *College English* 51 (March 1989): 262–76.

"Statement of Principles and Standards for the Postsecondary Teaching of Writing." *College Composition and Communication* 40 (Oct. 1989): 329–36.

Tate, Gary, and Edward P. J. Corbett, eds. *The Writing Teacher's Sourcebook*. 3rd. ed. New York: Oxford University Press, 1994.

"Teaching Writing [Symposium]." *College Teach* 39 (Spring 1991): 44–64.

Tobin, L. "Reading Students, Reading Ourselves: Revising The Teacher's Role in the Writing Class." *College English* 53 (March 91): 333–48.

Troyka, Lynn Quitman, with Gerber, Lloyd-Jones, et al. *A Checklist and Guide for Reviewing Departments of English*. New York: Modern Language Association and Associated Departments of English, 1985.

———. "Perspectives on Legacies and Literacy in the 1980s." *College Composition and Communication* 33 (Oct. 1982): 252–62. Reprinted in *Sourcebook for Basic Writing Teachers*, edited by Theresa Enos. New York: Random House, 1987.

Wiener, Harvey S. *The Writing Room: A Resource Book for Teachers of English*. New York: Oxford University Press, 1981.

PART ONE
CHAPTER TWO

The Impossible and The Possible: Realistic Goals for Courses in Writing

Well before the bell signals the first class meeting, teachers of writing must have come to terms with goals which are realistic for a college writing course. In other words, we must understand what is possible given the constraints of time and the backgrounds and attitudes of our students. Many teachers get so caught up in trying to teach the impossible that frustration clouds their vision of the possible.

The best confidence builder—and one too often neglected by most of us—is a long, hard look at what is possible during a term. Although the following list of goals is not comprehensive, most teachers would agree that these goals are realizable for most students in a single course in composition.

1. We can help students understand that they can learn to write. Building a positive attitude is essential. We can build the kind of confidence that will ensure an interest in writing long after the students have left our classes.

2. We can help students become aware of the role of writing in their lives. It is both possible and essential to show students that even in this age so often dominated by images, writing plays a major part in everything they do—from checking the weather in the newspaper to looking at the menu in a fast-food restaurant to playing a computer video game. We can help them see the need for learning to write.

3. We can help students realize that writing is a tool for learning about themselves and the world. We can help students discover that a paper is taking a direction they have not planned on. From that point, we can show them that this departure from their expectation is teaching them what they are really trying to say. We can show students that brainstorming a topic and writing a draft of a paper can give rise to questions that lead them to new ideas and connections. (See Troyka, *The Simon & Schuster Handbook for Writers*, Chapter 2, hereafter referred to as *Troyka*.)

4. We can help students realize that writing is a process. Many students think that writers are born being able to write and that a piece of writing springs, fully finished, from the brain of a "real" writer. We can certainly show students that all writing involves stages and that each stage can be learned. (See Troyka, Chapters 2 and 3.)

5. We can help students understand that a piece of writing is never finished. As a part of learning the stages that make up the process of writing, students can learn that writers finally let go of a piece of writing when they have revised it enough to satisfy the demands of the situation but that they rarely think they have written something that is perfect and defies improvement. (See Troyka, Chapter 3, Section c.)

6. We can help our students understand the importance of structure in writing. We can show students the relative merits of various kinds of sentences, the effectiveness of various kinds of paragraph structure, and the effectiveness of structure in an essay. Students may not be able to apply all of the principles of structure that we show them, but making them aware of structure is important and possible. (See Troyka, Chapter 1, Sections b and d, Chapter 4, and Parts III and IV.)

7. We can help our students understand what a paragraph is and how to write a coherent one. We can acquaint students with various methods for developing paragraphs that suit the audience and topic with which they are working. Chapter 4 of the Troyka handbook explains many methods of paragraph development and gives interesting, easy-to-grasp examples of each. It also provides a clear explanation of how to make paragraphs coherent and unified. By teaching students how to write effective paragraphs, we can help ensure the sturdiness of the groundwork on which they will eventually build coherent, effective essays.

8. We can help students understand the importance of making clear connections between ideas. It is possible to teach students to draw logical conclusions, to make their thoughts coherent, to support their generalizations with evidence. We can teach them how to make connections among ideas in their own writing and to look for them in the writing of others. (See Troyka, Chapter 4, Sections d and e, and Chapter 5, Sections a–d.)

9. We can help students understand the nature and the importance of the audience. Too many students think that English papers are written only for the English teacher. In making this assumption, they do not realize that many choices they make as writers depend on defining the audience for a given piece of work. We can help students realize that as writers they belong to a community of readers and writers. In

short, we can teach students that they do not write in a vacuum. (See Troyka, Chapter 1.)

10. We can help students understand that good grammar is not the same thing as effective writing. Although good grammar helps make writing clear and more acceptable to some audiences, it is a far different thing from the process of writing. We can, and must, clarify this important point for students. Part II of Troyka's handbook clearly presents basic grammar, but it does so in a positive way that should minimize students' feelings of inadequacy with grammar.

11. We can help our students understand that inflated diction does not equal sophisticated thinking. In the same way that many students equate good grammar with "good" writing, many students equate big words with elevated style and thought. We must show students that the most effective writing is that which puts clear, simple language together in a coherent and interesting way. (See Troyka, Chapters 20 and 21.)

12. We can help our students see the importance of revision. We can use peer critiquing and our own comments to help students see that papers grow slowly through definite stages, each of which requires full development, with revision being perhaps the most important. We can show them that revision is more than patching up problems with usage and mending a few awkward sentences, and instead that it involves several stages of reconceiving the purpose of the paper and reviewing its effect on the audience. (See Troyka, Chapter 3, Section c.)

13. We can help students understand what an essay is. Experienced teachers know that even the brightest students have read few essays and that most students have only vague notions of what an essay really is. Students frequently call them "stories," and they think that essays, invented by English teachers, are found only in school. Helping students define the term *essay* is important, as is showing them where they can find good essays being published today.

14. We can help our students understand how to use a dictionary. Students think that all dictionaries are created equal, and they think of a dictionary as a place to look up a word to check spelling or meaning. We need to acquaint them with the aids for using the dictionary, given in each one, and we need to show them the value of the prefatory matter in the dictionary. We can help them see the value of both desk dictionaries and unabridged dictionaries. (See Troyka, Chapter 20.)

15. We can help students learn to use a handbook to find answers to questions they have about writing. Too often many of us assume that

because we know what's in a handbook and how to find it, students will as well. We should take some time to show students how to use the book we have chosen. To a great extent, knowledge is knowing where to find out what one needs to know. Encouraging students to read Troyka's "Preface to Students" likely will help students feel that they are part of the book and that Troyka has considered their needs. The easy-to-find information inside the back cover, "How to Use Your Handbook," will also help students become independent learners.

16. We can help students understand that they have a responsibility to be critical readers. Most students think that if something is published, it must be important or "good." We can help them understand how to recognize the flaws in scholarship and logic tht make much published work inferior. (See Troyka, Chapter 5.)

17. We can help students see that they live in a community of readers and writers, a community which can grow in mutual understanding and respect only through careful, sensitive reading and writing that will promote dialogue between groups of different genders, ethnic origins, ages, socio-economic class, and geographic areas.

18. We can, and must, help students realize that writing is neither "good" nor "bad." Too often our students come to us having been labeled by themselves or by others as "good" writers or "bad" writers; but we can help them see that a better way of judging writing is to consider the effectiveness of a piece of writing in its context.

Taking stock of what we can do in a single course contributes significantly to our own sense of confidence in our ability to teach a stimulating class. My own experience has shown me clearly that students respond with more assurance and interest when they sense my confidence in achieving these goals.

SUGGESTED READING

Anderson, Chris. "Teaching Students What Not to Say: Iser, Didion, and the Rhetoric of Gaps." *Journal of Advanced Composition* 7, no. 1 (1987): 10–22.

Baumlin, James S., and Tita French Baumlin. "Bettetrism, Cultural Literacy, and the Dialectic of Critical Response." *Freshman English News* 16, no. 2 (Fall 1987): 2–8.

Cheney, Fred. "If It Isn't a Dialog, It Isn't Communication." *Journal of Teaching Writing* 7, no. 1 (Summer 1988): 51–55.

Devine, T. G. "Caveat Emptor: The Writing Process Approach to College Writing." *Journal of Developmental Education* 11 (Fall 1990): 2–4.

Elbow, Peter. *Writing with Power: Techniques for Mastering the Writing Process.* New York: Oxford University Press, 1981.

Enos, Richard Lee, and Elizabeth Odoroff. "The Orality of the 'Paragraph' in Greek Rhetoric." *Pre-Text* 6, no. 1 (Spring 1985): 51–65.

Finegan, Edward. *Attitudes Toward English Usage: The History of a War of Words.* New York: Teachers College, 1980.

Laib, N. K. "Good Writing Cannot Be Taught Effectively as an Empty Collection of Rules." *Chronicle of Higher Education* 35 (July 5, 1989) A36.

Madigan, Chris. "Applying Donald Murray's 'Responsive Teaching.'" *College Composition and Communication* 39, no. 1 (Feb. 1988): 74–77.

Ong, Walter J. "Writing is a Technology that Restructures Thought." In *The Written Word: Literary in Translation*, edited by Gerd Baumann. New York: Oxford University Press, 1986. 23–50.

Rose, Mike. "Rigid Rules, Inflexible Plans, and the Stifling of Language: A Cognitivist Analysis of Writer's Block." *College Composition and Communication* 31 (Dec. 1980): 389–401.

Schwartz, Helen J. "Writing with the Carbon Copy Audience in Mind." *College Composition and Communication* 39, no. 1 (Feb. 1988): 63–65.

Troyka, Lynn Quitman. "Closeness to Text: A Delineation of Reading Processes as They Affect Composing." in *Relating Writing and Reading in the College Years*, edited by Thomas Newkirk. Boynton/Cook, 1986.

———. "The Writer as Conscious Reader." In *Sourcebook for Basic Writing Teachers*. Edited by Theresa Enos. New York: Random House, 1987.

Wall, Susan V. "The Languages of the Text: What Even Good Students Need to Know about ReWriting." *Journal of Advanced Composition* 7, no. 1 (1987): 31–40.

Wallace, D. L., and J. R. Hayes. "Redefining Revision for Freshmen." *Research in the Teaching of English* 25 (Feb. 1991): 54–66.

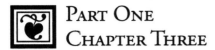

PART ONE
CHAPTER THREE

Using a Handbook: Why and How

Tyrant or tool, or something in between—one of these is the role that a handbook of grammar and usage generally plays in a course in writing. To play a vital role in a student's experience of learning to write and a teacher's experience in teaching writing effectively, the best role for a handbook like the *Simon & Schuster Handbook for Writers* is that of tool.

Many of us have seen the handbook as tyrant. Either as students, observers of other composition teachers, or new teachers of writing, we have seen the handbook become the focus of the course. In this scenario bad grades are often used to browbeat students into virtually memorizing the handbook. The teacher equates rules with writing. Instead of concentrating on the positive features of a piece of writing, the teacher points out all the rules it has violated. Revision becomes a belabored effort to "fix" the mistakes in the paper. The product of a handbook-as-tyrant class is frustrated students who come to fear using the handbook because they think that they can never fix their writing to reflect its perfect standards. Of course, a byproduct is a frustrated teacher who works hard and cannot see why the students are not improving.

In the ideal scenario, students view the handbook as a means to effective writing. They look upon it as a tool in the same way they consider a dictionary, a notebook, or a computer disk a tool.

But, we all know that it is totally unrealistic simply to plunk copies of the handbook down on students' desks and instruct the students to use the handbooks as tools. Few students know how to use a handbook, and, given their previous experience with writing classes and handbooks, many of them do not even want to try.

Teachers must help students figure out the apparatus of the handbook to make using it second nature, and, equally important, they must help students see that being able to use the handbook well as independent learners can improve both their writing skills and their sense of self-confidence as students. Initially, at least, students probably learn the together the apparatus and the confidence to work with the book on their own.

In addition to helping make students familiar with the handbook—and comfortable and confident using it—teachers are faced with important decisions about how large a role the handbook should play in the syllabus for the course. They also must consider ways in which they will use the handbook in marking students' papers.

The Handbook as Text

Although the handbook rarely works well as a central text for a course in writing, many teachers are successful in assigning parts of it for class discussion or as the basis for written assignments. We should be open to possibilities for using it that require us to deviate from the order of information in the text; that is, we should not be afraid to mix and mingle parts of the handbook to suit our students' interests and needs.

Depending on the focus of the individual teacher's class, several sections of the *Simon & Schuster Handbook* may be used separately or together as useful information for class discussion or writing assignments. Since Chapter 4 of this supplement gives sample syllabi which include sections of the handbook, the following are only general suggestions.

1. Choose to teach a unit on language, grounding it in Section Five of the handbook, "Using Effective Words." Since this section is not made up of "rules," it offers the teacher a good beginning point for creating a positive interest in writing rather than a negative one.

Most students are keenly interested in improving their vocabularies, though often for the misguided notion that big words equal important ideas. They also know very little about dictionaries and etymology. The first chapter of the section, Chapter 20, "Understanding the Meaning of Words," can provoke some substantial discussion, especially when coupled with a look at several kinds of dictionaries, including the *Oxford English Dictionary* (*OED*). This chapter works well alone or with Chapter 21, "Understanding the Effect of Words." Students often have lively discussions on such topics as sexist language, jargon, slang, doublespeak, and cliches. These discussions can be effective springboards into some energetic writing about language.

2. Choose to teach a unit on research and assign parts of Section Seven, "Writing Research," perhaps Chapter 32 ("The Process of Writing Research"), Chapter 34 ("Case Study of a Student Writing Research"), Chapter 36 ("Comparing the Different Disciplines"), Chapter 37 ("Writing about Literature"), and Chapter 38 ("Writing in the Social Sciences and Natural Sciences"). In using these chapters, emphasize that you want

the students to get an overview of the range of audiences for which research is done and the common methods respected in the many communities that rely on research. Many students are unaware of how much research is done in businesses and service industries,and some good class discussions can explore the real-life uses of reseach. We want to teach them that research is not something that only chemists and English teachers do.

Class discussions which grow out of a reading assignment from this section of the handbook should focus on the process of research and the process of writing information found in research. Discussions can make clear to students that knowing how to do research and write about their findings is much more than knowing the proper forms of documentation to use in research papers. This kind of assignment can combat the negative experiences that many students have had with term papers, especially if they begin to see that research is an essential part of most kinds of careers and fields.

In addition, this unit offers a great opportunity to help students understand the role of computers and electronic data bases in current research. Although some students will be experienced with the "information highway," even they will enjoy discussing the strengths and weaknesses of electronic searches. Less computer-literate students need to be introduced to the possibilities of electronic research. All students need help with learning to document material from electronic sources, and they need to learn what constitutes plagiarism in the world of electronic sources. Chapters 32 and 33 of the handbook offer such help. (For help with integrating computers into your teaching, see the Computer and Writing Supplement in the *Prentice Hall Resources for Composition* package.)

3. Choose to teach a unit on argument, basing it on Chapter 5, "Thinking and Reading Critically." Many students believe that anything in print is useful and true, and they will respond with interest to this informative section which shows why critical reading is important and how they can learn to read critically. Most of them have had little or no exposure to logic, and they will find the discussions of evaluation and reasoning informative and stimulating. The new edition of Troyka's handbook features a section in Chapter 6 which includes Steven Toulmin's ideas about argument.

This chapter can be a useful basis for assignments, both oral and written, which ask students to evaluate the arguments in books, movies, editorials, or advertisements. Once students learn about inadequate evidence and about inductive and deductive reasoning, they enjoy scrutinizing ads or letters to the editor for flaws in reasoning.

4. Choose to teach a unit on the paragraph, for which you assign Chapter 4, "Writing Paragraphs." Many teachers like to begin composition courses by having students learn to write well-unified, coherent paragraphs before they tackle a whole essay. Others like to do a unit on developing paragraphs after they have discussed the essay as a whole.

In either case students can usually benefit from discussing varieties of methods for developing paragraphs. They will particularly enjoy the information in this section if they to locate samples of paragraph development and critique the paragraphs of classmates.

5. Choose to teach a section on revision and assign Chapter 3, "Drafting and Revising." Many teachers prefer to teach revision as the third major step in the process of writing, but others find that pulling revision out of the chronology and emphasizing it help students understand that revisions are a major element of producing an effective piece of writing and that they are far more than patchwork repairs to grammar and spelling.

6. Choose to teach a unit on planning a piece of writing and assign Chapter 2, "Planning and Shaping." This unit should bring about some lively discussion, especially if you illustrate the chapter's points by having students work in class in groups to generate ideas and shape them into manageable topics for papers or paragraphs.

Many students complain that they cannot think of anything to write about, or they turn in topics that are worn out or too large for even a multivolume work. These students can benefit from reading this section of the text, but they will benefit much more if they are assigned activities that reinforce the skills introduced in the chapter. Unless students actually practice these skills, the information does not really register.

7. Choose to do a unit on effective sentences and assign Section Four. Especially fun for students are discoveries they make about wordiness (Chapter 16), coordination and subordination (Chapter 17), and variety (Chapter 19).

Even students who are improving their skills at the slowest rate take pleasure in crafting effective sentences, and the brighter students enjoy working with the possible variations of form for a single sentence.

8. Choose to teach a unit on the importance of audience and assign Chapter 1, "Purposes and Audiences." Many teachers like to begin writing courses by introducing students to the concept of audience, but oth-

ers prefer to introduce this idea after students have begun to work on paragraphs, research, or even whole essays.

Nevertheless, audience and purpose are two of the most important concepts that beginning writers need to know about, and most students do not. This chapter of the text presents information that is stimulating to students because it is largely new and nonthreatening in terms of "rules." They generally enjoy class discussions of alterations one would need to make in a piece of writing for a change in audience.

9. Choose to help students improve their performance when they must write under the pressure of exams or in note-taking. Using Chapter 40 ("Writing Under Pressure"), you can help students not only improve their success in these situations, but in the process you can also help them learn writing skills such as organization and conciseness that may be unusually appealing in a context which offers immediate practical rewards.

10. Choose to help students improve their writing skills by teaching a unit on Business Writing, the topic of Chapter 39 in the handbook. Most students are eager to learn about employment letters and resumes, and most also enjoy writing other kinds of letters and proposals. Such a unit allows us to help them see the importance of organization, precision with diction, grammar, and spelling, a clear view of purpose and audience, and attention to conventions of address and format.

In fact, business letters work better than many kinds of assignments to help students see the importance of careful planning of their message as well as careful revision and proofreading. We can help them see that personal pride in their work can be communicated in letters and other business documents. Students enjoy writing letters of complaint about real problems they have experienced with products or services, and they enjoy responding to one another's complaints. You might choose to have them write to local companies requesting information useful for research projects or samples of business documents the company routinely processes. Whatever the assignment, students usually take the business writing tasks more seriously than other writing requirements because they see an immediate value for this knowledge. For this reason, many teachers like to do some business writing early in the term to help motivate students to write and to make connections between business writing and extremely important concepts like audience and purpose, which should figure prominently in later writing assignments.

In a class, all of these sections of the handbook work well *as* text. They are not concerned with right and wrong usage and are thus nonthreatening to students. Most of these sections contain concepts which the students are only marginally knowledgeable about, if at all, and the information generally stimulates them to have a more positive attitude toward the whole process of writing.

The Handbook as an Aid In Marking Papers

Many teachers like to use a handbook as an aid in marking papers. The numbers listed inside the front cover or the symbols given at the back of the book make it easy for a teacher to indicate in an abbreviated way both what the problem is and where in the text the student can find an explanation and examples to help in the revision. Certainly the ease with which these numbers and symbols can be used makes them an attractive feature to busy teachers. For example, see the teacher's comments on Dawn Seaford's second draft in Chapter 3 of the handbook. But numbers and symbols are best used in conjunction with some written comments by the teacher. Such comments help remind the student that a human being has read the paper and is interested in it. (See Chapter 5 of this supplement, on Evaluation.)

The following paragraphs from students' essays show how a teacher can use these symbols and numbers along with written comments to help students understand how to revise their work and to help them feel that they can, in fact, continue to improve.

Studying does not take place with our group of friends. Late at night everyone
             20b

becomes tired and begin to act silly. We want to know what happened throughout
             11g

the day. Questions and laughter gorge the air. Kevin and Jeffrey bombard Natalie
             20b

and I with pillows. Each time I finally reach a state of concentration outside noise
     9b   24b

shatters the silence I find in my mind. The many distractions of a relaxed envi-

ronment force Natalie and I back to our room. Attempts to complete homework in
             9b

the boy's friendly, noisy and busy room always fail.
    27a3   24c

—Holly Burnette

Holly,
    You're off to a good start here, but can you flesh out the paragraph with more details? You'll also want to revise the mechanical problems I've marked.

Whether they choose Topps, Fleer, Donruss, or Upper Deck, millions of Americans
1b   10e
delight in the collection of baseball cards. For 75 cents, you can buy a pack of ten

cards, and if the brand is Topps a piece of gum will accompany the cards. Some col-
not quite clear
lectors strive to obtain a certain team, while others attempt to gain as many
awkward phrasing
cards as possible. Whatever the quantity, the idea of the trading card still exists,

as the collector's favorite pastime may be trading cards with a friend or local deal-
see 21b   see 16c
er. The baseball card collector can be a boy in the seventh grade or possibly a so-

phisticated business executive. Card collection is not restricted to males, as girls

can easily be found with their Barbie and baseball cards. Clearly this American

tradition truly entertains a wide variety. of?

Great topic, Steve.   —Steve Weathers
Try to make the sentences more specific and clearer.

If we have given our students a preliminary introduction to the
handbook during the first few days of class, they have little trouble using
the symbols and numbers marked by the teacher to find the explanation they need.

Often, in addition to marking symbols or numbers or both, teachers
indicate exercises that they want the student to do to strengthen particular skills. Sometimes they have students write a revision as well as certain
exercises before they meet with students about the paper. Of course writing exercises can be simply busywork unless the teacher carefully moni-
tors the students' use of them and encourages the students to see that the
exercises are not ends in themselves but means to strenghtening the revision. And having students work on a revision and exercises can help students become more independent learners.

The Handbook as a Tool For Students

Perhaps the most important function of a handbook is as a tool for
the students to use independently. But before we can expect them to use
it, or even to want to, we must show them how to make the handbook
work for them. One good way is to take two or three class meetings at the
beginning of the term to acquaint students with the handbook's features
and to give them an overview of its contents.

A simple but effective beginning, especially for weaker students, is to have them read the "To the Student" part of the Preface and write answers to the following questions (or similar ones):

1. What will Troyka discuss in this book?
2. How many chapters are in this book?
3. What three ways can you look something up in this book?
4. What appears on the inside back cover?
5. What does the degree symbol (°) mean when it appears after a term in the book?

Even though the students write out the answers, you will usually need to have them discuss their findings and do some exercises on locating material to ensure that everyone in the class has absorbed the information in the Preface. For all levels of students, discussion of the handbook seems to work better than individual written responses since students are capable of mechanically writing information without understanding or processing it.

In-class group exploration of the handbook can stimulate learners of all levels, and it can be a good ice-breaker to help students get to know one another during the first few class meetings. You may wish to have each group respond to more detailed versions of the questions above, perhaps giving a couple of examples to support each answer. In addition you may wish to have students do exercises that show them how to locate kinds of information in the handbook. These kinds of exercises not only teach students to find their way around in the book, but, more importantly, they build the students' confidence in their own ability to use it.

In using these kinds of exercises, you should emphasize, however, that the point is not the answer itself but the process of learning how to use the handbook. Following are some sample exercises that you may find useful models for your own versions.

1. Suppose you want to find out when to use *myself* and when to use *me*. Where could you learn the difference?

Most students would probably begin with the index to solve this problem since few of them would know that the *-self* forms are reflexive or intensive pronouns. When they found the entry in the index, they would notice that it was boldfaced and not followed by a page number. This discovery would send them to the directions for using the index, where they would learn that boldfaced terms are included in the Glossary of Usage. Looking up *myself* there, the students would find the degree symbol after *reflexive pronoun* and would go to the entry for it in the Glossary of Grammatical and Selected Composition Terms. There the students would find a both a brief definition of the term and a reference to Section 9h of the handbook, where the *-self* forms are discussed in detail. Those who did know that these terms are pronouns could quickly find the reference to Section 9h by looking in the inside front cover under Case of Nouns and Pronouns, where the last entry is "*-self* pronouns."

2. Suppose you are confused about the placement of quotation marks with commas. Where would you find some help?

If the students first looked up *commas* in the index, they would find an entry "with quotations," which would direct them to Section 24g. There they would find examples that would illustrate the placement of the two marks.

If they first looked up *quotation marks* in the index, they would be directed to Chapter 28, where section e discusses the conventions of using quotation marks with other punctuation.

If they first looked at the inside front cover of the text, they would find "Other Punctuation" as subdivision e of Chapter 28, and they could use the tabs to find this section. Similarly, if the students first looked at the back cover, the symbol for *quotation marks error* is followed by a reference to Chapter 28.

3. Where can you find out how to revise your essay to rid it of sexist language?

If the students looked up *sexist language* or *nonsexist language* in the index, they would be directed to two sections, 11n–2 and 21b. Looking up Section 11n–2, students find a shaded box labeled *How to Avoid Using Only the Masculine Pronoun to Refer to Males and Females Together*. If they look up Section 21b, they would find a more detailed shaded box, *How to Avoid Sexist Language*.

Although most students are not sophisticated enough to look under *pronoun* in either the index or front cover of the text, many could find *nonsexist language* by looking under Effect of Words in the front cover. The abbreviation *sxt* in the correction chart also refers students to Section 21b.

4. Your teacher has indicated that you have trouble making transitions both within your paragraphs and between paragraphs. Where can you learn how to make smooth transitions?

If students looked up the word *transition* in the index, they would find both a reference to Section 4b and a degree symbol directing them to the Glossary of Grammatical Terms. Looking in the Glossary, they would find further references to the terms *transitional expressions, pronouns,* and *parallelism.* If they looking these terms up in the glossary, they would find brief explanations of their function as transitional devices, and they would find references to Section 4b, which illustrates how to use transitions both within and between paragraphs.

5. Where would you find out how to cite a multivolume work internally in your essay and how to list it in your bibliography?

A look in the index under *multivolume work* would direct students to the section on parenthetical-references style (under bibliographic citations), Section 33b, with specific page numbers for multivolume works. If the students turned to those pages in that section, they will find an entry for Multivolume Work—MLA. The index also directs them to Section 33d (to specific page numbers) where students can see an example of an entry in a bibliography.

If the students looked up *citation* in the index, they would be told to see *documentation.* Looking at the entry for *documentation,* they would find a subheading for *parenthetical references,* followed by a reference to Section 33b. In this section students could find both an explanation of how to cite works parenthetically and some examples.

Students who tried to find the answer to the question first by using the inside front cover of the text would find references to two potentially helpful sections under Documenting Sources: Parenthetical References, Section 33b, and MLA Forms & APA Forms, Section 33d.

Here are other sample questions for this kind of exercise:

1. Where can you find out how to omit information from a quotation or to add explanatory words to it?

2. Your teacher has indicated that you frequently write dangling modifiers. Where can you find an explanation of this problem and some examples of ways to correct dangling modifiers?

3. You are writing a term paper which often quotes lines of poetry. Where can you find guidelines for conventions of quoting lines of poetry?

4. Your teacher has said that your writing is wordy. You don't quite understand the term *wordy,* and you want a further explanation of this concept and some suggestions for improvement. Where can you find them?

5. Your teacher has commented on your paper that your style is choppy and monotonous because you use too many short, simple sentences. The teacher has said that you need to subordinate more. Where can you find out what *subordination* means and how to put it into practice?

Such exercises will go a long way towards alleviating the fear and feeling of helplessness that handbooks often inspire in inexperienced writers and will help the students feel more confident that they can find in it what they need to know. After they use the handbook for a couple of weeks, most students will begin to regard it as a tool and an important reference work that they will want to keep for writing beyond the English classroom.

SUGGESTED READING

Boyd, Richard. "Mechanical Correctness and Ritual in the Late Nineteenth-Century Composition Classroom." *Rhetoric Review* 11, no. 2 (Spring 1993): 436–55.

Glasser, Marc. "Grammar and the Teaching of Writing: Limits and Possibilities." *Journal of Technical Writing and Communication* 22, no. 4 (Winter 1993): 23–32.

Reynolds, Patricia R. "Evaluating ESL and College Composition Texts for Teaching the Argumentative Rhetorical Form." *Journal of Reading* 36, no. 6 (March 1993): 474–80.

Shuman, R. Baird. "Grammar for Writers: How Much Is Enough?" *The Place of Grammar in Writing Instruction: Past, Present, Future*. Ed. Susan Hunter and Ray Wallace. Portsmouth, NH: Boynton/Cook, 1995.

Whichard, Nancy Wingardner, et al. "Life in the Margin: The Hidden Agenda in Commenting on Student Writing." *Journal of Teaching Writing* 11, no. 1 (Spring–Summer 1992): 51–64.

Williams, James D. *Preparing to Teach Writing*. Belmont, CA: Wadsworth, 1988.

——. "Rule-Governed Approaches to Language and Composition." *Written Communication* 10 (October 1993): 542–68.

PART ONE
CHAPTER FOUR

The Course Syllabus: Some Models

The term **syllabus** is our own jargon for the plan or outline of the purpose, goals, and form of our course. The syllabus is meant to be a tool for teachers and students—a guide, not a remonstrance constantly reminding us that "at my back I always hear / Time's winged chariot hurrying near." The term conjures up images of shackles for some teachers and steamrollers for others. But it's a safe bet that teachers who view a syllabus in these negative ways have been victims rather than its masters. A syllabus, an essential anchor for our teaching, is relatively easy to prepare and use if we approach its construction with some guidelines and some enthusiasm.

Twenty years ago handing out a syllabus on the first day of class was the exception, not the rule. Teachers were more likely to write the names of the texts on the blackboard and make an assignment orally for the next class. Those teachers who did hand out a syllabus usually gave their students a much more succinct statement of the policies of the class than what we have come to view today as a typical syllabus.

Today the syllabus comes in various forms, but it is generally more detailed than it was even a decade ago. One form is the departmental syllabus, often devised by a committee in those departments which teach numerous sections of basic courses. But even these fairly rigid guidelines need fleshing out, and teachers must do so, on paper, before the term begins, modifying as necessary throughout the term.

These changes in the nature of the syllabus and the frequency of its use have come about for several major reasons. Many department chairs and deans have urged faculty to give their students fairly detailed syllabi because having course policies and assignments in writing helps prevent misunderstandings which, in extreme cases, can result in lawsuits. Spelling out attendance policies, grading policies, the goals of the course, and the skills required of students earning credit for the course makes a kind of contract between teachers and students.

Also, in this age of accountability, students like to know what will be expected of them and that the requirements are not going to be changed drastically and arbitrarily (or, as they perceive it, whimsically) in the middle of the term. A syllabus—even a demanding one—is a security blanket of sorts.

From the teachers' point of view, however, the real advantage of having a syllabus is that it gives a game plan for the term. To be effective, such a game plan, affords teachers much leeway in strategy, but at the same time it clarifies for teachers the material that they think is realistic and manageable for them to cover in that term. Teachers who begin a composition course with no syllabus often run the risk of getting to the last two weeks of the term and realizing suddenly that there's no time to do the four additional papers required by the department or that only two of the twelve goals they have set for the course have been met.

Thus, legalities and students' security aside, handing out some kind of a syllabus makes good pedagogical sense. Having chosen to give students a syllabus, however, teachers are still faced with some major decisions about it: How detailed should it be? How much should it control the class? To what extent can the teacher feel free to deviate from it?

A syllabus should include the obvious information about the course: the teacher's name, the catalogue number of the course, the classroom number, the attendance policy, the grading policy—perhaps only a brief statement about what percent of the final grade will be made up of class work, essays, exams, and so forth. In addition, the syllabus should contain a statement of the overall goals of the course. Often this statement will be one formulated by a department or freshman writing committee. Also, many teachers like to include as part of the syllabus a statement defining plagiarism and the penalties for it.

In addition to this basic information, teachers usually give an outline of the course. This outline may be as specific as a day-by-day list of assignments for the entire term, or it may be as general as a list of dates on which specific assignments are due. Students like the day-by-day list of assignments because it helps them plan their work around that demanded by other courses, but teachers find it more problematic. With a day-by-day list of assignments, teachers often find themselves behind on the second or third day so that the syllabus either will be inaccurate throughout the course or will require constant revision. This kind of syllabus leaves little room for the slowing down or speeding up that will be motivated in all classrooms by the students themselves. Teachers may begin to feel that this kind of syllabus is a set of chains.

Conversely, the syllabus which lists only the dates when major assignments are due frustrates the students somewhat because they have a hard time juggling the seemingly arbitrary assignments that the teacher sporadically makes to supplement the syllabus. More importantly, such a syllabus may also be too vague to help the teachers pace themselves.

A good compromise is the kind of syllabus which breaks the course into weekly chunks and gives the goals and major assignments for the week. This kind is usually detailed enough to allow students to plan well with their other courses and to allow teachers to get through the allotted material during the term.

Writing a course syllabus effectively also requires that we consider both the length of the term and the emphasis we want to impose on the material. There's really no such thing as a generic composition course: the teacher's own interests or the philosophy of the department or freshman committee dictates a particular goal or emphasis for the basic college course in composition. These goals must be considered realistically in light of the length of the term.

In composition courses time is extremely relative; that is, the forty-five or so contact hours required for most three- or four-hour courses are not equally efficacious if one compares a long term to a short, compressed one. Obviously, time is required for process of writing to take root and for the students to begin to have confidence in their ability to write. The closer together the class meetings are and the longer the class sessions are, the more difficulty students have assimilating the principles we are trying to teach them. Thus, in arranging the syllabus we should keep in mind that less work is often more learning. Of course, those teachers in departments who require an absolute number or papers per term have less flexibility with this idea of less is more, though they can perhaps adjust the subjects and lengths of papers with this concept in mind.

Among the many possible focuses for a basic composition course, one of four approaches is used frequently by most teachers. Many prefer to emphasize:

> ➤ *the whole essay*, showing students seven or seven or eight rhetorical types of development;

> ➤ *the paragraph*, working up to the whole paper at the end of the term, a method often favored particularly by those in developmental studies;

> ➤ *research skills*, perhaps having students write papers for disciplines other than English and focusing on critical reading skills and attention to audience;

> ➤ *language*, often with much attention to sentence strategy, an approach which works especially well with both developmental students and extremely bright students.

These approaches are illustrated in the sample syllabi which follow. This chapter gives sample syllabi for using all four approaches in a fifteen-week semester, and it gives models for focusing on the whole essay and on language, respectively, in a ten-week quarter. Finally, it gives a sample syllabus for a six-week summer session which emphasizes the whole essay.

To approach the course in any one of these four ways, teachers will find the *Simon & Schuster Handbook for Writers* easy to use, although the book's usefulness is certainly not limited to these four approaches.

The order in which these syllabi assign kinds of essays, paragraph or the kinds of mechanical errors and stylistic features to be reviewed is fairly arbitrary, a personal order developed during my more than fifteen years of teaching. Each teacher develops his or her own expertise with regard to sequence and should experiment.

In general, my students seem to respond best if I begin with kinds of writing that are most immediate to them, narrative and descriptive, and if I begin a review of grammar with the least conventionally acceptable kinds of mechanical errors, usually comma splices, fragments, and agreement problems. Even with this rule of thumb, I often deviate from my syllabus if I sense that a class needs or wants to learn more about something I had planned to do later in the term.

SYLLABI FOR SEMESTER (FIFTEEN-WEEK) COURSES

These syllabi are based on the assumption that teachers are using the *Simon and Schuster Handbook for Writers* as well as a reader.

Emphasis on Whole Essay and Types of Development

This syllabus shows students how to develop essays which are narration, description, classification, compare and contrast, cause and effect, definition, argument, and process. It does not include an essay developed by illustration nor does it include a paper that would require evaluation and summary alone, though these could easily be substituted for two of the types of development included. This syllabus also assumes that the argument paper will require research and allows several weeks' work on that essay.

Since students are fresher and have more energy at the beginning of a term, the assignments are more rigorous early in the course. Also, this syllabus begins with narration and description, not necessarily because they are easier than some other types of development (as some teachers argue) but because students feel more comfortable writing narrations and descriptions. As students first begin to study the writing process, these more accessible types of development ease them into writing papers that are more analytical and for many students more difficult.

Before the students write the assigned essays, the syllabus includes a paragraph writing assignment which introduces the type of development that the next whole essay will require. Thus they understand the concept by practicing it in a small piece of writing first.

This syllabus also assumes that some of the work will be done in class, especially review of mechanics and grammar. Some teachers will spend more time with this than others.

Week One

Goals:	Learn how to use the handbook
	Learn about the importance of audience
Review:	Comma splices, fused sentences, fragments, manuscript form
Assignments:	Write narrative paragraph
	Read Chapters 1, 13, 14, and Appendix B in the handbook
	Read narrative essays in the reader

Week Two

Goals:	Learn how to plan an essay
	Learn how to write a rough draft
	Learn about writing across the curriculum
	Learn about narration as a method for developing an essay
Review:	Agreement of subjects and verbs, agreement of pronouns and their antecedents

Assignments: Write narrative essay
                  Read Chapters 2, 11, and 35 in the handbook

WEEK THREE

Goals: Learn how to revise
                  Learn about writing about literature
                  and other humanities
                  Learn about writing in the social sciences
Review: Pronoun case and pronoun reference
                  Subordination and coordination
Assignments: Revise narrative essay
                  Write descriptive paragraph
                  Read Chapters 3, 36 and 37 and review Chapters 9, 10, and 17 in the handbook
                  Read descriptive essays in the reader

WEEK FOUR

Goals: Learn about paragraph unity and coherence
                  Learn about description as a method for developing an essay
                  Learn about writing in the natural and technological sciences
Review: Shifts in person, number, voice, tense, mood, and quotations
Assignments: Write a descriptive essay
                  Write a classification paragraph as preliminary work for the next kind of essay
                  Review section 15a and read sections 4a–b in the handbook
                  Read classification essays in reader

WEEK FIVE

Goals: Learn about the arrangement and development of paragraphs
                  Learn about classification as a method for developing essays

Review: Uses of the comma

Assignments: Revise the descriptive essay
              Read sections 4c–d in the handbook
              and review Chapter 24

WEEK SIX

Goals: Learn to write introductions, conclusions, and
          transitional paragraphs
          Learn about comparison and contrast as a method
          for developing essays

Review: Conciseness

Assignments: Write a classification essay, reinforcing pattern
              introduced in the paragraph last week
              Write a comparison-and-contrast paragraph
              to introduce skills for the next essay
              Read section 4e and Chapter 16 in the handbook
              Read comparison-and-contrast essays in the reader

WEEK SEVEN

Goals: Learn to think critically
          Learn about cause and effect as a method
          for developing essays

Review: Parallelism, misplaced and dangling modifiers

Assignments: Revise the classification essay
              Write a cause-and-effect paragraph as preparation for the
              cause-and-effect essay next week
              Read Chapters 5 and 6 and review Chapter 18 and
              sections 15b–c in the handbook
              Read cause-and-effect essays in the reader

WEEK EIGHT

Goals: Learn about dictionaries and language
          Learn about definition as a method of developing essays

Review: Dictionaries, exactness, and vocabulary

Assignments: Write a cause-and-effect essay reinforcing
              skills learned in the paragraph last week

Write a definition paragraph as preparation
for writing next week's essay

Read Chapter 20 in the handbook

Read definition essays in the reader

WEEK NINE

Goal: Learn about levels of language

Review: Paraphrasing, summarizing, and quoting

Assignments: Revise the cause-and-effect essay

Read Chapters 21 and 31 in the handbook

WEEK TEN

Goals: Learn to define a research topic

Learn to plan a strategy for a research project

Review: Use of quotation marks, the dash, the slash, parentheses,
brackets, and the ellipsis

Assignments: Write a definition essay reinforcing the skills
learned in writing the paragraph last week

Read sections 32 a–c and review Chapters 28 and 29
in the handbook

Generate a topic for an argument paper
that will require research

WEEK ELEVEN

Goal: Learn to use the library

Review: Uses of the colon

Assignments: Write a proposal for research project

Read sections 32 d–j in the handbook
and review Chapter 25

Read argument essays in the reader

WEEK TWELVE

Goals: Learn to document sources in a research paper

Learn to draft a thesis statement for a research paper

Review: Uses of the semicolon

Assignments: Write the bibliography cards and notecards
for a research essay
Write the thesis statement for the research essay
Read section 32k and review Chapter 26
in the handbook

WEEK THIRTEEN

Goal: Learn to write the rough draft of a research paper
Review: Capitals, italics, abbreviations, and numbers
Assignments: Write the rough draft of the research essay
Read Chapters 33 and 34 and review Chapter 30
in the handbook

WEEK FOURTEEN

Goals: Learn to revise the research paper
Learn about process as a method of developing essays
Review: Uses of the apostrophe
Assignment: Revise the research paper
Review Chapter 27 in the handbook

WEEK FIFTEEN

Goals: Review the achievements of the term and note areas
which still need work
Assignments: Write a process paragraph
Read process essays in the reader
Take the final exam

Emphasis on Paragraph Development

WEEK ONE

Goals: Learn how to use the handbook
Learn about the importance of audience
Review: Comma splices, fused sentences, fragments
and manuscript form

Assignments: Write a narrative paragraph
    Read Chapters 1, 13, 14, and Appendix B
    in the handbook
    Analyze paragraphs in one narrative essay in reader

WEEK TWO

Goals: Learn what a paragraph is and how to unify paragraphs
   and make them coherent
   Learn about ways to develop paragraphs
Review: Agreement of subjects and verbs, agreement of pronouns
   and their antecedents
Assignments: Write a paragraph arranged from general to specific
    and a paragraph arranged from specific to general
    Read sections 4 a–d and Chapter 11 in the handbook

WEEK THREE

Goal: Learn about the writing process and gathering ideas
Review: Pronoun case and pronoun reference
Assignments: Write a chronological paragraph
    and a climactic paragraph
    Read Chapter 2 and review Chapters 9 and 10
    in the handbook
    Analyze examples of chronological and climactic
    paragraphs in the reader

WEEK FOUR

Goals: Learn to write rough drafts
   Learn to revise
Review: Shifts in person, number, voice, tense, mood,
   and quotations
Assignments: Write a descriptive paragraph, and revise two of
    the earlier paragraphs
    Read Chapter 3 and review section 15a in the handbook
    Analyze paragraphs developed by descriptive detail
    in the reader

WEEK FIVE

Goal: Learn to vary sentence patterns and lengths

Review: Misplaced and dangling modifiers

Assignments: Write a paragraph developed by process and a paragraph arranged spatially

Read Chapter 19 and review sections 15b–c in the handbook

Read process essays in the reader

WEEK SIX

Goal: Learn how to use language economically

Review: Parallelism and uses of the comma

Assignments: Write a paragraph developed by classification, a paragraph developed by cause and effect, and a paragraph arranged from problem to solution

Read Chapter 16 and review Chapters 18 and 24 in the handbook

Read classification essays and cause-and-effect essays in the reader

WEEK SEVEN

Goal: Learn to use subordination and coordination effectively

Review: Meaning of words

Assignments: Write a paragraph developed by comparison and contrast and a paragraph developed by definition

Read Chapters 17 and 20 in the handbook

Read comparison-and-contrast and definition essays in the reader

WEEK EIGHT

Goal: Learn about the levels of language

Review: Paraphrasing, summarizing, and quoting

Assignments: Write a paragraphs developed by example and a paragraph developed by analogy

Read Chapters 21 and 31 in the handbook

Read essays developed by illustration and example in the reader

Week Nine

Goal: Learn to develop special kinds of paragraphs

Review: Uses of the colon and semicolon

Assignments: Generate a topic for a narrative essay

Write an introduction and plan for a narrative essay

Read section 4e and review Chapters 25 and 26 in the handbook

Analyze introductory and concluding paragraphs in several essays in the reader

Week Ten

Goal: Learn to think critically

Review: Uses of the apostrophe

Assignments: Generate a topic for an argument essay

Read Chapter 5 and review Chapter 27 in the handbook

Read argument essays in the reader

Week Eleven

Goals: Learn to define a research topic

Learn to plan a strategy for a research project

Review: Use of quotation marks, the dash, the slash, parentheses, brackets, and the ellipsis

Assignments: Write a proposal which explains the research strategy to be used in finding evidence to support your argument

Read sections 32 a–f and Chapter 29 in the handbook

Analyze the kinds of evidence used in several argument essays in the reader

Week Twelve

Goal: Learn to use the library

Review: Capitals, italics, abbreviations, and numbers

Assignments: Write a preliminary bibliography of works to be used in the argument essay

Read sections 32g–j and review Chapter 30 in the handbook

WEEK THIRTEEN

Goals: Learn to document sources in a research paper

Learn to write the rough draft of a research paper

Review: Conventions of business writing

Assignments: Write the rough draft of the research paper

Read Chapters 33 and 34 in the handbook and review Chapter 39

WEEK FOURTEEN

Goals: Learn to revise the research paper

Learn about writing in other disciplines

Review: Methods for developing the whole essay

Assignments: Revise the research paper

Write a letter of application for a job and a resume

Read Chapters 35–38 in the handbook

WEEK FIFTEEN

Goal: Review the achievements of the term and note areas which still need work

Assignments: Write an analytical essay (comparison and contrast, cause and effect, process, classification, or definition) which does not require research

Take the final exam

Emphasis on Research Skills

WEEK ONE

Goals: Learn how to use the handbook

Learn about the importance of audience

Review: Comma splices, fused sentences, fragments,
              and manuscript form
Assignments: Write a cause-and-effect paragraph
              Read Chapters l, 13, 14, and Appendix B
              in the handbook
              Read cause-effect essays in reader

Week Two

Goals: Learn how to plan an essay
              Learn how to write a rough draft
Review: Agreement of subjects and verbs, agreement of pronouns
              and their antecedents
Assignments: Write a cause-effect essay
              Read Chapters 2, 3, and 11 in the handbook

Week Three

Goal: Learn about writing research
Review: Conventions of quoting
Assignments: Write a proposal for a research paper
              about a current issue
              Read and sections 32 a–i and review Chapter 28
              Read argument essays in the reader

Week Four

Goal: Learn to think critically
Review: Shifts in person, number, voice, tense, mood,
              and quotations
Assignments: Write an analysis of the arguments in two essays
              from the reader
              Read Chapters 5 and 6 and review section 15a
              in the handbook

Week Five

Goals: Learn to use the library
              Learn to document sources in a paper
              and to write a bibliography

Review: Conciseness

Assignments: Read Chapters 33 and 16 in the handbook
Write a bibliography of possible sources
for the research project

WEEK SIX

Goal: Learn to summarize, paraphrase, and quote

Review: Misplaced and dangling modifiers

Assignments: Write a summary of two or three articles from magazines or scholarly journals to use in the research paper

Read Chapter 31 and review sections 15b–c
in the handbook

WEEK SEVEN

Goal: Learn about paragraph unity and coherence

Review: Parallelism

Assignments: Write a rough draft of the research project

Read sections 4a–b and Chapter 18 in the handbook

WEEK EIGHT

Goals: Learn about the arrangement and development
of paragraphs

Learn to revise a research paper

Review: Uses of the comma

Assignments: Write a revision of the research paper

Read sections 4c–d and review Chapter 24

WEEK NINE

Goal: Learn to write introductions, conclusions,
and transitional paragraphs

Review: Uses of the colon and semicolon

Assignments: Write a proposal for a comparison-and-contrast essay
on two pieces of literature or art by the same writer or artist

Write a bibliography and notecards for four sources
which support this topic

Write an introduction and outline for the
comparison-and-contrast essay

Read section 4e and review Chapters 25 and 26
in the handbook

Read and analyze comparison-and-contrast essays
in the reader

Week Ten

Goals: Learn about the meanings of words

Learn about definition as a method of developing essays

Review: Dictionaries, exactness, and vocabulary

Assignments: Write the comparison-and-contrast essay

Write an analysis of the meanings of a current
slang term based on definitions given in at least
three specialized dictionaries

Read Chapter 20 in the handbook

Read the definition essays in the reader

Week Eleven

Goal: Learn about levels of language

Review: Uses of the apostrophe

Assignments: Write an analysis of the meanings of the term *mug*
offered by the *Oxford English Dictionary*

Write a brief paper explaining how language changes
over time, using as examples your analysis of *mug* and
your analysis of the slang term from last week

Review Chapter 27 in the handbook

Week Twelve

Goal: Learn how differences in audience affect style

Review: Techniques for achieving variety and emphasis

Assignments: Find a journal article of two or three pages
and find a magazine article of two or three pages,
both on the same topic (weight loss, for example,
or insomnia or drug use among athletes)

Write an essay comparing and contrasting the

differences in style dictated by the differences
in the intended audience of each periodical

Read Chapter 19 and review Chapter 30
in the handbook

WEEK THIRTEEN

Goal: Learn about process as a method for developing an essay

Review: Capitals, italics, abbreviations, and numbers

Assignments: Use the library to learn about how to get started with
a new hobby in an area which interests you and then write
a process essay which would explain to someone less knowledgeable than you how to pursue this hobby

Review Chapter 30 in the handbook

Read process essays in the reader

WEEK FOURTEEN

Goal: Learn about classification as a method
for developing an essay

Review: Subordination and coordination

Assignments: Write an introduction and a plan for a classification
essay about a topic in an area different from your major
(for example, if you're a humanities major, choose a
topic in science or the social sciences)

Read Chapter 17 in the handbook

Read and analyze classification essays in the reader

WEEK FIFTEEN

Goals: Learn about the kinds of writing people do
in various kinds of careers

Review the achievements of the term, and note areas
which still need work

Assignments: Choose a business or profession that interests you and
interview two or three people, in person or by telephone,
and find out about all of the kinds of writing they do each
week on their jobs. Use the library to add to your findings
about the kinds of writing people do in this area

Write an essay about writing in this specific area and illustrate it with information from your interviews and research

Take the final exam

Emphasis on Language

WEEK ONE

Goals: Learn how to use the handbook

Learn about the importance of audience

Review: Comma splices, fused sentences, fragments, and manuscript form

Assignments: Write a narrative paragraph in informal language, and write two additional versions, one in slang and one in formal English

Read Chapters 1, 13, 14, and Appendix B in the handbook

Read the narrative essays in reader

WEEK TWO

Goal: Learn about meanings of words

Review: Misplaced and dangling modifiers

Assignments: Look up a common word (*cup* or *beef,* for example) in both a current desk dictionary and the *Oxford English Dictionary* and write a brief essay about the difference and similarities in the two definitions

Read Chapter 20 in the handbook and review sections 15b–c

WEEK THREE

Goals: Learn about levels of language

Learn to plan an essay

Review: Use of quotation marks, the dash, the slash, parentheses, brackets, and the ellipsis

Assignments: Revise last week's essay about two definitions

Write a proposal for a definition essay

Read Chapters 2 and 21 and review Chapters 28 and 29 in the handbook

Read definition essays in the reader

WEEK FOUR

Goals: Learn to write a rough draft

    Learn about sentence variety and emphasis

Review: Uses of the apostrophe

Assignments: Write the rough draft of the definition essay planned last week

    Write an analysis of the sentence structure in a single paragraph from essays by two authors in the reader and be prepared to explain to the class in what ways these authors use sentences differently

    Read Chapters 3 and 19 and review Chapter 27 in the handbook

WEEK FIVE

Goal: Learn about basic sentence patterns

Review: Parts of speech

Assignments: Write sentences in each of the basic sentence patterns

    Write an analysis of the sentence structure in one paragraph of a definition essay from the reader

    Write a revision of last week's definition essay

    Read Chapter 7 in the handbook

WEEK SIX

Goal: Learn about effective subordination and coordination

Review: Uses of the comma

Assignments: Write a descriptive paragraph

    Plan a narrative or descriptive essay

    Read Chapter 17 and review Chapter 24 in the handbook

    Read narrative and descriptive essays in the reader

WEEK SEVEN

Goals: Learn to write introductions, conclusions, and transitional paragraphs

    Learn about comparison and contrast as a method for developing essays

Review: Uses of the semicolon and colon

Assignments: Write the narrative or descriptive essay
                planned last week

                Read section 4e and review Chapters 25 and 26
                in the handbook

WEEK EIGHT

Goal: Learn to write coherent, unified paragraphs

Review: Capitals, italics, numbers, and abbreviations

Assignments: Choose two often-confused words (*hero* and *celebrity*,
                for example) and look them up in the *Oxford English
                Dictionary* and a current desk dictionary

                Plan a paper that will compare and contrast these two
                terms in an effort to distinguish their meanings and
                write an introduction for it

                Read sections 4a–b and review Chapter 30 in the
                handbook

WEEK NINE

Goal: Learn about the arrangement and development
            of paragraphs

Review: End punctuation

Assignments: Write the comparison-and-contrast essay planned
                last week

                Read sections 4c–d and review Chapter 23
                in the handbook

                Read comparison-and-contrast essays in the reader

WEEK TEN

Goals: Learn about economy in language
            Learn how to use the library

Review: Paraphrasing, summarizing, and quoting

Assignments: Find two articles (one or two pages each) in the
                library, both on the same subject, one of them in a
                popular magazine and the other in a scholarly journal

                Write an analysis of the difference in conciseness in each

and the kinds of sentence structure used by each

Write a summary of each article

Read Chapter 16 and sections 32e and 32f and review Chapter 31 in the handbook

Week Eleven

Goals: Learn to use cause and effect as a method for developing an essay

Learn to identify a research topic and plan a strategy for a research project

Review: Parallelism

Assignments: Write a proposal for a research project on a current issue

Write a cause-and-effect paragraph

Read sections 32a–d and 32g–i and review Chapter 18 in the handbook

Read cause-and-effect essays in the reader

Week Twelve

Goals: Learn to think critically

Learn to document sources in a research paper

Assignments: Write a bibliography and notecards for the sources you plan to use in the cause-and-effect essay

Read argument essays in the reader

Read Chapters 5 and 6 and 33 in the handbook

Week Thirteen

Goal: Learn to outline, draft, and revise a research paper

Assignments: Write the rough draft of the cause-and-effect paper

Read Chapter 34 in the handbook

Week Fourteen

Goal: Learn to write an argument essay

Review: Writing in other disciplines

Assignments: Write a plan for an argument essay on a local issue
Write notecards and a bibliography for sources you will
use in the argument essay
Read Chapters 35–38 in the handbook

Week Fifteen

Goal: Review the achievements of the term and note areas
which still need work
Review: Conventions of business writing
Assignments: Write the argument essay
Review Chapter 39 in the handbook
Take the final exam

Syllabi for Quarter-Length (Ten-week) Courses

Even though the quarter-length term offers the same number of contact hours with the students as the semester system, some teachers find that for students to master the principles of writing covered in the course, they should do fewer papers with more time between or write shorter papers. Because of these individual preferences, the models that follow may be adjusted for more or fewer papers than are suggested. And like those for the semester-length term, these syllabi also make use of a reader in addition to the handbook, though teachers may adjust them to use only the handbook.

The two syllabi here focus on the whole essay and on language, respectively. The models in the previous section that focus on research skills and on the paragraph may easily be adapted to accommodate the shorter terms, as the two here have been. In adapting a syllabus to a shorter term, many teachers generally find that they have more success if they require slightly fewer papers and more detailed work on those they do require. Simply squeezing the requirements of a semester-length course into ten weeks or less does not give students the time they need to absorb the principles they are being taught.

Emphasis on the Whole Essay and Types of Development

WEEK ONE

Goals: Learn how to use the handbook

Learn about the importance of audience

Learn how to plan an essay

Review: Comma splices, fused sentences, fragments, and manuscript form

Assignments: Write a narrative paragraph

Plan a narrative essay

Read Chapters 1, 13, 14, and Appendix B in the handbook

Read the narrative essays in the reader

WEEK TWO

Goals: Learn how to write a rough draft

Learn how to revise

Learn about writing in other disciplines

Review: Agreement of subjects and verbs, agreement of pronouns and their antecedents

Assignments: Write the narrative essay planned last week

Read Chapters 2, 3 and 11 in the handbook and review Chapters 35–38

WEEK THREE

Goals: Learn about paragraph unity and coherence

Learn about description as a method for developing an essay

Review: Pronoun case and pronoun reference

Subordination and coordination

Assignments: Revise the narrative essay

Write a plan for a descriptive essay

Read sections 4a–b and review Chapters 9, 10, and 17 in the handbook

Read descriptive essays in the reader

WEEK FOUR

Goals: Learn about the arrangement and development
of paragraphs

Learn about classification as a method
for developing essays

Review: Shifts in person, number, voice, tense, mood,
and quotations

Assignments: Write the descriptive essay planned last week

Write a classification paragraph

Write a plan for a classification essay

Read sections 4c–d and review section 15a
in the handbook

Read classification essays in the reader

WEEK FIVE

Goals: Learn to write introductions, conclusions,
and transitional paragraphs

Learn about comparison and contrast as a method
for developing essays

Review: Conciseness and dangling and misplaced modifiers

Assignments: Write the classification essay planned last week

Write a comparison-and-contrast paragraph

Write an outline and introduction for a comparison-
and-contrast essay

Read Chapter 16 and section 4e
and review sections 15b–c in the handbook

Read comparison-and-contrast essays in the reader

WEEK SIX

Goals: Learn to think critically

Learn about cause and effect as a method
for developing essays

Review: Parallelism

Assignments: Write the comparison-and-contrast essay
planned last week

Write a cause-and-effect paragraph

Write a plan and introduction for a cause-and-effect essay

Read Chapters 5, 6, and 18 in the handbook

Read the cause-and-effect essays in the reader

WEEK SEVEN

Goal: Learn about the meanings of words
and the levels of language

Review: Paraphrasing, summarizing, and quoting

Assignments: Write the cause-and-effect essay planned last week

Write a definition paragraph

Read Chapters 20, 21, and 31 in the handbook

Read definition essays in the reader

WEEK EIGHT

Goal: Learn to define a research topic and to plan a strategy
for a documented argument essay

Review: Use of quotation marks, the dash, the slash,
parentheses, brackets, and the ellipsis

Assignments: Write a proposal for an argument essay on a current
issue, a paper that will use at least five sources

Read sections 32 a–i and review Chapters 28 and 29 in
the handbook

Read argument essays

WEEK NINE

Goals: Learn to use the library

Learn to document sources in a research paper

Review: Conventions of business writing

Assignments: Write a rough draft of the argument essay

Read Chapters 33 and 34 and review Chapter 39
in the handbook

WEEK TEN

Goal: Review the achievements of the term and note areas
which still need work

Assignments: Write the final draft of the argument essay
Take the final exam

Emphasis on Language

WEEK ONE

Goals: Learn how to use the handbook
Learn about the importance of audience.
Learn about narration and description as methods
for developing paragraphs and essays

Review: Comma splices, fused sentences, fragments,
and manuscript form

Assignments: Write a narrative paragraph
Write a descriptive paragraph
Read Chapters 1, 13, 14, and Appendix B in the handbook
Read narrative and descriptive essays in the reader

WEEK TWO

Goals: Learn about basic sentence patterns
Learn about sentence variety and emphasis

Review: Parts of speech and uses of the comma

Assignments: Write an analysis of the sentence structure in one
paragraph of a narrative or descriptive essay in the reader
Write an analysis of your sentence structure
in last week's descriptive paragraph
Read Chapters 7 and 19 and review Chapters 6 and 24
in the handbook

WEEK THREE

Goals: Learn how to use subordination and
coordination effectively
Learn to plan an essay and to write the rough draft
of an essay

Review: Uses of the apostrophe

Assignments: Write an analysis of the sentence structure in a single paragraph from essays by two authors in the reader and be prepared to explain to the class the ways in which these authors use sentences differently

Plan a narrative or descriptive essay, and write the rough draft

Read Chapters 3 and 19 and review Chapter 27 in the handbook.

WEEK FOUR

Goals: Learn about the meanings of words
Learn about the levels of language

Review: Misplaced and dangling modifiers, use of quotation marks, the dash, the slash, parentheses, brackets, and the ellipsis

Assignments: Revise the narrative or descriptive essay

Write a plan for a definition essay

Read the definition essays in the reader

Read Chapter 21 and review sections 15a–b and Chapters 28–29 in the handbook

WEEK FIVE

Goals: Learn to write introductions, conclusions, and transitional paragraphs

Learn about comparison and contrast as a method for developing essays

Review: Uses of the semicolon and the colon

Assignments: Write the definition essay planned last week

Write a plan and introduction for a comparison-and-contrast essay about two often-confused words (*hero* and *celebrity*, for example), looking them up in the *Oxford English Dictionary* and in a current desk dictionary. Your essay should compare and contrast these terms in an effort to distinguish their meanings.

Read section 4e and review Chapters 25–26 in the handbook

Week Six

Goals: Learn to write coherent, unified paragraphs
             Learn about the arrangement and
             development of paragraphs
Review: Capitals, italics, numbers, and abbreviations
Assignments: Write the comparison-and-contrast essay
             planned last week
             Read sections 4a–b and review Chapter 30
             in the handbook
             Read comparison-and-contrast essays in the reader

Week Seven

Goals: Learn about economy in language
             Learn how to use the library
Review: End punctuation, paraphrasing, summarizing, and quoting
Assignments: Find two articles (1–2 pages each) in the library, both
             on the same subject, one in a popular magazine and the
             other in a scholarly journal. Write an analysis of the
             difference in conciseness in each and the kinds of sentence
             structure used by each. Write a summary of each article.
             Read Chapter 16 and sections 32e–f
             and review Chapters 23 and 31 in the handbook

Week Eight

Goals: Learn to use cause and effect as a method
             for developing essays
             Learn to identify a research topic and plan a strategy
             for a research project
Review: Parallelism
Assignments: Write a proposal for a research project on a current
             issue, a paper that could be developed largely by cause
             and effect
             Write a cause-and-effect paragraph
             Read cause-and-effect essays in the reader
             Read sections 32 a–i and review Chapter 18
             in the handbook

Week Nine

Goals: Learn to think critically

Learn to document sources in a research paper

Assignments: Write a bibliography and notecards for the sources
to be used in your cause-and-effect research project

Write the rough draft of your research paper

Read Chapters 5, 6, and 33 in the handbook

Read argument essays in the reader

Week Ten

Goals: Review the achievements of the term and note areas
which still need work

Assignments: Revise the research paper

Take the final exam

Syllabi for Summer-School (Six-week) Courses

Planning courses for such intensive terms as summer school requires great care. Classes in these sessions, normally about six weeks, are generally scheduled daily for about two hours, a long enough period for the teacher to allow in-class work on papers. A big advantage of the short term is that teachers can observe students while they write and help them in the process, lending immediacy to the process. A second advantage, shared by the quarter-length term, is the continuity of class meetings, which usually occur daily.

Along with the more constant teacher-student contact that this schedule provides comes the down side—the much more intensive pace. Teachers must decide if they can have students do numerous short papers or several long ones. Those whose departments demand the same number of papers for summer school as for a regular term have little choice but to require shorter ones. Those with more control over the syllabus may choose fewer papers, one per week, for example, or several revisions of only one or two essays. In any case, teachers need to pace themselves carefully so as to avoid the "If it's Tuesday, this must be narration" syndrome.

The model given in this section is, therefore, skeletal. Teachers will find that fleshing out the syllabus depends somewhat on knowing the level of students they will have in such a short term. This model is intended for use with average students, mainly freshmen, in their first writing course.

Like the other sample syllabi here, this one assumes the use of a reader. Also, it approaches the course by teaching ways to develop the whole essay. Teachers who wish to emphasize paragraphs, research skills, or language may adapt the previous models to accommodate the shorter term.

Emphasis on the Whole Essay and Types of Development

Week One

Goals: Learn how to use the handbook

Learn about the importance of audience

Learn how to plan an essay and write a rough draft

Review: Comma splices, fused sentences, fragments, and manuscript form

Assignments: Write a plan for a narrative or descriptive essay

Write the rough draft of this essay

Read Chapters 1–3 and review chapters 13 and 14 and Appendix B in the handbook

Read narrative and descriptive essays in the reader

Week Two

Goals: Learn how to revise

Learn about paragraph unity and coherence

Learn about classification as a method for developing essays

Review: Agreement of subjects and verbs, agreement of pronouns and their antecedents

Assignments: Revise the narrative or descriptive essay

Write a plan for a classification essay

Read sections 4a–b and review Chapter 11 in the handbook

Read classification essays in the reader

WEEK THREE

Goals: Learn about the arrangement and development
of paragraphs

Learn to write introductions, conclusions,
and transitional paragraphs

Learn about comparison and contrast as a method
for developing essays

Review: Pronoun case and pronoun reference

Subordination and coordination

Assignments: Write the classification essay planned last week

Write a plan and introduction for
a comparison-and-contrast essay

Read sections 4c–e and review Chapters 9, 10,
and 17 in the handbook

Read the comparison-and-contrast essays in the reader

WEEK FOUR

Goals: Learn about cause and effect as a method
for developing essays

Learn how to use the library

Review: Shifts in person, number, voice, tense, and mood,
quotations, and conciseness

Assignments: Write the comparison-and-contrast essay
planned last week

Write a plan and introduction for a cause-and-effect essay

Review sections 15a and 32a–j and Chapters 16 and 28.

WEEK FIVE

Goals: Learn to think critically

Learn how to write an argument

Review: Paraphrasing, summarizing, and quoting

Assignments: Write the cause-and-effect essay planned last week

Write a plan and introduction for an argument essay

Read Chapters 5 and 6 and review Chapter 31

Read argument essays in the reader

WEEK SIX

Goals: Review the achievements of the term and note areas
which still need work

Assignments: Write the argument essay

Revise one earlier essay

These syllabi are by no means comprehensive. They are intended as starting points for new teachers of composition or for teachers new to the *Simon and Schuster Handbook*. All teachers eventually come up with combinations of mechanics and rhetoric that work well together in any given class. Therefore, these models are offered only as guidelines until teacher's own creativity with using the handbook takes over.

SUGGESTED READING

Belanoff, Pat, et al. *The Right Handbook*. Upper Montclair, NJ: Boynton, 1986.

Gold, R. M. "How the Freshman Essay Anthology Subverts the Aims of the Traditional Composition Course." *Teaching English in the Two-Year College* 18 (Dec. 1991): 261–65.

PART ONE
CHAPTER FIVE

Evaluation by the Teacher: Using Grading to Help Students Develop their Writing

Evaluation of writing presents many challenges which quite naturally give pause to the new teacher sharpening up the red pencil to pass judgment on the first set of papers. But even experienced teachers fret over obvious inconsistencies among philosophies of grading and inconsistencies between theory and application. Evaluation of writing is possibly the single most difficult task required of us, yet it may well be the most important part of our job insofar as helping individual students.

Careful evaluation has the potential not only to improve students' writing dramatically but also to boost students' confidence in themselves as important members of a community of writers. As teachers certainly we have the power to use grades to browbeat students—to show them every flaw in their mechanics and every crack in their logic. But, more important, we have the power to use evaluation to foster students' interest in writing, to help them develop a sense of confidence in their own ideas and their ability to express those ideas, to awaken their excitement as they discover the satisfaction of finally being able to say what they mean—and be understood by others. Whether we influence our students negatively or positively largely depends on the way in which we go about grading their papers.

It's no wonder our students sometimes think their grades result from luck or the teacher's mood. Far too many teachers view grading as a chore defined by vague concepts or harsh, absolute categorization of errors. In some departments grading policies are spelled out in a sort of "theme penalty sheet" so that the student earns grade *X* if he or she *avoids* certain kinds of errors. This kind of absolute, negative grading teaches the students only that they know how to write well if they succeed in avoiding problems in grammar and punctuation. Surely this kind of misconception is not what we wish to teach. Good writing is much more than avoiding mechanical problems, and our methods of grading need to make this point loudly and clearly.

Even before we begin to think about grading individual papers, however, we must decide how to consider the whole body of work a student does during the term. Three of the most current and common ways are using portfolios, using a contract system, and weighting each assignment.

Portfolio Assessment

One of the newest and most successful kinds of grading is using portfolios to determine a student's final grade in the course. Although some teachers find that, initially, at least, portfolio grading takes more time than other methods of assessment, many agree that in the long run this technique is worth their attention because it gives students the kind of individual assessment that such a personal skill as writing requires. Instead of squeezing each student into standardized notions of time required for a paper and number of revisions needed, this method comes closest of all forms of evaluation to personalizing grading. Therefore, it offers rich rewards to both students and teachers alike when they see that grading is part of a dialogue that helps each student work at an individual pace to overcome individual problems and feel a sense of accomplishment at having done so.

Teachers who want to use this kind of assessment, however, should have a clear strategy of what the portfolio will contain, when and how often they will grade it, and what the grades will mean. Some teachers want to have all assignments in the final portfolio and grade all papers at the end of the course, having made written comments throughout the term on individual papers and revisions. Others set a number of papers the student must include in the portfolio. Some teachers choose which assignments will ultimately determine the grade; some teachers allow students to make the choice. I prefer to allow students to choose, because they know which papers are working well for them in terms of interest and revision. Of course, it is important to have enough variety in the required assignments to ensure that many types of writing skills are finally graded, not just the one type that the student may have always been good at. Students who are allowed some choice about what will be assessed for their final grade seem to feel more invested in the course and to take the grading more seriously.

Students usually do not like waiting until the end of a term to get some grades. They would rather be reassured several times during the term that the grades have some connection to what they perceive of as the work they are doing. For this reason, I like to grade portfolios at least two or three times during the term, announcing the dates on the syllabus so that they may plan their work from the first day. Such scheduling also teaches them to be responsible about deadlines and commitments.

One problem teachers find with portfolio grading is that consistency from student to student is more difficult to maintain in terms of the equation between letter grade and quality of work. Many portfolio-graders are influenced by improvement and effort, especially because students who revise over and over usually believe they are improving and that this improvement deserves better grades. Of course, not every student who revises improves the paper, and not all assignments are equally appealing to all students. Thus, teachers should clarify for themselves at the outset what standards they will apply, how much they will reward effort and improvement, and how closely they will monitor consistency in grading overall.

Contract Grading

Some teachers like to use contracts with their students, but these contracts take many forms. Some teachers make contracts for each grade, contracts that spell out precisely what proficiency level a student must reach and the amount of work which will show that level in order to receive a specific letter grade for the term.

Other teachers like to use contracts to allow students to choose how they want certain assignments weighted. For example, in a course which requires six essays, a journal, ten paragraphs, and an essay test, the teacher might allow students to decide what percentage of the final grade (perhaps within a range) would be from the essays, what percentage from the journal, and so on. The teacher might even allow students to weight each essay a different percentage.

The major advantage of contracts is that they allow students to enter into dialogue about grading and to feel that they have had a say about something important to them. Contracts also allow students to learn the responsibility of sticking to commitments once they are made.

The disadvantages may discourage some teachers from using the technique, but they become relatively minor once a teacher has tried this method once and learned from the experience. The major problem is the time-consuming bookkeeping that must keep track of the value of each assignment for each student, all assignments possibly having a different weight. However, a computer program or handwritten spreadsheet will reduce the confusion. Another problem for some teachers is the time and tact necessary for dealing with those students who, having signed the contract during the first few days of class, want to change it at one time or another during the term, once the student sees how the grades are going. I recommend not opening the Pandora's Box of altering contracts. Students can learn from the process of contracts that they must make decisions and abide by them. On the other hand, some teachers think that students are justified in requesting a change or two during the term, because they believe that students don't always know at the beginning where their strengths and weaknesses lie. Whether a teacher decides to alter contracts or not, he or she must have made that decision and explained it clearly to the class at the beginning of the term.

Weighted Grading

Many teachers believe that they should decide the relative value of assignments, because, they argue, students don't really know enough about the course's goals to be able to make or enter into those decisions. Therefore, they assign a certain percentage toward the final grade to each assignment or group of like assignments.

This traditional method, probably the most common kind of grading in college writing courses, can, however, be more or less effective, depending on the teachers' methods of weighting assignments and factoring in revision. Certainly, it makes little sense to say to students that each of the ten assignments that count toward the final grade will count ten percent of the final grade. Such a technique offers no reward for improvement and seems to suggest that the assignments are totally isolated from one another. Students work harder and improve more, it seems to me, if we weight the earlier assignments as much less than later ones and if we allow revision a high percentage.

No matter how lenient or harsh our letter grades are—and there is a good deal of leeway here—we must seek ways of grading that will help students, not demoralize them. These methods include such decisions as the color of ink we use and the tone of our remarks, as the following suggestions show:

1. CHANGE INK. Many teachers have found that as simple a change as switching from red ink to pencil or blue ink has a positive effect on the students' attitudes. No one denies the authority of red ink, but the students are more likely to see pencil comments as less threatening. By choosing another color, the teacher in effect says that he or she is just another critical reader in a world of readers.

2. CHANGE TONE. The old saying that "you can catch more flies with

honey than with vinegar" applies significantly to grading papers. Students who are bombarded with "don't do this" and "don't do that" soon give up altogether. Naturally we cannot say that a poor piece of work is great just to make students feel good, but students' improvement is directly related to how we tell them the work is poor.

Throughout the paper as we are marking ineffective features of the writing, we should also take the few seconds needed to write in the margin "I like this image," "These details really help make your point," or "Your transition is especially skillful between these two paragraphs." More important, we should begin the first part of a final note with comments about the strengths of the paper. Then we can comment on the parts that need work, but we should end with an additional positive comment. All of us like to be complemented, and students especially respond well to compliments. By beginning and ending our notes with positive statements, we show students that we're not in the business of simply hunting for errors but that we also notice what they do well.

As the term goes on, these comments should, if possible, emphasize the improvement we are seeing regarding particular features of the students' writing. And even when we're hard pressed to find new elements to compliment, we can always end with a statement like, "I'm really looking forward to seeing your revision of this piece. You've got some strong ideas here that I know will come together well in your final draft." If the students believe that we are genuinely interested in what they are saying, they will work hard to come up to our expectations as far as mechanics are concerned.

3. CHANGE PRIORITIES. Don't mark everything that's wrong all at once. It stands to reason that if we mark all the errors and stylistic problems in a piece of writing—especially in red ink—the student who looks at this sea of red ink is likely to give up in the face of his or her hopeless inadequacy. Some teachers think it is dishonest to leave errors unmarked. They argue that by doing so, we only mislead the students into thinking that they are much better writers than they in fact are. Other teachers— and these seem more successful, in the long run—believe that it's what the students know at the end of the course that matters and that keeping them involved in improving and enthusiastic about their writing is ultimately more important than absolute tyranny in marking errors.

Those teachers who are selective about the errors they mark each time vary with regard to the criteria for marking papers in a given week. Some mark only the most serious mechanical errors early in the term (comma splices, fragments, subject-verb disagreements, and fused sentences) and comment only on major problems in content and style (adequate transition within and between paragraphs, enough evidence and detail, clear thesis and topic sentences, for example). Others mark only matters of content and organization first, inspiring students to think clearly about the subject, and gradually mark mechanics as the term proceeds. Some teachers mark matters of content and organization first as well as whatever mechanics they review during the period in which the students are working on the essay (usually these teachers, too, begin reviewing the most serious mechanical problems first). As the term goes on and students gain confidence in their ability to express their ideas in coherent paragraphs that support a clearly stated thesis, teachers have more success with criticizing problems of style (wordiness, adequate subordination, inconsistency of diction, and in effective sentence structure).

Some teachers find that students respond especially well to written comments if the students have communicated to the teacher the degree of detail with which they wish the teacher to mark the essay. Agreeing with the teacher about this helps create a sense of shared responsibility for the grading that can make students more responsive to the comments the teacher does make.

Once we have decided how densely to mark errors and in what order we ought to point out problems to the writer, we still have to make the difficult decision about what letter grade to assign the essay. As with other matters of grading, this decision is sometimes made largely by departmental consensus on what kinds of achievements merit certain letter grades. In some departments this consensus can take the form of the rigid "theme penalty sheet," which dooms papers with certain errors to the grade of *F* or *D*. Fortunately, in most cases departmental consensus is meant as a guideline for the teacher, not as an absolute set of criteria.

Though standards vary from school to school with regard to some features of writing, in general the following standards seem to be generally acceptable guidelines. Some teachers find that handing these kinds of guidelines to their students makes grading seem less arbitrary to students.

A – Most teachers recognize as an *A* paper one which has a spark of true originality. It has few if any mechanical errors, and it has clear organization, smooth transitions, exceptional detail, consistent diction and tone, and sophisticated sentence structure. Its thesis and evidence are specific and intriguing, not dull and predictable.

B – A *B* paper is one in which the writer organizes the material into coherent, well-unified paragraphs which have clear topic sentences. The writer does not violate the tone by shifting levels of diction, nor does the writer make serious or numerous mechanical errors. The evidence is fairly detailed, and the sentences are somewhat varied in terms of structure and length. The thesis, while perhaps not as insightful or original as in an *A* paper, is nevertheless neither dull nor obvious.

C – In a *C* paper teachers find evidence that the student is learning. *C* is not a negative grade: it means "satisfactory." Students often think that this grade means "mediocre" or "unsatisfactory," but with our positive comments about what they have done well in the paper, we can help students take pride in the considerable accomplishment that goes into the paper which earns a *C*.

A *C* paper usually has several serious mechanical errors, and it may have problems in content. Its thesis may need to be narrowed, and the paper often needs more detail and evidence. The paper may need better transitions both within and between paragraphs, and some paragraphs may need better topic sentences. This kind of paper typically is wordy and has inadequate subordination as well as illogical coordination. Its sentences are often monotonous in terms of structure and length. The paper may shift tone and levels of language.

D – A *D* paper is one which has numerous mechanical problems, including some problems in sentence boundaries (comma splices, fragments, fused sentences) that make the ideas unclear. Usually it lacks a clear thesis and clear organization, and its language is often much too general and dull. It offers no real evidence to support its points. Its sentences are wordy and unvaried in terms of length and structure. This kind of paper often shifts levels of language and tone. A *D* paper can, however, be relatively free of mechanical errors but have so many serious problems with content and organization that it seems unfocused and even garbled.

F – An *F* paper is one which has no clear thesis, no clear organization, little specific detail, and many mechanical errors, especially problems with sentence boundaries (comma splices, fragments, and fused sentences). This kind of paper usually has problems with diction and wordiness, and its sentences are unvaried in terms of structure and length. The writer often coordinates ideas which do not belong together. Paragraphs lack coherence and unity.

Some teachers like to give split grades, that is, one grade for content and one for mechanics. Although this kind of grading reduces the complaints from students about not getting enough credit for their good ideas, it also teaches students that conventions of writing are relatively unimportant. As teachers we know the extent to which writing loses credibility in our culture when it does not follow the conventions. Thus, it seems misleading to separate the grade in this way and, as a result, foster the notion that the conventions are not part of the content.

Many teachers avoid discouraging students with low grades by simply refusing to put grades on the papers until late in the term when presumably students have learned what it takes to write an effective paper. Some teachers give grades from the beginning but stipulate that students must continue to revise papers until they are of at least *C* quality. And within reason, some teachers manipulate grades to avoid giving a string of *C*'s or *D*'s to a student: that is, even if the fourth or fifth paper deserves another *C* or *D*, the teacher might give it a *B-* or *C-* simply to encourage the student. Teachers who use grades in this way must be aware of the disappointment the student feels if the next grade is lower and perhaps should let the student know that the standards for grading get slightly harder as the term progresses: a *C* early in the term is weaker than a *C* later in the term.

As they mark papers, most teachers find it convenient to use a numerical chart or symbols referring to sections in the handbook. These numbers or symbols make it easy for the teacher to direct the student to the appropriate rule or explanation he or she needs in order to revise well. The *Simon & Schuster Handbook for Writers* contains both a chart of symbols and a numerical chart. In addition to using these numbers or symbols, most teachers like also to write some comments in the margins, particularly comments about whatever skill or concept the class is working on that week or about the most serious problems. Certainly teachers should also use these marginal comments to compliment students on mastering particular skills.

Following are two copies of a student's paper, one overmarked and too harshly graded and the other less heavily marked and more affirmative. (This comparison-and-contrast paper was the fourth essay in a one-term composition course, preceded by a narrative essay, a cause-and-effect essay, and a classification.) Both copies are marked with numbers and symbols from the *Simon & Schuster Handbook*. The second example is the kind of grading that seems to be most helpful in terms of inspiring students to care about revising and continuing to learn about writing. It asks the student questions rather than dictating changes, and the tone of the marginal comments is friendly, not sarcastic and insulting to the student.

Overmarked

Sinatra Versus Vandross

Power surges into the radio. The music blares from the speakers with

this is not — intensity. But what really is music? Music has many definitions according
at all clear
All of them? That must be tough.
to each individual's taste. Multitudes of singers strive to fulfill these

You're get- — different definitions to achieve success. Both Frank Sinatra and Luther
ting less and
less clear
Vandross fulfill two of these contrary definitions of music. On the surface
10a, 10c
it appears as though they are inherently dissimilar, but upon closer

evaluation they share certain specific details in common. Comparing the

emotional quality of their music, the importance placed on lyrics, and their
24c   *wordy*
use of rhythm, can reveal that even the most diametrically opposed singers

share important similarities.   *if it's background music,*
it has been utilized
For both Sinatra and Vandross, the utilized background music

indicates their different styles of music. Vandross's style best fits into the

category of soul music. Vandross does not sing straight soul; however, he

What are you takes certain elements from jazz. In some forms of jazz, instrumentation
comparing and
contrasting in takes a secondary role as the voice develops into the key element. Vandross
this ¶? I don't
understand uses this element to accent his voice to become the most important
what you mean.
element in his music. Sinatra, unlike Vandross, gears his music toward
sp
older genenrations His music relates back to the big band era as he uses

the violin and brass sections of the band in many songs. The violin and the

piano play an important part in the majority of his love songs while the

brass section communicates the stalwart feeling in others. The large band

helps to make his music more diverse as his voice cannot produce much
equal to what?
variety. The band plays an equal role in complimenting Sinatra's voice yet

not overpowering it.

For both Sinatra and Vandross, the emotion communicated through

wordy! their songs plays a vital role. The majority of Vandross's music deals with
16
sexual connotation of love. This does not mean that he directly sings of

awkward diction – 20b

sexual <u>confrontation</u>, but rather his singing brings physical stirring within the listener. His voice makes the listener appreciate the emotion he or she feels. Vandross also communicates loneliness and solitude in songs dealing with the loss of love. Through Vandross's voice, the listener has the capacity to feel the loneliness and pain associated with losing a special love. Vandross has the ability to relate love to other topics as well. In the *transition – 4d* song "A House is Not a Home," Vandross uses this theme to present the idea of what a real home should entail. He combines love with the idea of a home and makes a point of the importance of having a home with love present

This ¶ is too long

within. For Sinatra as well, the theme of love appears in many songs. In *10c* Sinatra's songs, however, <u>he</u> emphasizes more emotional and innocent love. *hyphen* Songs like "Tell Her" sing of a never ending love that needs to be renewed *two words* *11m* everyday by telling that special person that they are love. Indirect reference to sexual love commonly occurs but only using subtle undertones. Sinatra also has the ability to relate love to inanimate objects. Several of his most famous songs are about cities like New York and Los Angeles and how he finds them special or unique. More frequently Sinatra's songs deal with lost love and reminiscing over past loves. Instead of making the listener feel sorry for his condition like Vandross, he imparts a message of stalwartness to hold on to hope for the future. The song "That's Life" is *20b* expressly <u>donated</u> to this idea. This message of hope gives Sinatra a more optimistic message than Vandross. But on the same idea, Vandross can be

confusing

considered a more realistic singer. Sometimes a listener may not want to hear about the defiance of love's importance which Sinatra sings about. In this case they listen to Vandross who makes the listener come to grips with *you're awfully absolute here* *sexist! 11g* *10c* his true feelings. Sinatra cannot do <u>this</u> as his voice does not allow him to relate the pain associated with lost love on a realistic level. Vandross lets *is this really what you mean?* *15b* the listener relate to the <u>pain he or she feels through the song and his voice</u>.

To achieve the intended emotion in their songs, both Vandross and *10c* Sinatra utilize strikingly different methods. For Vandross, <u>this</u> is <u>done</u> through his remarkable vocal ability. One can understand the emotion he *he's trying to convey by listening?*

15b
tries to convey <u>by just listening to his voice.</u> He can attain any range of

10c
notes <u>which</u> gives his music flavor and uniqueness. He uses this indirect

method to convey the desired emotion to the listener. Sinatra, on the other

hand, depends on his lyrics and not on vocal ability. To express himself,

Sinatra tells an emotional story through his songs. <u>To receive the full effect</u>

15c   *awk*
<u>of this emotion,</u> the complete song must be listened to. <u>Like in a fairy tale,</u>

the complete story makes it magical and not just the individual parts. The

lyrics play such an important role in songs such as "The September of My

Years" that the sadness of growing old would not be understood had the

                                 wordy   *awk*
lyrics not been listened to completely. ~~Taking~~ songs <u>where</u> both Sinatra and

Vandross sang the words "I love you" reveals striking contrasts in how

each conveys emotion. For Sinatra, the surrounding lyrics give these words

meaning. Taken in context, they derive their meaning. Vandross, on the

other hand, can make a person weep by saying these words. The listener is

                                wrong preposition
able to understand whether Vandross is <u>reminiscing of a past love,</u> has just

dangling modifier   15c
lost a love, or is currently in love, <u>by singing just these three words.</u> His

vocal ability gives him this talent.

       When people listen to music, no two people hear exactly the same

thing. Singers like Frank Sinatra and Luther Vandross each fit different

definitions of music. The rhythms they use and the way they convey

       wordy
their ideas may be <u>different,</u> yet they still share important similarities.
                         11p   24a   *sp*
Each imparts love as their main theme for music and they also (ütilize)
                       don't split infinitive   20b
appropriate background music <u>to properly accent</u> their <u>different</u> vocal

wordy abilities. For both Sinatra and Vandross they utilize every aspect of their

music to accent the strengths and reduce the weaknesses of their music.

Even though on the surface two singers may appear to be totally contrary

to each other like Sinatra and Vandross, even the most opposite singers

share important similarities.

       Steve, you've got the beginning of a paper here — but this
       needs much more work to get it up to an acceptable level. –D

More Affirmatively Marked

Sinatra Versus Vandross

Can you be more precise here? How do these ideas relate to what you're exploring in this paper?

Power surges into the radio. The music blares from the speakers with intensity. But what really is music? Music has many definitions according to each individual's taste. Multitudes of singers strive to fulfill these different definitions to achieve success. Both Frank Sinatra and Luther Vandross fulfill two of these contrary definitions of music. On the surface it appears as though 10a, 10c they are inherently dissimilar, 24c but upon closer evaluation they share certain specific details in common. Comparing the emotional quality of their music, the importance placed on lyrics, and their use of rhythm, can reveal that even the most diametrically opposed singers share important similarities.

This is a good idea, but you need to focus a bit more clearly

Steve, you've got the idea of comparison and contrast, but you are looking at different kinds of things in this ¶. You need to look again.

For both Sinatra and Vandross, the utilized background music indicates their different styles of music. Vandross's style best fits into the category of soul music. Vandross does not sing straight soul; however, he takes certain elements from jazz. In some forms of jazz, instrumentation takes a secondary role as the voice develops into the key element. Vandross uses this element to accent his voice to become the most important element in his music. Sinatra, unlike Vandross, gears his music toward older sp generations. His music relates back to the big band era as he uses the violin and brass sections of the band in many songs. The violin and the piano play an important part in the majority of his love songs while the brass section communicates the stalwart feeling in others. The large band helps to make his music more diverse as his voice cannot produce much variety. The band plays 15e an equal role in complimenting Sinatra's voice yet not overpowering it.

very interesting!

For both Sinatra and Vandross, the emotion communicated through their songs plays a vital role. The majority of Vandross's music deals with a sexual connotation of love. This does not mean that he directly sings of

wordy see 16

20b
sexual <u>confrontation</u>, but rather his singing brings physical stirring within the listener. His voice makes the listener appreciate the emotion he or she feels. Vandross also communicates loneliness and solitude in songs dealing with the loss of love. Through Vandross's voice, the listener has the capacity to feel the loneliness and pain associated with losing a special

transition – 4d

Can you sub-divide this ¶ to make more well focused points?

love. Vandross has the ability to relate love to other topics as well. In the song "A House Is Not a Home," Vandross uses this theme to present the idea of what a real home should entail. He combines love with the idea of a home and makes a point of the importance of having a home with love present within. For Sinatra as well, the theme of love appears in many songs. In Sinatra's songs, however, he emphasizes more emotional and innocent love. Songs like "Tell Her" sing of a never ending love that needs to be renewed

You have given some good ex-amples and details—can you give even more?

everyday by telling that special person that they are love. Indirect reference to sexual love commonly occurs but only using subtle under-tones. Sinatra also has the ability to relate love to inanimate objects. Several of his most famous songs are about cities like New York and Los Angeles and how he finds them special or unique. More frequently Sinatra's songs deal with lost love and reminiscing over past loves. Instead of making the listener feel sorry for his condition like Vandross, he imparts a message of stalwartness to hold on to hope for the future. The song "That's Life" is

20b
expressly <u>donated</u> to this idea. This message of hope gives Sinatra a more

can you make this more precise?

optimistic message than Vandross. But on the same idea, Vandross can be considered a more realistic singer. Sometimes a listener may not want to hear about the defiance of love's importance which Sinatra sings about. In

can you make this less absolute?

this case they listen to Vandross who makes the listener come to grips with

11q   10c
<u>his</u> true feelings. Sinatra cannot do <u>this</u> as his voice does not allow him to relate the pain associated with lost love on a realistic level. Vandross lets

15b – misplaced modifier

the listener relate to the pain he or she feels (through) the song and his voice.

good topic sentence

To achieve the intended emotion in their songs, both Vandross and

10c
Sinatra utilize strikingly different methods. For Vandross, <u>this</u> is done through his remarkable vocal ability. One can understand the emotion he

15b
tries to convey by just listening to his voice. He can attain any range of
10c
notes which gives his music flavor and uniqueness. He uses this indirect

method to convey the desired emotion to the listener. Sinatra, on the other

hand, depends on his lyrics and not on vocal ability. To express himself,

Sinatra tells an emotional story through his songs. To receive the full effect
15c
of this emotion, the complete song must be listened to. Like in a fairy tale,

the complete story makes it magical and not just the individual parts. The

lyrics play such an important role in songs such as "The September of My

Years" that the sadness of growing old would not be understood had the
awkward, wordy – see 16
lyrics not been listened to completely. Taking songs where both Sinatra and

Vandross sang the words "I love you" reveals striking contrasts in how

each conveys emotion. For Sinatra, the surrounding lyrics give these words

meaning. Taken in context, they derive their meaning. Vandross, on the

other hand, can make a person weep by saying these words. The listener is
wrong preposition
able to understand whether Vandross is reminiscing of a past love, has just
15c
lost a love, or is currently in love, by singing just these three words. His

vocal ability gives him this talent.

When people listen to music, no two people hear exactly the same

thing. Singers like Frank Sinatra and Luther Vandross each fit different

definitions of music. The rhythms they use and the way they convey
16
their ideas may be different, yet they still share important similarities.
↘11p
Each imparts love as their main theme for music and they also utilize
20b
appropriate background music to properly accent their differing vocal

wordy | abilities. For both Sinatra and Vandross they utilize every aspect of their
16 |
music to accent the strengths and reduce the weaknesses of their music.

Even though on the surface two singers may appear to be totally contrary

to each other like Sinatra and Vandross, even the most opposite singers

share important similarities.

Steve, Sinatra-lover that I am, I'm intrigued with your topic. You have some
great ideas to support your comparison and contrast. In a few places you
need to focus your ideas more precisely, and some mechanical problems
weakened the paper. On the whole, though, you're off to a great start.
I'm looking forward to the next draft! –D

Grading can set the tone for a class and largely determine a student's attitude toward writing. If we use grading carefully, along with peer evaluation and conferences, we can motivate students to tackle their problems with enthusiasm.

SUGGESTED READING

Allen, Jo. "Approaches to Teaching: A Machiavellian Approach to Grading Writing Assignments." *Technical Writing Teacher* 15, no. 2 (Spring 1988): 158–60.

Anderson, Larry, et al. "Reader-Response Theory and Instructors' Holistic Evaluating in and out of Their Fields." *Teaching English in the Two-Year College* 21, no. 1 (Feb. 1994): 53–62.

Baker, N. W. "The Effect of Portfolio-Based Instruction on Composition Students' Final Examination Scores, Course Grades, and Attitudes toward Writing." *Research in the Teaching of English* 27 (May 1993): 155–74.

Bartholomae, David. "The Study of Error." *College Composition and Communication* 31 (Oct. 1980): 235–69.

Belanoff, Pat, and Marcia Dickson, eds. *Portfolios: Process and Product.* Portsmouth, NH: Boynton/Cook, 1991.

Bullock, Richard. "Spreading the Word... and Possibly Regretting It: Current Writing about Portfolios." *Journal of Teaching Writing* 12, no. 1 (1993): 105–13.

Christensen, N.F. "Avoidance Pedagogy in Freshman English." *Teaching English in the Two-Year College* 18 (May 1991): 133–36.

Christian, Barbara. "Freshman Composition Portfolios in a Small College." *Teaching English in the Two-Year College* 20, no. 4 (Dec. 1993): 289–97.

Connors, Robert, and Andrea A. Lunsford. "Teachers' Rhetorical Comments on Student Papers." *College Composition and Communication* 44, no. 2 (May 1993): 200–23.

Daiker, Donald. "Learning to Praise." *Writing Response: Theory, Practice, and Research.* Ed. Chris Anson. Urbana, IL: National Council of Teachers of English, 1989. 103–13.

Dragga, Sam. "The Effects of Praiseworthy Grading on Students and Teachers." *Journal of Teaching Writing* 7, no. 1 (Summer 1988): 41–50.

Duke, C. R., and R. R. Sanchez. "Giving Students Control over Writing Assessment." *English Journal* 83 (April 1994): 47–53.

Elbow, Peter. "Ranking, Evaluating, and Liking: Sorting Out Three Forms of Judgment." *College English* 55, no. 2 (Feb. 1993): 187–206.

Fuller, David C. "Teacher Commentary That Communicates: Practicing What We Preach in the Writing Class." *Journal of Teaching Writing* 6, no. 2 (Fall 1987): 307–17.

Greenberg, Karen L. "Assessing Writing: Theory and Practice." *New Directions for Teaching and Learning* 34 (Summer 1988): 47–58.

Haswell, Richard, and Susan Wyche Smith. "Adventuring into Writing Assessment." *College Composition and Communication* 45, no. 2 (May 1994): 220–36.

Hillenbrand, Lisa. "Assessment of ESL Students in Mainstream College Composition." *Teaching English in the Two-Year-College* 21, no. 2 (May 1994): 125–29.

Hodges, Elizabeth. "The Unheard Voices of Our Responses to Students' Writing." *Journal of Teaching Writing* 11, no. 2 (1992): 203–18.

Krest, Margie. "Time on My Hands: Handling the Paper Load." *English Journal* 76, no. 8 (Dec. 1987): 37–43.

Lawson, Bruce, Susan Sterr Ryan, and W. Ross Winterowd. *Encountering Student Texts: Interpretive Issues in Reading Student Writing.* Urbana, IL: National Council of Teachers of English, 1989.

Metzger, Elizabeth, and Lizbeth Bryant. "Portfolio Assessment: Pedagogy, Power, and the Student." *Teaching English in the Two-Year College* 20, no. 4 (Dec. 1993): 279–88.

Norton, L. S. "Essay Writing: What Really Counts?" *Higher Education* 20 (Dec. 1990): 411–42.

Olson, Mary W., and Paul Raffeld. "The Effects of Written Comments on the Quality of Student Compositions and the Learning of Content." *Reading Psychology* 8, no. 4 (1987): 273–93.

Peckham, Irvin. "Beyond Grades." *Composition Studies Freshman English News* 21, no. 2 (Fall 1993): 16–31.

Purves, Alan C. "Reflections on Research and Assessment in Written Composition." *Research in the Teaching of English* 26, no. 1 (Feb. 1992): 108–22.

Roemer, Marjorie, Lucille M. Schultz, and Russel K. Durst. "Portfolios and the Process of Change." *College Composition and Communication* 42 (1991): 455–69.

Shaughnessy, Mina. *Errors and Expectations.* New York: Oxford University Press, 1977.

White, E.M. "Language and Reality in Writing Assessment." *College Composition and Communication* 41 (May 1990): 187–200.

PART ONE
CHAPTER SIX

Peer Evaluation:
Opinions That Matter

Many teachers today recognize that their own painstaking comments, made with measured tone and affirmative intention, have much less impact on students' writing than even the most superficial and offhand comments by their peers. Increasingly teachers have worked diligently to harness the power of peer evaluation and to shape it to suit their pedagogical aims. The result of this experimentation is the realization that generally the kind of evaluation most helpful to students combines carefully directed peer critiquing and carefully thought out paper grading by the teacher.

Peer evaluation, if well directed by the teacher, can rival—if not surpass—the teacher's criticism in terms of impact on student writers. The teacher's control of peer evaluation and careful direction to students about the goals of it are critical. If teachers do not give students specific goals, the criticism that results is likely to be vague and impressionistic and not worth the time devoted to it. Some help with these guidelines is to be found in section 3c5 of the *Simon & Schuster Handbook,* "Knowing How to Be a Peer Critic." Following these or similar guidelines can produce surprisingly fruitful results that will excite students about the possibilities inherent in their work. Such critiques work so well perhaps because students believe that their classmates understand their vision better than we do or—heaven help us!—that their classmates' eyes are less clouded by matters of grammar and style and are thus more capable of keen insight. When classmates tell a student that the thesis is fuzzy of that they don't understand why four different topics are included in a single paragraph, the student usually believes the criticism and revises accordingly. Often an identical criticism from the teacher wins a shrug and a puzzled look that forecast a hit-or-miss, unenthusiastic revision.

But how do we get good critiques from students? And how often in a term and at what stages in the composition process should we use peer critiquing?

As with most techniques in teaching, we do not want to use critiquing by classmates to the point that it becomes trite, predictable, and dull. Varying the frequency and complexity of this kind of evaluation helps maintain the students' interest and helps make critiquing an activity that the students look forward to participating in each time.

Peer critiquing can be employed usefully at any point in the development of an essay. But before we use this tool, we need to establish some ground rules. We need to remind students that what is being criticized is the piece of writing, not the individual who wrote it. We need to remind them that both taking and giving negative criticism are hard but that honest comments are essential. We need to remind students that the word *criticism* implies much more than "bad" or "wrong"; it also implies "good" and "effective." Most students believe *criticism* is a pejorative term. We must show them that all effective criticism points out strengths and discusses weaknesses of a piece of work best in the context of the potential of the piece of writing. In other words, students should point out the weaknesses in the writing by making positive statements about the effectiveness that will result from revision.

Once students understand what criticism means, they are ready to practice. One good exercise in critiquing is to have them comment only on the introduction of a paper in its earliest stages. Students can be instructed to bring to class a legible rough draft of their introductions. (Having them write on every other line and on only one side of the sheet makes the writing more readable, and having them number their lines down the left margin provides reference numbers for the reader to use when making suggestions.)

To begin, the teacher might hand each student's paper to another student in the class, having requested the students' permission to share their work. Many teachers find that students are less inhibited by peer critiquing if they do not know the name of the author whose work they are reading, and others believe that students should have the courage of their convictions and directly address the students whose work they are critiquing. I have found that having students address one another by name in the written reviews makes them somewhat more serious in their approach.

As teachers get to know their students, they sometimes find it useful to give weaker writers' papers to other weaker writers and stronger writers' papers to stronger writers. Initially at least, a weak writer is likely to feel intimidated and utterly discouraged reading a paper written by a strong writer. In addition, the weak writer's capacity to help the strong writer is somewhat limited. Later in the term, once students have become more familiar with the terminology and the process and once they feel more confident about their opinions, trading papers between writers of different ability can be useful. Then the weaker writer can see a good model, and the stronger writer will receive better criticism than would have been possible in an early critique.

Once each student has a classmate's introduction, the students need to be given specific directions for critiquing. You might do this by listing questions on the board or on a handout. Some teachers make up forms for this kind of exercise. And, it might even be useful to have students help compile a list of the elements they think they need help with. For this particular exercise in analyzing strengths and weaknesses of only the introduction, the following questions might be asked:

1. What ideas are particularly effective and interesting?

2. Considering the thesis stated in the introduction, what information do you need to have in the introduction which you do not find there? What further background information do you need to understand this thesis or the purpose of the essay?

3. Do you have trouble understanding how the writer gets from one idea to the next? Are the transitions smooth?

4. Which sentences are particularly effective? Which words, phrases, or sentences do you find especially strong? Which details do you especially like?

5. Are there places where the writer needs to be more specific and less abstract?

6. Who seems to be the audience for this essay? How do you know? What words or phrases has the writer used which suggest the audience?

7. Do you see any grammatical or punctuation problems which weaken the credibility of the paper?

8. What specific suggestions can you make to this author to help him or her strengthen this introduction?

Students need ample time to read the introductions more than once and to write full answers to these questions. They should begin their written critiques with a salutation—"Dear Sally"—and at the end of their comments they ought to sign their names. Using names reminds the students that they are talking to a human being who has feelings. Students generally are not embarrassed to have their work read by classmates or to give honest criticism if teachers explain that the students are a community who can teach one another the way more experienced writers do in workshops. If teachers appeal to students in a professional way, students usually respond enthusiastically.

If time allows, you may wish to have students critique two papers in the same session. Doing so gives each writer two sets of suggestions, suggesting to him or her that as brief a piece of writing as an introduction can impress readers in different ways, often widely different. Having two or three responses to the introduction can also help students begin to understand the concept of audience. And using only part of an essay for a critique provides a quicker way of helping the students begin to think critically about the writing process.

Some teachers like to monitor the critiques before they go to the students whose work is being criticized, but others think that students perceive the teacher's interference as threatening or as somehow diluting the impact of their peers' thoughts. Monitoring the first critiques, however, helps teachers spot the students who need help learning how to respond to a piece of writing. A conference with them early in the term can often help them respond more beneficially to their classmates. In addition, the teacher's help may be needed after the critiques have been given to the writers whose work was being scrutinized. Faced with what may seem like really bad advice, students usually ask the teacher's opinion—as they should be invited to do—before they incorporate the peer's suggestions into their papers. Furthermore, having several critiques of early papers and having to evaluate these critiques for possible benefit to the paper sharpen the writer's own critical sense: he or she must consider the relative merits of the critiques. And even if the student incorporates some bad advice into the essay, it is likely that critiques of a later draft will send up a red flag in time.

Although students are certainly capable of taking others' papers home to critique them, the process does not work as well at home as it does in the classroom. Divorced from the presence of their classmates and the energy of the class, students are less willing to take the time required to do a careful critique. In the classroom the spontaneity creates excitement that is missing in the dorm room. Students like the energy produced by instant feedback.

Some teachers prefer to use peer critiquing only on a draft of the whole essay, and some prefer to wait until the student has revised several times. But no matter what stage of the essay's development is evaluated, the process should be more or less the same: the teacher should give specific questions for the readers to answer in writing, and students should be given ample time both for reading the paper several times and for writing their responses.

In some programs teachers operate their classrooms like real writers' workshops, at least for one or two class meetings a week. During the workshop sessions students are asked to present their own papers to the class for discussion. A fifty-minute period allows for two such presentations per session. For such classes the students who will present their work are responsible for bringing enough copies of their paper so that each member of the class will have one. Some teachers prefer to have the papers distributed several days before the discussion, and others prefer that the students read the papers a couple of times just before the discussion.

Sitting or standing in front of the class, the student whose paper is up for discussion explains what the purpose of the paper is and its intended audience. The student also tells the class the specific problems encountered in writing the essay, explaining as clearly as possible why these trouble spots seemed to present problems. Then the student opens up class discussion of his or her essay.

Like other kinds of peer critiquing, this process can benefit students in several ways. But this kind of face-to-face discussion also requires good preparation. Many of us have had the experience of trying to lead a class discussion in which an apathetic class participated only through groans and the occasional monosyllabic response to a question designed to evoke a lively conversation. Students who are told simply to discuss an essay written by a classmate will respond in a similarly apathetic way, particularly if they think that grammar and usage are the focus of the discussion. They must be prepared with a vocabulary of critical terms, and they must be taught what kinds of features to notice in an essay. And, as in written critiques, they need to be shown how to make suggestions for improvement that will sound positive and affirmative, not negative and hurtful. This vocabulary and preparation may be provided in a handout of basic critical terms and a teacher's demonstration of a critique.

Some teachers using the workshop method have found that they must pull back from the group (literally pull their chairs away from the circle so as to be unobtrusive) and not speak at all until the end of the class, even when long pauses tempt them to rush in and explain the weaknesses and strengths of the paper under discussion. If the students know that the teacher is observing, not participating, they are far more likely to take control of the discussion.

Teachers who want to spend less time with peer critiquing may reap some of the benefits of the workshop method with in-class criticism of single paragraphs, perhaps taken anonymously from one or two papers in the process of revision by class members. Even a brief exercise like this helps acquaint students with the vocabulary they need as writers and thinkers, and it helps reassure weak writers, who may be reluctant to speak, that their unspoken ideas are the same as those articulated by stronger writers in the class who do not mind speaking out.

Peer critiquing reinforces the important concept that writing involves not only the writer but also the reader. And it makes students aware, as they likely have never been before, that the ultimate reader is no longer the English teacher. The teacher's written comments on the paper and the grade can help the student improve, but comments by peers contribute substantially to students' learning about their own writing and that of others.

Suggestions for planning and incorporating collaborative writing and collaborative learning may be found in the *Collaborative Writing* section of this supplement.

SUGGESTED READING

Barron, Ronald. "What I Wish I Had Known about Peer-Response Groups but Didn't." *English Journal* 80, no. 5 (Sept. 1991): 24–34.

Berliner, David, and Ursula Casanova. "The Case for Peer Tutoring." *Instructor* 99 (April 1990): 16–18.

Bishop, Wendy. "Helping Peer Writing Groups Succeed." *Teaching English in the Two-Year College* 15, no. 2 (May 1988): 120–25.

Hughes, J.A. "It Really Works: Encouraging Revision Using Peer Writing Tutors." *English Journal* 80 (Sept. 1991): 41–42.

Leverenz, Carrie Shively. "Peer Response in the Multicultural Classroom: Dissensus—A Dream (Deferred)." *Journal of Advanced Composition* 14, no. 1 (Winter 1994): 167–86.

Liftig, R.A. "Feeling Good About Student Writing: Validation in Peer Evaluation." *English Journal* 79 (Feb. 1990): 62–65.

McManus, Ginger, and Dan Kirby. "Using Peer Group Instruction to Teach Writing." *English Journal* 77 (March 1988): 78–80.

McKendy, T. F. "Legitimizing Peer Response: A Recycling Project for Placement Essays." *College Composition and Communication* 41 (Feb. 1990): 89–91.

Spear, Karen. *Sharing Writing: Peer Response Groups in English Classes.* Portsmouth, NH: Boynton, 1988.

Sultan, Gerry. "No More Sixes, Nines, and Red Lines: Peer Groups and Revisions." *English Journal* 77 (Sept. 1988): 65–69.

PART ONE
CHAPTER SEVEN

Conferences: Student and Teacher One-on-One

Some of the most valuable time that we spend with students is time we spend in conference, one-on-one, in our offices. Conferences can give us the opportunity to make students more confident of their ability to write and can give us the opportunity to nurse along the weak writers who, without our interest, would simply give up. Conferences are the times when we try to overcome the inequities inherent in teaching writing to a group of students with different abilities, problems, and levels of commitment.

One of the important early realizations that we writing teachers come to is that if we have twenty-two students in a class, for all practical purposes we are teaching twenty-two different courses. Each student's problems are so individual that some of them cannot be addressed satisfactorily in class. Thus, the conference becomes useful as a means of dealing with concerns that lie outside the interests of the class as a whole. All students need the extra attention to individual problems that conferences offer, but the strong students and the weak ones particularly benefit from this attention to their needs, which normally are not addressed when circumstances force us to teach more to the average students.

In an effective student-teacher conference, the teacher is learning along with the student. The conference can teach us what we are not clarifying in the classroom and what concerns and needs among students we should respond to in our assignments.

But how do we get the students into our offices willingly for help? How do we use this valuable time to the best advantage to achieve both our goals and those of the students?

Many departments stipulate that instructors must devote a given number of hours per week to office hours, and teachers in such departments dutifully post the hours when they will be available to students. Students do not, however, always come. Thus the teacher sits in the office waiting for students who often want help but are too frightened of the teacher or formality of office suites to seek it. Unfortunately, many students have grown up with the notion that it is a sign of weakness to ask a teacher for help, and too many of them have been told that the big bad college teacher is interested not in helping students, but flunking them.

One good solution to the problem of getting students into the office is simply to require each student to sign up for a ten-minute get-acquainted conference during the first week of school. Yes, that is heavy traffic for the teacher, but it is time well spent. During such a visit the teacher might ask the students to explain their experiences with writing in high school and their current feelings about their writing. Students usually begin to relax in this kind of conference, and they seem to appreciate the new teacher's interest in their past. Teachers who have large classes may find it helpful to take notes immediately following the conference so that they will be able to recall the meeting when the student comes in again.

In addition to showing students that we don't maim and torture them in our offices but are, instead, interested in them, these short, early-in-the-term conferences show them that we are available in our offices to help them continue to learn about writing. These mandatory get-acquainted conferences show them where our offices are and emphasize that we expect them to come there regularly. The conferences also help the students see that being a member of a community means taking responsibility for getting help with their work.

Even with these early required conferences, many students still will not come regularly when they need help, and some won't come at all until they've received a low grade or two. Therefore, some instructors schedule mandatory conferences three or four times during the term to go over problems that students have had up to that point. Other teachers, however, believe that they waste their time in requiring students who really do not want help to come for conferences, and they believe that they are not teaching the students responsible behavior if they force-feed students. Some teachers simply do not have the luxury of this choice because the available time for conferences is severely curtailed by other responsibilities and by having too many students in writing classes. Thus teachers must decide for themselves if they want to do more than extend an invitation for students to come in during office hours.

Even before we can decide how to use conferences most efficiently, they must decide what to do about the outpouring of personal problems that frequently occurs in conferences about writing. Because students in composition classes share information about their personal lives in papers they do for us, even in non-narrative essays, it stands to reason that they will talk with us about their personal lives. After all, we are already submerged in their personal lives by virtue of having read their essays. For many of us this kind of personal sharing is one of the allures of teaching: We want to know that we are dealing with human beings. On the other hand, teachers who hear about students' personal lives can find themselves in serious dilemmas about how to proceed with a student and sometimes how to evaluate a student's work.

Most of us can deal effectively, if not painlessly, with certain kinds of personal problems, for example, problems of the heart. We have learned simply to listen and not to offer advice. And we've learned to steel ourselves against the appeals to pity. What we have a harder time with are students who come ostensibly to talk with us about a paper but who really come because they need help with a serious problem: parents who are getting a divorce, siblings or friends who have betrayed them, friendships that depend on drugs, sexual abuse by family or other adults, and serious financial threats, even homelessness.

What do we do in the face of these serious issues? They are not remotely related to comma splices and paragraph coherence, yet we cannot teach students who are threatened by problems of such magnitude. Since we have read our students' papers about what they think and feel, students recognize that we know them better than most teachers do—and even, perhaps, better than most adults do—and they seek us out as confidants and counselors.

But we must remember that we are not trained counselors, and we must therefore resist the temptation to offer advice. We may give the wrong advice, seriously wrong. Of course, few teachers want to turn their backs on students who really need help. What we must do is get the right kind of help for them insofar as we are able to do so.

We might, for example, suggest that the student see a trained counselor in the infirmary or counseling center. Most colleges have such personnel, but often students (and many faculty) do not know about them, or they believe that these counselors are for "mentally ill" people, not someone with problems like theirs. Often a student who is reluctant to seek such help beforehand will go if a teacher he or she respects suggests it. The teacher may even intervene to the extent of calling to make the appointment while the student is there. Such action conveys the teacher's concern. Students don't usually think the teacher is trying to get rid of them or sidestep the problem if the teacher has listened carefully to the student and has explained that this problem warrants a kind of advice that the teacher is not trained to give.

Sometimes several sessions in which the teacher only listens and reacts sympathetically help the student think through the problem. In serious cases, when the student refuses to seek counseling, a concerned teacher may want to call the staff therapist or the dean, or the department head or a dorm counselor and alert him or her to the student's problem—preserving confidentiality, of course.

Finally, teachers must decide if what a student is telling them is really a crisis or is a ploy to win sympathy and easier grades or exemptions from deadlines. Dealing with the genuine malingerer may requires some sympathy, but usually we help this kind of student more by showing firmness in requiring them to meet deadlines and practice responsible behavior. Some students must be shown that they are responsible for the consequences or their actions or inaction. The best technique for dealing with these types of students, however, is to make writing so stimulating and so dynamic that they will want to do the assignments. One of the ways to interest the lagging student is to have a conference in which the teacher really excites him or her about writing. Such conferences should also reinforce and intensify the interest of the hard-working, responsible student.

To work well, a conference must put students at ease, not on the defensive. We should greet them pleasantly and ask how they are doing generally. If the students have requested the conference, we should invite them to voice the concerns that prompted the conference. Often these will be specific questions about a specific paper. We can answer these questions fully—but we should do so only with the student's help; that is, we ought to question students about how they would go about solving the problem they've brought to us, but we must to question them in a nonthreatening, supportive way. These questions help us understand where communication in the classroom is breaking down, and they help teach the student more about independent problem-solving.

More often, however, the conference is prompted not by specific questions about a particular assignment but by the student's vague feelings that he or she is failing, is lost, is depressed about his or her progress, or just discouraged. These kinds of conferences require more skill than those prompted by specific questions.

First, we should try to get the students to articulate insofar as possible how they are feeling about the process of writing and why they feel this way. Typically they say that no matter what they write, teachers don't like it and it's no good, or they say that they just can't think of anything to say and they feel stupid, or they say that they've never been any good at writing before and they don't sense that it's getting any better now.

Then we can ask them to explain how they go about the process of writing: how long they spend brainstorming, how long they spend drafting a paper, what forms their revision and proofreading take. We want to try to show them, of course, the direct correlation between their work habits and their attitudes. In most cases students who are discouraged are not spending enough time or they are badly misusing the time they spend writing.

No conference should end, however, with simple platitudes about spending more time and proofreading better, though we usually do want to make these points. What we want to do in the conference is get the student excited about some piece of writing he or she is working on.

Often the reason students struggle with writing is that they cannot focus well enough on a suitable topic. They try to develop topics that are much too general, usually because they have not practiced brainstorming. In a conference we can help by asking questions that lead them from the outer layer of a topic to the core where their real knowledge, interest, and excitement lie. Such questions should be easy, in a conversational tone reflecting genuine interest in the subject. After the students work through our brainstorming questions and get to the focus of the topic, where their answers are enthusiastic and full, we can illustrate on paper the kind of process they have gone through in getting to the topic: We can show them our own diagram of their thought processes, as they have articulated them, and we can show them the suggestions for brainstorming in Chapter 2, section d, of the handbook. Then we should listen while they talk through their ideas for the work at hand and make some sketchy notes on how to proceed. Usually students led through this process will leave our office geared up to write. Teachers need to realize, however, that they can talk too much during a brainstorming session and end up telling the student more or less what to write. This kind of "overtalking" does not help the student learn to think through the topic and become an independent learner.

Other kinds of problems bring students in for conferences. Some students who are discouraged have written papers that were well-focused but in need of major revision in terms of content, organization, mechanics—or all of these. In these cases we want to spend the conference talking with the students in such a way that they will feel proud of the achievements they have made in the paper up to this point so they will feel confident in their ability to revise the paper and excited about doing so. To this sense of achievement we can add a sense of the independence they will have in learning to use the handbook to help answer questions as they write.

To foster this positive response, we want to reinforce orally the compliments we originally wrote in the margins of the paper. Instead of bowling the students over with negative comments about their inadequacies, we want to emphasize what they have done well. We can, for example, compliment them on choosing a uniquely interesting topic and focusing it well, or we can talk about particular images and phrasing that are especially evocative and original. Perhaps we can pull out a particular paragraph that has exceptionally good coherence and unity and structure, or we can comment on the excellent sentence variety in a place or two. (Of course, sometimes these strengths in the writing have come about accidentally, but our comments make the students aware of what they are doing well so that they will continue to do it, whether or not it has been an accident this time.)

Once we have made the students feel good about their achievements, we can explain what they need to do to strengthen the paper. If they believe that we like it up to this point and that the paper is worth working on—that they in fact have an interested reader—they will be eager for our suggestions for improvement. Even so, these suggestions should not be a list of errors. As much as possible, we should ask the students to explain what they think they should do to strengthen a particular passage, the organization, or the examples. Our gentle questioning makes the students feel more in control of their writing and helps them become more independent thinkers.

Whatever problem students bring to our offices can usually be handled best by beginning with positive assumptions about their ability to write and their interest in writing. No matter how positive we may be, however, students who have just received a paper with a low grade generally are anything but positive. Thus, it is a good idea to tell them that we are happy to make appointments—but not on the day we return papers. We should tell them that we expect them to go home and look at our written comments and look up the references to the handbook so that our conference with them will be really productive. Certainly if students have taken their papers home and spent some time trying to figure out what the problems are and how they can be solved, they are more likely to have useful questions when we do have our conference.

Often the students' questions should be the focus of the conference with the teacher doing little more than listening and asking other questions. The Socratic method works well with many students. Sometimes the right question opens the student's imagination or memory so that he or she goes away from the meeting eager to get the new ideas down in writing. The judicious question helps teachers avoid talking too much and inadvertently dictating the paper. Questions also work well when teachers see several students at once.

In a conference with several students teachers can focus on a problem common to those students. Although many teachers prefer to have only one-on-one conferences, heavy teaching loads sometimes mean that a conference with several students at a time is the only way to see everyone. These multistudent conferences often help the student more than the teacher alone can—the interaction with other students can help make the student more independent and more excited about writing.

Although a few students may resist our efforts in conferences to help them improve, most will appreciate the time we spend with them and will use our guidance to think in positive ways about their writing. It's human nature to enjoy personal attention, and most students thrive on our interest in their lives and their writing—and especially the intersection of the two.

SUGGESTED READING

Arbur, Rosemarie. "The Student-Teacher Conference." *College Composition and Communication* 28 (Dec. 1977): 338–42.

Carnicelli, Thomas A. "The Writing Conference: A One-to-One Conversation." *Eight Approaches to Teaching Writing.* Ed. Timothy R. Donovan. Urbana, IL: National Council of Teachers of English, 1988. 101–31.

Flynn, Thomas, and Mary King, eds. *Dynamics of the Writing Conference: Social and Cognitive Interaction.* Urbana, IL: National Council of Teachers of English, 1993.

Kuriloff, Pesche E. "Reaffirming the Writing Conference: A Tool for Writing Teachers across the Curriculum." *Journal of Teaching Writing* 10, no. 1 (Spring/Summer 1991): 45–57.

PART ONE
CHAPTER EIGHT

Some Ideas for Assignments and Classroom Activities

Before we meet our students the first day of class, we need to have analyzed the skills we want to teach them and formulated some assignments and classroom activities which will help them develop those skills. Certainly making a syllabus (see Chapter 4 in this supplement) helps us come to terms with how much we can realistically expect to teach and the order in which we should introduce the skills we want our students to master. But carefully planning our assignments and use of time in the classroom can further ensure that we meet our goals.

For most of us, the list of basic skills we want our students to have when they leave us includes:

1. Clear sentences in terms of diction and phrasing.
2. Coherent organization of both paragraphs and essays.
3. Transition between and within paragraphs.
4. Adequate subordination and economy of language.
5. Different methods for developing paragraphs and essays and the ability to make the appropriate choice of methods for a given purpose and audience.
6. Focused topics and narrow theses.
7. Critical thinking, the ability to detect weaknesses and strengths in the arguments of others and to support their own arguments with appropriate evidence.
8. Basic use of the library and other resources for research.
9. Up-to-date documentation.
10. Conventional mechanics.

Certainly other, more sophisticated skills would be expected of accelerated students, but these are the basic skills for most students in their first college writing course. Our task is to design assignments and activities that will teach and reinforce these skills.

Before students write anything, they need to begin thinking in terms of the purpose of what they are writing. Are they writing to inform their audience or to persuade their readers? Many teachers prefer to begin the course by having students discuss both audience and purpose and their interrelatedness. (See Troyka, Chapter 1.) An obvious but effective way to generate meaningful discussion of audience and purpose is to have students bring to class samples of various kinds of writing. Teachers may direct these choices or simply ask students to bring two different kinds of writing to class for discussion. Interesting discussions can result from students' assessments of the purpose and audience for writing such as letters to the editor in a newspaper or magazine, advertising copy, the preface to a book, directions for assembling a toy or an appliance, a poem or a piece of fiction, a sales letter, an article in a teen magazine, an article in a technical journal, and so on.

Class discussion of audience can include speculation about the educational level and perhaps even the social and economic level of the intended reader.

Many teachers are finding that letter-writing and journal-writing can help students understand audience and purpose. A good way to help students learn to be comfortable in the class at the beginning of the term is to pair each student with one or two others and have the students write letters to one another following specified instructions that will help you achieve your purpose. For example, you might ask the students to write about what points in the class discussion confused him or her and speculate on the causes of the confusion. Similarly, using a journal for a group of five or six students for the entire term might afford the students to learn something about audience and purpose if you specify the kinds of issues and topics the group is to address each week. I have found that these work best if I grade only for the ideas and only mark major mechanical errors. Students naturally enjoy writing to their peers and reading what their classmates think, and we should design assignments that take advantage of this kind of writing that seems more like pleasure than work.

An effective exercise to follow up this discussion is to have students choose one piece of writing that they have brought into class and to have them rewrite it, or part of it if it is long, for a different kind of audience. For example, a student might choose to rewrite an article about general nutrition that is aimed at retired Americans so that it would appeal to teens. In struggling to rewrite the article, the student would have to grapple with important choices of vocabulary level and sentence structure and tone.

Another effective exercise, especially useful early in the term, is to ask students to write a paragraph that gives directions to a carefully specified audience (a babysitter, a mechanic, a parent, etc.), directions which explain how to do something, and then ask them to rewrite the directions for a totally different, perhaps more general audience. You may even ask students to write an analysis of the kinds of changes they made and the reasons for them.

This same kind of exercise works well in helping students understand purpose. Too often students have the mistaken impression that certain kinds of topics are informative—always—and that other kinds of topics are persuasive—always. Students usually gain valuable insight if we have them write a paragraph or brief essay which is informative in its purpose and then have them rewrite it to make it persuasive. A written analysis of the changes students made in this revision may also help them see the critical importance of determining purpose before they write.

Some teachers ask students to identify the purpose and intended audience as part of the students' plan for the essay. They may even ask the students to explain how their choice of purpose and audience will affect other choices they must make as writers—choices of vocabulary level, tone, sentence structure, paragraph structure, and so on. Other teachers ask students to write the intended audience and the purpose in the upper corner of the first page of the essay. Even this simple act emphasizes to the students the importance of these decisions.

An example of a cover sheet which identifies audience and purpose is this title page for the essay given in Chapter 5 of this supplement:

Title: Sinatra Versus Vandross   January 30, 1996   Steve Feyl
Comparison-and-Contrast Essay   Dr. Julian, English 11K

Audience: This essay is written for a friend on my hall, Eric Fuller. At the beginning of the year we had extensive conversations about each other's taste in music.

Purpose: The purpose of this essay is to take an unbiased position on the topic to show Eric that even in our different opinions about music, there also are similarities.

Thesis: Comparing the emotional quality of their music, the importance placed on lyrics, and their use of rhythm can reveal that even the most diametrically opposed singers share important similarities.

Difficulties in writing the essay: The chief difficulty in this essay came with research. I know a lot about Frank Sinatra but relatively little about Luther Vandross. Eric Fuller gave me help with this as he gave me one of Vandross's tapes and directions about what to look for in his music. Grammatically, linking verbs still gave me the most trouble. I also had trouble making the essay flow together with proper transitions.

No matter what method of organization a teacher chooses for the writing course, some attention to purpose and audience are essential early in the term.

Some teachers prefer to organize their course by theme. They may ask students to write several papers on a subject of general interest to the students. Organizing the course by topic provides teachers an ongoing opportunity to have students explore differences in purpose and audience.

Using this approach, the teacher might ask students to write an informative essay on a topic which the students have specialized knowledge of, rock music or clothing fads, for example. The students would tailor the essay to whatever audience they chose. Then the teacher might have the students expand the essay into a research project and change the audience significantly. Next the teacher might have the students make the paper persuasive, for a totally different audience than that of the first two essays. Other variations are possible and instructive. Combining this topical approach with a rhetorical approach also works well for some instructors.

Many teachers prefer to organize their course by rhetorical type. In this organizational plan the teacher's most important decisions are choosing the order in which to present the types of development and making appropriate assignments for each.

Beginning with narrative and descriptive writing puts students at ease because these kinds of development draw on the students' own experiences and feelings. Although some students have a hard time finding something to say even about themselves, most students can write a personal narrative more easily than an essay developed by other methods. Beginning with personal narrative helps weak writers who are intimidated by the writing process. Because they are writing about something they know well, they do not have to struggle with both form and content at once, at least not to the degree that later papers will require.

A good beginning assignment is a topic like "Until I experienced X, I had never understood Y." If the event (X) being described is limited to something which happened in a couple of hours, the student has a manageable narrative chunk to control in the essay. A useful exercise is to have each student write three versions of this topic sentence, each version completing the blanks with a different experience. Then teachers—or classmates—can choose the topic that will lend itself best to an interesting narration.

While the students are working on this essay, however, the teacher can teach several skills at once. As students begin to brainstorm in an effort to narrow their topics, they should discuss the purpose of the essay and the intended audience. On all outlines and drafts of the paper, students should write the intended audience in the corner as well as the level of formality dictated by that choice. Thus when classmates critique the essay, they can comment on whether or not the writer is considering the needs of the audience that he or she has chosen.

In addition to audience and purpose, a narrative essay as a first essay is a good place to begin teaching various related kinds of paragraph development. In class students can practice developing paragraphs by chronology. We can show them the differences between chronological narrative paragraphs, chronological process paragraphs, and chronological climactic paragraphs.

A narrative essay also gives us the opportunity to talk about topic sentences in narrative and descriptive writing—to say that they are not always stated but that they can be. A useful classroom exercise is to take a hypothetical version of the topic they are working on and have the class break the narration down into segments that could become paragraphs. They then can write topic sentences for each segment. The class can do this assignment independently and then discuss their versions, or the class can collaborate on an outline and topic sentences for the sample topic, with the teacher writing their suggestions on the board.

The narrative essay is also a good place to begin a discussion of descriptive detail. It's a good time to make the point that no piece of writing is entirely narrative or descriptive or expository or argumentative but that we classify according to the dominant mode. We can ask them to imagine the lack of interest they would create in a version of "Little Red Riding Hood" if they were allowed to tell only what happened and not to describe the big, bad wolf or the dark forest.

In discussing the relationship between narration and description, we can begin to emphasize the need for specific, original detail in writing, a point that we need to make over and over during the course. One good way to help students think about detail is to do a classroom exercise in which each student must write five sentences about the classroom, one sentence evoking each of the senses (taste, touch, smell, hearing, and sight). After students share their sentences, it's fun to have them do sentences again, this time making similes and metaphors. Exercises requiring all the senses help them realize that good description means doing more than simply saying how something looks. Having done this exercise, we can even insist that the narrative essay have sentences evoking each of the senses at least once. Such an arbitrary, artificial exercise impresses upon students the need to create for their reader the world which is part of narration.

Moving from narrative writing to the descriptive essay, we can show students that although descriptive essays often relate events, their primary goal is to convey a sense of place and mood. A good topic is something like "Why X-place makes me feel Y-emotion." Some teachers like to have students describe a place on campus, looking for the unusual features that make it unique. Having students write an in-class description of the classroom or of a common place can make it easy for the teacher to talk about cliches and the need for fresh, specific detail.

Good choices for the third paper are comparison-and-contrast writing or classification. Both are a little harder for the students than narrative and descriptive writing because they require some analysis, but they are less difficult at this point than, say, cause and effect or definition or argument.

Compare-and-contrast is a type of development that most students have been taught in high school; thus they are usually receptive to learning a more sophisticated version of it. This type of development offers a lot of flexibility with regard to the kind of topic, depending on what skills we want to teach along with it.

We can appeal to the interests of the class with this kind of essay, by having art students, for example, compare and contrast paintings or statues by the same artist, or engineering students compare and contrast methods for solving some kind of problem. Obviously teachers who are using a reader can easily have students compare and contrast essays with regard to content or style. Most students enjoy comparing a movie with its sequel or a book with the movie made from it, and they enjoy comparing television shows or magazine ads or fast-food restaurants— any topic, in fact, which draws on what they experience.

A topic which works well for the teacher who is interested in teaching stylistic elements early in the course is to have students compare and contrast the styles of two movie reviews. This assignment can teach several important skills: it can teach students how to use the library to find movie reviews, it can teach them about conventions of quoting, paraphrasing, and summarizing, and it can teach them about elements of style.

Teachers can also couple comparison-and-contrast writing with definition. A good assignment is to have students compare and contrast definitions of the same word in several dictionaries. This assignment helps acquaint students with various kinds of dictionaries. Now that students use computers which have spell-checks and thesauruses, it's more important than ever that we help them understand how to use a dictionary and why they should want to. Many students are unaware of the differences between abridged and unabridged dictionaries, and few of them have had any experience with the *OED*. Thus a comparison of a couple of dictionaries or definitions teaches much more than the method of comparison and contrast.

Classification works well after comparison and contrast because the idea of comparison and contrast is implicit in classification. Certainly topics like "types of horror movies" or "types of golf swings" work well, but students also enjoy classifying groups of people. If we allow them to write on such topics as "types of drivers" or "types of basketball fans," we can teach them about the dangers of stereotyping and the need for qualifying our generalizations.

Since the organization of a classification essay is implied by the topic, the time we normally would have to devote to explaining structure—obviously important with comparison and contrast, for example—can be devoted to work on transition between and within paragraphs and varieties of introductions and conclusions. This assignment also gives students further practice in using effective descriptive detail.

Equally useful because of its relatively simple organization is the process essay. This kind of essay provides a perfect way to teach attention to audience. We can have students explain a process in the second person and have them rewrite it into the third person. We can have them assume that the audience is somewhat familiar with the process or is not familiar with it at all and do a version suitable in each case. Particularly useful for weak writers, process writing can really boost the understanding of transitions and assumptions made by the writer.

As a prelude to argumentation, many teachers find it helpful to do a definition essay. Students believe that if they don't know the meaning of a word, they should simply look it up in a dictionary. To correct this misconception, we must show them that disagreement about definitions of abstract terms is at the root of many issues. We can ask them, in fact, to find editorials to share in class that argue about terms like *pornography* or *freedom* or *democracy* or *liberal* without defining the terms.

Before we ask students to write a definition of one of these kinds of terms, though, having students write paragraph-length definitions of a slang term or newly-coined term like *yuppie* or *airhead* can teach them about the subtleties of definition. Within this paragraph they can practice citing the dictionary meaning (more practice in quoting accurately) and expanding it by giving examples, defining in terms of negatives, comparing the term with terms closely related to it, exploring the source of the quality or thing, explaining how our culture generally defines the term, and stating, finally, their personal definition.

As an essay assignment, we can have the students choose from a list of abstract terms like *pornography, art, fun,* or *selfishness,* or we can give them more practice with comparison-and-contrast writing by having them compare and contrast often-confused terms like *right* and *privilege, selfishness* and *self-esteem* or *hero* and *celebrity.* In making these kinds of assignments, we want to emphasize that in argumentative writing, careful writers define their terms early in their arguments and do not shift the meaning of these terms. Some careful attention to audience and purpose in definition is also important.

Argumentative writing requires a lot of preparation by the teacher, but it allows us much flexibility in teaching some secondary skills. Many teachers prefer to teach argument only in the context of a research project since students usually know too little about most issues to argue their positions without research. But whatever kind of argument topic we decide to assign, we need to do some preliminary work with the class to discuss the difference between inductive and deductive reasoning, kinds of acceptable evidence, fallacious thinking, and definition of terms.

Far too many of students believe that if something is printed it is good and true, and, therefore, one of our first chores is to explain that all sources and all arguments are not equal. We must communicate that the quality of a writer's argument reveals much about the usefulness of the information he or she presents.

One good way to begin teaching students about the relative merits of arguments is to bring in to class some letters to the editor from the local newspaper. These nearly always contain fallacies, often memorable ones. After going through the basic kinds of fallacies, we can ask students to look for further printed examples of fallacious thinking. This assignment also reinforces the importance of attention to audience and purpose.

A useful kind of essay to have the students write at this point is a cause-and-effect essay that will require some research. This assignment allows us the opportunity to teach students to distinguish between sufficient and contributory causes, and it is a good opportunity to emphasize the dangers of hasty generalization.

Students can also learn much about argument by writing critiques of arguments. A good exercise that can be done in two stages to teach the difference between summary and evaluation involves such a critique. We can give students a set of brief newspaper arguments as the raw materials for a couple of essays—the point/counterpoint arguments that appear daily on the editorial page of *USA Today* work well for this. In the first of these essays, we may choose to teach the students to summarize the main points each writer makes and point out the fallacies and other weaknesses in each argument. The students should also consider the audience and purpose each writer seems to intend. With this assignment students practice comparison-and-contrast technique, and they must come up with a thesis that is non-evaluative. They must also continue to develop their ability to quote accurately and to handle quotations gracefully. Once they have done the essay summarizing the arguments of the two editorials, students should then be assigned a paper that evaluates the arguments and argues that one is a better argument than the other.

Assigning a full-fledged argument paper requires some careful thought by teachers. If we want to offer students a useful alternative to the traditional, argumentative, library paper, we can have them do some research of a primary nature. A useful topic is to have students tackle some school issue, interviewing appropriate authorities, polling students with their own questionnaire, and observing and analyzing the problem. Then they can support their findings with secondary material.

Similarly, students can do an interesting argumentative paper by investigating a particular kind of job or career and arguing its strengths and weaknesses. To do this essay, they might shadow someone who has that kind of job, interview others who are in the profession, and read about that field, including government predictions about the profession.

These kinds of assignments are useful not only because they teach argumentative skills but also because they help make the point that the kinds of writing and research students are doing do not end with graduation but that research, argument and the writing process are important to us all throughout our lives.

Similarly, in assigning more traditional library projects, we ought to encourage our students to write about other disciplines. We should help them see writing as a life skill, not something one does for English teachers. Forcing students to write a paper on Keats' poetry simply because they are registered in an English class is folly: Our own partiality to Keats' poems should not blind us to the fact that students will pursue writing projects with real enthusiasm only when they are interested in the topic.

Encouraging a biology major to write about the greenhouse effect will help him or her learn more about the writing process—and its continuing role in our lives—than forcing down another paper on *Hamlet* or Greek mythology. Presumably a few of our students will propose literary topics.

Whether or not we choose to organize our course by rhetorical type, these assignments can be modified to suit classes organized in other ways, for example, those emphasizing research skills, language, or paragraph development and sentence structure. And in addition to using rhetorical types for essays, they can be applied to paragraphs to strengthen the skills the students are learning, and some work with sentences also helps both stylistic and grammatical problems as well as punctuation. One useful method of reviewing mechanics is to present "Oops!" sentences to the class each week, that is, a list of sentences we take from their own papers to illustrate problems with mechanics that the class as a whole is having. These are particularly good supplements to the handbook because, unlike the handbook, they present several problems at once. Students seem to enjoy going over these sentences because they are "real" in a way that the handbook's exercises are not.

Whatever method of organization teachers choose, the best teachers are always looking for new assignments and new ways to improve those they've found to be helpful. We need to keep files of particularly effective and ineffective sentences, paragraphs, and essays. We need to collect effective and ineffective arguments. We need to pay attention to our students' interests, always thinking how we can merge their interests with our goals.

SUGGESTED READING

Arrington, Phillip. "A Dramatistic Approach to Understanding and Teaching Paraphrase." *College Composition and Communication* 39, no. 2 (May 1988): 185–97.

Bizzell, Patricia. " 'Contact Zones' and English Studies." *College English* 56, no. 2 (Feb. 1994): 163–69.

Black, K.M. "Audience Analysis and Persuasive Writing at the College Level." *Research in the Teaching of English* 23 (Oct. 1989): 231–53.

Carter, Michael. "A Rhetorical (and Teachable) Approach to Style." *Teaching English in the Two-Year College* 14. no. 3 (Oct. 1987): 187–94.

Capossela, T.L. "Students as Sociolinguists: Getting Real Research from Freshmen Writers." *College Composition and Communication* 42 (Feb. 1991): 75–79.

Fick, V.G. "A History-Based Research Paper Course." *Teaching English in the Two-Year College* 17 (Feb. 1990): 34–35.

Gillis, Candida. "Writing Partners: Expanding the Audiences for Student Writing." *English Journal* 83, no. 3 (March 1994): 64–67.

Horner, Winifred Bryan. *Composition and Literature: Bridging the Gap.* Chicago: University of Chicago Press, 1983.

Hourigan, M.M. "Poststructural Theory and Writing Assessment: 'Heady, Esoteric Theory' Revisited." *Teaching English in the Two-Year College* 18 (Oct. 1991): 191–95.

Kari, Daven M. "A Cliche a Day Keeps the Gray Away." *Teaching English in the Two-Year College* 14, no. 4 (Dec. 1987): 265–72.

Krest, Margie. "Monitoring Student Writing: How Not to Avoid the Draft." *Journal of Teaching Writing* 7, no. 1 (Spring 1988): 27–39.

Lent, Robin. "'I Can Relate to That...': Reading and Responding in the Writing Classroom." *College Composition and Communication* 44, no. 2 (May 1993): 232–40.

Matthews, Mitford M. "The Freshman and His Dictionary." *About Language.* Ed. William H. Robert and Gregoire Turgeon. Boston: Houghton, 1986.

Meyer, Charles F. "Teaching Punctuation to Advanced Writers." *Journal of Advanced Composition* 6 (1985–86): 117–29.

Moxley, Joseph M. "Reinventing the Wheel or Teaching the Basics: College Writers' Knowledge of Argumentation." *Composition Studies Freshman English News* 21, no. 2 (Fall 1993): 3–15.

Pullman, George L. "Rhetoric and Hermeneutics: Composition, Invention, and Literature." *Journal of Advanced Composition* 14, no. 2 (Fall 1994): 389–412.

Rafoth, B.A. "Audience and Information." *Research in the Teaching of English* 23 (Oct. 1989): 273–90.

Raymond, R.C. "Personal and Public Voices: Bridging the Gap from Comp 101 to Comp 102." *Teaching English in the Two-Year College* 17 (Dec. 1990): 273–82.

Roemer, M.G., et al. "Portfolios and the Process of Change." *College Composition and Communication* 42 (Dec. 1991): 455–69.

Spivey, N.N. "The Shaping of Meaning: Options in Writing the Comparison." *Research in the Teaching of English* 25 (Dec. 1991): 390–418.

Thaden, B.Z. "Derrida in the Composition Class: Deconstructing Arguments." *Writing Instructor* 7, no. 3 (Spring 1987): 131–37.

Wall, Susan V. "The Languages of the Text: What Even Good Students Need to Know about ReWriting." *Journal of Advanced Composition* 7, no. 1 (1987): 31–40.

Wallace, D.L., and J.R. Hayes. "Redefining Revision for Freshmen." *Research in the Teaching of English* 25 (Feb. 1991): 54–66.

Washington, Eugene. "Yes-No Questions in Teaching Writing. *Journal of Teaching Writing* 4, no. 2 (Fall 1985): 204–09.

PART ONE
APPENDIX

Further Suggestions For Reading

No matter how hectic the pace in our classes, we must—as professionals—try to keep up with the scholarship in our field. In the last twenty years much useful information about the theory of teaching composition has appeared, information that can enrich our teaching significantly if we can eke out the time to delve into the theoretical underpinnings of what we do. Recent scholarship has also made available a wealth of practical applications that can enhance our teaching and our usefulness to students.

Each chapter in this supplement ends with a brief bibliography, necessarily selective, and this additional bibliography lists both practical and theoretical books and articles of a more general nature than those appended to chapters.

Adams, P. D. "Basic Writing Reconsidered." *Journal of Basic Writing* 12 (Spring 1993): 22–36.

Carpenter, Carol. "Exercises to Combat Sexist Reading and Writing." *College English* 43 (1981): 293–300.

Carrell, P. L., and L. B. Monroe. "Learning Styles and Composition." *Modern Language Journal* 77 (Summer 1993): 148–62.

Cope, Bill, and Mary Kalantzis, eds. *The Powers of Literacy: A Genre Approach to Teaching Writing*. Pittsburgh: The University of Pittsburgh Press, 1993.

Fox, Thomas. "Repositioning the Profession: Teaching Writing to African American Students." *Journal of Advanced Composition* 12, no. 2 (Fall 1992): 179–93.

Harris, Helen J. "Slice and Dice: Response Groups as Writing Processors." *English Journal* 81, no. 2 (Feb. 1992): 51–54.

Heilker, Paul. "Nothing Personal: Twenty-Five Forays into the Personal in (My) Composition Pedagogy." *Writing Instructor* 12, no. 2 (Winter 1993): 55–65.

Hindman, Jane E. "Reinventing the University: Finding the Place for Basic Writers." *Journal of Basic Writing* 12, no. 2 (Fall 1993): 55–76.

House, Elizabeth B., and William J. House. "Problem-Solving: the Debate in Composition and Psychology." *Journal of Advanced Composition.* 7, no. 1 (1987): 62–75.

Howatt, A. P. R. *A History of English Language Teaching.* Oxford: Oxford University Press, 1984.

Johns, A.M. "Written Argumentation for Real Audiences: Suggestions for Teacher Research and Classroom Practice." *TESOL Quarterly* 27 (Spring 1993): 75–90.

Kinneavy, James L. "The Process of Writing: A Philosophical Base in Hermeneutics." *Journal of Advanced Composition.* 7, no. 1 (1987): 1–9.

Lindemann, Erika. *A Rhetoric for Writing Teachers.* 3rd ed. New York: Oxford, 1995.

Murphy, James J., ed. *A Short History of Writing Instruction from Ancient Greece to Twentieth-Century America.* Davis, CA: Hermagoras, 1990.

North, Stephen M. "Research in Writing, Departments of English, and the Problem of Method." *ADE Bulletin.* 88 (Winter 1988): 13–20.

Rose, Mike. *Writer's Block: The Cognitive Dimension.* Carbondale, IL: Southern Illinois University Press, 1984.

Roy, Emil. "Freshman Composition with a Business Focus." *Teaching English in the Two-Year College* 14, no. 4 (Dec. 1987): 285–93.

Smithson, Isaiah, and Paul Sorrentino. "Writing Across the Curriculum: An Assessment." *Journal of Teaching Writing* 6, no. 2 (Fall 1987): 325–42.

Tchudi, Stephen, and Diana Mitchell. *Explorations in the Teaching of English.* 3rd ed. New York: Harper & Row, 1989.

Troyka, Lynn Quitman. "The Phenomenon of Impact: The CUNY Writing Assessment Test." *Writing Program Administration* 8 (Fall–Winter 1984): 27–36.

Whitaker, E. E. "A Pedagogy to Address Plagiarism." *College Composition and Communication* 44 (December 1993): 509–14.

PART TWO

Collaborative Writing

Patricia Kelvin
Youngstown State University

Scott A. Leonard
Youngstown State University

PART TWO

Teaching Collaborative Writing

This is a manual for practitioners, for the hard-working teacher striving to give students an understanding of rhetoric and the writing process. Whether you have been teaching composition for years and are ready to try something now or you are new to the teaching of writing, we hope this manual can refresh and renew your sense of excitement about teaching. The student comments you will read in this chapter are quoted (with the names changed) directly from the "process logs of memos" that we ask each student to keep for their own, as well as our, evaluation. You will also find some collaborative assignments that have worked in our classrooms. Some of the ideas presented here may work for you in your environment while others will not. But they should be a springboard from which you can dive into your own pool of ideas. While we have mentioned some of the best-known scholars working in the field of collaborative learning and writing throughout our text, we have compiled a more extensive bibliographic essay at the end for those who would like to read further on the subject.

Collaborative writing can be an extremely rewarding experience for both teacher and student. When things work well, students gain confidence in their ability to write and to work with a team. The teacher will feel energized working with a class of active, enthusiastic learners. What could be better than a writing pedagogy that encourages students to discuss every dimension of writing from topic selection to word choice? What more can the writing teacher want than a way to encourage students to view effective writing as a process within their conscious control? Collaboratively written papers, like single-authored texts, go through a series of drafts. But, unlike single-authored texts, collaborative papers will actively integrate concepts of audience, tone, planning and purpose into the writing process because at every step student must explain to one another what they think the paper needs and why.

Why Teach Students to Write Together?

Collaborative Learning is Good Pedagogy

The basic premise of what John Trimbur, Kenneth Bruffee and others have called **collaborative learning** is that peer influence is a "powerful educative force" (Bruffee 638). It is the conversation of students working together that disseminates information more surely and erects conceptual scaffolding more efficiently. In the context of the group, the internalized conversation of human thought becomes the externalized authority of the collective. The pedagogy that has developed from these assumptions has transformed both classroom architecture and the teacher's role. Those accustomed to a teacher-directed lecture or discussion classroom might wonder whether organizing students in small groups to discuss course content can lead to anything but idle chat. But those who have assigned small group exercises that give students hands-on practice in generating paper topics, or in appropriately punctuating works-cited entries, or in identifying the cohesive devices that published writers employ, know the power of collaborative learning. Providing students with opportunities to talk and work together in small groups allows them to remember and exchange points of view about what they read for class, to develop concepts more extensively than they could on their own, and for weaker student to learn from their stronger peers. Indeed, collaborative learning is excellent pedagogy because it organizes and focuses the natural human impulse to create knowledge through small-group discussion even as it fosters learning by doing. Those instructors who use response groups in their classes already know the value of collaborative learning. Collaborative writing takes the process even further.

Collaborative Writing is Good Pedagogy

Asking students to write together takes advantage of the substantial benefits derivable from collaborative learning. Student groups of two or more authors working on a single document are able to combine their individual strengths, tackle large and complex projects, share information, challenge each other to think longer and harder about the demands of a writing situation, and model for one another the learnable skills of writing. In groups, students can also divide the work of reading, writing, organizing, and editing.

For almost a decade now, we have observed that writing collaboratively impels students to think about the learning process in ways that individuals writing alone might not. Because writing groups must negotiate everything from meeting times to paper organization to word choice, the individuals within those groups must explain what they think will work for a paper and why—a phenomenon that makes every aspect of text production an occasion for discussion, questioning, and information-sharing. In addition, because students must arrange work time in advance, they tend to procrastinate less and work with a specific sense of what they want or need to accomplish at a given time. Thus, most students, having a limited time to work on a project each week, will begin to see their project as a series of tasks, and pace their work rather than do everything they have time for the night before it is due.

Moreover, our students have often told us that they enjoy the experience of writing and researching together. One student remarked that it felt good having "someone to talk to about [a] project—about how to do it and what to say." The collaborative writing classroom frequently buzzes with energetic conversation, joking, and the excitement of discovering just the right words for a complex idea. But even when all is quiet, or when the conversation is not so jovial, students derive many benefits from the experience. For example, our students frequently report experiencing what cognitive psychologists have called *decentering* effects. As one young woman put it, "working with others in this quarter has really opened my eyes to different perspectives on how to write and on life in general." Other students confirm what many researchers have long suggested: Collaboration is good for students because it allows them to pool their resources. "Jim was our researcher," reported Allison in her process log, "while Kim's editing skills really helped us out at the end."

Collaboration is Typical Work After College

Learning and writing together is more than just good pedagogy; it is the ideal preparation for our students' careers after college. Lunsford and Ede (1990), after surveying seven professional organizations, report that approximately half of all writing in the workplace is, broadly defined, collaborative. Newspaper editorial boards, for example, routinely engage in "peer response" critique and in group brainstorming when determining the position their paper will take on a given issue. Such technical fields as computer science, engineering, or pharmaceuticals consider the planning and writing and editing of multi-author documents standard procedure. Small groups of workers in such nontechnical fields as insurance, psychology, and social work also share the work of creating a wide variety of written products. When Patal from public relations, Chen from economics, and Jastrow from product pricing sit down to draft a corporate report, they pool their expertise to accomplish that task. Writing teachers whose pedagogical goals include helping students prepare for careers are better served by incorporating practice in writing together rather than by teaching only as though they subscribed to the Romantic ideal of the inspired poet-prophet, alone in his or her garret, struggling to put sublime visions to paper. After all, even poet-prophets like Wordsworth and Shelley benefited greatly from sharing ideas and manuscript copy with their friends.

Collaboration Affords Several Advantages

Students can undertake more complex projects when they write together than when they work alone. As writing instructors, we like the fact that, even in a ten-week quarter, collaborative writing projects can be considerably larger in scope than traditional single-writer assignments. Not only can group-members divide the workload but they can also tackle several tasks simultaneously. As Jeanine wrote in her process log:

> After leaving your office, we decided how to split up the work. I had a wedding to attend this weekend and Randy had to work the Memorial [Golf] Tournament. Our time was very tight as the end drew near. (So melodramatic!) [*sic*] For a remedy to this problem, Randy and I thought it would be a good idea for three of us to work on the ethics paper while the others worked on the revision to our earlier paper.

Students writing together can emphasize their strengths rather than their individual weaknesses. Unlike many individual projects in which students' deficiencies stand out, group projects allow students to contribute what they are best at while at the same time learning, from their peers, ways to improve areas in which they are weak. As Jenny wrote in her post-paper analysis memo,

> It took a long time to decide how we were going to do this paper because each of us had different ideas, and we really didn't want to let them go. But finally we decided that Glenn was faster in the library and so he would do the research. I would do the writing, [and] Mel would be the technical expert—he got

everything into the computer. We actually got a draft done two days early and we all worked on the revision. I surprised myself by coming up with some better ideas for digging up the research and I had to admit that Mel and Glenn improved the way I'd worded the draft.

Collaboration also encourages social interaction and promotes understanding of and respect for others. We find that collaborative learning and writing provide students with a sense of community so often missing in large general-education classes. Most of our students begin the term as strangers, but often become friends as well as coworkers. Dan and Frank were Air Force officers in training, majoring in engineering. Eliza, the third member of their group, was a Singaporean national in Hotel Management. She wrote,

> I do enjoy being in the group and I thank you ... for putting me in this group. It amazes all three of us that we did not have any major disagreements with one another.... For this meeting I brought some "hot roasted peas"—a Chinese delicacy for them to taste and they really enjoy it. [*sic*] They are good friends and colleagues to work with.

In addition, collaborative assignments promote originality because each group's approach to an assignment will be as unique as the group that generates it. While we did not begin teaching our students to write collaboratively as a way of discouraging recycled papers from other classes or generic "frat file" themes, we have since discovered that having our students work in groups has virtually eliminated plagiarism. We are continually encouraged to find that students working in groups work harder at topic selection because they must arrive at an approach on which everyone is willing to work.

Creating a Collaborative Classroom

Reshape the Classroom Landscape

Have you ever wanted to re-create a room? Your garden? Yourself? Creating a collaborative classroom gives you that personal and professional opportunity—imagine sowing an annual garden where you once had only perennials. Like the carefully planted linear rows of the traditional formal garden, the traditional classroom features rows of desks that face the front of the room where the instructor directs classroom activities. By contrast, the collaborative classroom is more like a country garden where the aesthetic is not rigidly constrained but is allowed to flower randomly and exuberantly. Desks are no longer always and only arranged in rows but can be clustered around the room to allow student groups space to talk among themselves. The collaborative classroom is an active and noisy place rather than a quiet and passive one. But the alternative to orderly formality is not unproductive chaos; rather, the noise you hear is the sound of knowledge being created.

Teaching in the collaborative classroom, then, works better with desks that can be moved. Ideally, the collaborative classroom will have round tables and moveable chairs, an arrangement that allows students to work together or singly and to have room enough to spread out and share their in-class assignments, research materials, and drafts. (After all, how many resources can be laid out on the typical student desk?) The overall effect of this arrangement is to direct students' attention away from the teacher and toward themselves and their peers.

Rethink the Role of the Writing Teacher

The traditional model of the teacher posits one who directs, plans, assigns, grades, controls, and judges, and positions the instructor at the center of activity as *the* decision maker, *the* authority, *the* expert. Obviously, most of us excelled in traditional classrooms, even if some did not thrive in such learning environments. But if the goal of our instruction is to equip students with a working knowledge of sound rhetorical principles and compositional strategies in the surest and most efficient way possible, it should not matter to us whether we drive the car or lay the road. The role of the teacher in a collaborative classroom is considerably different from that conceived in the traditional model. In the collaborative model, the teacher provides the theatre and drafts the script, but the students take center stage. Standing in the wings, the teacher of collaborative writing facilitates, encourages, advises, and nurtures students who can learn by doing in a semi-structured environment.

Does the teacher of collaboration simply walk away from her students and leave all learning entirely in their hands? Emphatically no. While some theoretical positions assert the importance of decentering authority in the collaborative classroom, complete decentering is impossible. So long as a teacher's assessments of papers are the most authoritative response they get, and so long as he or she retains the power to assign permanent grades, the instructor has all the power that matters to most students.

Rather than looking to an impending Students' Paradise where all traces of hierarchical teacher-student power relations have been erased, we prefer to think of the teacher in the collaborative classroom as *sharing* power and using her or his authority to motivate students and to construct a learning environment that will encourage students to grow as thinkers and as writers. In our own teaching practice, we generally find ourselves playing one (or more) of three roles: the reassuring listener (counselor); the dispenser of information and clarifier or assignments (teacher); and the mediator of disagreements (referee). The teacher may well have the ultimate institutional authority, but she can also work *with* students on invention and organizational strategies in nondirective ways, negotiating evaluative standards that recognize students' own measures of success.

Encourage Students to Take Responsibility for Learning

The most exciting and professionally liberating part of teaching collaborative writing is that we stop managing and directing the flow of information and conversation in our classrooms and start creating a dynamic learning space in which *students* take the responsibility for learning. In the collaborative learning environment, the teacher moves away from the chalkboard or the overhead projector and organizes students into groups that work together on the many aspects of the writing process. Teacher-centered classrooms place the onus on the instructor to present information that we hope our students will absorb, albeit passively. But in a classroom where students work in small groups requiring them to create solutions to the problems they identify, the burden for learning is instead placed on the learners.

Teaching Collaboration: Conceptual Vocabulary and Group Behaviors

Remind Students as they Work Together that Collaborative Groups are Groups of People

While it may sound obvious, one must always remember that, like the individuals who compose them, collaborative groups are unique and human. Students differ in degree of motivation, type of learning style, and overall skill level. Accepting these differences and adjusting one's expectations appropriately will decrease the instructor's frustration. Equally obvious and important to remember is the fact that collaborative writing groups are social in nature. Some students (and some writing teachers) worry that joking around, passing campus gossip, or sharing information about friends and family is counterproductive. However, seemingly off-task chat is not only normal to collaborative groups, it is absolutely necessary. People who have developed a friendly working relationship can be candid with one another. It is very hard to tell a stranger that his or her ideas or writing need work. Therefore, the writing teacher should encourage social interaction within groups but prepare them beforehand for the adjustments that individuals will need to make in order to work successfully with others.

We teach our students the following "Ten Commandments" of working together:

I. COMMIT YOURSELF TO THE SUCCESS OF THE GROUP. When it is just you, you can decide whether or not you want to work hard on a project or come to class. But you do not have that luxury when you work with a group. When you miss class or a group meeting, you owe your group the courtesy of a phone call. And you should make up any time lost to the group.

II. REMEMBER THAT EACH MEMBER OF YOUR GROUP IS AN INDIVIDUAL; getting to know each other's strengths, capabilities, and personalities will help your group immensely.

III. RESPECT THE DIVERSITY OF ABILITIES AND BACKGROUNDS IN YOUR GROUP. These differences may be, at times, frustrating, but diversity is actually the greatest benefit of working in a group.

IV. ASSUME A DIFFERENT IDENTITY WHEN YOU WORK IN A GROUP. Your identity as a member of a group differs from that of the solitary scholar. When your groups writes or speaks, it is "we" and "us," not "me" and "I."

V. ALLOW PLENTY OF TIME FOR COLLABORATIVE WORK. It takes longer to work with someone else than it does to work individually—but the product is invariably stronger. Give your group time for spontaneous, informal talk; many times, this is where the best ideas come from.

VI. ACCEPT SOME CONFLICT. More creative solutions are found with some conflict that without it. However, focus your disagreements on ways of approaching a task and arriving at a satisfactory solution and not on individual personalities or abilities.

VII. DISCUSS CONCERNS AND FRUSTRATIONS OPENLY WITH EACH OTHER. It is best to work problems out as they occur rather than to allow them to fester, unattended, until a crisis brings them out. If members' work habits or attendance bother you, tell them so in a nonthreatening way.

VIII. MAKE IT A GROUP PROJECT TO FIND A SOLUTION TO GROUP PROB-
LEMS. If the group cannot find a solution, talk to the instructor immediately.
    IX. LISTEN TO EACH OTHER AND ASK CLARIFYING QUESTIONS. Many
problems are simply matters of poor communication.
    X. COMPROMISE. Face it, you simply will not get your own way all
the time.

Teach Group Roles

The traditional top-down management model of group behavior desig-
nates one person the leader and all other group members as followers.
Typically, the leader solicits information from the followers, decides what
the group should do, and organizes the rest of the group to implement
the plan. However, the top-down management approach is rarely successful in the classroom because not all self-appointed (or even elected)
leaders have true leadership qualities, and not all followers are completely
sanguine about their subservient roles. Furthermore, in the collaborative
writing classroom, the top-down management model often inhibits members of a student group from making rhetorical and compositional decisions. In a writing course, everyone needs to learn how to organize, to
choose an appropriate topic, and to develop a workable approach to a
task. Consequently the instructor in the collaborative writing classroom
should work hard to assure that responsibility for projects is equally shared.
More often than not, when someone "takes charge" a general breakdown
in communication and motivation results. For that matter, vote-taking
and a "majority rules" approach to decision-making can cause disaffected
group members to drop out of the process. *Everyone* has to buy into the
topic and the process, or it is no longer a group effort.

Appropriate behaviors for successful group work can be learned. They
should not be regarded as intrinsic personal qualities, despite conventional practice. Rather, behaviors should be thought of as contributing to
the group's success or detracting from it. First, we teach students to identify and practice a wide range of positive and negative roles that a member of a group might play. We stress that these roles are not permanent,
but will vary *during* a group meeting as well as from day to day.

Early studies by social scientists (notably Benne and Sheats) have identified three kinds of behaviors associated with group member performance:
group-building roles, group-maintenance roles, and group-blocking roles.
We have modified their lists of roles to apply to the writing classroom.

Group Building Roles

The Initiator

➤ suggests new or different ideas for discussion

➤ proposes new or different approaches to the group's process (for problem solving or for writing)

The Elaborator

➤ elaborates or builds on suggestions made by others

➤ gives relevant examples

The Tester

➤ restates problem

➤ evaluates the group's progress toward completing assignments

➤ looks for holes in the plan

➤ pulls together or reviews the discussion

The Task-designer

➤ raises questions about member preferences for styles or working

➤ suggests the tasks that the group will need to accomplish its goals

The Responder

➤ evaluates written work with suggestions for revision

Group Maintenance Roles

The Facilitator

➤ makes sure all group members have a chance to speak

➤ supports the contributions of others

The Vibes-watcher

➤ focuses on the group's process

➤ mediates differences of opinion

➤ reconciles points of view

➤ calls for a break if discussion gets too warm

THE TIME-KEEPER

➤ focuses on task completion

➤ maintains the forward progress of the meeting

➤ when necessary, shifts the group's work back to accomplishing its stated goals

Group Blocking Roles

THE AGGRESSOR

➤ deflates status of others in group

➤ disagrees with others aggressively

➤ criticizes others in group

THE BLOCKER

➤ stubbornly disagrees with and rejects others' views

➤ cites unrelated personal experiences

➤ returns to topics already resolved

THE WITHDRAWER

➤ will not participate

➤ daydreams during group meetings

➤ carries on private conversation within group

➤ is a self-appointed taker of notes

THE RECOGNITION SEEKER

➤ tries to show his or her importance through boasting and excessive talking

➤ is overly conscious of his or her status

THE TOPIC JUMPER

➤ continually changes the subject

THE CONTROL FREAK

➤ tries to take over the meeting

➤ tries to assert authority

➤ tries to manipulate the group

THE LOBBYIST

➤ tries to get group to work on his or her own special interests

THE CLASS CLOWN

➤ wastes the group's time by constantly showing off and telling funny stories

➤ acts with nonchalance or cynicism

THE BOOR

➤ talks endlessly and irrelevantly about his or her own feelings or experiences

THE DEVIL'S ADVOCATE

➤ when he or she is more devil than advocate

Giving students the conceptual vocabulary necessary to identify and discuss both positive and negative group roles is essential for healthy collaboration. We provide the "Ten Commandments" and the Roles List as handouts. For students to try out these behaviors, we conduct the following role-playing exercise early in the term.

We print out several copies of the Roles List, cut them apart, and number enough roles to place at least one builder, one maintainer, and one blocker in groups of three to five. (Say, we have a class of twenty-four. We number building roles from one through eight, maintaining roles from one through eight, and blocking roles from one through eight. We will, of course, repeat some roles.) Students draw a slip of paper with a role on it and look for the others in the class who share the same number (all the *one's* work together, all the *two's*, etc.).

Telling the students not to reveal their roles, we offer them a humorous prompt for discussion (such as coming up with a nonviolent sport to replace football; developing unusual ways to use the library after hours for fund-raising, and the like). We give them five to ten minutes to talk about the prompt while playing their assigned roles. We then repeat the exercise with new groups, sometimes enlarging the groups to expand the numbers of roles.

Afterwards, we ask the class to discuss what happened. They find not only that they can recognize the behaviors but that they *can* assume unfamiliar roles. They also learn how disruptive a blocker can be and how little progress takes place when no one assumes a group-building role. While we reiterate the need for everyone to work on group-building behaviors, we suggest that for each meeting, one member take on the facilitator's role, one the vibes-watcher's, and one the time-keeper's. Rotating these tasks from meeting to meeting helps group cohesiveness and minimizes antagonism.

Other Useful Group Behaviors

We have found that groups manage their time better if they set goals for each meeting—preferably at the end of the previous meeting. Our more successful groups usually agree to an agenda in advance of a meeting and then the timekeeper checks that the previously established goals have been met before the group plans its agenda for the next meeting. When groups discover that they have diverged substantially from the agenda, they can take that occasion to review the group's goals and discuss whether adjustments are necessary.

During all group meetings, everyone should take notes. Too frequently, one of the group's female members is directly or indirectly assigned "secretarial" duty. Alternatively, one person offers to take notes in order to control decision-making. We require everyone to record the group's activities and decisions. At the end of each meeting, group members compare notes to assure that they all agree on what happens next. To encourage everyone to take responsibility for keeping track of what is going on, what got said, what got done, and when the group will meet next and why, we usually assign a post-paper memo or journal in which students are asked to report what happened at all group meetings. This memo serves as more than a diary; it also provides an ideal occasion for students to reflect upon the writing process, group interaction, and the ways in which their project evolved from topic selection to final draft.

About Conflict

A number of researchers distinguish between procedural, affective, and substantive conflicts (particularly Putnam, 1986, and Burnett, 1993) as important sources of both positive and negative friction among group members. If the collaborative project is to move forward, substantive conflict, which comprises negotiations about the scope of the project, the nature of the problem, possible solutions, and the form and content of the written product, must occur. Frequently, though, students confuse this vital form of conflict with its destructive counterfeits, affective conflict and procedural conflict. Affective conflict occurs not at the level of ideas, but between individuals who are either pitted against one another in a bid for control of the group or who simply rub each other the wrong way. While teaching consensual group behaviors can minimize conflict arising from a naked power grab, it is virtually impossible to mitigate personality conflicts short of reassigning one or more members of a group. Procedural conflict issues from misunderstandings over who is responsible for what or what the group's next move should be. Discussions emanating from procedural conflict can be quite productive if everyone has an equal say. Groups that work to mitigate against affective conflict usually emerge from the process stronger and with a clearer sense of direction.

Substantive conflict originates in a group's discussion of the form and content of its essay. This form of conflict—even if it is quite spirited—can be the most productive of all. Students who argue with one another for or against the inclusion of illustrative examples, the positioning of information within an essay, and which issues to cover or to exclude are not necessarily fighting. Rather, they are learning about how to write effectively by testing ideas out on their peers. Obviously, group-maintenance roles are extremely important in preventing substantive conflict from degenerating into counterproductive interpersonal exchanges. The communications expert needs to insure that everyone has a chance to voice an opinion and the nurturer needs to draw attention to the strengths in everyone's ideas. Writing instructors should actively encourage lively debate among coworkers who know that they are being heard and appreciated for what they bring to the group.

Responding to Peers in the Collaborative Group

The value of the peer response group is well established in composition pedagogy, and some even consider the peer response group as synonymous with the collaborative writing group. However, the work of the collaborative writing group goes beyond responding to the single-authored drafts of fellow students. In the collaborative group, students develop topics and approaches to writing as well as doing the writing itself. Peer response is a continuous action. Collaborative groups integrate the benefits of peer response into a group's writing process. Students cowriting a document must explain specifically to one another what features of a draft require revision and why.

Responding to and Revising Each Other's Work

We have found that the following advice makes a good handout to guide individual responders and collaborating writer/readers:

➤ Feel free to evaluate and make changes to each other's work.

➤ Remember that it is very difficult for people to relinquish ownership over anything they have written. Here are some suggestions for making this process easier:

❏ As a writer, try to create an objective attitude toward your work. People are responding to the words on the page, not to *you* as a person.

❏ As a reader/responder/reviser, the best rule is *The Golden Rule*: "Treat others as you would like to be treated." A little sensitivity will go a long way in dealing with your peers' writing.

❏ If you recommend changes in something someone else has written, be sure to explain to the writer how and why you changed it. If you do not, you risk alienating that person from your team.

Collaborative groups, like individual writers, can lose sight of the way their writing reads to others. When entire groups exchange papers for response, they will develop a greater sense of writing for a "real" audience if they know that others will be responding to their work. Those who are teaching more than one composition class might exchange papers across classes, which usually minimizes the "kid glove" attitudes with which some students appraise the work of their classmates.

Groups can also form a revision collective with members developing specific areas of expertise for a given assignment. For example, the members of each group can divide the *Handbook's* revision checklists (pages 56–57) so that all questions are addressed. As an added advantage, having beginning responders work through scripted response sheets like these will help them avoid engaging in either unnecessarily harsh critique ("This stinks—you should drop out of college!") or unhelpfully vague praise ("Sounds great to me—have you considered publishing it?"). On responding days, teachers should direct the focus of comments. It is not appropriate for students to pinpoint typos and usage errors in the first draft when they should be addressing such crucial global issues as organization, point of view, and sufficiency of included information. By the second or third draft, students can pay attention to usage, word choice, and transitions. As a means of building your students' repertoire of response techniques, you can—after some preliminary explanation—ask them to build their own lists of issues they should check for at each stage of the drafting process.

Assigning Groups

Assigning Groups is Too Important to Trust to Luck

Although group assignment has received little research attention, teacher lore reveals a number of methods by which students are groups: dividing students alphabetically; pulling names from a hat; counting students off by threes, fours, or fives; requesting student preferences; classifying students by academic major; or assuring a strong and weak writer in each group, to name a few. These more-or-less random methods can be very useful for breaking the ice (see below), however, when assigning groups for major projects we consciously try to put students together in ways what will assure the highest possible level of group success—both academically and interpersonally. In class on the first day of the term, we sample writing abilities by asking students to write us letters in which they discuss:

> ➤ their reason(s) for being in the class and their expectations from it,

> ➤ their level of motivation for the class,

> ➤ their previous experience with writing, and,

> ➤ their career expectations.

A week later, we ask students to write a more formal memo to us telling us what to know before placing them in groups, paying particular attention to (a) work and academic schedules, work habits and style (e.g., driven vs. laid-back), (b) previous experience with groups and attitudes about group-work, (c) other relevant personal data (e.g., whether students think themselves shy or likely to dominate a conversation), and (d) any preferences they might have for working or not working with particular students in the class. After students prepare an initial draft of these memos, we require private conferences which give us a chance to discuss their writing and the information in the memos, and also to let us get to know them better.

In addition, during the first two weeks of class, we introduce small group activities and role-playing exercises for students to learn successful collaboration techniques. These in-class activities also provide opportunities for us to observe how students work together—who is quiet, who assertive, who stays on task, who gets sidetracked, and so forth. Toward the end of the second week, we assign groups of two to five members according to the following priorities:

➢ Student schedules should permit at least two non-class hours per week in which all could meet. Often this consideration supersedes all others. After all, students must be able to work *together* on shared work. Even were groups to meet in class only, students could work toward the group's goals by completing individual responsibilities outside class and then merging their work during class time.

➢ Students should be similarly motivated. Hard workers with high grade motivation should not be placed with those who cannot or will not spend adequate time for the class or who are simply passing. Many theorists believe that strong students should be identified and placed with weak students to encourage peer mentoring. While we find the idea philosophically noble, we have repeatedly found that differing motivation levels create the most significant roadblocks on the journey to success. Highly motivated weak students have the potential to do well and learn a great deal on their own whereas unmotivated students of whatever ability level are the source of most student complaints about collaboration.

➢ Students are not placed with those they had asked not to work with—generally a result of their having worked together in a prior class. If possible, students are placed with students they do ask to work with.

➢ Students with special needs (e.g., non-native speakers, returning older students, shy students, minority students) are placed with those that intuition suggests might be more accepting of them.

In general, we find that large groups (four to six members) work best for in-class discussion-oriented activities whereas small groups (two or three members) work best for multi-draft writing assignments. Because writing with others—especially at first—generate numerous procedural questions, we "roam" the classroom spending time with each group listening and/or participating as needed. We also require each group to attend a private faculty-office conference for each major assignment. Most groups, however, ask for more than one conference.

Determining Group Longevity

In our ten-week quarters, there is barely enough time for students to get to know each other, let alone to build the comfort and trust necessary to create effective working relationships. Thus, barring catastrophes, we prefer to keep student groups together for the length of the term. Some teachers vary group membership so that students can benefit from exposure to a range of work styles and personality types. However, we have found that such logistical considerations as time availability outside of class usually make a general reshuffling of writing groups unworkable. To give our students the benefits of working with a wide variety of others, we "scatter" the members of collaborative writing groups when we work on in-class group non-writing activities.

What to Do about Ungroupable Students

We always emphasize the necessity of collaborative work and outline in our syllabi, and, during the first class meeting, the unique demands it will place on students (e.g., responsibility to others, required work outside of class, the understanding that writing takes longer with a group than writing solo). Even so, we have occasionally found students for whom working in collaborative groups outside of class poses an exceptional burden. We remember, for example, one student who, in addition to a seventeen-quarter hour academic load, spent four to five hours or road work a day training for an Olympic bicycling event. He could spare only one hour, one day a week, to work with his group. Obviously, a student who cannot meet with others outside the classroom will be unable to contribute fully to his or her group. In this particular case—and the principle applies more widely—the student was allowed to undertake individualized, scaled-down versions of the class's writing projects and thus to fulfill the course requirements.

More frequently, we have encountered students who perform so poorly that they pose a significant liability for their groups. We have had students who seemed almost pathologically driven to subvert the group's efforts through habitual tardiness, failure to complete promised tasks, or by being chronically critical or obstinate. Usually we resolve these difficulties by allowing the problematic student to work alone. Cooperative students should not be forced to bear the burden of another's obdurate intransigence.

Developing Group Ground Rules

Urge each group to develop its own drafting process. Some groups are happier if each member drafts a separate section of the document which the group will merge later as a complete draft. Other groups prefer to have each member draft the entire document, with the group picking and choosing the best parts of each. Still other groups prefer to huddle around a single computer and write the entire document together from scratch. Groups whose members have a hefty campus commute appreciate the ability to conduct at least some of their work independently or by telephone. We have even had groups who faxed sections of their papers to each other.

In any case, student groups should develop their own work styles, determine their internal management rules, and allocate tasks however they see fit. The instructor can monitor these arrangements by asking students to keep a detailed, confidential log of each group meeting—both in and out of class. The quality of these logs varies of course: high-achieving students might write pages; low-achieving students might write but a few paragraphs, generally focusing on tasks rather than ideas or behaviors.

Aiming the Groups Toward Success

Success in the Collaborative Writing Classroom

No matter how many drafts a group project undergoes, as some point the text must be evaluated. But what measures of success are appropriate to a collaborative project? In the traditional writing classroom, the answer is straightforward enough. If a text is logically organized, well-articulated, presented from an interesting point of view, and more or less free of mechanical errors, it can be considered a success. In the collaborative writing classroom, the issue of what constitutes a "good paper" is more complicated. Naturally, a final draft of a collaborative project featuring the above hallmarks of a well-written paper is—at least at the discursive level—successful, but in the collaborative classroom one teaches both how to write and how to work well with others. For this reason, we consider both pedagogical emphases during grading. Some groups collaborate very well together, but for a variety of reasons produce a less than perfect product. Other groups produce an excellent product, but do so by subverting the aims of collaboration. Because we believe the goal of the collaborative writing classroom is to teach both collaboration and writing, then success can only be defined as a combination of good collaboration and a well-written document. Thus, while grading, we consider a student text "good" only when produced by a truly collaborative group.

Obviously, our increasingly grade-conscious students want to know what, exactly, an "A" paper is—especially when they learn that "good collaboration" is a class requirement. We include our students in the process of defining an excellent collaborative paper by asking them to create a list of discursive features and group behaviors that distinguish an "A" paper. First the small groups draw up their lists, and then prioritize them. The class discussion that follows can provide an excellent occasion to talk about what makes a piece of writing interesting to a reader and what kinds of group behavior constitute good collaboration. As groups report what they came up with, we write their ideas on the board and by the end of class have a list of criteria that the students agree should apply to the final evaluation of their writing. This exercise is important not only because it allows collaborative groups input into the grading process, but also because students remind one another of the criteria for a good paper and good collaborative techniques as they work together.

Introduce Collaborative Work Sequentially

An informal survey of collaborative assignments in the writing class indicates that they generally fall into four broad categories:

➤ BRIEF ASSIGNMENTS, perhaps short textbook problems, that can be completed within the classroom, usually within one or two class periods. For example, the *Handbook's* exercises in the sections on tone [1d], or distinguishing between primary and secondary evidence [5h] can be performed collaboratively and result in a brief written summary of findings.

➤ SHORT ESSAYS OR BRIEF RESEARCH PAPERS of relatively short duration but which require that groups meet outside class. As preliminary exercises for extended research papers, collaborative groups can be sent to the library to do exploratory research on their topic. After consulting all information resource systems, students can collaboratively write a report that discusses their topic's major issues.

➤ MAJOR PROJECTS, such as multipart reports, which are long-term assignments of several weeks duration requiring extensive non-classroom work for completion. (See below for examples of major collaborative projects.)

➤ TERM-LONG PROJECTS, whether quarter or semester, which are the focus of a course. Ideally, term-long projects should be undertaken in the second of a two-term sequence after students have had several opportunities to write with others.

We find that teaching collaboration works best if it is introduced gradually and sequentially over the course of the term. In the beginning, we assign short-term projects that minimize logistical difficulties and give us an opportunity to assess individual and group dynamics. In addition, several short-term assignments, undertaken early in the semester or quarter when the class is focusing on group roles and peer response techniques, gives students a chance to adapt their customary approaches and behavior patterns to the requirements of collaborative group work before embarking on longer assignments. These brief, out-of-class assignments can also serve as group invention exercises, providing students with an occasion to gather and organize information even as they refine their paper topics. At last, after several brief in-class assignments and at least one short out-of-class exercise, students should be sufficiently comfortable with their group members' working styles and the unique requirements of collaborative writing to embark on a major project. In our classrooms, major projects take about three weeks to complete, which allows time for two or three drafts and for at least two in-class peer response sessions. While we think it is important to ease students into collaborative writing, we also think that students should work on several assignments simultaneously. Life is rarely one discrete task after another, and being required to turn in drafts of major projects even as they begin short writing tasks relevant to their next major project teaches them to manage their time and intellectual activity.

Breaking the Ice

It is important for the instructor in the collaborative writing classroom to recognize the essential nature of writing teams. Therefore, it is good practice to allow a little time at the beginning of each class meeting for groups to chat. (At first, you might have to explicitly tell students that they have about five minutes to catch up on group gossip before class gets rolling.) Before groups are assigned—and certainly right after they have been—it will be necessary to orchestrate some ice-breaking exercises that will give individual students a chance to meet one another and to find out that collaborative writing can actually be fun. Here are some ideas for getting the ball rolling:

Warming Up: In-class Collaborative Assignments

➤ Students compile the group's schedule and phone list.

➤ Students interview each other and report back to the group what they have discovered. This can also lead to the enumeration of expertises, equipment, or capabilities that each member brings to the group.

➤ While students understand the concept of audience in a general way, they also find writing for others intimidating. The following collaborative exercise can help students overcome this anxiety and simultaneously explore the concrete characteristics of an audience.

☐ Divide the class into groups of three to five

☐ Ask your class to envision a group of refugees rescued from the primitive conditions of nomadic life and brought to a modern American city. Even after being shown how to operate the lights and faucets in their apartments, the refugees remained so innocent of the technologies that we take for granted that they washed their clothes by soaking them in the sink and then pounded them with heavy objects—just as they had done by river banks for generations.

☐ Ask each group to craft a set of instructions that would tell the refugees how to wash and dry their clothes using a modern washer and dryer. Students will have to bear in mind that they cannot take what they would consider "common knowledge" for granted. Even simple commands like "open the lid" or "check the lint filter" will require careful explanation— perhaps even illustration.

In this exercise, the social nature of the interaction forces students to *articulate and practice* what they know about audience needs. By visiting each of the groups as they work, you can gather a few representative comments demonstrating what your students already know about their audience to share with the entire class when it comes time to synthesize what was learned during the activity.

Create an Ongoing Discussion about Writing Projects

Another way that the collaborative writing instructor can point student groups toward success is to require numerous individual writing assignments that ask students to reflect consciously on what they are learning as a result of writing with others. We usually require three kinds of analytical writing from our students in addition to the brief, short, and major assignments described above:

1: THE WORK PLAN—a descriptive essay that specifies the group's paper topic and outlines the way they anticipate addressing it. The work plan takes the form of a collaboratively produced memo addressed to the instructor which spells out how the work will be organized and the labor divided. Work plans should specify which paragraphs and/or sections each group member will write, who will type the drafts, who will make copies (if required for peer response work), who will proofread, and who will be responsible for the paper getting in on time. In addition, the work plan can be used to encourage students to think about group roles—who will act as facilitator, or questioner, or idea person. There are several advantages to this assignment:

> ➤ by introducing "first-timers" to collaborative writing through a comparatively short, concrete project, you give them a chance to adapt to each others' working and writing styles with minimal grade pressure;

> ➤ by asking group members to assign themselves specific tasks during the drafting process, you encourage them to think in detail about how they will organize their writing in advance; *and*

> ➤ by getting students to commit to a plan of action, you can evaluate and respond to the "do-ability" of their projects before too much time and energy has been expended on ideas that will not work. While a work plan constrains students to plan their writing in advance, it need not suggest—as traditional outlines sometimes do—an inviolably rigid structure into which all ideas discovered during writing must fit. In fact, for another short, graded writing task that encourages a critical awareness of the writing process, you can ask students to write a follow-up report that analyzes the ways in which producing the final draft differs from the work plan.

2: **THE COLLABORATIVE LOG**—an ongoing diary of what the group is doing even as they do it. The collaborative log should articulate the group's agenda for each meeting and should report on who came to the meetings, what each person contributed, and evaluate the degree to which the group's agenda was met. To insure that students keep their collaborative logs up, the instructor can collect them for review about halfway through a major project. As an alternative effort to keep abreast of developments within the group, we have occasionally asked that students write progress reports based on their collaborative logs.

3: THE POST-PAPER ANALYSIS—a synthesis and analysis of how and to what degree the group's project changed from the time of the work plan until the day the final draft was handed in for evaluation. The post-paper analysis (one of our students renamed this paper the "postmortem") should also summarize how the student felt about the work his or her group did. Does the writer consider the group's effort to be good collaboration? What grade does the student think the paper deserves and why? Should everyone receive the same grade?

These writing assignments tend to represent all of James Moffet's "modes of discourse" from the basic *recording* and *reporting* of experiences in collaborative writing groups (as formalized by the collaborative logs) to *generalizing* and *theorizing* (as made available in the post-paper analyses and work plans, respectively). The collaborative writing classroom as we have envisioned it requires many different written products, and the assignments have been created to teach the "content" obtaining to the writing classroom while at the same time encouraging students to make *how* they write an object of reflection and analysis. Thus, we can, through one series of short writing assignments, reinforce classroom discussions of readers' needs and Moffet's modes of discourse, gather "insider" information into the workings of collaborative groups, and give students plenty of practice in writing.

Leave Room for Innovation and the Imagination

Recent research on small group dynamics suggests that the quality and number of ideas generated by invention is enhanced by having group members first engage individually in such prewriting activities as mapping, clustering, and focused free-writing before coming together for group brainstorming. During group brainstorming, collaborative groups should select a "scribe" to record all reactions and ideas that surface as the group works on an assignment. Before the group pursues its topic any farther, have them repeat the individual-first, group-second prewriting process on the new, narrower idea.

If you are lucky enough to be a classroom equipped with tables and moveable chairs, you can supply each group with large sheets of butcher paper so they can map out invention topics seated around a table. Group mapping also works if your room has multiple chalkboards. Just be sure your groups are supplied with enough chalk to map their ideas at one of the boards. When students map together they can pool their resources for generative topic ideas and organizational strategies.

Designing Collaborative Writing Assignments That Work

Selecting a Topic

In general, we think that students rather than instructors should select paper topics. Student motivation is stimulated when they are allowed work on subjects that pique their interest. Of course, the teacher can point students in productive directions. We find that supplying students with a general purpose or genre provides them with a lens through which to focus their interests. Thus, instead of handing students a menu of paper topics, we assign papers dealing with specific themes (see below). For example, the paper on public policy asks student groups to gather as much information as possible on any issue that is an object of law. Within the large purpose of reporting all sides of a public policy debate—or the history of a public policy that directly affects them—students have the freedom to select any of a hundred topics ranging from legislation concerning drinking and voting ages to proposals for solving the nation's growing health-care crisis to the debate surrounding gays in the military. The principle of using topic selection to encourage student motivation can also apply within the groups themselves. Thus, you will want to emphasize to your students the importance of choosing a topic that everyone in the group agrees to. *Consensus* rather than *majority rule* is the key to successful collaboration. A student left out of the initial decision may feel no subsequent commitment to the group effort.

Once groups have selected a topic, we ask each group to write a well-developed audience profile. Have the groups articulate exactly whom they would expect to read their work. For example, if the group decides to write a paper on the parking problem on campus, group members should be clear about whom they see as their primary audience. Do they perceive a secondary audience for their writing as well? What can they assume their primary and secondary audiences know and do not know about the parking problem? How much background will they need to include in their paper to be sure that their readers fully understand the issues they raise? What kind of tone is appropriate for the audiences they have identified? Writing a statement of purpose for their writing can be a useful preliminary to tackling a major project: for example, "This paper will persuade the administration to schedule classes in a way that minimizes parking lot overcrowding at eight in the morning." Alternately, the individual members of the group could write separate statements of purpose, comparing and combining them afterwards.

The Teacher's Role in Drafting

As described above, the teacher in the collaborative learning and writing and environment moves to the periphery of the learning activity in order to allow students to step up and take responsibility for their educations. This in no way minimizes the importance of the teacher. The instructor must create an environment hospitable to collaborative learning by creating a variety of in-class and out-of-class exercises that will give students hands-on experience with the vast array of principles and skills that conduce to good writing. Though working around the edges of classroom activity, the teacher must be alert to the sometimes subtle signals that a group is struggling, and must then decide when and if to intervene. The teacher must also be able to move from group to group, and be ready to suggest alternatives, answer questions, point students toward useful resources, or simply to share a joke.

Thus, even punctuation lessons can be an opportunity for student interaction. Instead of defining such abstract notions as what commas are and why participle, infinitive, and absolute phrases need them [24b2], the teacher can set a task that will require students in groups to read, review, analyze, and use the comma rule information in their *Handbooks*. Or students can identify such sentence-level units as restrictive and non-restrictive clauses [24e], coordinate adjectives [24d], and transitional and parenthetical expressions [24f] in their own writing. To encourage them to synthesize and apply the abstract information in the *Handbook* to their own, very concrete writing, students also could be asked to create short documents that report how many of which kind of unit they discovered and whether or not a comma should be used in such a case. Thus even learning punctuation rules can be fun when students learn, analyze, and apply their new-found knowledge together. Ask each member of a group to be the "expert" on a particular mark of punctuation: commas, periods, semicolons, colons, quotation marks, and so forth. In proofreading, let each "expert" find the errors and explain to the writer how to correct them. On successive papers, have the students rotate the punctuation assignments, so that each gains expertise in all areas of punctuation. For under-prepared students, starting with just commas, say, or periods, is less intimidating than learning and applying all punctuation rules at once. Peer discussion and reinforcement of the rules provides a more effective learning experience than asking individual students to correct teacher-marked errors.

Modify Assessment and Grading

Some instructors assign a single grade to the entire group; others assign grades individually, and others use some combination of the two methods, each student receiving both a group grade and an individual grade. While it is typical practice to assign grades based on the technical quality and discursive maturity of the final text, the success of a collaborative assignment should derive from other bases as well:

> ➤ the completion of the project

> ➤ the finding of an appropriate solution or resolution to the problem or case

> ➤ the group's equitable allocation of work or tasks

> ➤ non-written aspects of the completed project (such as oral presentation, visuals, and the evaluation and presentation of numerical data)

> ➤ the students' sense of successful completion

> ➤ the students' having learned something about group processes

Whether an instructor measures these factors in formal assessment or informally for course development, we believe that each represents an important part of what is taught through the collaborative project. We have heard it jokingly suggested that teaching collaborative writing will diminish an instructor's workload by having students work collaboratively. Would that it were true! We have found that even though the collaborative method causes the exchange of twenty-five individual papers and drafts for eight or so collaboratively-produced papers and drafts, the time it takes to evaluate collaboratively produced papers evens the scale. And, of course, instructors must also judge the information they gain from all those smallish writing assignments that help students analyze and synthesize the writing process.

Creating Prompts That Encourage Analysis, Synthesis, and Self-reflection

For the collaborative writing instructor, the most demanding expenditure of creative energy is planning writing assignments that can accomplish many goals simultaneously. As discussed above, the writing instructor must deploy a wide range of writing assignments—and at the right time—in order to teach students how to collaborate effectively and how, when collaborating, to write with precision and power. Despite the difficulty of creating workable prompts, we usually follow a few general principles:

> ➤ Prompts should lay out an activity that encourages conversation, information exchange, and speculation, and that results in a written product.

> ➤ Prompts should ask students either to analyze a content-oriented issue in a sample text or synthesize the group's discussion of the prompt.

> ➤ Prompts should make it the students' responsibility to discover what principles apply to a given problem. It defeats the purpose of collaborative learning if you tell them what they will find if they look closely enough at the situation you have drawn to their attention. Likewise, prompts should ask students to engage in an activity that gives them practice using a particular concept (e.g., the audience analysis and discovering purpose exercise described above).

> ➤ Prompts should solicit self-reflection. Individuals should be urged to respond personally to the situations and issues that your prompts bring into focus.

In addition to this general advice about creating prompts, we further suggest that you avoid leading groups into discussing and writing about volatile, irresolvable subjects. Collaboration works when students can share and develop concepts and ideas. Positions set in stone are rarely amenable to any kind of modification, and an inability to negotiate a position on an issue will likely make negotiation of writing processes impossible as well. Topics like abortion, gun control, religious beliefs, or family values do not work very well as discussion or paper topics because—despite our students' natural attraction to them—they are not conducive to the development of congenial relations among group members nor to the development of balanced papers.

Diagnosing Problems in the Collaborative Group

Collaborative learning, collaborative writing, and collaborative projects are extraordinarily useful, but not unproblematic, tools for the teacher of writing. As teachers new to collaborative writing soon learn, despite their best efforts, sometimes collaborative projects simply do not work. While the benefits of collaboration in the writing classroom are manifold, it is important to be aware of what we call "collaborative breakdown." Because the dynamics of each class can vary widely, *monitor each group's progress.*

Among the clues to incipient breakdown are:

➤ Individual student anxiety as interim or final deadlines approach;

➤ A group's inability to decide what to do or how to do it;

➤ Students asking to change groups or have an assignment modified; and

➤ A work load that seems inequitably distributed.

To increase the likelihood that the instructor will learn of any problems in time to intervene, part of every collaborative project should include individual assessments by the students. These can take the form of conferences, journals, or the memos and/or progress reports we referred to above. Equally important, the instructor should schedule group work on regular class days so that he or she can sit in on each group to evaluate how well they are functioning.

Watching for the Five Fields of Dissonance

In our studies of student collaborative work, we have identified five major causes of trouble: 1) logistical difficulties; 2) personality conflict; 3) differing cognitive abilities; 4) differences in epistemological development; and 5) differences in social background. While these vexing spirits can rarely be cast out by the instructor, being able to identify them may permit a teacher to modify an assignment or better evaluate its success.

THE LOGISTICS OF COLLABORATION. Perhaps there are a fortunate few instructors who have no students who are working at least one job to make ends meet and gain work experience while they are in school. But many of us expect that at least half our students will have one or two part-time jobs in addition to their full-time class load. In one of our early collaborative writing classes, Chuck reported, "Tom, Michelle, and I all work different hours, and getting together to write out drafts of our paper was impossible." Competing demands on our students' time may make it impossible or extremely difficult for them to work outside the classroom as a group and, as we have already mentioned, the instructor should make every effort to minimize scheduling conflicts.

DIFFERENCES IN COGNITIVE ABILITY. Another area of difficulty that can work against successful collaboration is differing cognitive maturity. Cognitive development specialists tell us that the composing process comprises a tremendous variety of mental operations, ranging from understanding the assignment, to remembering relevant facts, to imagining and seeking to meet the needs of an audience, to organizing data in such a way that it may be presented in a clear and logical manner (e.g., Flower and Hayes, 1984), but it also includes the basics of literacy—reading and writing. Thus, when we speak of the cognitive maturity of a writer or a group of writers we are referring to the facility with which that writer or that group can usefully conceptualize and execute the requirements of a writing task. And of course, not all students are created with equal abilities. Some students will be able to conceptualize problems and propose solutions posed by and directed toward a writing task more adequately than their facility with the language will allow them to demonstrate on paper. Conversely, there are writers who are extremely facile with the language, but whose thinking is nevertheless superficial.

In the context of collaborative work, a form of cognitive dissonance occurs when students with varying levels of cognitive maturity tackle a problem together—a situation which holds both pedagogical promise and peril. The promise is that students, regardless of maturity, can learn problem-solving techniques and efficient strategies for reading, writing, and organization more effectively from one another than from a textbook or a teacher (Daiute, 1986). The peril lies in the fact that cognitive dissonance frequently leads to frustration and impatience, and even to the formation of factions or the dissolution of the group itself. The more cognitively mature student may become impatient with her less advanced group members and usurp control of the project.

EPISTEMOLOGICAL DEVELOPMENT IN CONFLICT. In his study of Harvard students, William G. Perry (1970) proposed a nine-stage scale of epistemological development along which the individual moved from **dualism**—an authoritarian, black-or-white view of the world, to **multiplicity**—the recognition of other points of view; and finally a commitment in **relativism**—taking a personal stand while also accepting other points of view. Epistemological dissonance occurs when different members of a group are at different stages along Perry's continuum. The problematic for classroom collaboration is not only that students may be operating at different epistemic levels, but also that students cannot comprehend the "ways of knowing" of their co-members. The dualist, regardless of the sophistication of his or her writing abilities, cannot understand how the group can develop alternative solutions to a problem. A student at the multiplistic stage may be able to recognize views other than his or her own, but be unable to evaluate their relative strengths. Achieving consensus can be difficult when a member of a group does not know how to compare and choose among alternative solutions that may appear to have equal merit. Such a student may bow to the loudest voice or, unsure of his or her own position, say simply "do what you guys want to do." Even a student who may have attained the upper reaches of Perry's scale (and we do not believe that "a commitment in relativism" is the likely endpoint for most individuals) may not tolerate the dogmatism or apparent "wishy-washyness" of the less epistemologically advanced student and may react either by withdrawing from the group or by attempting to dominate it.

PERSONAL DISSONANCE. Most instructors know when they have a personality problem in class. A student's aberrant behavior or argumentative stance manifests itself early in the term. In a work setting, such an individual would be weeded out—or at least pruned—early in his or her employment history, but rarely is a student so disruptive that he or she is ejected from class. Yet even a small disruptive element is antithetical to group process, and a perverse streak may totally sabotage a group's work. Other personality problems are the aggressive student whose personality force dominates the other students and the shy or quiet student who is unable to present his or her views or is unable to take on the parts of the assignment that he or she is best suited for. Related to this phenomenon is the dissonance that can arise from students who have differing levels of motivation. Students who need high GPAs in order to qualify for scholarships in their majors will not appreciate being grouped with students who are taking your class credit/no-credit. Even without considering grades, students do not always come to class with the same priorities and degree of commitment. The instructor cannot change a student's personality or supply motivation, but she can teach students about the ways in which personality and motivation factors can affect group interaction. The teacher can also consider these factors when assigning groups—when logical considerations do not completely dictate groupings.

SOCIAL DISSONANCE. This little-discussed area of interpersonal friction can be defined as the clashing work behaviors that derive from differing socioeconomic backgrounds and which influence task representation, work ethic, and degree of imagination or risk-taking. Rather than viewing the matter in stereotypical terms—"working class attitudes," "women's ways of knowing," etc.—we see this area of dissonance as deriving from differing "dialects of behavior." Although what we have called the "dialect of behavior" shares much conceptually with a "discourse community," we believe that the behavioral dialect encompasses more than shared discourse. It was only after teaching at three very different institutions that we became aware of the considerable differences in response that could be engendered by the same assignments. For example, in responding to an ethics case regarding a corrupt politician, students in Arcata, California and Columbus, Ohio saw it as only the behavior problem of one individual. Students in Youngstown, Ohio, on the other hand, assumed mob connections and a general corruption in politics. In Arcata, environmental concern among students is taken for granted; in Columbus, it is much less widespread. As another example, in the Youngstown area, positions of authority and responsibility are accorded considerable deference. Thus, on second reference in a newspaper, a lawyer is identified as "Attorney Smith." Professors with doctorates are always "Dr." In both Columbus and Arcata, "Dr." is usually reserved for physicians and dentists, and attorneys are not accorded special status.

Behavioral dialect may also account for the degree of comfort a student experiences with hierarchical or non-hierarchical structures; the degree to which a student resists responsibility for her or his education; and the expectation the student has for the location of authority—all of which have implications for the decentered, non-hierarchical, shared-authority collaborative classroom. Such social factors can cause collaborative breakdown when members of a group do not share the same behavioral dialect or when a shared behavioral dialect does not permit satisfactory completion of an assignment. Interestingly, factors attributable to behavioral dialect often supersede attitudes or behaviors predicted from class, ethnic, or gender theory.

Mediating Conflict

While there are many potential sources of collaborative breakdown in the writing classroom, those considering teaching collaborative writing for the first time should know that complete breakdown is the exception and not the rule. Most groups instinctively compensate for tensions and imbalances—if for no other reason than they want to pass the class. But most frequently, collaborative groups demonstrate that human beings are thoroughly social animals with considerable reserves of tolerance,

understanding, and humor to smooth their ways to successful completion of a shared task—whatever the perceived reward. This table distills
responses that experience has shown can help teachers of collaborative
writing nurture students' innate social strengths:

Field of Dissonance	Instructor Response
Logistical	• Acknowledge students' scheduling difficulties by showing flexibility on due dates and course expectations. • Allow in-class group work time. • Arrange groups with consideration for schedules.
Personal	• Solicit students' self-appraisals and preferences. • Provide alternative models for behavior in groups (suggest such roles as "idea person," "elaborator," and "group scribe") to minimize reliance on traditional leader-follower paradigm. • Be willing to give a disruptive personality an individual assignment rather than insisting on group participation.
Cognitive	• Recognize that all students are not created with equal abilities nor does their cognitive development proceed at the same pace. • Graduate the complexity of assignments over the course of the term to permit what development can take place to take place. • Group students at different cognitive levels only when motivation appears equal. • Accept that students' intellectual contributions may not be equal.
Epistemic	• Recognize that students at the lower end of the development scale cannot perceive the views of those in positions above them. • Because students at the lower end of the epistemic scale may be incapable of responding to open-ended assignments or assignments in which a group is expected to develop its own approach, be prepared to provide explicit directions.
Social	• Develop awareness of and adjust to local knowledge. • Provide in-class opportunities for encountering and discussing other perspectives, other norms.

Assignments That Work

Some Field-tested Prompts To Get You Started

Ultimately, the only way to learn how to teach writing in a collaborative classroom is to devise the best syllabus you can and give it a whirl. All of the advice presented in these pages derives from years of trial and error, and while we have had some spectacular failures along the way, we do not think that those classes where failures occurred learned less about writing that those we conducted according to the more traditional model. Collaborative writing, like democracy, may be the worst way to teach writing—except for all other ways of teaching it. What follows are several assignments that have proven winners in many collaborative writing classes. We hope that, like us, you will be amazed at how creative students can be when they are fully engaged in the learning and writing process.

RESEARCH PAPER 1: THINKING GREEN

Everyone is talking about our deteriorating environment—deforestation, strip mining, acid rain, overfishing, over-fertilization, the difficulties of disposing of toxic and nuclear wastes. But what are the facts? What do you really know about any environmental issue? Where does your information come from? How reliable is it? This assignment lets you gain some expertise in at least one area of environmental concern and draw your own conclusions.

WHAT INFORMATION YOU WILL NEED: Once you have decided on a topic, you will need to dig up information on at least three issues: 1) the physics of the problem—how the environmental impact occurs; 2) the biology of the problem—what happens to the plants and animals affected by the problem, and 3) the socioeconomics of the problem—the human activities and needs that occasion the environmental impact. (Some papers will also have to consider the "chemistry of the problem"—what chemical compounds are released as a result of the environmental impact and what chemical reactions result from this release.)

How you actually organize the paper will, as always, be dependent on the logic that best explains your chosen topic. However, generally speaking, the reader can understand the biology of a problem better then he or she already understands why the affected organisms are in harm's way in the first place. It may be, though, that you find it more sensible to explain the socioeconomics of the problem you are studying even as you relate how that problem occurs. In any case, you will need to work out a provisional strategy and present it in your work plan.

EDITORIAL

As stated in the syllabus, you will work collaboratively with several other students to develop and write a persuasive essay on a subject upon which you all agree. To get to this point, you will need to do some legwork.

STEP 1: Write brief papers (approximately 350–500 words) in which each of you explains the significance of the issue you have chosen.

STEP 2: Each member of the group will write a paper explaining the facts of the issue.

STEP 3: Divide the group. One half will write a pro paper and the other half, a con paper.

STEP 4: Finally your group will reach consensus on the issue and write a persuasive essay advocating the position you have agreed on. You will use secondary sources to build your case.

GRADING: Significance: 3 points, Facts: 5 points, Pro/Con: 7 points, Final Essay: 10 points—for a total of 25 points.

As you have learned from the editorials that you have read and those shared in class, educated opinions are the basis of strong persuasion, and facts are the basis for educated opinions. Persuading others to follow the course of action you advocate—whether voting for a candidate, contributing to the United Way, or wearing seat belts—requires that you not only provide sound reasoning but that you consider the audience you are trying to persuade and the purpose you have in persuading them.

While it may be said that "everyone is entitled to his or her opinion," everyone is not entitled to have that opinion listened to. There are good opinions and bad ones; part of your job in this assignment is to determine which opinions are valid and which are not.

In general, opinions whose credibility relies on higher authority (the government, the Constitution, the Bible, etc.) are not arguable and only rarely can they be used to bring about change in the hands of the editorial writer. Thus, any argument you wish to advance that uses the Bible or other religious work as authority will probably be inappropriate in this class. Rather, your job is to seek out the facts that explain and issue—taking great care in the source of those facts—sort through those facts, write opinions that support each side of an issue (for example, on using or not using motorcycle helmets) and then write an editorial, or public policy statement, on that issue—a fact-based persuasive essay.

Pick a subject all of you are content with. Obviously, any topic on which you cannot be objective is out: no gun control, abortion, prayer in the schools, or anything else which causes members of the group to raise their voices. Instead, select a subject which is interesting, which is under contention, and for which information is readily available.

A good editorial runs about 500 to 750 words, almost never more. However, an explanation of the facts and a discussion of opinion may, in fact, run a lot longer. One of the jobs of the editorial is to distill those facts to educate the reader.

While your facts and opinion essay must be documented, the final editorial should not be.

RESEARCH PAPER 2: HOW PUBLIC POLICY IS CREATED

It is easy to criticize government officials: to say they are crooks, they don't keep promises, they aren't principled, they just do not use common sense. But these easy criticisms fail to consider the difficulty of creating laws that are simultaneously intelligent, fair, and politically possible. The question remains: What influences shape public policy? What information is considered? What pressures do special-interest groups exert? How do such abstract and occasionally relative moral values like right and wrong figure in the making of public policy? The ultimate goal of this assignment, then, is to pick a public policy issue, to figure out what is being said about it and by whom, and to explain to your readers how power, fact, opinion, and belief have influenced (or are influencing) law and behavior.

WHAT INFORMATION YOU WILL NEED: Choose an area of public policy that interests you, read all you can about it, and write a report that explains what you found out. The possibilities are almost endless—health care, gays in the military, the discussion about whether nicotine should be labeled a controlled substance, America's role in Haiti (or anywhere else), the distribution of tax money for schools, term limits, campaign finance reform, whether or how to manage the environmental Superfund—*you* name it. But watch it! This is *not* a persuasive paper; you will not be arguing one point of view or another. Instead, you will be presenting *all* the points of view on a given issue in a way that fairly represents them.

Stuck for ideas? Read through the front sections of the *Washington Post* or the *New York Times* or *Los Angeles Times* for the last couple of weeks and see what public policy issues they are discussing. Your group should find something you think is crucial.

ORGANIZING YOUR RESEARCH: You will probably find it most logical to begin by discussing the problem that the public policy you are investigating has been proposed to solve. What is its history? What is its social impact? Who is affected? What would the proposed policy do to change the status quo? What is the hoped-for result? It would be all right to give more weight to the legislative history of your issue than its social effects, but you must discuss some of both.

More About Collaboration

While collaborative writing has become an important focus of composition studies in the past ten years, the idea of an individual's copyright to "intellectual property" is relatively new. The history of writing extends back five thousand years, but the notion that a solitary individual can create "original" written work and then possess that work as property has only existed for a little over two hundred years (cf. Ede and Lunsford 1–6). Prior to the seventeenth century, books frequently compiled the written work of others and only infrequently cited the original writers. Prior to the seventeenth century, written ideas, like talk, belonged to everyone in a linguistic community. Indeed, before mass literacy and the widespread availability of inexpensive printed materials, written ideas were only available to most through oral transmission. These communal notions about intellectual property gradually changed as it became increasingly possible for individual writers to achieve fame and fortune through their pens. Yet, even as novelists, poets, and playwrights became increasingly more concerned with the ownership of their words, the industrial revolution created its own species of corporately owned language (Ede and Lunsford 5). Throughout the nineteenth century and into our own time, written discourse in science, business, and industry has become a corporate product. Most scientific reports rely on the work and ideas of teams of researchers. Corporations frequently distribute information to shareholders and the public that acknowledges no one but the company.

Today our students are bewildered by the range of views on intellectual property. While software companies and the music and movie industries wage international war on copyright "pirates," those same companies ask their employees to imagine their individual efforts as contributions to a large team. One might well create a new software program for Microsoft, but one should not expect authorship credit. Preparing for their careers, students pass through an academic establishment that is deeply concerned that students *do their own work*. Plagiarism and cheating are represented as moral bankruptcy while the sharing of information is discouraged. Graduate students in the sciences might well find themselves conducting experiments and writing reports for senior scientists for which they receive no name credit in institutions where they could be expelled for passing off the words of others as their own. English majors could easily find themselves taught to value the individual genius and unique creative power of Virginia Woolf in classes entitled "Woolf and the Bloomsbury Circle."

It is in this conflicted context that recent research on collaborative writing has been conducted. Beginning as early as 1963, Derek J. de Solla Price noted the increase in the number of scientific articles written by large teams. From the mid-sixties until the early seventies, Price (1963), Hagstrum (1964), Clarke (1964), Price and Beaver (1966), Zuckerman (1967), Weinberg (1970), and Crane (1972) identified the research and reporting practices of those working in the sciences and social sciences. In 1973, Kenneth Bruffee introduced the fledgling discipline of composition studies to "practical models of collaborative learning." Response to Bruffee's early work was slow in emerging, however. In the 1970s, composition studies were largely preoccupied with the claims of "expressivist" and "writing-as-process" schools of thought—both of which emphasized the importance of the *individual's* voice, ideas, and composing processes. It was not until the early 1980s, when Richard Gebhardt (1980) and John Clifford (1981) each published essays discussing the ways in which collaboration affects writing pedagogy, that a large number of researchers began to examine collaborative learning and writing from the compositionist's point of view.

Since the early 1980s, research on collaborative writing has divided itself into three main strands: 1) studies and analysis of collaboration in "nonacademic settings"; 2) defining and describing models of collaboration; and 3) the interpersonal dynamics of collaborative groups. Beginning with Faigley and Miller's "What We Learn Writing on the Job" (1982), it is clear that research into the collaborative activities of those working outside the academy has become the most important research site. Odell and Goswami's *Writing in Nonacademic Settings* (1985) is perhaps the most logical starting place for those interested in off-campus collaborative activity. Introduced in Odell and Goswami's collection are several oft-cited essays on collaborative writing research, including Paul Anderson's "What Survey Research Tells Us about Writing at Work" and Paradis, Dobrin, and Miller's "Writing at Exxon ITD: Notes on the Writing Environment of an R&D Organization." Yet, despite the historical importance of Odell and Goswami's collection, the "seminal" text on collaborative writing is Ede and Lunsford's superbly researched *Single Texts/Plural Authors* (1990) which presents a history of notions of authorship, statistical information on what kinds of writing really are done in the world outside the academy, and a rationale for a collaborative pedagogy. Other important texts on nonacademic collaboration are Lay and Karis's *Collaborative Writing in Industry: Investigations in Theory and Practice* (1990) and Burnett and Duin's *Collaboration in Technical and Professional Communication: A Research Perspective* (1995).

The second important area in collaborative research is composed of those studies which consider the various kinds of collaboration. While many of those investigating what collaboration is and how it works do their work in nonacademic settings, the emphasis on models of collaboration can derive from any research base. Killingsworth and Jones's and Couture and Rhymer's 1989 studies, for example, pay particular attention to defining what workplace collaboration is and when it occurs, while Beard, Rhymer, and Williams focus their 1989 essay on how properly to assess collaborative writing groups. Several essays describing nonacademic models for collaboration, including those by Debs and Selzer, can be found in Fearing and Sparrow's collection *Technical Writing: Theory and Practice* (1989). One can also find important essays discussing conceptual frameworks for understanding collaboration in Forman's *New Visions of Collaborative Writing* (1992). Other useful texts discussing models of small groups are Hare's somewhat dated *Handbook of Small Group Research* (1976), Swap's *Group Decision Making* (1984), and Hirokawa and Poole's *Communication and Group Decision-Making* (1986). Those particularly interested in how collaborative models drawn from industry have been translated into collaborative writing pedagogy should consult Phillips's *Teaching How to Work in Groups* (1990).

The last major area in collaborative writing research investigates the "sociology" of small groups. In addition to the aforementioned collection by Forman, one will find a good overview of relevant small-group dynamics in Blyler and Thralls's *Professional Communication: The Social Perspective* (1993). Included in this volume is Burnett's "Conflict in Collaborative Decision-Making" which those new to teaching collaborative writing should find valuable as a summary of research into how conflict can either mediate or enhance the quality of collaborative efforts. Our own "Fields of Dissonance in the Collaborative Writing Classroom" builds on

Burnett's work by presenting an even more complex picture of the small group working dynamic. In addition to small group "conflict," gender studies perspectives have also been brought to bear on research into collaboration. Lunsford and Ede's "Rhetoric in a New Key" (1990), for example, distinguishes between a predominantly male "hierarchical mode of discourse" and the predominantly female "dialogic mode." Lay's "The Androgynous Collaborator: The Impact of Gender Studies on Collaboration" (1992) also asserts the importance of gender in determining interpersonal dynamics in groups, suggesting that attention must be paid to gender stereotyping when students evaluate their collaborative groups. Raign and Sims's 1993 "Gender, Persuasion Techniques, and Collaboration" amplifies the issues raised in Lunsford and Ede and also in Lay. In addition to these important articles, Nadler, Nadler, and Todd-Mancillas's *Advances in Gender and Communication Research* (1987) provides a good starting point for those interested in exploring communications theory, gender, and language. Still other researchers have urged the importance of incorporating self-monitoring strategies into collaborative work—most notably, Forman and Katsky's article discussing the importance of groups remaining aware of both writing and group processes (1986). To build a solid general background in how small groups work we suggest reading around in Morse and Phelps's *Interpersonal Communication: A Relational Perspective* (1980), Klauss and Bass's *Interpersonal Communication in Organizations* (1982), Rolloff and Miller's *Interpersonal Processes: New Directions in Communication Research* (1989), Ross's *Small Groups in Organizational Settings,* Napier and Gershenfeld's *Groups: Theory and Experience* (fifth edition, 1993), and Frey's *Group Communication in Context* (1994).

Works Cited

Beard, John D., Jone Rymer, and David L. Williams. "An Assessment System for Collaborative-Writing Groups: Theory and Empirical Evaluation." *Journal of Business and Technical Communication* 3 (1989): 29–51.

Bruffee, Kenneth. "Collaborative Learning: Some Practical Models." *College English* 35 (1973): 634–42.

———. "Collaborative Learning and the 'Conversation of Mankind.'" *College English* 46 (1984): 635–52.

Burnett, Rebecca E. "Conflict in Collaborative Decision-Making." *Professional Communication: The Social Perspective.* Eds., Nancy R. Blyler and Charlotte Thralls. Newbury Park, CA: SAGE, 1993. 144–62.

Burnett, Rebecca E. and Ann Hill Duin. *Collaboration in Technical and Professional Communication: A Research Perspective.* Hillsdale, NJ: Erlbaum, forthcoming 1995.

Clarke, Beverly. "Multiple Authorship Trends in Scientific Papers." *Science* 143 (1964): 822–24.

Clifford, John. "Composing in Stages: The Effects of a Collaborative Pedagogy." *Research in the Teaching of Writing* 14 (1981): 37–53.

Couture, Barbara and Jone Rymer. "Interactive Writing on the Job: Definitions and Implications of 'Collaboration.'" *Writing in the Business Professions.* Ed. Mura Kogan. Urbana, IL: National Council of the Teachers of English, 1989.

Crane, Diane. *Invisible Colleges: Diffusion of Knowledge in Scientific Communities.* Chicago: University of Chicago Press, 1972.

Daiute, Collette. "Do 1 and 1 Make 2?: Patterns of Influence by Collaborative Authors." *Written Communication* 3 (1986): 382–408.

De Solla Price, Derek J. *Little Science, Big Science.* New York: Columbia University Press, 1963.

De Solla Price, Derek J. and Donald Beaver. "Collaboration in an Invisible College." *American Psychologist* 21 (1964): 241–63.

Ede, Lisa and Andrea A. Lunsford. *Single Texts/Plural Authors: Perspectives on Collaborative Writing.* Carbondale, IL: Southern Illinois University Press, 1990.

Faigley, Lester and Thomas Miller. "What We Learn from Writing on the Job." *College English* 44 (1982): 557–69.

Fearing, Bertie E. and W. Keats Sparrow. *Technical Writing: Theory and Practice.* New York: Modern Language Association, 1989.

Flower, Linda and John R. Hayes. "Images, Plans, and Prose: The Representation of Meaning in Writing." *Written Communication* 1 (1986): 120–60.

Forman, Janis. *New Visions of Collaborative Writing.* Portsmouth, NH: Boynton/Cook, 1992.

Forman, Janis and Patricia Katsky. "The Group Report: A Problem in Small Group or Writing Processes?" *The Journal of Business Communication* 23 (1986): 23–35.

Frey, Lawrence R. *Group Communication in Context: Studies of Natural Groups.* Hillsdale, NJ: Erlbaum, 1994.

Gebhardt, Richard. "Teamwork and Feedback: Broadening the Base of Collaborative Writing." *College English* 42 (1980): 69–74.

Hagstrum, Warren O. "Traditional and Modern Forms of Scientific Teamwork." *Administrative Science Quarterly* 9 (1964): 241–63.

Hare, A. Paul. *Handbook of Small Group Research.* New York: Free Press, 1976.

Hirokawa, Randy Y. and Marshall S. Poole. *Communication and Group Decision-Making.* Beverly Hills: SAGE, 1986.

Killingsworth, M. Jimmie and Betsy G. Jones. "Division of Labor or Integrated Teams: A Crux in the Management of Technical Communication?" *Technical Communication* 36 (1989): 210–21.

Klauss, R. and B.M. Bass. *Interpersonal Communication in Organizations.* New York: Academic, 1987.

Lay, Mary M. "The Androgynous Collaborator: The Impact of Gender Studies on Collaboration." *New Visions of Collaborative Writing.* Ed. Janis Foreman. Portsmouth, NH: Boynton/Cook, 1992. 82–104.

Lay, Mary M. and William M. Karis. *Collaborative Writing in Industry: Investigations in Theory and Practice.* New York: Baywood, 1990.

Lunsford, Andrea A. and Lisa Ede. "Rhetoric in a New Key: Women and Collaboration." *Rhetoric Review* 8 (1990): 234–41.

Moffett, James. *Teaching The Universe Of Discourse.* Boston: Houghton Mifflin, 1983.

Morse, B.W. and L.A. Phelps. *Interpersonal Communication: A Relational Perspective.* Minneapolis: Burgess, 1980.

Nadler, Lawrence B., Marjorie K. Nadler, and William R. Todd-Mancillas. *Advances in Gender and Communication Research.* Lanham: University Press of America, 1987.

Napier, Rodney W. and Matti K. Gershenfeld. *Groups: Theory and Experience.* Boston: Houghton Mifflin, 1993.

Odell, Lee and Dixie Goswami. *Writing in Nonacademic Settings.* New York: Guilford, 1985.

Perry, William G. *Forms of Intellectual and Ethical Development in The College Years.* New York: Holt, 1970.

Phillips, Gerald M. *Teaching How to Work in Groups.* Norwood: Ablex, 1990.

Putnam, Linda L. "Conflict in Group Decision-Making." *Communication and Group Decision-Making.* Eds., Randy Y. Hirokawa and Marshall S. Poole. Beverly Hills: SAGE, 1986. 175–96.

Raign, Kathryn Rosser. "Gender, Persuasion Techniques, and Collaboration." *Technical Communication Quarterly* 2 (1993): 89–104.

Rolloff, M.E. and G.R. Miller. *Interpersonal Processes: New Directions in Communication Research.* Beverly Hills: SAGE, 1989.

Ross, Raymond S. *Small Groups in Organizational Settings.* Englewood Cliffs, NJ: Prentice Hall, 1989.

Swap, George and Associates. *Group Decision Making.* Beverly Hills: SAGE, 1984.

Thralls, Charlotte and Nancy Roundy Blyler. *Professional Communication: The Social Perspective.* Newbury Park: SAGE, 1993.

Trimbur, John. "Consensus and Difference in Collaborative Writing." *College English* 51 (1989): 602–16.

Weinberg, Alvin M. "Scientific Teams and Scientific Laboratories." *Dædelus* 99 (1970): 1056–75.

Zuckerman, Harriet. "Nobel Laureates in Science: Patterns of Productivity, Collaboration, and Authorship." *American Sociological Review* 32 (1967): 391–403.

PART THREE

Help For Writing Instructors: Using Portfolios for Learning and Assessment

Laurel Black
St. John Fisher College

PART THREE

Help For Writing Instructors: Using Portfolios for Learning and Assessment

Introduction

I began using portfolios the first semester I ever taught. As a graduate student enrolled in a summer course to train teaching assistants, I was overwhelmed by all that I had to learn in such a short time. We spent part of one class talking about portfolios as an option for grading. The professor was experienced at using portfolios, and I'm sure what he told us was much more complex than what I got out of his presentation. However, all I heard in my anxiety about grading papers was that I could let students revise as often as they wanted and not grade them until the final portfolio. They could pick some papers to put into a folder, I'd average the grades of the pieces, and the whole scary grading process would be over in one fell swoop at the end of the semester when I was more secure in my ability to evaluate writing. It wasn't much, but it was a plan.

I went into that semester without any real theoretical understanding of portfolios, nor any sense of structuring my class around any goals other than to avoid embarrassment and confrontation. I didn't think of portfolios as part of a larger context of assessment issues. My first-year students were also new to portfolios and saw the revision and selection process—and the deferral of grades—as a wonderful improvement over high school English. They responded enthusiastically and evaluated the course highly. I decided I would keep using portfolios—they had done the job for me. However, as colleagues asked me questions about how I constructed my class, I realized how little I had thought about the relationship between the shape of my course and my pedagogical beliefs, that I had never thought seriously about the connections between assessment and goals, and that I couldn't explain and didn't understand the theory undergirding the practice of portfolios.

I am still using portfolios in almost every class I teach. My students still respond enthusiastically to them; we are both still learning about writing and assessment through their use. Recently, one student told me, "It's hard work to put one of these together, but you know, it's kinda cool, too, to work like this." What does "like this" mean? What are portfolios, and how are students and teachers prepared to work with portfolios? What follows helps define portfolios but is not "definitive": one of the hallmarks of portfolios is their ability to be shaped to meet the demands of local contexts. It is important to remember that writing portfolios are constructed in a context, usually a classroom. This context helps shape portfolios. In fact, Sandra Murphy ("Portfolios and Curriculum Reform," 1994) asks us to consider the way in which a "portfolio culture" is developed in a classroom. Each institution, each class presents its own challenges. Thus my suggestions for preparing students to work with portfolios and my advice to help instructors avoid problems aren't all-encompassing. If you choose to use portfolios as part of your classroom, however, they should help you understand better the opportunities and difficulties they present.

What Is a Portfolio?

As an object, a portfolio is simply a collection of items. In fact, Peter Elbow writes that a portfolio is "nothing but a folder, a pouch—an emptiness: a collection device and not a form of assessment" (1994, 40). In fact, a teacher may use portfolios in her classroom and not change much in her practice at all—students simply collect their writing at the end of the semester and the teacher can see the body of work all at once.

But portfolios are most often defined by the activities involved in constructing them; they are most often seen as part of a process that eventually results in a product. What are often called the defining features of portfolios (Yancey, 1995, 84) are actually the defining features of the *work* of constructing portfolios, work done by both teacher and student. The features usually considered in defining a portfolio include *collection, selection, revision, reflection, presentation,* and *evaluation.* Yancey also includes communication among her list of features; this is certainly part of portfolios, just as it is part of any text. While these features are easily listed separately as products—that is, a student could say, "Here is a selection of my writing"—they are inseparable in practice. When a student presents a portfolio that is a selection of work completed over the course of a semester or unit, all of the processes above have gone into its construction.

Collection

Students *collect* materials for a portfolio. Often, everything a student has written is collected in what is called a "working portfolio": first notes for a paper, journal entries connected to essays, drafts, revisions, responses and evaluations from teachers and peers, and all other related materials. I've had students save notes passed in class, letters to a girlfriend, and hard copy of electronic mail correspondence—all writing that they felt was important or representative of the kinds of writing they do by assignment or choice.

Selection

From the messiness of this writer's portfolio the student is usually asked to *select* materials for a "showcase" or "presentation" portfolio. When portfolios are used for assessment purposes (they need not be, as Edward White (1994) and Peter Elbow (1994) both point out), it is usually the presentation portfolio that is evaluated. When students select particular pieces for a presentation portfolio, they may follow guidelines set for them by the teacher (who may be following guidelines set for her by a department or university), or they may select pieces based on principles they themselves have determined. It may be that a teacher and student have negotiated the selection principles, or perhaps the class as a group has worked with the teacher to determine how pieces will be selected.

Revision

While the pieces that have been culled from the working portfolio may be presented "as is," it is often the case that students will *revise* at least some of the chosen pieces before they are presented. They may revise to meet specific criteria or they may revise in response to earlier suggestions offered by peers or their teacher. In many classrooms, work on the remaining pieces in the working portfolio is left off; the students focus on the selected pieces instead.

They may revise because the purpose of the portfolio has changed or the audience for the piece has changed. For example, a student may rework a piece drawn from a child psychology course to present it as part of a portfolio for an English class.

Reflection

Reflection appears to be a crucial defining feature of a writing portfolio and of the learning that we hope will take place as students construct a portfolio. Whether the portfolio is specifically for assessment or learning, a piece of writing that could be considered reflective distinguishes a writing portfolio from a simple collection in a folder. In some cases, students write an introduction to their portfolio which goes beyond simple description of the portfolio components, while in other cases, students assess themselves and their writing. The form of the reflection may be a single piece or may involve "memos" attached to each piece in the portfolio. For many teachers and students, writing reflectively is a new experience and an exciting part of a portfolio-based course.

Presentation

Students *present* their portfolios to someone. That someone may be a teacher, a peer, or even themselves, especially if the portfolio is being used as a learning portfolio and not for formal assessment. In presenting a portfolio, students acknowledge that they have written in a social context, that readers—or the writer's concept of potential readers—of the portfolio have shared in some way in its construction. Even when a portfolio is a learning portfolio, the student is attempting to understand what the portfolio "re-presents" about himself as a writer. This feature, too, separates a portfolio from a simple collection in a folder.

Evaluation

Not all portfolios are *evaluated* formally. However, in most writing classrooms, a final portfolio will be evaluated by a teacher and possibly also by peers. Grant Wiggins (1990, 1993) argues that criteria for evaluation of any performance be clear and available to the student before he or she attempts that performance. As students select and revise pieces for a portfolio, then, they are probably taking those criteria into account, practicing evaluation on their own.

These processes are interconnected. In selecting pieces to showcase or present, a student evaluates and reflects; in revising, a student also evaluates and reflects, and in both selection and revision, the knowledge that this portfolio will be presented to someone will be a part of the process. A student may return to the original collection after working for some time on a piece and ultimately rejecting it; the process begins again as she reflects on this decision and selects another piece from the working portfolio to revise and present to a reader for response and/or evaluation.

Why Use Portfolios?

When I chose to use portfolios, the rationale I offered my students was that a final grade based on how well they wrote at the end of the semester—instead of an average of grades over the course of a semester—was a more valid grade. I still feel that's right, although as I confessed earlier, that's not why I came to use portfolios. Many teachers (particularly at the high school level) are required by administrators to use portfolios; this is also sometimes the case with new teaching assistants who must, at least initially, follow departmental guidelines. I have continued to use portfolios because they are a central part of a classroom that is student-centered, process-oriented, and focused on active and collaborative learning, and they lend themselves to learning *and* assessment. I like, too, that portfolios create a space for diverse voices to be heard, that they change the way time is used in the classroom and in learning, and the ways they support a sense of the social nature of writing and learning.

Diverse Voices

Because portfolios are shaped by the local context, particularly the classrooms in which they are constructed, they permit teachers to adapt assessment to the students. Teachers of nontraditional and ESL students often come to portfolios because they feel they change the whole nature of the classroom, making it less frightening for their students. Pat Belanoff (1994) points out that in many classroom nontraditional students, students of diverse backgrounds, cultures and language outnumber "traditional" college students. We cannot assume any longer that our students are homogeneous and that traditional ways of teaching and assessing are a match for every classroom. Portfolios are a way of allowing diverse voices to be heard. Sandra Murphy suggests that particularly for students whose native language is not English, portfolios reduce some of the stress associated with the structure of traditional ways of teaching and assessing writing where one essay follows another in quick succession and the demand for each is perfection ("Writing Portfolios," 1994).

Portfolios are used to demonstrate progress, to showcase writing, to evaluate students' writing and thinking, and to encourage collaborative learning and reflection. Colleagues have asked me why the same things can't be achieved without using portfolios; my response is that they can, but it is often more difficult for both teacher and student. There are a number of reasons why this is so.

Time

Portfolios change our sense of time in significant ways. Because portfolios are at the very least collections of work, they must be constructed over an extended period of time. This is very different from an essay that must be written by Monday (and too often is composed on Sunday night!), followed by another two weeks later, followed by another one. . . . Because portfolios are usually selections of work, they require that students examine their work as it appears over time; this consideration helps them understand what it is they have learned and how what they've learned has manifested itself in writing. They are constantly looking both backwards at what they have collected and forward toward the portfolio they will create.

When students have little time to think about each essay, when they feel pressed to create, they often fall back on what they are most familiar with, continuing to use the time-honored strategies that have gotten them decent grades in the past, ignoring what we are trying to teach them about writing in this new collegiate setting. Because students begin a portfolio course knowing that not all they write will "count" in the usual way (but all of it can be acknowledged), they often feel free to explore and experiment. Thus some pieces will count for a grade, but all pieces can count for learning. They have the freedom to decide how much time they will spend on these different pieces and processes.

"Why can't I achieve the same thing by allowing students to revise all semester?" teachers ask. Certainly, knowing they have that option relieves some of the pressure on students. But many writers, particularly those least familiar with the demands of college level writing, have difficulty writing each essay, let alone juggling revisions of multiple essays. Most teachers will admit that student writing often improves if the students have time to think over what they've written and how their audiences responded to it. Portfolios are one way of creating that time for students. It also changes the way we teach and respond. When the decision what and how to revise rests more firmly with the student, our responses to writing as teachers may be less geared toward a grade and more like the way we respond to all the other writing we read without having to assign a grade or ranking, more formative and less summative. We are not simply "putting off" grading; we are grading when the "time is right."

Collaboration

Because students must make decisions about what to include in a portfolio, they must pay attention to what their peers and teacher say about their writing. In this way, collaboration is fostered. In cases where the choice of portfolio contents is left largely to the student, portfolios may vary greatly in their shape. If students share their portfolios with one another in peer response groups which are part of most process classrooms, then writers must explain the kinds of writing they've included and help focus discussion in order to receive the level of response that will help them revise. In essence, they must teach their peers about their writing. This kind of interaction encourages active learning on the part of students; they must make critical decisions about their writing, educate peers and teacher about those decisions, and accept responsibility for the quality of the writing.

If we see writing as performance—like art, theatre, or dance—then portfolios offer one of the best ways to judge that performance (Black, et al., "Connecting Current Research," 1994). Portfolios are complex documents which reflect the complexity of the act of writing. Furthermore, they can be firmly a part of the classroom context, reflecting local standards and concerns. They speak to teachers' and students' needs to learn and assess in ways that standardized tests and externally generated assessments and criteria do not.

Preparing to Use Portfolios

New teachers often inherit or are given syllabi that reflect someone else's sets of beliefs or purposes. When they try to integrate portfolios that reflect their own beliefs into the pre-existing curriculum, or when they try to tack on to a course a portfolio designed for a different purpose or even simply a different section of the same course, they are likely to find a mismatch. Sometimes, teachers have not thought through clearly what is implied by their practice.

But for portfolios—or any kind of assessment—to support learning, it is important to be able to answer some questions for yourself before your students ask them of you.

When students enter the classroom and read for the first time through a syllabus which states they will be working all semester toward a final portfolio, many of them will be confused and not a little anxious, particularly if they are new to college anyway. It is helpful to provide them with some guidelines, even if those have not been fully worked out yet. They want to know something about what a portfolio is and why they are constructing one; they want to know what it might or should include, how they will organize it, and how it will be assessed. They want to know who will read it.

In order to answer the seemingly simple questions students might pose, an instructor must deal with some thorny issues beforehand. What are the goals for my course? How do these reflect institutional goals? What purpose does my course serve? What purpose does the portfolio serve? What do I believe about learning and writing? How does the portfolio I want my students to construct reflect my beliefs?

Pedagogical Beliefs

As mentioned earlier, it's entirely possible for a teacher to use portfolios and change very little that he or she does in the classroom. Students could still be assigned topics to write on and modes to write in; could still work individually without discussing writing with peers; and could place all their work in a folder with their name on it and submit it to their teacher, who would average all the grades together and give the student a final grade. The instructor controls all learning from the beginning. However, what I've tried to point out above is that the features of portfolio use—and their benefits in terms of learning—come about when students are permitted to share in their learning. What would the portfolio described above communicate about the beliefs of the teacher and the structure of the classroom?

Clearly, portfolios can be designed to serve a number of purposes, and when we consider how we will shape the portfolios that are parts of the courses we teach, we must consider not only what our goals are for the course, but what we believe about learning; we must examine our pedagogical theory. As Sandra Murphy points out, portfolios not only allow students to demonstrate skills or explore issues in depth, they also reflect our theoretical perspectives on teaching and learning ("Portfolios and Curriculum Reform," 1994). She describes several kinds of portfolios and how they reflect differing beliefs. A behaviorist portfolio, for example, would manifest the belief that learning is both observable and measurable as a set of discrete skills; such a portfolio might be a collection of skills in the form of worksheets. In a classroom where the focus is cognitivist, that is, focused on the processes by which we think and learn, portfolios would be constructed to demonstrate the student's ability to collaborate, reflect, self-assess, revise, etc. They would be evaluated not just for evidence of these processes but the level at which they are performed. So, for example, in an institution where there is concern about first-year students' abilities to punctuate properly, two teachers may use portfolios to address those concerns, but in one case the portfolio may show little evidence of "skills and drills," instead seeing skills as inseparably part of various learning processes, while another portfolio may focus more on worksheets and exercises.

One Course Among Many

In designing a course that uses portfolios, we need to think, too, about possible connections between courses. First-year English classes are often considered "service" courses, or may be part of a sequence of writing/English courses. In institutions with strong writing across the curriculum and writing in the disciplines programs, the first-year writing course may be interdisciplinary in nature, filling more than just a niche in the basic skills or "core curriculum" of the institution. Just as any individual assignment within a course is part of a larger context of assignments and learning, each course is part of a larger context of learning. In such cases, teachers must ask themselves questions beyond their own, personal pedagogical goals. These are institutional questions. Does my course prepare students for another course? A series of specific courses? How will my use of portfolios affect student learning and colleagues' expectations for my students when they enter those courses? These are questions that are best discussed in a large forum with all the faculty involved. In reality, however, that rarely takes place.

Teachers must consider all stakeholders in the assessment. Peter Elbow points out that portfolios

> help us demand the high quality that we want or some other constituency wants: the hard texts themselves, 'the real thing,' the bottom line. We don't have to accept ineffective writing and justify it to ourselves or to colleagues with defensive talk about the lovely process that lies behind it. On the other hand ... portfolios reward students for using a good writerly process: to explore a topic in discussion and exploratory writing; to complicate their thinking; to allow for perplexity and getting lost; to get feedback; to revise; and to collaborate. (1994, 41)

Yet I have heard complaints from colleagues that portfolios "distort" what a student is capable of doing. These colleagues are concerned that the time allowed for revision, the collaborative nature of the writing process, and the selection of texts for evaluation produces grade inflation—what I am grading in each portfolio is the work of *all* my students, and not all the work at that. This complaint may seem at first wrong-headed, but for someone in a field that does not focus on the processes by which they learned to write, in a field where collaboration is less visible and where it is not the writing that is extensively revised but the activities that lead up to the writing, the complaint is very real and must be discussed seriously. This is a case where discussions among faculty, as well as discussion in the classroom about contexts for writing and disciplinary expectations is important.

Using Portfolios

Sandra Murphy lists a number of purposes for portfolios, ranging from

> tracking student development over time, showcasing student response to a range of assignments, evaluating student work across the curriculum, motivating students, promoting learning through reflection and self-assessment, and evaluating students' thinking and writing processes, to program implementation, program assessment, evaluating curriculum, or establishing exit requirements. The possibilities are multiple. ("Portfolios and Curriculum Reform. . . ," 1994, 179–80)

Clearly, the portfolios designed to meet the purposes listed above will each be different. A portfolio used to place students into the proper level course will likely contain writing that is similar to the kinds of writing taught in the courses under consideration. A portfolio to demonstrate development over time would include writing from a student's earliest courses as well as from later courses, and perhaps from courses in a variety of disciplines. A number of models exist, but portfolios need to grow out of the local context. Regardless of how portfolios are to be used, instructors need to make decisions about content, the kinds of choices available for students will have as they construct their portfolios, how portfolios will be organized, and how they will be evaluated.

Contents

The contents of a portfolio reflect its purpose and the classroom it grows out of. For example, in a writing course offered for developmental writers, the emphasis of the portfolio might be progress. Rather than constructing a portfolio that showcases only her best work, a student might include her first paper and papers written midway and at the end of the semester. She might also include journal entries that reflect development, drafts of papers showing increasing sensitivity to the needs of readers, and written critiques of others' papers that show how she has learned to constructively respond. If she is required to self-assess, she may not focus on how her final papers deserve an "A" by some outside standards, but on how much she has learned over the semester and how a reader might see that demonstrated in the artifacts in front of him. She might discuss what has been difficult for her to learn and what she wants to get out of the next course she will take.

Such a portfolio will be very different from one constructed by students near the end of their college work who are showcasing their writing for potential employment or graduate school. Such a portfolio would be much more product-oriented than process-oriented, focusing on achievement rather than development. It might include a reflective essay which explores career and life goals, examples of different types of writing—technical, "academic," reports, creative writing, journalism or scientific writing—that are important to the field which the student wishes to enter, and even a resume or cv.

A sample of portfolio contents for a course in creative writing follows.

English 372
Poetry

Your portfolio must include at a minimum:

➤ Five poems

➤ Two critiques of classmates' poetry

➤ A revised, two page section of your critical essay

➤ A reflective essay

Other items you could include:

➤ additional poems

➤ materials generated from your class presentation

➤ additional critiques

➤ entries from your writer's log

The portfolio contents shown here reflect both my attempt to create in the class a culture of poetry, and the students' desires to keep the focus squarely on the writing of poetry and their development as poets. Responding to poems, speaking about and teaching poetry, and writing critically—extensive reviews, an examination of a particular aspect of poetry, or exploring an issue in poetry—seemed to me to be part of the life of a professional poet in this country. My purpose in the portfolio was for students to present their abilities to write in the range of genres and purposes typically visited by a poet. My students, however, wanted to emphasize in their portfolios their creative writing and their ability to reflect upon their work. Many included several more poems, much draft material, and wrote extensive reflective pieces.

Reflection

In the portfolio guidelines above, I ask students to include a reflective essay. Many find this both the most difficult and most interesting piece they write for the portfolio. Writing reflectively is often a new experience for students. Some students may have kept diaries, but a diary isn't necessarily reflective; it may simply list the day's activities without comment. Reflection can take a variety of forms. In some cases, the reflective essay acts as an introduction to the portfolio. In such an instance, the student's reflection usually touches on most of the items that will follow. The student may discuss the organizing principles she used to construct the portfolio, the relationship between pieces, the purpose she sees her portfolio serving, or may answer direct questions from the teacher. The reflective piece may be entirely separate from the introduction. A student might then focus more on one aspect of her writing or development rather than touch on all the pieces we've read. If the reflective essay is placed last, she can assume certain kinds of knowledge on the reader's part, gained from their experience of the rest of the portfolio. Reflection doesn't necessarily involve evaluation; it may be more descriptive, comparative, or ruminative. However, many teachers ask students to engage in some self-assessment in their reflective piece.

It is important to consider the kind of "reflection" you want students to engage in, to consider the purpose of the essay as part of the portfolio and as part of the whole learning process. Students may need extensive practice in writing reflectively for different purposes; such practice can be built into the curriculum.

Choice

One crucial issue in portfolios is choice. Who will decide what constitutes a portfolio and who will decide the criteria by which it will be evaluated? For students to feel they have ownership over their learning, they must be actively involved in making those choices. A portfolio driven by a constructivist pedagogy, Murphy notes, provides "a means for engaging students in self-reflection and for acknowledging their role as collaborators in the learning process" ("Portfolios and Curriculum Reform . . . ," 1994, 190). In most courses, the teacher sets the goals before the students even settle into their seats, before they even register for the class. When that happens, it's difficult for students to consider themselves "collaborators" in their learning. Yet it is possible to accommodate students' goals, as well as allow students choices in how they meet the goals you have set for them. If one course goal is for students to understand the political and ethical dimensions of their writing and the writing of others, for example, not every student needs to demonstrate that in the same way. Making choices is part of active learning. Students benefit most when they solve problems connected with constructing their portfolios, when they make critical decisions about the shape and quantity of the contents, when they articulate and explore the beliefs and goals that shape their individual portfolios. If all the important decisions have been made and room for choices has been narrowed to almost nothing before students even begin to understand what a portfolio is, then many of the perceived benefits of portfolio learning and assessment that convinced a teacher to use portfolios have been lost. When developing the syllabus for a portfolio course, then, it is important to consider how student voices will be heard as each set of choices must be made.

Organization

The organization of the portfolio may also be a matter of the student's choice. The order in which items are to be read can be significant. Perhaps the student wants to emphasize his understanding of his writing process; he might ask us to read first the notes, then the drafts, then the final version for each essay. Perhaps another wants to emphasize that each essay selected has an important connection to a particular issue or concern of the student. She might then organize the portfolio in a circular way, one that emphasizes the recursive nature of her thinking and the items that provoked it. Students often use a table of contents, which may be annotated; they may also use an introduction which not only tells readers what they will be reading but explains the organizing principle and develops a context for reading.

Evaluating Portfolios

How will you evaluate a portfolio? What will the criteria be? Will the criteria assume that development or progress will take place? Or will development be given credit in some way, as many students request? What would development look like on paper? Are the criteria understood by everyone? For example, if "understanding the writing process" is part of the criteria, does that mean a theoretical writing process—collecting and generating ideas and information, developing that information alone and with peers, focusing the topic more tightly, ordering material to meet the needs of the audience as well as the writer, continuing to develop and revise the writing and still meeting an external deadline—or the writer's own process, which may be very different? How would a student demonstrate such an understanding? Through self-assessment? Through responses to peers?

Often as teachers we are so imbedded in the language and assumptions of our fields that we forget that once we, too, didn't know what these words meant. And sometimes, we have never articulated these understandings to ourselves, let alone students. Such articulation is, however, more than just a valuable exercise. It is an important part of demystifying evaluation and opening up the process to those being evaluated. Students may even be involved in establishing criteria for evaluation, particularly if their goals for the course have been built into the portfolio. Some teachers who use portfolios ask their students to participate in the final assessment process, as they have been involved throughout the semester in many ways in their peers' effort to construct a portfolio.

Typically, portfolios are evaluated holistically. That is, each piece is not graded separately, but all of them together present a picture of the writer. A journal entry, which may have errors in punctuation and spelling, missing words, sentence fragments, and other differences from conventional written English, may be an important part of a writer's strategy of demonstrating the ability to generate, develop, and support ideas. Seen in a later form, perhaps an essay, the ideas have been shaped to fit an audience and presented following the conventions of standard written English. Which piece is more important? How do you separate out the journal entry—the generative material—from the product in the portfolio? Such variety in form, purpose, and audience among pieces in a portfolio demand a holistic reading.

Some teachers who use portfolios create a rubric that they share with students. In such a rubric, defining features of an "A" portfolio are described, as are the features of portfolios that fall into other grade ranges. (See Appendix C for one such rubric.) Students and teacher can refer to the rubric as they are constructing the portfolio and afterwards, as grades are being anticipated and assigned. Some teachers use the reflective essay as an integral part of evaluation. If a student makes a claim in such a piece that she has improved her ability to organize a long essay, then the teacher may look for evidence in the rest of the portfolio to support such a claim.

At some institutions, portfolios are read by an instructor other than the student's. In such cases, the student's instructor can act as a coach rather than a grader; it radically changes the teacher/student relationship. Others use a process called "team-grading" or group grading. Instructors exchange portfolios according to a set pattern. Each portfolio may receive multiple grades. Discrepancies between grades are usually resolved through discussion or an additional reader. This method reflects the complexity of reading and grading any written texts, but especially a document as varied in its parts as a portfolio.

Preparing Students for Portfolios

When the use of portfolios has radically changed the ways in which students participate in learning and writing, even the most familiar practices may be altered, may seem strange or unfamiliar. For example, because I want students to pay attention to one another and to emphasize the social nature of the classroom, I ask students to arrange their desks in a circle. While this doesn't automatically keep students from only addressing me, it works much better than when students are arranged "theatre style" and see only the backs of the students in front of them. But this simple change is problematic for many students, and often it takes weeks to teach them that when they come into class, they should automatically place their desks in a circle. If this small change is so difficult, imagine how difficult it is for students to understand the changes in writing, learning, and assessment that can take place in a portfolio culture!

While the use of portfolios is becoming more widespread, it is still a new concept for many students. We must remember as teachers that if we want students to perform in certain ways and at a particular level at the end of the semester, we must give them practice throughout the course. We cannot reasonably expect students to understand and apply criteria for evaluation without exposure and practice, nor can we expect them to write a reflective essay to include in a portfolio without any exposure to the various forms such writing can take.

Introductory Portfolios

One way to begin is with introductory portfolios.* These portfolios include items that introduce the student to his or her classmates. Students select a small number of items that represent various aspects of their lives or selves and write a brief introduction to the items. Often, these items include a photo of the student and family and friends; awards; an example of something the student collects; something to represent the student's career goals. One of my students brought in a large wall map to represent her interest in geography; another brought in a can of children's band-aids to represent her goal of becoming a pediatrician. Another brought in his hockey skates, and yet another brought in a corn-husk doll made for her by her grandmother.

As students share these portfolios, they ask each other questions about the items and what they represent; the student whose portfolio is being discussed begins to articulate more clearly her criteria for selection. After sharing is through, students can reconsider items—based on their peers' responses, would they choose something different if they could do it again? They consider what they included in their written introductions. Now that they have heard the responses evoked by the items in their portfolios, would they introduce them differently? As a class and individually, they begin to learn about collection, selection, revision, presentation, and evaluation. This is an example of portfolios for learning, not assessment.

Writer's Memo

Most students are used to handing in essays without generative or draft materials, as if the piece had written itself or sprung from their pens or computers fully developed. Usually, too, students hand in essays without any accompanying explanation of their intent, their process, their successes and failures in the piece as it stands. And typically there's no reason why they should; after all, the teacher assigned it, gave them the topic, and knows more about their writing and why they would write such an essay than they themselves do. But in a portfolio culture, where decision-making and problem-solving are part of the learning environ-

---

* I borrowed this wonderful assignment from John Gaughan several years ago.

ment, drafts and discussions of essays are important. Jeffrey Sommers (1989) champions the use of "writers' memos" which explain what the student was intending to accomplish by writing this portfolio, what process she used in constructing it, where she encountered difficulty and where it was easiest, what her concerns are, and what she would like the reader to focus on. In writing such a memo, the student looks back through the drafts that preceded the essay the teacher sees. In reflecting on her process and articulating her choices, she begins to understand the power the writer has over her work. In expressing her concerns about the piece, she is working with criteria for "good" or "bad" writing and is learning to evaluate her own work. Such writers' memos function to prepare students to write reflectively at the end of the semester as they provide a context for reading their portfolios. (See Appendix B for a sample writer's memo assignment.)

Mini-Portfolios

Some courses lend themselves to mid-semester portfolios and unit portfolios. These are ways of practicing in miniature and with less anxiety the process of putting together a portfolio. Mid-semester portfolios ask students to go through the same processes that they will engage in at the end of the semester. Although students have less to select from and those pieces are unlikely to have been extensively revised, a mid-semester portfolio provides a momentary point where learning and assessment clearly come together. It helps to highlight the structure and process of their learning, something particularly important for new students. Unit portfolios help students reflect on learning at points throughout the semester when material changes. They are particularly effective in content-courses. I have used them myself in first-year literature courses, asking students to construct portfolios organized around a single text or perhaps two texts. Such portfolios have contained journal responses, class notes, one or more formal essays, notes on the reading, responses to study questions, and other materials. One student included as part of her discussion on her learning process a copy of the cover of the *Cliff's Notes* for the text we were reading—she had purchased it in hopes of "sounding more intelligent," but found it disappointing after our class discussion. Another included a copy of the playbill for a play she was performing in as part of her discussion of why she chose to work with a dramatic text rather than a poetic one.

Rubrics, Scoring Guides, and Team-Grading

Students need practice in evaluating writing if they are going to be asked to make decisions on selecting "best" works or in revising their own or responding to others' work. They can participate in describing in a rubric what "good" writing includes and then modifying that description depending upon the assignment. They can also read and respond to writing in "team grading" sessions. Typically, writing that has already received a grade from teachers is distributed to students for discussion and grading following the guidelines of a rubric. The teacher explains what grade the paper received and why after students have offered their grades. As the discussion continues, students and teacher can begin to articulate what "organized" or "focused" or "creative" mean both in the context of the classroom and in terms of external standards.

Students can respond, assess, and evaluate each other's portfolios and essays. Although most students are reluctant to give a grade, at least initially, they will place writing into categories such as "young," "teenaged" or "mature" (see Appendix C). They can assess with the assistance of rubrics which they have helped to design. And with a variety of sample portfolios and papers that they have discussed during team grading, they can offer suggestions for improvement. "Well, this one got a B from the teachers and we gave it a B+ and the writer does this," they might say. "You might try that in here." Having practice in writing memos, the author whose work is under discussion can help focus the responses, can explain with more clarity his intent and difficulties.

Students can also participate in creating the final guidelines and criteria for evaluation. Even if the teacher had initially established criteria, it may well be that the course has shifted in focus, or that the goals that students articulated have shifted the course to some extent. It has been my experience that when I ask students what an "excellent" portfolio should include, should look like, should communicate, they demand far more of it than I would. If they have had practice all semester, they will likely have internalized many of the criteria that the teacher has offered them. They will have some of their own as well, and as a teacher, I have always learned important things from listening to what my students value in writing. (Appendix A includes evaluation questions.)

In such a course, the defining features of the process of creating a portfolio are foregrounded again and again. The structure of the course itself and the theory that drives the practice are often on display and under question. Using portfolios often means giving up some of the control traditionally exercised by the teacher. But it is usually an even deal. When control is shared, so is learning.

Pitfalls and Problems in Portfolio Use

Borrowing Portfolios: Make Your Own Recipe

When teachers share stories of "what worked in my class" with each other, it's always tempting to simply take a strategy that was successful in one class and apply it to another. But as I've pointed out above, a portfolio—even one designed for another section of the same course—reflects a whole set of beliefs about teaching and learning. Without a serious consideration of what you believe and what goals you have set for the course, it is unlikely that you can simply tack on a portfolio designed by another teacher and find success. The most successful portfolios grow out of the local context: the beliefs, goals, and abilities of the teacher and students who will construct them.

Supporting Portfolios with Course Design

Another difficulty is designing a course to support portfolios. Portfolios flourish in courses with a lot of writing and interaction. In a literature course that involves a great deal of lecture, a limited amount of group work, and a midterm and final, the foundation for portfolios is shaky. In order to make choices in selecting pieces for a portfolio, students must have a sufficient body of work to select from. If students write only three papers over the semester, there are few tough decisions to make when they are asked to select two of them for a portfolio. For a portfolio to include writing other than formal essays, for example, journal entries, drafts, responses to study questions, critiques of peers' work, writing from other courses, or even texts that aren't written—videotaped peer group work, perhaps—students must have the opportunity to produce such texts. They also need to produce them in a quantity sufficient to give them practice in such writing—and presumably then, the opportunity for improvement over time—and to give them a large enough collection to be able to select examples to include in a final portfolio. Thus, if students are asked to write critiques of each other's work only once during the semester and the rest of the time they respond orally, yet in the final portfolio they are asked to demonstrate that they can respond constructively to a peer's text, they will either have to submit their first written critique (quite probably not their best work) or make arrangements to submit an audio- or videotape of their performance.

What is important to remember here is that portfolios cannot simply be "added" to a course. Assessment and curriculum dance with one another in tight steps. They drive one another. If in a traditional literature course the lectures all "teach to the test," which is a single-sitting, timed, final exam, then in a course where students will construct a final portfolio, we must teach to that form assessment, too. Opportunities for practicing the kinds of writing that will be required in the final portfolio must be built into a syllabus. If a portfolio is to be sensitive to student goals and writing desires, then the syllabus must be flexible enough to support that as well. If you are going to offer students the chance to place a text of their choice in the portfolio, it's important to remember that the chosen text might be a poem or short story they wrote. Will there be time built into the syllabus for such personal or experimental writing? Will there be time built in for the revision and reconsideration of texts at points throughout the semester?

Lost Drafts and Papers, Erased Disks

Most instructors hear at least once a semester: "I left my paper in the library and someone took it" or "I had the whole thing done and then it got deleted somehow off the disk." This problem is magnified when a student loses a whole portfolio or the working portfolio from which she will select material for presentation. One solution is to ask students to submit copies of drafts and papers to you as they work on them or turn them in. This produces its own logistical problems, even when using disks. Another solution is to have students team up in a "buddy system" and submit copies of all their materials to at least one other student.

Muddy Waters: Grading Portfolios

Reading a portfolio is not entirely unlike reading a single essay, but it does present some additional challenges. When we read a single essay or paper, we may find we have formed an opinion about the writer's skills very early in our reading, perhaps in the opening paragraphs. This opinion may well be correct, particularly if the paper is short; after all, in a five paragraph theme we will have read one-fifth of the paper after one paragraph! But a portfolio often contains many pieces, and those pieces may vary widely in their quality.

It is tempting to read an introductory portfolio essay and feel confident in your evaluation of the writer's abilities. But it is likely that within the next few pieces your evaluation will shift back and forth. An insightful journal entry may prompt us to expect the next piece to be a wonderful paper; we may discover, however, that the student had difficulty making a transition from informal to formal writing. We also know as readers of many papers at one sitting that if we read a merely competent essay right after a very poorly written essay, the competent essay may receive a higher grade than it otherwise would. It is important to practice reading portfolios to get a feel for the ways in which these "glow" and "roller coaster" effects within portfolios influence our grading (Sommers *et al.*, 1993). The ability to withhold judgement is crucial when reading portfolios. In some ways they are like collages; they do not always have the same kinds of coherence that single essays do.

Holistic grading is unfamiliar not only to most students and many faculty, but also to some administrators. This may present a problem. Will you as the instructor be able to explain holistic grading well enough to satisfy a student unhappy about a grade? A student's parents if necessary? If a grade is challenged, will the departmental administrators—the department chair or the Writing Program Administrator—support a holistic portfolio grade, that is, a "C" for an entire body of work? If you are in the position of "pioneering" portfolio use, you may find it necessary to acquaint some of your colleagues or administrators with your grading practices.

Reading the Writer, Not the Writing

There is another aspect of reading portfolios that is also important to remember. Most of us have found ourselves at one point or another really offended by what one of our students has written. We may have found ourselves judging and grading the student more than the writing. When we draw back a bit and think about it, we realize that we are reading just one paper, probably not a very long one at that, and the student's views are probably much more complex than what appears in the essay. Portfolios, however, provide us with not just a more complete picture of the writer's abilities, but of the writer him or herself. The more complete and complex the picture, the more likely it is that we will respond to some aspect of the portfolio that is not part of the agreed upon criteria. It becomes easier to "like" or "dislike" the author of a portfolio, and more difficult to maintain the kind of professional stance—that tightwire act we juggle all the time when we respond honestly to our students and their work—that we need to draw on when grading.

Reflective essays are especially sites where the personal aspects of the writer/student/teacher/evaluator relationship may become even more complicated than usual. As Glenda Conway (1994) and Nedra Reynolds (1994) point out, it is in a reflective essay (often used to both self-assess and introduce the portfolio) that students try most apparently to negotiate that relationship. They are aware keenly of their audience, but the multiple purposes of the essay often become entangled. Depending upon the assignment for the essay, students may be compelled to discuss their weaknesses as a writer, even though the portfolio is supposedly their best work. They may feel compelled to compliment the teacher (I really liked the way you responded to my work, I think you could relate to me), evaluate the course (I'm weak because I didn't get any practice in this area), or even adopt a stance that sets them apart from their classmates and teacher (while you want this portfolio to showcase work, I want to emphasize effort and progress). Given that reflective essays are often introductory essays and likely to be the first substantive materials in a portfolio, they are often given more weight and importance than other pieces. They set the tone and establish the relationship between reader and writer. This is very problematic when the reader must also actually grade the portfolio. Practice in writing reflectively, attention to issues of audience, and attention to the final portfolio's shape are important. One solution is to place annotated tables of contents or clearly introductory essays first and reflective essays last. Another is to examine the ways in which description becomes evaluation. Finally, Conway suggests that each teacher examine the ethics of asking students to draw attention to weaknesses in such an essay.

Grading Logistics: Dealing with the Paper Load

I have heard colleagues say they don't use portfolios because there is too much to evaluate during the last week of a semester—the grading load is overwhelming. Often, these same colleagues have never used portfolios, but they see as unwelcome the prospect of reading three essays and many other pieces from each student when their own desire to assess fairly and completely combines with the fast-approaching deadline for a final grade. It has not been my experience, however, that grading portfolios takes much more time than grading final essays and then averaging together the grades for various essays, quizzes, etc. completed over the course of the semester. In fact, I've often found that I have more difficulty assigning a final grade I feel comfortable with when I am considering one piece of writing as the major source of that grade: final exams often count for 40% or more of the final course grade. I am reading responses to the same questions over and over, trying to distinguish one from another by the time I've reached the end.

Even a well designed final exam seems inadequate to me after the experience of reading the multitextual, complex body of work that is a portfolio. My sense is that most teachers would prefer to be able to sit down with a student and talk together over a large quantity of her writing, identifying strengths and weaknesses, areas of great development, and directions for further writing. When I read a portfolio, I feel as if I could and wanted do that; I also feel as if my students could participate in such a conversation without the usual apologies for test performance: "Well, it was timed, I could've done better with more time;" "I read the book and I thought it was neat that X did this or that but I couldn't remember the name of the guy who . . . . so I missed that question . . . . "

Portfolios are usually read holistically, which means that I can sit back with my coffee cup and read straight through without a pen in my hand. Most of the writing is familiar to me; I have seen it in draft several times, and I have a sense of the history of each piece as I read. The most recent piece, a reflective essay, is the least familiar to me and often the piece my students play with the most. It is a joy to read essays so full of voice and hope and learning. Each is different from the next.

My students and I have created and discussed the grading rubric; we understand the terms we are using, the criteria which are flexible and those that are not. Each portfolio has a copy of the rubric in it. I usually write a quick narrative response, highlighting the strengths of the portfolio and using some of the key words from the rubric. There is little else to consider for the final grade—perhaps a whole semester journal, a classroom presentation, or participation or attendance. Even these aspects of a grade have been discussed and negotiated in my courses.

There is certainly no less work involved in using portfolios instead of a more traditional approach. Like other teachers, I think long and hard about my syllabus as I am constructing the outline of the course; I put time into creating materials to support the various kinds of writing my students are asked to do or may choose to do on their own; I spend a great deal of time helping my students learn to do much of the work themselves as the course progresses. In the end, they give me for a grade a multilayered artifact that we both can say presents their best work—not their best work under the circumstances. Because I am not grading each piece individually, because I have responded to most of this work in earlier drafts, because my response is global and holistic, I can respond swiftly and comfortably to each portfolio.

Connecting Portfolios to the Simon & Schuster Handbook for Writers 4/e

Much of the material in the handbook can also be applied to the construction of a portfolio. The handbook concentrates on writing to inform and persuade, as these are two of the most common purposes of writing in an academic setting. However, a course designed around writing for these purposes can offer opportunities for both personal and public writing, writing that is expressive and transactional. An instructor might encourage writing that is poetic *and* persuasive—are listeners persuaded by the lyrics of a song? By the imagery of a poem? Such a course may in addition be organized topically, with students selecting one topic to explore over the course of the semester. A final portfolio for such a course might include journal entries about the topic selected, for example, the effect of television violence on viewers. The journal entry is private writing: the audience is the writer and the purpose may be exploratory, an attempt to discover. But in response to assignments that vary audience and purpose, a writer may: produce a mini-research paper in which she summarizes the positions generally taken on the topic and the support offered for each; attempt to persuade a local cable company not to offer a particular channel, arguing the violence is damaging to children; write a short children's story which teaches them about television violence; or write up limited original research after surveying peers about their viewing preferences. A final course portfolio could be used to provide information and persuade readers of the writer's position at the end of the semester. The reflective essay for such a portfolio might include a TV viewing autobiography and consideration of the connections between the writer's TV viewing and the position, arguments, even the imagery used in the rest of the portfolio.

In an alternative, non-topical final portfolio, rather than focusing on one topic the writer might include essays on various topics and for various audiences, selected and organized to show the writer's increasing sensitivity to the demands of each rhetorical situation.

As students begin working on a portfolio, they might be reminded of the what they have learned about the various processes that are part of writing. For example, students often want their portfolios to showcase their best work, to demonstrate the breadth of their writing skills, and to provide evidence of progress and effort. But too many purposes will make it difficult to select pieces and revise them. As they construct their final portfolio, students will need to apply when they've learned about narrowing a topic when writing individual essays.

Similarly, the instructor must think carefully about the purpose of the reflective essay and the ways in which the audience for such an essay will effect "reflection." In honest reflection in a private journal, I might admit that I really didn't read the whole book I wrote about for one essay; I just read a few chapters and listened to what was discussed in class. I might wonder how much more I might have learned if I'd read the whole thing, and I might consider how that would change my essay. Personally, I think that's worthwhile reflecting on. But if I knew that my reader was also going to grade me on my portfolio and that essay is part of it, I would be tempted instead to write about why I was interested in the topic of the portfolio—something safe and relatively easy. Students and instructor need to talk about purpose and audience for the reflective essay, as well as topic. Are there some things that the student *must* discuss? Or is the topic wide open, as long as there is some connection to the portfolio?

Students might look back at Chapter 5 in the *Handbook* and consider how they will "think beyond the obvious" as they write an introduction to their portfolio. The reader will make obvious connections, but what are the connections he might not see, and what are the implications of connecting these pieces together in such a way? Instructors might, too, point out the ways that introductions and reflections may appear to be informational in purpose, but are very important in persuading a reader to adopt a certain position as she reads and finally evaluates.

Conclusion

I hear about portfolios everywhere I turn now. They are being required by administrators who have not read one themselves, explored and even mandated by state legislative bodies, and are following students from grade to grade at all levels of learning. They are being used to place students in courses, to evaluate programs, and to demonstrate competency in major fields. They are being used by teachers themselves in rank and tenure applications. They are being tacked onto courses at all levels of learning and at institutions nationwide.

Portfolios present unique opportunities for both learning and assessment because they focus our attention at various times on both the processes of writing and the products that we construct. They are often complex and challenging both to create and evaluate. But they are one assessment instrument among many, and are certainly not the only way to help students learn. By themselves they are not a panacea for the problems presented by standardized testing, essay tests, and the passivity that can result from lectures and a lack of student involvement in everyday classwork. When they are part of a carefully considered and designed curriculum, however, they can support and help create active learning, collaboration, and the development of critical learning skills such as problem-solving, small-group communication, generating, developing and supporting ideas, and critical thinking and questioning. They do not make teaching easier, but they do change its shape. Faculty who use portfolios as an integral part of their teaching may rediscover themselves as learners. Teachers who have constructed a portfolio themselves, either as a participant in their own class or as part of their professional responsibilities—a teaching portfolio for rank and tenure considerations—find that the processes of learning and writing are foregrounded in ways they have not been for years as we have written professionally, working on individual pieces in the kind of academic writing we are comfortable with. Instructors using portfolios in their classrooms may rediscover or discover for the first time how much their students really know. Too often we see students as their essays, as three pages here, four there. Portfolios show us our students as more than the sum of their parts.

Further Reading and Resources

There are a number of newsletters and journals which are devoted to assessment, some exclusively to portfolio use. In addition, there are several recently published collections of essays about portfolio use that may prove helpful. The articles cited in this introduction provide a good starting place for specific questions you might have about portfolios. And professional conferences in English studies usually offer a number of sessions on portfolio assessment.

The following journals and newsletters are available at many academic libraries. Publishers of these journals may also offer additional instructional aids and resources for study.

AAHE Assessment Forum. American Association for Higher Education. One Dupont Circle, Suite 600, Washington, DC 20036-1110.

Assessing Writing. Ablex Publishing Corporation, 355 Chestnut St., Norwood, NJ, 07648.

CWA Newsletter. Missouri Colloquium on Writing Assessment. Missouri Western State College, St. Joseph, MO 65407.

Notes from the National Testing Network in Writing. National Testing Network in Writing. CUNY, 535 East 80th St., New York, NY 10021.

Portfolio Assessment Newsletter. Northwest Evaluation Association. 5 Centerpoint Drive, Suite 100, Lake Oswego, OR 97035.

Portfolio News. C/o San Dieguito Union High School District, 710 Encinitas Boulevard, Encinitas, CA 92024.

Portfolio — The Newsletter of Arts PROPEL. Harvard Project Zero, 323 Longfellow Hall, Harvard Graduate School of Education, 13 Appian Way, Cambridge, MA 02138.

Quarterly of the National Writing Project and Center for the Study of Writing and Literacy. Graduate School of Education, University of California, Berkeley, CA 94720.

❋ ❋ ❋

The following recent collections offer essays dealing with the theory and practice of portfolios at levels from elementary through professional.

Black, Laurel, Donald A. Daiker, Jeffrey Sommers, and Gail Stygall, (Eds.). *New Directions in Portfolio Assessment: Reflective Practice, Critical Theory, and Large-Scale Scoring.* Portsmouth, NH: Heinemann, Boynton/Cook, 1995.

Belanoff, Pat, and Marcia Dickson, (Eds.). *Portfolios: Process and Product.* Portsmouth, NH: Heinemann, Boynton/Cook, 1991.

Yancey, Kathleen Blake (Ed.). *Portfolios in the Writing Classroom.* Urbana, IL: NCTE, 1992.

Works Cited

Black, Laurel, Edwina Helton, and Jeffrey Sommers. "Connecting Current Research on Authentic and Performance Assessment Through Portfolios." *Assessing Writing* 1.2 (1994): 247–266.

Belanoff, Pat. "Portfolios and Literacy: Why?" *New Directions in Portfolio Assessment.* Eds. Laurel Black, Donald A. Daiker, Jeffrey Sommers, and Gail Stygall. Portsmouth, NH: Heinemann, Boynton/Cook, 1994. 13–24.

Conway, Glenda. "Portfolio Cover Letters, Students' Self-Presentation, and Teachers' Ethics." *New Directions in Portfolio Assessment.* Eds. Laurel Black, Donald A. Daiker, Jeffrey Sommers, and Gail Stygall. Portsmouth, NH: Heinemann, Boynton/Cook, 1994. 83–92.

Elbow, Peter. "Will the Virtues of Portfolios Blind Us to Their Potential Dangers?" *New Directions in Portfolio Assessment.* Eds. Laurel Black, Donald A. Daiker, Jeffrey Sommers, and Gail Stygall. Portsmouth, NH: Heinemann, Boynton/Cook, 1994. 40–55.

Murphy, Sandra. "Writing Portfolios in K–12 Schools: Implications for Linguistically Diverse Students." *New Directions in Portfolio Assessment.* Eds. Laurel Black, Donald A. Daiker, Jeffrey Sommers, and Gail Stygall. Portsmouth, NH: Heinemann, Boynton/Cook, 1994. 140–156.

———. "Portfolios and Curriculum Reform: Patterns in Practice. " *Assessing Writing* 1.2 (1994): 175–206.

Reynolds, Nedra. "Graduate Writers and Portfolios: Issues of Professionalism, Authority, and Resistance." *New Directions in Portfolio Assessment.* Eds. Laurel Black, Donald A. Daiker, Jeffrey Sommers, and Gail Stygall. Portsmouth, NH: Heinemann, Boynton/Cook, 1994. 201–209.

Sommers, Jeffrey, Laurel Black, Donald A. Daiker, and Gail Stygall. "The Challenges of Rating Portfolios: What WPAs Can Expect." *WPA: Writing Program Administration* 17.1–2 (1993): 7–30.

———. "The Writer's Memo: Collaboration, Response, and Development." *Writing and Response: Theory, Practice and Research.* Ed. Chris Anson. Urbana, IL: NCTE, 1989. 174–86.

White, Edward M. "Portfolios as an Assessment Concept." *New Directions in Portfolio Assessment.* Eds. Laurel Black, Donald A. Daiker, Jeffrey Sommers, and Gail Stygall. Portsmouth, NH: Heinemann, Boynton/Cook, 1994. 25–39.

Wiggins, Grant. "Assessment: Authenticity, Context, and Validity." *Phi Delta Kappan* (1993): 200–214.

———. "The Truth May Make You Free But the Test May Keep You Imprisoned: Toward Assessment Worthy of the Liberal Arts." Paper presented at the fifth American Association for Higher Education (AAHE) Conference on Assessment, Washington, D.C., 1990.

Yancey, Kathleen Blake. "Portfolios for the Writing Instructor: Some Definitions, Some Guidelines, Some Recommendations." *Resource Guide, 12th ed. Prentice Hall Handbook for Writers.* Eds. Melinda G. Kramer, Glenn Legget, C. David Mead. Englewood Cliffs, NJ: Prentice Hall, 1995. 82–104.

PART THREE
APPENDIX A

Advanced Composition: English 251

Course Writing Assignments:

1. Minimum two entries weekly in a journal
2. Introductory portfolio
3. Five essays: four open and one reflective essay
4. Grammar Presentation and Workshop
5. Written responses to a peer's paper

Final Portfolio Requirements

1. Table of Contents
2. Reflective Essay
3. Two essays, revised from earlier drafts
4. Five journal entries

OPTIONAL: Additional journal entries, worksheets, critiques, in-class writing exercises, ?—What else have you been working on that you'd like to include?

Final Course Grade

The class has decided that final course grades will be computed using the following formula:

Portfolio: 60%

Journal: 15%

Presentation: 5%

Participation: 20%

Evaluating Portfolios for English 251

As I read through your portfolio, I will be asking myself the following questions. These questions are based on our discussion over the course of the semester, and particularly on our discussion on "excellence" last week. As you construct your portfolios, you can ask yourself the same questions.

> ➤ Does the writer demonstrate the ability to develop and support a thesis where necessary?

> ➤ Does the writer demonstrate the ability to ask questions of her material that allow her to fully explore her topic?

> ➤ Does the writer demonstrate the ability to think critically about the material with which he is working?

> ➤ Does the writer demonstrate the ability to make what he or she writes interesting to a reader?

> ➤ Does the writer engage the reader?

> ➤ Does the writer demonstrate the ability to use language appropriate to the rhetorical situation?

> ➤ Does the writer demonstrate the ability to write following the conventions of standard written English?

> ➤ Does the writer demonstrate the ability to write for a variety of purposes?

I don't ask these questions about each single piece in the portfolio, but I ask them when they are appropriate. I won't ask that a journal entry be free from error, but I do expect that your essays be free from error. I may feel that you have suggested some abilities and demonstrated others as I read through the whole portfolio. The more you are able to demonstrate, rather than suggest, the higher your portfolio grade will be. You and I will have met in a conference as you are making portfolio decisions, and we will read and respond to each other's rough portfolios in class before they are due.

PART THREE
APPENDIX B

Writer's Memo Assignment

A **writer's memo** is a way of letting readers in on the purpose you had in composing your essay. It also helps readers understand the process you used in constructing your writing. Readers will be better able to understand why you put this particular piece of support here, an anecdote there, why you chose your title, why you concluded what you did. A writer's memo is a way of following your essay around, explaining the things you might if you were sitting with your readers, talking about your writing.

When this memo is intended for a teacher who will give you response and a grade, it provides other kinds of information as well. For example, the teacher may come to understand that you have definite ideas and plans for your writing but have difficulty turning plans into writing in certain situations. She may then be able to offer you some advice or guidance. The teacher may also be better able to understand how you evaluate your writing and share with your her evaluation.

Another way the memos help you is the practice they give you in writing reflectively and writing about writing. Over the course of multiple drafts and a whole semester, you will have written a number of these memos. If you look back at them at the end of the semester, you may be able to see how you have developed successful techniques for approaching assignments, that you have learned how to write about writing, or that you have continued to struggle with one aspect of your writing but been successful with others.

As you write your memo consider giving the reader answers to the following questions:

> ➤ When did you start thinking about this paper? What ideas did you consider? Why did you reject the others and select this one to work with?

> ➤ When did you actually start writing the paper? What prompted you to write or what kept you from writing? Did you use a different process when writing this paper from one that you used in the past?

181

➤ What were the major decisions you made while writing the first draft? When you revised? Why did you decide what you did?

➤ What did you learn—if anything—from writing this paper? Should we as readers be able to tell what you learned as we read the paper?

➤ What are the strengths of this paper? Why?

➤ What parts of the paper aren't quite as strong? Why?

➤ What grade would you give this paper right now and why?

➤ What would you like your readers to get from this paper?

➤ What would you like your readers to focus on as they prepare to respond to the paper or prepare suggestions for revision?

As you write your memo, imagine you are having a dialogue with an interested reader, someone who wants to know how you did what you did and why, someone whom you trust to respond honestly and constructively.

 PART THREE
APPENDIX C

Portfolio Response Rubric*

YOUNG PORTFOLIO – A portfolio that is full of possibilities not yet realized. The reader has a sense that the portfolio as a whole is undeveloped. It is often short and lacks substance. The writing may be free from errors, but it does not possess a strong voice. There may be no clear sense of audience or purpose. There may also be recurring problems in content and style. The reflective essay may substitute surface narrative and summary for reflection. The writing may rely on formulas and cliches. On the other hand, there may be moments of effective writing, places where the writer hints at strengths that are yet to be developed.

TEENAGED PORTFOLIO – In this portfolio we see pretty clearly the shape of things to come. The writing is competent in both content and style. There may be an unevenness of quality or underdevelopment in places—perhaps the reflective essay doesn't offer a full picture of the writer's work, or several pieces seem to need attention to bring them up to the level of development seen in another piece. The reader may want "more" to be fully convinced of the writer's ability to use language effectively. But the writer takes more risks with her work. Her voice is stronger, more original. She has a clearer sense of where she stands with her writing and her audience.

MATURE PORTFOLIO – This portfolio is substantial in development and accomplishment. It engages its readers, invites them into a mature dialogue. It uses language effectively and creatively. The reflective essay moves well beyond summary to help provide a context for understanding the writer and the writing. At the upper range of this group, mature portfolios take risks that work and challenge their readers by trying something new.

Remember: no portfolio is perfect, and each of these groups represent a range and a variety (a thirteen-year-old is different from a nineteen-year-old, yes?). So as you respond to your peers, keep in mind that you might make even finer, more accurate analogies for them.

---

* These descriptions draw on Miami University's scoring guide for placement portfolios. Edwina Helton suggests the terms "starting," "working," and "polished" for these three levels. I have found students enjoy the category descriptors used above, even adding a few of their own in close-knit peer groups: "infant" and "old man."

PART FOUR

ESL Writers in the Composition Class

Cynthia Myers
Iowa State University

PART FOUR

ESL Writers in the Composition Class

Introduction

When I was in my second semester of teaching freshman composition as a graduate student, I had an articulate and motivated Colombian student in my class. I enjoyed having Julio in class and optimistically hoped that my course could help him mature as a writer. One day after class, he approached me with a paper I had corrected and kindly asked me to explain a few of the mistakes he had made: He wanted to thoroughly understand which situations required the present perfect and which required the past perfect. I launched into an explanation, but as I talked, I suddenly realized that I had only a vague notion of the answer. I knew it had something to do with time frame, but why exactly couldn't Julio say "I have lived in Kansas since six months ago"? It was not something I had ever really considered, nor was it a grammar question that had come up in my teaching of high school English to native speakers.

I began to notice how many grammar errors I had corrected on Julio's paper: the page was covered with green ink. I also began to suspect that my corrections were probably not going to help him avoid making the mistakes another time. I noticed how few substantive comments I had made to help him with revising his material and reorganizing his ideas. I began to feel embarrassed, and then apologetic, and finally inadequate. How could I help him improve his writing without becoming mired in long and confusing grammar explanations? How could I help him improve his grammar when I had such an incomplete understanding of the language myself?

I tell the story because I believe my feelings of incompetence at that time have probably been felt by many teachers suddenly faced with non-native students whose questions and whose presence in a class with native speakers are disquieting. As teachers of writing, we want to help all students, but without specialized training we may be uncertain how to proceed. Will we embarrass a quiet Japanese student if we ask him to share an especially poetic description with the rest of the class? Is it useful to mark the many errors that appear on an Indonesian student's first draft? Should we tell a Puerto Rican student that her lateness to class is disruptive since we know that her Latin American sense of time is different from our own? Should we avoid calling on a Chinese student whose spoken English is difficult to understand? And, in addition to the many questions we may have about individual non-native speakers, how do we handle classroom dynamics to encourage the native speaking students to include non-native speakers when they choose collaborative or peer review groups? How can we foster an atmosphere in which all students feel empowered?

My role as coordinator of a program of cross-cultural freshman English classes at a large state university has given me some insights into the challenges faced by composition teachers who work with classes made up of half non-native and half native speakers, particularly when the teachers have little experience in teaching ESL (English as a second language). It has also given me a new appreciation for the stimulating diversity of a composition class with students from varied backgrounds and also for the benefits to the U.S. students in a class with international classmates.

Whether international students comprise half a class or are scattered more sparsely throughout sections of freshman English, the insights and experiences of international students can enrich any class. Students learn to collaborate with students from different backgrounds, gaining skills that will make them more cosmopolitan citizens of the world. Goals of a writing course may include encouraging students to draw material from multiple perspectives, growing beyond a narrow view of the world, and thinking critically, goals which can be facilitated when differing views are represented. Regardless of their cultural background, students can learn to tolerate ambiguity and avoid automatic judgments, and having a culturally mixed class can broaden the perspectives of both U.S. and international students. Students can also learn that culture is much more than an assemblage of curious customs, that it is at the very root of our personalities, ideas, and beliefs.

Though ESL students may be initially apprehensive about taking a composition course, they have much to gain from the experience. In many universities, freshmen enroll primarily in large lecture classes; a composition class may be one of the few in which professors know their names, or in which they have a chance to get acquainted with their classmates. Some international students spend much of their time associating with a support group of other students from their own cultures; though they may wish to make American friends, international students often do not find opportunities to get well-acquainted with U.S. students. The intimate setting of a composition class can be an ideal opportunity for an international student to make U.S. friends. Additionally, the more chances an international student has to practice listening, speaking and writing the more likely she will be to improve her abilities to communicate in English. This practice occurs with more intensity and frequency in the writing classroom than in many content area classes.

The first section of this chapter examines cultural issues that make studying in the United States a challenging situation for many international students and suggests ways in which a composition teacher can integrate international students into the classroom. It also discusses some of the general concerns in cross-cultural education and provides insights into the differing perspectives of international students. The second section describes some of the difficulties new international students may have in speaking and listening. It discusses classroom activities that have proved useful in helping ESL students improve their listening comprehension and speaking abilities. The third section looks more specifically at writing pedagogy for the ESL student, covering such issues as understanding differences in rhetorical expectations of native and non-native students, handling errors in ESL student's writing, and adapting pedagogical techniques like peer review and collaborative writing to a class including non-native students.

Cultural Issues

New international students face big adjustments when coming to the U.S. to study. Not only is the language a challenge, but even well-meaning Americans can cause distress for newly-arrived students. Mui, from Malaysia, wrote this in her journal:

> When I first came, I was very frightened because I did not understand the American way of doing things. I can clearly remember my first time on the campus. It was a afternoon, but the campus was as quiet as midnight because the university was closed for winter break. I was walking alone with a campus map in my right hand and worrying that I would not be able to find all my classes. An American guy approached me as I walked along the sidewalk. As he got closer, he said "Hi." I looked around and there was nobody else except the two of us. "He must be saying hi to me," I thought. I was so scared! I whispered in my

heart, "My goodness, I hope he won't attack a helpless girl like me. He must be a crazy person." I walked faster with my head down and ignored him. My heart was beating and I could hardly breath. I just couldn't believe it when he passed me by without any assault! Later, as I was here a longer time, I realized that saying "hi" or smiling to strangers was to be friendly to them. I hoped that the guy wouldn't misinterpret that foreigners were cold and unfriendly.

Reading her journal, we cannot help but sympathize with Mui's terror. If this situation caused her to panic, one might imagine that other, more complex situations could be very confusing. New international students sometimes have great difficulty knowing what is appropriate or expected in a given situation. For example, a new student in one of my ESL classes confided to me that he had been unable to sleep for a week because his American roommate would enter their dorm room at two or three in the morning talking loudly to friends, would turn on the light and the stereo, and would often not go to bed until dawn. To the international student, his roommate's behavior was incomprehensibly rude, yet my student was uncertain whether or not this unkindness was inappropriate for an American. He had no idea whether or not he should complain, either to the roommate or to someone else. And in the meantime, he was attempting to attend class and study through a blur of exhaustion.

These two situations were resolved favorably: Mui noticed the differences in greeting customs and began to feel comfortable with them; my tired student spoke to his RA and eventually arranged to move into another room. But other situations may continue to provoke uneasiness, discomfort, or confusion. The anthropologist Edward Hall (1959) explains that ". . . culture is more than mere custom that can be shed or changed like a suit of clothes" (p. 46), and ". . . culture controls behavior in deep and persisting ways, many of which are outside of awareness and therefore beyond conscious control of the individual" (p. 48).

Some students may never feel entirely comfortable with the relaxed, "anything goes" atmosphere in an American classroom: It violates all they have been taught about the teacher's proper authority and the respect owed by a student. Though they may manage to understand and function in a U.S. classroom, they may never feel completely "at home" in a class where students interrupt the teacher or pack up their books to leave while the teacher is still talking. Another student may grow to understand that American friends are not intending to be rude when they say "Let's get together sometime?" but never call, yet it may continue to seem impolite.

We need to recognize rather than trivialize the differences in deeply-rooted cultural values. As Hall (1959) points out, the most useful aspect of learning about cultural differences is gaining a deeper understanding of one's own culture. "The best reason for exposing oneself to foreign ways is to generate a sense of vitality and awareness—an interest in life which can come only when one lives through the shock of contrast and difference" (p. 53). If teachers understand the complex challenges facing their international students, they can work to make the composition classroom a place where some cultural issues can be explored. At the very least, they can provide a supportive atmosphere where U.S. and international classmates can learn together.

It is also well worth remembering that international students are an amazingly diverse group of people. They come from backgrounds very different from one another, have widely varying goals and attitudes about studying in the United States, and certainly have different skills. My comments are not meant to minimize these differences, nor am I intending to "lump" all international students into one large, easily-explainable group. However, certain difficulties reappear among students from many backgrounds, and several issues about cross-cultural communication are worth exploring. The following suggestions may help to clarify areas confusion, misinterpretation and difficulty experienced by many international students.

Nonverbal Communication

Anyone who has done reading on cultural diversity is aware that students from other cultures may interpret matters of personal space and body language very differently than the "average American." My consciousness was raised about this issue during my first semester as a teaching assistant. A Nigerian student in my class frequently came for office hours to get extra advice about his writing. I enjoyed talking with him and got to know him well from our frequent conversations. We would begin the conference with me behind my desk and him on the chair to the right of the desk where all my students sat when they came in to talk to me. As we talked about his writing, he would invariably gather up his papers and move his chair so that we were sitting side by side. Though I didn't feel threatened by him, I found myself feeling uncomfortable sitting with our shoulders touching, and I would unconsciously edge my chair farther away. As we talked, my student would scoot his chair closer; I would move farther. I finally realized what was happening when I found that I was leaning into the wall at the left side of my desk: inch by inch, he had pursued me there. He felt comfortable at a closer distance than I did—a phenomenon I had read about but never experienced before.

Hall (1959) provides insights into this phenomenon for his U.S. readers:

> In Latin America the interaction distance is much less than it is in the United States. Indeed, people cannot talk comfortably with one another unless they are very close to the distance that evokes either sexual or hostile feelings in the North American. The result is that when they move close, we withdraw and back away. As a consequence, they think we are distant or cold, withdrawn and unfriendly. We, on the other hand, are constantly accusing them of breathing down our necks, crowding us, and spraying our faces. (p. 209)

Students from other cultural backgrounds may also have differing conventions for who may touch whom and in what circumstances. A Japanese student may feel that her space has been invaded if an American student puts his feet on the back of her chair. Asian students often express surprise at U.S. couples publicly hugging or kissing, yet may find the taboo against same-sex touching odd. One assumes, until one has reason to know otherwise, that all people operate under the same unspoken rules for nonverbal appropriateness, and it may come as a disquieting shock to realize that one's own internalized rules are not held by others. "Since most people don't think about personal distance as something that is culturally patterned, foreign spatial cues are almost inevitably misinterpreted" (Hall & Hall, 1990, p. 12).

Eye gaze varies across cultures, too, with some cultures encouraging direct eye contact and others considering direct eye contact too forward or insulting. Once during a discussion of this topic, a student told me that he would never stare at a woman's eyes. He felt that she would certainly interpret this as him indicating sexual interest in her. When I asked what place was the appropriate spot for his eyes, he responded seriously, "Her chest." It is often pointed out that Vietnamese students show respect by directing their eyes downward, not by making direct eye contact. Conversely, students from the Middle East may feel that Americans do not keep eye contact long enough.

Teachers tend to be focused on the verbal channel of expression, and may not have a conscious awareness of nonverbal communication (Morain, 1978). They should educate themselves about some of the differences in nonverbal communication, especially if international students comprise a good portion of their students. Differences in gesture, eye contact, touch and movement are interestingly discussed by many writers. Particularly accessible are collections by Valdes (1986), and Byrd (1986) as well as the classics by Hall. ESL texts can also be interesting resources for a teacher interested in cross-cultural differences. Genzel & Cummings (1994) and Levine, Baxter, & McNulty (1987) are good resources.

Trying to define one's own cultural expectations for nonverbal communication can be an interesting topic of class discussion if several nationalities are represented. A teacher can have students discuss questions like these:

➤ How do you enter a classroom if you are late and arriving after the class has begun?

➤ How do you greet a friend of the opposite sex after not seeing him/her for several months? Of the same sex? How do you greet a friend when you see him/her for the second time in the same day?

➤ What body language would you use when you meet your parents at the end of the school year?

➤ In what circumstances, if any, would you expect to be able to smell a friend? Would you find it offensive, normal, embarrassing?

➤ In what circumstances would you walk hand in hand or arm in arm with a friend?

➤ What gestures are considered rude in your culture? Why?

Although issues such as these do not go to the root of cultural differences, they can raise students' awareness and make them more sensitive not only of their classmates but also their own cultural assumptions.

Time Codes

Most North Americans have heard of the Spanish term "mañana" and realize that the expression says something about the relative cultural importance of being on time or doing things "right now." U.S. residents assume that this stereotype simply means that Latin Americans "put off for tomorrow what they should do today," yet the underlying cultural values are much more complex. Levine (1985) interviewed Brazilian students to better understand their sense of time, and noted that the Brazilian students felt less regret about being late and were less likely to be bothered that someone else was late than students from North America. As a matter of fact, the Brazilian students believed that a consistently late person was probably more successful than one who was on time.

Hall & Hall (1989) describe the distinction between "monochromatic" and "polychromatic" time. People who are monochromatic focus on one thing at a time, while in polychromatic cultures, people are comfortable with doing many things at once. The U.S. is a monochromatic culture: time is seen as linear, and it is scheduled, compartmentalized and talked about as if it were tangible. It can be "'spent,' 'saved,' 'wasted,' and 'lost'" (p. 13). In polychromatic cultures, keeping to a schedule is less important than interacting with people, and students with a polychromatic sense of time may have trouble understanding why it is important to their teachers for them to come promptly to class or an appointment. Students would opt to be late for an appointment rather than rudely end a conversation they are having with a friend.

Being aware that a student is not intentionally trying to be rude may help a teacher interpret this behavior correctly. Though they may occasionally be late for class, Latin American or African students may also stay after class to chat, and will likely not be among the group packing up their backpacks to head out the door before the class is over. And of course, many students who would not worry about the clock in their home countries will make an effort to be on time when they are in the United States.

An American student wrote about her growing understanding of a Puerto Rican classmate's different sense of time:

> I talked to Ana one day during class and she mentioned that she was uncomfortable with the way people here said, "Hi, how are you!" without waiting for a response. She said it was rather shallow. It didn't dawn on me that I said those words often until I heard myself saying them to Ana herself two days later. I was in a *big* hurry to get to one of my classes and I saw Ana on one of the paths. I was practically running when I saw her, and because I was happy to see Ana, I said 'Hi, how are ya!' as I kept on going. As soon as the words came out of my mouth, I knew I

had said something really stupid. I stopped to talk to her for awhile and I left feeling a little happier. Even though I was in a hurry, I still made it on time.

This kind of insight into another person's perspective is exactly what we can hope for in a class where students are working together with others from different cultures.

Sensitive Cultural Issues

One of the instructors in our program recently raised an interesting question: "What if an ESL student writes a paper setting forth cultural values that the teacher simply cannot accept?" (Falck-Yi, personal communication). This teacher was imagining a situation in which a student made a claim that men were superior to women, or that an oldest child was evil if he did not care for aging parents, or that one's government must be obeyed blindly.

It is certainly true that students from other cultures will have, and will express, values that are not shared by many U.S. teachers. However, this also occurs in writing classes for U.S. students: the teacher with a liberal perspective will feel uncomfortable about a student's praise of Rush Limbaugh; many writing teachers have disagreed with student papers containing racist comments. Given that the situation is not uncommon, most teachers will attempt to approach such writing with sensitivity. A teacher can ask the student questions to help him more clearly define his ideas, a teacher can suggest alternative viewpoints or point out inconsistencies in his arguments, but in the end, a teacher must respect the student's right as an individual to hold differing beliefs.

At times, teachers may find they have unexpectedly strayed into "taboo" areas. Several years ago, I thought I would try a creative descriptive assignment in an ESL class. I brought several varieties of apples to class, gave one to each class member, and asked them to describe the apples in detail. I suggested they look carefully at the outside of the apple, but also that they take several bites to describe the taste and texture. The class included two students from Malaysia, one from Indonesia, one from Saudi Arabia and one from Egypt, and I noticed several minutes into the activity that none of them were eating their apples. Suddenly, it struck me: we were in the month of Ramadan when Muslims fast during daylight hours! I was momentarily afraid that I had offended them, but they graciously took the opportunity to explain their religious beliefs to the rest of the class. My mistake provided an opportunity for learning. Some culturally sensitive topics are worth exploring in the classroom. Teachers may find that with some international students, they not only need to explain techniques for avoiding sexist language (Section 21b in the handbook), but also may need to explain the rationale behind the concept. In addition, with current concerns about sexual harassment, students from different cultures may need to be sensitized to the fact that their "normal" manner of approaching people of the opposite sex can be misinterpreted. A student from Honduras recently told one of the teachers in our program that when he saw college women sunning themselves on public lawns, he assumed he would be welcome to go up next to them, sit down, and begin a conversation. When his American classmate said that the sunbathing woman might think he was harassing her, the student was puzzled. "Why is it worse to go up and talk to someone," he asked, "than it is to stare at them without speaking the way the U.S. men do?" To the Honduran student, the impersonal staring of the American men was more insulting than the approach he perceived as direct and friendly.

Tyler (1994) describes a situation in which an male tutor from India was working with an American female undergraduate in a volunteer situation. The female student complained that the tutor had made sexual advances during the tutoring session because his leg had brushed against hers several times and he had not apologized. Tyler notes that it was clear that the touch had been unintentional, and that the Indian tutor had not recognized that this casual contact required an apology.

Teachers should be aware that students from some cultures may not feel at all comfortable criticizing their government or their parents, will balk at topics that offend their religious sensibilities, and may have differing attitudes about relations between the sexes. Teachers should attempt to understand their students' viewpoints and appreciate the diversity they bring to the classroom. At the same time, giving the international students more complex insights into U.S. culture can also be a useful goal.

Listening and Speaking Skills for ESL Students

Although the focus of a composition course is writing, an international student needs to be able to comprehend and speak in order to participate fully in the class. U.S. students can be sensitized to the difficulties facing the international students, and a teacher can encourage communication between native and non-native speakers.

Listening

Especially for newly-arrived students, coping with average American's idiomatic, connected speech can be challenging. Many students from East Asian countries have learned a sort of "textbook" English, focusing on translation, memorizing model texts, and rigorously studying formal English grammar. Some have never taken a class in which they had to speak; some have never communicated with a native speaker; many have learned from British English models. Imagine the surprise a Korean student feels when she hears her American partner on the first day of class say something that sounds like "Whaddayawanna do?" She can, without difficulty, read the words "What do you want to do?" but her classmate's pronunciation is unexpectedly confusing.

Of course most native speakers realize that English is not always spoken the way that it is written, that words like *thought, throughout,* and *rough* share common spelling but have different pronunciations. However, many native speakers don't realize that the natural speech patterns for Americans are not easily predictable from written text. Words within phrases are linked, as in the previous example, and vowels in unstressed syllables may be reduced (not pronounced clearly) or omitted entirely. For instance, the phrase *back and forth* will be spoken *back 'n forth* and *wants to go* is said *wants t' go.* Native speakers probably write *should of* rather than *should have* because, as it is spoken, the word sounds more like *of* than *have.*

Sound changes also occur—are said to be assimilated—when certain consonants occur together. For example, *could you* becomes *couldja* where the *d* and *y* combine into a sound like *dj,* or "What was your name?" becomes "What *wazshur* name?" Finally, stress patterns in English sentences can affect meaning in a way quite unusual in other languages. "He's leaving on *Friday,*" "*He's* leaving on Friday" and "He's *leaving* on Friday" are appropriate in slightly different contexts. Similarly, "I went to the white *house*" is not the same as "I went to the *White* House!" It's no wonder that new international students sometimes appear puzzled! (See pronunciation texts like Gilbert, 1994 for detailed explanations of these phenomena.)

Academic idioms can make understanding classroom spoken English even more difficult for a new student. Academic discourse is rife with idiomatic expressions: "Will you *pass back* the *handout*"; "There's a *pop quiz* today"; "I'll *post the scores* at *midterm*"; "You can take a *make-up test.*" The vocabulary of the writing classroom may be just as opaque for a new international student. *First draft, peer editing, brainstorming,* and *prewriting* may not only be unfamiliar terms, but may not link into an already existing schema in the international student's mind.

Even more troublesome for international students are the many idioms and slang expressions that native speakers use unconsciously in their informal speech. "That was over my head"; "It's on the tip of my tongue," and "I'm between a rock and a hard place" are not immediately transparent to a non-native speaker. Sports idioms like "way out in left field," "pinch hitter," or "couldn't make it to first base" are used frequently in everyday language, but are meaningless to a student who is unfamiliar with baseball. And slang expressions from "grunge" to "nerd" also can confuse the second language learner.

Many non-native students are eager to learn new idioms, but they may not always have an effective strategy for acquiring them. I recall one diligent student who was studying a small paperback book as I walked into class. When I asked Ming what he was reading, he told me he was learning American slang from his book, which provided translations into Chinese. I expressed enthusiasm for his efforts, and asked him to give me an example. He looked down, and read his most recently learned idiom: "Paint the town red." I explained that that particular idiom was rather outdated, and commiserated about the difficulty of keeping up-to-date on slang. I confided that I frequently had to ask my teenage children to explain popular expressions. Ming decided to ask some of his American friends for current alternatives before he began to say "Paint the town red."

The complexities of comprehending spoken English may seem overwhelming, but encouraging the non-native speakers to use their native classmates as "slang informants" is useful for both the U.S. and international students. The non-native students should be encouraged to bring their questions about idiomatic expressions; it is an enlightening experience for the native speakers to attempt to define terms that they use without thinking, and identifying idioms can raise their awareness. For example, international students frequently ask "When I thank people, why do they say 'sure' or 'you bet' instead of 'you're welcome'?" or "What exactly should I say when an American says 'What's happening'?" A student recently asked me, "What's the difference between 'Oh boy' and 'Oh man'? Why don't you say 'Oh girl' or 'Oh woman'?" Struggling with questions like these makes a native speaker more sensitive to his or her own language. If the non-native students seem to feel uncomfortable asking their classmates for help with idioms, students can use their journals for recording expressions and terms they don't understand. This allows a teacher to give feedback privately.

Often, students who are not following class discussion or who do not understand something their teachers have said may not indicate that they are having trouble; the problems only become evident when the teacher collects a homework assignment. Students may be reluctant to show that they do not understand because they consider asking questions insulting, since it would communicate that the teacher had not explained well enough. Other students may simply be too shy or fearful to tell the teacher that they don't understand. Putting instructions in writing can be a helpful way of backing up oral comments, as indicated in the handbook teaching tip sidebar, p. 749. Additionally, encouraging students to come for individual help in an office conference can be a nonthreatening way for them to ask questions.

Native speaking students may need some guidance to respond to their ESL classmates in a helpful way. Levine, Baxter & McNulty (1987) quote a non-native speaker who was frustrated talking with an American, "When I say . . . 'Please repeat,' he often repeats everything he said before, only louder, and faster. Why doesn't he speak more slowly when he repeats? Why does he repeat so many sentences? Usually, after he repeats, I still don't understand" (p. 65). If several non-native students in a class appear to be having difficulty with listening, the teacher may wish to address the issue directly. One can request that the native speakers speak slowly (not more loudly) and be willing to stop to explain expressions their classmates don't know. Additionally, rather than repeating the exact words that were initially misunderstood, a native speaker can try paraphrasing, using different expressions to communicate the same idea. The teacher can model this technique if it seems that students are having trouble communicating. Also, if the teacher occasionally stops to explain an idiom to the non-native students, the U.S. students in the class may wish to add their perspectives or suggest alternative idioms, and will become sensitized to the difficulties of the non-native speaker in understanding these expressions.

Speaking

While non-native students' listening problems may not be obvious, especially if they seem to be paying attention, their speaking abilities are often more apparent. A student may know what she wants to say, but not be able to articulate her ideas; another may speak quickly, but with impenetrable pronunciation.

Speaking fluency will improve with practice, and I encourage my students to take advantage of every opportunity to talk they can find. However, even students who wish to practice interacting may feel inhibited raising their hands in class and may never feel comfortable enough to interrupt a classmate. One should recognize that non-native students may have differing expectations regarding what goes on in a classroom. Students may feel that the best and proper way to learn is to sit silently and diligently take notes on the professor's lecture. They may be surprised to be expected to participate in class discussion, or they may attempt to participate but not find a way to "get a word in edgewise." Research into communication patterns reveals differences even between New Yorkers and Californians in their sense of the length of silent pauses between speakers or their tendency to interrupt one another (Tannen, 1984). If speakers from the U.S. differ, one can assume that speakers from various parts of the world will have very different unconscious expectations about how to get the attention of a classmate or how to take a turn in the conversation.

In a class with mixed nationalities, a teacher may find, at least initially, that the native speakers are dominating class discussions. However, a teacher can provide positive reinforcement when a non-native student does respond to a question, can call on the non-native speakers to encourage their participation, and should model supportive behaviors like repeating a difficult to understand comment so that the whole class can understand or providing an appropriate phrase or word if a student is struggling to find one.

Using Small Group Activities

Even though reticent students may never eagerly participate in a whole-class discussion, such students often open up in the safer context of a small group or pair. For this reason, using small groups for discussion of a reading, for examining sample student writing, or for a revision exercise can encourage the international students to participate. Other small group activities can include collaboratively gathering information, problem-solving, and annotating or evaluating readings (Reid, 1993).

Small group work may be a new experience for international students, but if the groups are structured carefully, they can be an effective way of encouraging discussion from quiet students. Assigning groups allows the instructor to mix international and U.S. students and avoids a situation in which the U.S. students choose their friends, leaving the international students to feel like the last ones picked for the seventh grade soccer game. On the other hand, a native speaker may feel excluded if several students from the same language background carry on a discussion in their language rather than in English, and ground rules about using English in class are sometimes useful.

Just as with native speakers, gender balance can also affect group dynamics; for example, a Muslim woman may feel more uncomfortable than a U.S. woman if asked to work with a group of male classmates. Ideally, the teacher of a culturally-mixed language class should avoid stereotyping her students (the Muslim woman might be just as outspoken and confident as her American classmate), but should remain sensitive to the cultural and gender makeup of student groups.

Of course native speakers can dominate the discussion of small groups, or they may take over a collaborative project without consulting the international students. It is often useful to specifically discuss some of the benefits and problems in cross-cultural communication before students are placed into groups. Additionally, one can set ground rules for discussions which include the participation of every member to encourage native speakers to solicit the ideas of the non-native students. Or, if students regularly discuss class readings in small groups, rotating the "chair" or "reporter" who summarizes the group's work will necessitate that all the students have a turn. Structuring the group exercises, too, can guarantee that each student gets a voice: for example, if the assignment requires recording responses and ideas from every group member and incorporating those ideas into a summary, then each student's opinions will, by the nature of the assignment, be solicited.

Group activities certainly allow students to use and develop listening and speaking skills in the writing classroom. (Schlumberger & Clymer, 1989) Additionally, teachers should not hesitate to encourage non-native students' participation in whole class activities and in group oral presentations. More specific comments on using peer review and collaborative writing will follow in the next section.

Writing Skills for ESL Students

New teachers should remember that international students vary widely in their writing abilities. A teacher should not automatically assume that the non-native speakers students will be the ones with the most pressing problems. On the contrary, teachers often say that the international students are among the best writers in their classes, willing to take on serious issues and work hard at improving their writing. Certainly, the non-native speakers are often highly-motivated students, and they may be more focused on their academic goals than some of their native speaking classmates.

In our multicultural society, a student with a non-English name and appearance may well be as "American" as the blonde Jane Smith sitting beside her. Second generation immigrants can have interesting cultural perspectives, but their writing skills will be indistinguishable from other U.S. students. A permanent resident, immigrant student who learned English in a U.S. Junior High School may be fluent in spoken English, yet may retain non-native-like problems in grammar or expression. Leki (1992) describes one such Vietnamese student who did not want to take an ESL class for "foreigners" because she clearly wished to be considered an American; however, the student struggled in the regular composition class because of her English abilities. At some U.S. universities, the distinction between first language basic writers and ESL writers has become blurred with the effects of bilingual education as well as the fact that students have immigrated at different ages (Santos, 1992). Certainly, too, students' educational backgrounds in their first languages will affect their abilities in the new language.

Given that there is no "typical" non-native speaker in a composition class, how can a teacher meet the diverse needs of international students in helping them gain greater writing skills? Teachers can be reassured that many of the techniques used to teach writing to native speakers work equally well with ESL students. However, understanding culturally-based writing differences and gaining insights into ESL students' expectations will help teachers evaluate their students needs more accurately.

Assumptions About Writing and Learning to Write

Since composition classes are such an expected feature of U.S. university curricula, it may come as a surprise that many students who come from different educational backgrounds have not had instruction in writing in their own language (Leki, 1992). In some cultures, writing instruction may embody very different values. I have already mentioned that students may feel uncomfortable with the casual atmosphere in U.S. classrooms and may be surprised that they are supposed to participate in class discussions. Other aspects of the U.S. composition class may also be unexpected.

If they come from university systems in which students can freely choose whether or not to attend lectures during the semester, students may feel that the frequent, daily homework assignments given in typical freshman level-classes are unnecessary busywork. One South American student commented that these classes were like high school classes, with the teacher always checking up on the student and attendance expected. He was accustomed to more freedom at the university level. On the other hand, some students adapt to these expectations and indicate that they appreciate the frequent practice and feedback. I often mention at the beginning of a course that a writing class is very different from most others: instead of absorbing a body of knowledge, students are developing skills. For this reason homework, frequent reading and writing, as well as regular attendance are essential in giving students practice in the skills they are learning.

Other differences may not be as obvious but may deeply affect a student's ability to write compositions. Students may have come from traditions in which the appearance of a piece of writing is judged as an important feature, and thus may be very uncomfortable handing in drafts that have cross-overs, arrows, or marginally-added phrases. I have frequently had to reassure students that I could read any but the most indecipherable handwriting and that I would not grade them on the neatness of their rough drafts. In fact, the concept of writing more than one draft may be surprising to them, and the rationale for asking them to do so should be carefully explained. Additionally, some students may have come from educational systems in which they were expected to do exactly as the teacher says. The respect and honor that they give to their teachers may be flattering, but a composition teacher can find it frustrating to find his own ideas and suggestions incorporated, whole cloth, into a student's papers. He may find that a student resists taking a strong personal stance in an argument or that, having taken a stance, the student does not feel a need to support or defend it. Teachers will probably resist students' requests for writing models to copy; they may not understand students' reluctance to critique an essay. These differences can make a mismatch between the teacher's and the ESL students' expectations in a class.

Rhetorical features

A student once mentioned that the Chinese have a saying to describe the way that writing should work: "Open the door and see the mountain." She explained that the Chinese writer would paint a picture for the reader, building detail by detail, until finally, the mountain was revealed. If, on the other hand, one considers "the mountain" to be the main purpose of a piece of English writing, then we might imagine that the appropriate approach when writing in English is to first tell the reader she is going to see a mountain before she ever opens the door! In other words, the approach a writer takes to a piece of discourse—the choices a writer makes about what a reader needs or wants, what evidence to include, and how to organize—is influenced by the conventions of her culture.

A number of researchers have found interesting differences in writing conventions deemed appropriate in different populations. In a series of studies, Purves (1986) found differences between national groups in aspects such as how personal or impersonal writing was supposed to be, whether writing should be abstract or concrete, and how a writer should provide text coherence. People of the same culture tend to agree on what is appropriate proof for an assertion: English readers expect facts and statistics and are not convinced by extensive use of analogy, metaphor, intuition and the authority of the ancients. "Yet conventions of argumentation in other cultures may require precisely that recourse to analogy, intuition, beauty, or shared communal wisdom" (Leki, 1992, p. 92). Hinds (1987) makes the distinction between "reader-responsible" and "writer-responsible" writing. The Japanese expect the reader to make inferences and may feel insulted if a writer is too explicit, while English readers may see the Japanese approach as circular and vague. I have had Latin American college students balk at my requests for personal examples: to them, a personal example seemed immature or babyish; they preferred theoretical generalizations.

In her introductory essay in the Annotated Instructor's Edition to the handbook (pp. 35–44), Reid summarizes Robert Kaplan's (1966) exploratory study of non-native students' organizational patterns. Though these patterns are certainly simplistic, Reid points out that the field of contrastive rhetoric can offer insights into some of the difficulties that the non-native writer faces in understanding the best way to organize a piece of writing in a specific context. As a matter of fact, I have occasionally drawn Kaplan's diagrams on the board, and asked ESL students to comment about whether or not these simplified patterns seem to represent patterns with which they are familiar. Showing the straightforward expectations of an English-speaking audience as an arrow often brings nods of understanding.

Matalene (1985), who spent a semester teaching in Taiyuan, China, explains that some of her Western expectations baffled her students. She wanted originality, directness, and self-expression; her students valued indirectness, memorization, and references to Chinese classics. Not only was the definition of good writing different, but so was the very function of rhetoric. She concludes that for teachers who work with students from varied backgrounds, "our responsibility is surely to try to understand and appreciate, to admit the relativity of our own rhetoric, and to realize that logics different from our own are not necessarily illogical" (p. 806).

The current theory about contrastive rhetoric does not hold the "deterministic view that speakers of other languages think differently" (Grabe and Kaplan, 1989, p. 264). Instead, literacy skills are learned, are transmitted through the system of education, and are culturally shaped; differences reflect preferred conventions. One should realize that, "as conventions, those that the United States espouses are no better or worse than those espoused in other cultures" (Purves, 1986, p. 50).

As writing teachers, we can be so influenced by our notions of appropriateness in writing, that we sometimes forget that we, too, are looking at writing through a cultural lens. Thus, rather than asserting that the U.S. approach is the "right" or "best" or "only" way of organizing or arguing, I usually present such material as a series of options. I may say that a native speaker of English will expect that a piece of writing be more, rather than less, direct; will prefer concrete, personal examples to an abstract statement of truth; will want explication rather than implications. When phrased in terms of the reader's expectations, learning these conventions becomes like learning customs. Understanding this, too, helps a teacher evaluate students' papers more fairly.

Plagiarism

Given the very different traditions of ESL students, one might expect differing conventions for citing or copying source material. There is a clear contrast between our emphasis on individuality and finding an "authentic voice" in writing and an emphasis on the commonality of knowledge and a reverence for the wisdom of the elders, and this difference may account for differences in views of plagiarism (Leki, 1992). Matalene (1985) emphasizes that basic literacy in Chinese requires amazing feats of memorization of the thousands of characters in the language. Combine that with the importance of learning texts from classical Chinese writing, memorization of set phrases and proverbs, and one can see that for a Chinese student, learning to write means memorizing, copying, and following well-proven patterns, something very different than the U.S. writing teacher's expectation of originality, authenticity, and creativity.

To students from many cultures, it is a novel idea that a writer owns his words, as if they were property, so students may be surprised at the anger and shock provoked in his teacher when he copies a source without citing it. Additionally, some students have learned to write by memorizing models on specific topics: they are able to churn out an error-free paper by writing the text they have memorized word for word. Students may feel that since the original author conveyed her message so clearly and beautifully, they would be foolish to put that message in their own clumsy prose.

Writing teachers can be sensitive to the fact that plagiarism is not considered as a serious transgression in all cultures. At the same time, one needs to clearly explain the expectations of a U.S. audience, for students certainly will be writing papers for other courses, may be working on scientific reports in graduate work at U.S. universities, and may write in many contexts in which they cannot copy verbatim. As with rhetorical features, I explain the underlying attitudes about plagiarism in the U.S. to my students, emphasizing the importance of learning to quote and paraphrase accurately as an expected skill in U.S. university classes.

These being skills that are also difficult for native speakers, many composition teachers will choose to spend class time practicing summary, paraphrase, and quotation. (See Handbook, section 31.) One should realize that these techniques are especially challenging for non-native speakers, and a teacher will find the time well-spent to help students practice and to explain the importance and usefulness of the skills.

Students' Goals

A more troubling issue is that international students often have very different goals for learning to write than do native speakers. Many international students intend to get an education and return to their own countries. Holding these students to the same writing standards that one would expect from U.S. students seems counterproductive (Land and Whitley, 1989). We can also question the goal of having non-native students use English for self-discovery, since native-language writing would surely be more appropriate for such a venture, and since some students may not see this as a natural purpose for writing (Leki, 1992; Matalene, 1985). If teachers are not aware of these important, and essentially political, issues, they may make unfair and unrealistic assumptions about their ESL students. Leki (1992) covers this problematic issue effectively.

Helping ESL Students in the Composition Classroom

The needs of ESL students are, as I have indicated, complex and varied, and teachers may wish to keep some of these issues in mind as they plan a syllabus, select a text, consider assignment topics, and respond to their ESL students' writing. For example, if a number of ESL students can be typically expected in a class, a teacher may wish to choose a cross-cultural reader that includes selections written from international perspectives. (See, for example, Holeton, 1995, Verberg, 1994, or Hirschberg, 1992). These readers can provide a springboard for stimulating class discussions, and they allow students from varied backgrounds to read about attitudes and perspectives different from their own.

Some other currently-available multicultural readers naturally focus on the diversity of the U.S. population, and although they can be an excellent choice for a class with immigrant and minority students, texts focusing on U.S. minorities may have a very "American" bias. Though they are inclusive of the U.S. population, they may not address issues that international ESL students find compelling. On the other hand, some teachers have chosen not to use a multicultural reader and have found that standard readers can be fascinating for ESL students who are trying to understand U.S. culture. Regardless of whether teachers choose a multicultural reader or one with standard U.S. readings, they should also consider their ESL students when choosing which readings to assign. Fiction written in dialect can be impenetrable for ESL students, and lengthy essays take much more reading time for an ESL student. A teacher may wish to consider providing some background for readings that assume a knowledge of U.S. history and culture and plan to give extra help orienting students to long or difficult readings.

Responding to ESL writing

Recognizing that ESL students have varied needs and goals, and that they may well have different notions about what makes a piece of writing effective, teachers can be reassured that strategies for responding to ESL writing are really little different from those for responding to native speakers. Most research discourages teachers from focusing on errors early in the writing process, assuming that an early focus on error will not allow a student to think about more substantiative matters. Providing opportunities for students to get feedback as they work on a piece of writing is also quite important. Research has shown that students tend not to pay attention to the comments written on penultimate drafts of their papers, and that these comments can be confusing, contradictory, and unclear (Zamel, 1985). Rather than seeing oneself as an evaluator, stepping in at the last minute to grade the final copies of students papers, a teacher should become involved early in the process. Encouraging students to come in for conferences, providing short mini-consultations during class with individual students, helping students work through the revision process are all useful methods of providing feedback. When one does provide feedback on a draft, focusing on content and organization before looking at errors is likely to be most productive.

Strategies for dealing with ESL errors

In order to help ESL students reduce their mistakes in grammar and mechanics, a teacher new to ESL teaching may wish to learn something about current theories of language learning. The following summary provides some abbreviated background.

Popularized in the 1950s and influenced by structural linguistics and behavioral psychology, the audio-lingual approach held that language was learned by conditioning (Brown, 1994). Teachers had students memorize pattern drills and dialogues so that they could learn without making mistakes: errors were considered bad, since they would compete for the correct forms, and language teachers paid much attention to students' mistakes. Though widely used for a time, this approach to language teaching was based on several misconceptions. Brown notes that "language was not really acquired through a process of habit formation and overlearning, that errors were not necessarily to be avoided at all costs..." (p. 71).

New views of language learning have necessitated changes in pedagogy. Now we know that language learning occurs as the patterns of the new language are internalized through meaningful communication in a variety of contexts. And pedagogical approaches have changed to provide these rich communicative contexts. Errors are considered a natural part of language learning, not something to be rigorously avoided: they occur for complex reasons, as a learner generalizes about incompletely learned patterns in the new language or guesses about the existence of forms in the new language which occur in the first (Leki, 1992).

Of course these changes in language teaching also affect the teaching of second language writing. Teachers influenced by ESL writing research now spend less effort in correcting errors or in attempting to keep students from making them. Leki (1992) points to two factors that have influenced this turn away from a focus on errors: some research shows that faculty from other disciplines have greater tolerance for ESL students' errors than do English teachers; and, second, correcting those errors has little effect on students' abilities to avoid making mistakes. If students will not be penalized in other courses for occasional non-native lapses, then what is the purpose of English teachers demanding native-like fluency? And why invest tremendous time and energy correcting errors if this activity has negligible results. For example, in a controlled research study, Robb, Ross, & Shortreed (1986) examined the effect of four types of feedback on written error. Regardless of whether teachers elaborately corrected all student errors, marked the type of error with a coding system, or simply indicated the location of the error, the groups did not show statistically measurable differences. Since error correction can be incredibly time consuming, most ESL teachers do not attempt to correct all the mistakes a student makes, and may wish to consider a certain number of errors as a kind of foreign accent in writing (Harris & Silva, 1993).

However, students may have different expectations about what kind of teacher feedback will help them improve. Leki (1991) points out that an ESL student's past success with learning English by memorizing grammar rules and focusing on errors may conflict with a writing teacher's wish to emphasize content. Her survey found that ESL students were very interested in their teachers pointing out errors and they claimed to look carefully at their teachers' corrections. However, she notes other studies which indicate that teachers' corrections have little effect on improving student writing. So, though ESL students may expect their teachers to mark all their errors, the usefulness of doing so is in doubt.

It is sometimes easy to lose perspective about the importance of different conventions when faced with ESL students' papers. I once listened to a group of experienced and well-meaning composition teachers who were debating how to handle the "spelling errors" that came from a student using British rather than American English. ("Colour," "practise," and "judgement" are examples.) I was surprised that such a topic would be an issue, first because there were so many more substantive issues to discuss about the students' writing, and second, that the Americans felt the British spellings were "errors"! A teacher can certainly encourage students to follow expected academic conventions—including formatting, punctuation, and spelling—but she would be wise to adopt a flexible attitude about these conventions when evaluating ESL writing.

The fact does remain, however, that ESL students may make more serious errors that are distracting and frequent. In his examination of research studies comparing native and non-native student writers, Silva (1993) notes that ESL students make a larger number of errors than native speakers in many categories, including vocabulary and semantic choice, control of syntax, and problems with verbs, prepositions, articles, and nouns.

Given that composition teachers want to help students reduce the seriousness and frequency of errors, what strategies can they use? First, teachers should avoid the impulse to make all the corrections for the students, and certainly they need not mark every error. It is sometimes possible to find a pattern that can be pointed out to a student or to focus on a particular type of error that seems distracting in a particular paper. For example, a control of verb tense shifts will be important in a paper that begins with generalized truths ("The relationship of parent and child is important"), moves to personalized statements indicating duration of time ("I have always loved my parents ..."), and then shifts to an example from the past ("But when I was thirteen ..."). Showing a student how the tense helps set the time frame of the sentence or paragraph could be productive if she is writing a paper where verb shifts are required. Also, focusing on one particular error may prevent a student from feeling overwhelmed by the many possible mistakes he has made. If I see that a student is having trouble with a particular structure, I may have the student proofread his next draft for that one structure only. The student can feel a sense of accomplishment, then, for spotting nearly all the subject-verb agreement errors, or all the sentence fragments, and this makes editing more manageable.

If teachers plan to choose one kind of error for the focus of comments, they can consciously choose a rationale to decide which kind of error to emphasize. Leki (1992) suggests several strategies. One approach is to focus on errors that are also made by native speakers such as subject-verb agreement or sentence boundary errors, since they may be the kind of errors that trigger assumptions about a person's educational background. Another approach is to look at more global errors, those that interfere with the reader's understanding, and to ignore the local errors which merely distract.

Yet another method is to focus on systematic, rule-governed grammatical features rather than those which are idiosyncratic. Leki gives the example of *assignments*, which takes a plural ending, and *homework*, which does not (1992, p. 131) as an idiosyncratic example that can't be learned by applying rules. On the other hand, students can learn the system for verb formation to avoid making mistakes like *He can goes*. They simply need to apply a predictable formula: following a modal verb (*can, could, shall, should,* etc.), the next verb takes the "bare infinitive" form (the infinitive without the word *to,* the most simple form of the verb). However, students will be much less likely to find errors in verbal complements:

> I hope *to go* and I dislike *going* are right, but
>
> *I hope *going* and *I dislike *to go* are wrong.

(Here, the rule is much less clear: verbs like *hope, want* and *decide* are followed by the infinitive, while verbs like *dislike, avoid, enjoy,* or *suggest* are followed by the gerund form. The problem is in deciding which kind of complement is required by the main verb.)

Though grammarians have invented complicated methods of deciding which category of verbs require infinitives and which require gerunds, the explanations are often so complex that students find them impenetrable. (See Celce-Murcia & Larsen-Freeman, 1983, for a summary.) These forms, like prepositions or phrasal verbs, nearly require memorization, since either the governing rules are not particularly systematic or the "system" is not transparent to the average ESL student. In order to correct errors of this sort, students can rely on lists of verbs (like those in the Handbook p. 773–4) and attempt to memorize those they use most frequently. But when choosing the type of error to have students focus on, it may be more productive for a teacher to suggest that students proofread for other kinds of errors—those which are more obviously rule-governed—and teachers may wish to focus on these more systematic issues in their comments.

A comprehensive ESL grammar series like *Grammar Dimensions,* (Larsen-Freeman, 1993) or a small ESL handbook like *Grammar Trouble-spots* (Raimes, 1992) can provide more background in ESL grammar for a teacher who needs extra help.

Teaching Suggestions

Many of the assignments and class activities that work for native speakers are also useful for non-native students. A nongraded journal, popular in many composition classes, can improve the fluency of non-native speakers. (Note the sidebar teaching tip in the Handbook Preface for ESL students, p. 744.) Providing students with frequent opportunities to revise, or using portfolio grading can be a useful way to help ESL students improve, taking the focus away from producing error-free early drafts. Avoiding this early focus on error is also important so that students can concentrate on more substantial matters of content and organization.

Other common practices are less effective for international students. For example, graded in-class writings are particularly difficult for international students. Under time pressure, they may not be able to write fluently, and certainly will produce many more grammatical errors than they would if they were allowed time to revise. Though for fluency practice, frequent writing is useful, an emphasis on graded in-class writing can be counterproductive, particularly if international students are held to rigid correctness standards. On the other hand, some composition teachers have had success in helping their students improve the ability to understand an essay exam prompt, and to organize and write answers to the kind of exam questions they might be asked on tests in other courses. If the focus is on interpreting the prompt, on organizing, and on finding a few clear details of support, then timed, in-class work can be useful.

It is also productive to guide students through the prewriting process, helping them find new ways of selecting topics, narrowing them, gathering and developing ideas. (See section 2 of the handbook.) If students choose their own topics for their papers, new ESL students may need guidance. Not having the background in writing the kind of personal or persuasive essays that are expected, they may have little idea of the kind of topic which would be appropriate. Showing them typical student papers or referring them to the handbook samples is a first start in helping them see a range of appropriate topics. Students may choose topics which seem extremely broad or vague for a composition class. Keeping in mind that a student is learning new expectations about appropriate conventions for U.S. compositions, a teacher can guide a student to narrow a broad topic or to find a personal angle in the same way that he gives that advice to U.S. students.

If an instructor assigns some of the writing topics for the course, care should be taken to choose topics which will allow international students to write from their own backgrounds and from their own perspectives. Most general topics work effectively: if a readings unit focuses on topics like family relationships, growing up, political change, education, language, an international student can write with a personal angle. Teachers in our program have also had success with some more culturally-based topics. Students have explored different versions of familiar folk tales like *Cinderella,* or examined the values expressed in movies like *The Joy Luck Club.* Additional topics have included childhood games, common superstitions, coming-of-age celebrations, and the cultural implications of the architectural design of homes.

If there are a number of international students in a class, focusing an assignment on familiar proverbs can be one way of opening students' minds to cultural differences. Several teachers in our program have had students bring "old sayings" from their culture and translate them into English. Small discussion groups compare their proverbs, looking for similarities and differences. For instance, the English "to lock the barn after the horse gets out" is much like the Chinese "to dig a well after one is thirsty." But the Chinese expression "You can still lock the door after the sheep have left" means that a person can learn from her mistakes, a rather different interpretation than the English idiom.

Students are often fascinated to learn sayings from their classmates' cultures, and the discussion opens students to understanding the power of figurative language. Some teachers have had their students write about what cultural values are represented by the proverbs of their culture. Have we adopted Franklin's "the early bird gets the worm" because we are a competitive culture? When you hear the Japanese saying, "The nail that sticks up will be hammered down," do you sympathize with the nail or the hammer, and does this say something about your cultural orientation? (For a similar assignment, see Reid, 1993, p. 170.)

Finally, directly examining the idea of cultural stereotypes can be enlightening for native and non-native students alike, particularly after students are comfortable enough with each other to discuss such a potentially threatening topic. Our world view is so shaped by our culture that reality is thought to be objectively perceived through our own cultural pattern, and a differing perception is seen as either false or 'strange' and is thus oversimplified" (Brown, 1994, p. 166). Stereotypes assume that general characteristics distinguishing a group are held by all members of that group: they can be accurate as far as a description of a "typical" group member but become inaccurate because they do not account for individual differences. Stereotypes can have positive effects in that they allow us to systematize our knowledge and make comparisons between the familiar and unfamiliar (Brown, 1994). However, they become destructive if we assume that every member of a group will fit neatly into the oversimplified and inflexible picture we have.

For example, one student wrote:

> As an individual from the Middle East, my image of the USA was not a very good one. I imagined the USA as a society full of crimes, drugs and all type of social problems. I never

imagined that I can leave my car opened and come back to find it. I never imagined that people would be friendly. All of that was the result of the stereotype of the USA in the Middle East. Yet that is not the only stereotyping problem I have seen. The Middle Eastern image in the USA is not much better. A large portion of the population here thinks that Middle Easterners are nothing but a group of rich crazy people with four wives.

One often finds in discussions of stereotypes, that U.S. students can be unaware of the stereotypes that others hold of them. A Canadian teacher in our program said that, in general, U.S. residents are seen as "rich, loud, and insensitive." U.S. students may respond to such a comment with astonishment. The following quotations from international students about the stereotypes they hold of American society can be useful starting points for discussion. Originally from Fieg and Blair (1975), they were cited by Kohls (1981).

FROM COLOMBIA: "The tendency in the U.S. to think that life is only work hits you in the face . . . "

FROM ETHOPIA: "The American seems very explicit: he wants a 'Yes' or 'No'—if someone tries to speak figuratively, the American is confused."

FROM IRAN: "To place an aged or senile parent in a nursing home is appalling for our people; taking care of one's parents is the children's duty. Only primitive tribes send their old and infirm off to die alone."

FROM KENYA: "Americans appear to us rather distant. . . . it's like building a wall. Unless you ask an American a question, he will not even look at you . . . individualism is very high."

FROM INDIA: "Americans seem to be in a perpetual hurry. Just watch the way they walk down the street. They never allow themselves the leisure to enjoy life; there are too many things to do." *(pp. 7–8)*

The topic of stereotyping can be an effective one for a writing class, and is often included in texts with readings on multicultural issues. Students can describe typical stereotypes of people from their own culture, explain where the stereotypes originated, and analyze how accurate or inaccurate they are. Becoming aware of the inaccuracy in stereotyping others is one of the great benefits that freshmen can gain in a composition class where these issues have been explored. (See Dunnett, Dubin, and Lezberg, 1986, p. 150 for a different assignment dealing with stereotyping.)

If teachers do choose to guide students in choosing writing topics, they should be careful to avoid topics that require knowledge of U.S. culture, or at the very least provide background for the non-native students. One student complained that it was impossible to write on the topics her teacher had assigned: high school dating and drugs in American high schools. She had never dated, since girls in her culture did not go out unchaperoned, and she had no knowledge beyond what she read in the papers about drugs in U.S. high schools. Another teacher suggested that a good topic for her half-international class was the meaning of Columbus's discovery of the Americas, yet none of her Asian students had an understanding of Columbus or the effect of his explorations on the New World. Instead, they had learned about the Chinese cultural revolution or the formation of Bangladesh. Imagine the difficulty U.S. students would have in giving a personal slant to these historical topics! On the other hand, the topic of Columbus might be an excellent one for Latin American students. A teacher simply needs to be sensitive to the ESL students in a class and approach topic suggestion with a certain flexibility.

Finally, a teacher should also respect the international students' wishes about sharing personal material or writing about cultural issues from the perspective of their nationalities. A Russian student in our program complained that all of his teachers wanted him to write about the effects of the fall of the communist government on Russian society. He said he was tired of the topic and that he did not find it interesting or compelling: he never wanted to be asked about it again! Other students may have lived through traumatic times and not wish to share these deeply personal memories with anyone. And others may wish to be assimilated into U.S. society and do not want to draw attention to their differences.

Using Peer Review and Collaborative Writing

Several researchers provide cautions about using peer editing and collaborative projects with ESL students. Bosley (1993) notes that the manner in which collaborative projects are structured may "represent a Western cultural bias" (p. 51). She points out cultural assumptions about the importance of individualism, of recognizing individual achievement, and of formulating assignments as problem-solving exercises. Similarly, the typical structure of peer review sessions in the U.S. classroom may not be comfortable for students from collectivist cultures like Japan and China. (Carson & Nelson, 1994) In the United States, writing groups often function for the benefit of the individual student: students listen to classmates' comments in order to improve their own piece of writing. But students from collectivist cultures are more accustomed to group activities which function for the benefit of the group. They may be reluctant to criticize classmates and may be "concerned primarily with group harmony at the expense of providing their peers with needed feedback on their compositions" (Carson & Nelson, 1994, p. 17). Other problems may relate to different communication styles leading to conflict among collaborators and differing understanding of what makes writing good (Allaei & Connor, 1990).

Keeping these concerns in mind, however, most teachers who have worked with international students do find a number of benefits in using peer review and collaborative writing. Authentic readers provide a greater motivation for students to revise, students receive feedback from multiple perspectives, they better understand how to meet the needs of their readers, and they may discover that other students are also struggling with putting their ideas into writing (Mittan, 1989).

Several suggestions can make peer review groups go more smoothly. Especially for the non-native students, it is important to explain clearly what they are going to be doing and what the expected outcome will be. If students have done other group activities—discussing readings, for instance—they will be more comfortable with the small group setting. Useful ideas include having students read and discuss articles on differences in cross-cultural communication, and modeling the peer review behavior with a sample piece of writing in front of the class before the peer review sessions begin (Allaei & Connor, 1990; Mittan, 1989; Reid, 1993). Teachers can also have students discuss student drafts from past semesters, photocopied so that students can use them in groups. (I have found my students quite generous in giving me written permission to use their papers anonymously.) This allows students to practice the skills of small group review before they take the emotional plunge of having their own work examined.

When students do bring in their own work, I always have them respond to specific questions, starting positively by identifying something that works well in the writing. Reid (1993) points out that "the goal of peer response/review is not so much to judge . . . as to cooperate in a communicative process, helping others in the classroom community to balance individual purposes with the expectations of the readers" (p. 209). Thus, I never ask my students "What grade would you give this paper?" or "Is this a good or bad paper?" Instead, I have students focus on their responses as readers, by answering questions like these: "Can you easily sum up the writer's main purpose in writing?"; "Was there any place that you wanted more information from the writer?"; and "Were there places where you had trouble following the argument of the writer?" Allowing plenty of time for peer review is important, and having students focus on spoken comments during the class period will avoid a silent classroom where students spend the hour writing their responses. Grimm (1986) suggests having students take their notes home to draft written comments for their classmates, and this idea seems especially useful for international students who will take longer to formulate their responses in writing. When peer review is effective, students gain a greater facility in identifying the aspects of their classmates' writing that give them difficulty as readers, and they will be able to transfer that knowledge to their own writing (Allaei & Connor, 1990).

Collaborative projects, too, can be effective in a class with international students. Assignments in which groups or pairs of students work together can draw on the basic understanding and interests of several students. One teacher in our program had his students work in groups to write final projects in which they did original research. One group went to the local mall and tested their hypothesis that the native speakers would be approached more quickly and more positively by the store clerks. Another group drew from their collective knowledge to write a guidebook for new international students who had just come to study at the university: the native speakers were able to contribute their greater knowledge of standard campus procedures and American customs, while the non-native speakers could provide insights to the problems faced by new non-native students.

Again, as with peer review groups, specific instruction will be helpful for collaborators. Burnett (1993a, 1993b) notes that co-authors who are willing to criticize one another's rhetorical choices and voice their disagreement in constructive ways produced higher quality documents than those students who simply nodded agreement to whatever their collaborators suggested. She suggests modeling this "substantive conflict" (1993a, p. 134) by providing students with specific information about successful collaborative behaviors and modeling particular "verbal moves" (1993b, p. 73) that a student can use for purposes such as prompting, challenging, or contributing information. Though Burnett's research focuses on native speaker collaboration, this suggestion is even more important for a class with non-native students who may lack the verbal repertoire for voicing disagreement. Also, showing students that they can provide feedback to their collaborators in a spirit of friendly disagreement may help students understand that it is possible to disagree without causing "loss of face." Burnett also suggests having the teacher model constructive criticism by working in front of the class with a student or colleague to illustrate how writers can improve their collaborations.

In short, the methods used to teach peer review and collaboration to native speakers can be adapted quite readily for a class with ESL students. Both techniques have the added benefits of getting quiet students more involved in the classroom, providing opportunities for speaking and listening practice for ESL students, and building understanding and group solidarity between the U.S. students and their international classmates. Additionally, of course, the most valuable benefit is that these techniques help students improve their writing skills.

Conclusion

A teacher of writing can welcome ESL students, knowing not only that the class can be a tremendous help to the students but also that the students may offer much to the class. The stimulating discussions that can occur in the small group setting of the composition class, the opportunity to share their cultural backgrounds and to learn about others' views, and the chance to more clearly understand U.S. academic expectations all benefit the ESL student tremendously. Additionally, in contributing their unique perspectives, ESL students add to the education of the U.S. students in the class. One U.S. student wrote this in his evaluation of a cross-cultural composition class:

> My feelings have definitely changed about people from other cultures since I've joined this class. Before this semester I carried with me many misconceptions. The main reason was because before now I had not had the opportunity to talk to people. This class has shown me that people from other parts of the world share my same frustrations, concerns, joy and happiness. I have learned to enjoy working with my classmates and working to become more open-minded.

In discussing the benefits of cross-cultural classes, Patthey-Chavez and Gergen write, "the presence of different voices and visions of the world can be transformed into an instructional resource" (p. 76). Whether a teacher has many ESL students or just a few, this resource can be a source of opportunity and inspiration.

REFERENCES

Allaei, S.K. & Connor, U.M. (1990). Exploring the dynamics of cross-cultural collaboration in writing classrooms. *The Writing Instructor,* Fall, 19–28.

Brown, H.D. (1994). *Principles of language learning and teaching* (3rd ed.). Englewood Cliffs, NJ: Prentice Hall.

Bosley, D.S. (1993). Cross-cultural collaboration: Whose culture is it, anyway? *Technical Communication Quarterly, 2,* 1, 51–62.

Burnett, R.E. (1993a). Decision making during the collaborative planning of co-authors. In A. Penrose & B.M. Sitko, Eds. *Hearing Ourselves Think: Cognitive Research in the College Writing Classroom* (pp. 125–146). New York: Oxford University Press.

Burnett, R.E. (1993b). Interactions of engaged supporters. In L. Flower, D.L. Wallace, L. Norris, and R.E. Burnett, Eds. *Making Thinking Visible: Writing, Collaborative Planning, and Classroom Inquiry* (pp. 67–82). Urbana, IL: NCTE.

Byrd, P. (Ed.). (1986). *Teaching across cultures in the university ESL program.* Washington, DC: NAFSA.

Carson, J. & Nelson, G. (1994). Writing groups: Cross-cultural issues. *Journal of Second Language Writing, 3,* 1, 17–30.

Celce-Murcia, M. & Larsen-Freeman, D. (1983). *The grammar book: An ESL/EFL teacher's course.* New York: Newbury House.

Dunnett, S., Dubin, F. & Lezberg, A. (1986). English language teaching from an intercultural perspective. In J.M. Valdes (Ed.), *Culture bound* (pp. 148–161). Cambridge: Cambridge University Press.

Genzel, R. & Cummings, M.G. (1994). *Culturally speaking: A conversation and culture text.* Second Edition. Boston: Heinle and Heinle.

Gilbert, J. (1994). *Clear Speech* (2nd ed.). Cambridge: Cambridge University Press.

Grabe, B. & Kaplan, R.B. (1989) Writing in a second language: Contrastive rhetoric. In D. Johnson & D. Roen, (Eds.), *Richness in writing: Empowering ESL students* (pp. 263–283). White Plains, NY: Longman.

Grimm, N. (1986). Improving students' responses to their peers' essays. *College English.* 27. 91–94.

Hall, E.T. (1959). *The silent language.* Garden City, NY: Doubleday & Co.

Hall, E.T. & Hall, M. (1990). *Understanding cultural differences: Keys to success in West Germany, France, and the United States.* Yarmouth, ME: Intercultural Press.

Harris, M. & Silva, T. (1993). Tutoring ESL students: Issues and options. *College Composition and Communication, 44,* 4, 525–537.

Hinds, J. (1987). Reader vs. writer responsibility: A new typology. In U. Connor & R. Kaplan (Eds.), *Writing across languages: Analysis of L2 text.* Reading, MA: Addison-Wesley.

Hirshberg, S. (1992). *One world, many cultures.* New York: Macmillan

Holeton, R. (1995). *Encountering cultures* (2nd Edition). Englewood Cliffs, NJ: Prentice-Hall.

Kaplan, R.B. (1966). Cultural thought patterns in inter-cultural education. *Language Learning, 16,* 1–20.

Kohls. L.R. (1981). *Developing intercultural awareness.* Washington, DC: The Society for Intercultural Education, Training, and Research.

Land, R.E. & Whitley, C. (1989). Evaluating second language essays in regular composition classes: Toward a pluralistic U.S. rhetoric. In D. Johnson & D. Roen (Eds.), *Richness in writing: Empowering ESL students* (pp. 284–294). White Plains, NY: Longman, Inc.

Larsen-Freeman, D. (Ed.). (1994). *Grammar dimensions* (four book series). Boston, MA: Heinle & Heinle.

Leki, I. (1991). The preferences of ESL students for error correction in college-level writing classes. *Foreign Language Annals, 24,* 3, 203–211.

———. (1992). *Understanding ESL writers: A guide for Teachers.* Portsmouth, NH: Boynton/Cook.

Levine, R. with E. Wolff. (1985) Social time: The heartbeat of a culture. *Psychology Today, 19,* (March), 28–37.

Levine, D., Baxter, J., & McNulty, P. (1987). *The culture puzzle: Cross-cultural communication for English as a second language.* Englewood Cliffs, NJ: Prentice Hall.

Matalene, C. (1985). Contrastive rhetoric: An American writing teacher in China. *College English, 47,* 8, 789–808.

Mittan, R. (1989). The peer review process: Harnessing students' communicative power. In D. Johnson & D. Roen, (Eds.), *Richness in writing: Empowering ESL students* (pp. 207–219). White Plains, NY: Longman.

Morain, G. (1986). Kinesics and cross-cultural understanding. In J.M. Valdes, (Ed.), *Crossing Cultures* (pp. 64–76). Cambridge: Cambridge University Press.

Patthey-Chavez, G. & Gergen, C. (1992). Cul ure as an instructional resource in the multi-ethnic composition classroom. *Journal of Basic Writing, 11,* 1, 75–96.

Purves, A. (1986). Rhetorical communities, the international student, and basic writing. *Journal of Basic Writing, 5,*1, 83–51.

Raimes, A. (1992). *Grammar troublespots: An editing guide for students* (2nd ed.). New York: St. Martin's.

Reid, J.M. (1993). *Teaching ESL writing.* Englewood Cliffs, NJ: Regents/ Prentice Hall.

Robb, T., Ross, S., Shortreed, I. (1986). Salience of feedback on error and its effect on ESL writing quality. *TESOL Quarterly,* 20,1, 83–93.

Santos, T. (1992). Ideology in Composition. *Journal of Second Language Writing, 1,* 1, 1–15.

Schlumberger, A. & Clymer, D. (1989). Tailoring composition classes to ESL students' needs. *Teaching English in the Two Year College,* May, 121–127.

Silva, T. (1993). Toward an understanding of the distinct nature of L2 writing: The ESL research and its implications. *TESOL Quarterly, 27,* 4, 657–676.

Tannen, D. (1984). *Conversational style: Analyzing talk among friends.* Norwood, NJ: Ablex.

Tyler, A. (1994). Sexual harassment and the ITA curriculum. *The Journal of Graduate Teaching Assistant Development, 2,* 1, 31–41.

Valdes, Joyce M. (Ed.). (1986). *Culture bound.* Cambridge: Cambridge University Press.

Verberg, C.J. (1994). *Ourselves among others: Cross-cultural readings for writers* (Third Edition). New York: St. Martin's.

Zamel, V. (1985). Responding to student writing. *TESOL Quarterly, 19,* 195–209

PART FIVE

Reading and Writing About Literature: A Primer for Students

Edgar V. Roberts
Lehman College
City University of New York

PART FIVE

Foreword

The following primer, which is modified and adapted from the eighth edition of *Writing About Literature* and the fourth edition of *Literature: An Introduction to Reading and Writing,* is written to students, and is designed for their use. It contains a condensed overview of the nature of literature, the ways of reading and reacting to a primary text (which here is "The Necklace," the famous story by Guy de Maupassant), and the methods of moving from early and unshaped responses to finished drafts of essays.

It would be most desirable to duplicate the entire primer for distribution to classes, but barring that, students should at least receive copies of the story and the sample essays to facilitate study and classroom discussion.

It is my hope that the overview provided here will stimulate students to carry out deeper and more methodical explorations of literary works. Literary understanding and appreciation should be acquired as early as possible, and students should never end their quests for the enjoyment, understanding, and power that literature provides.

— Edgar V. Roberts

PART FIVE

Reading and Writing About Literature

■ WHAT IS LITERATURE, AND WHY DO WE STUDY IT?

Although the word **literature** broadly includes just about everything that is written, we use the word more specifically to refer to compositions that tell stories, dramatize situations, express emotions, and analyze and advocate ideas. Before the invention of writing, literary works were necessarily spoken or sung, and were retained only as long as living people repeated them. In some societies, the oral tradition of literature still exists, with many poems and stories designed exclusively for spoken delivery. Even in our modern age of writing and printing, much literature is still heard aloud rather than read silently. Parents delight their children with stories and poems; poets and storywriters read their works directly before live audiences; plays and scripts are interpreted on stages and before moving-picture cameras for the benefit of a vast public.

No matter how we assimilate literature, we gain much from it. In truth, readers often cannot explain why they enjoy reading, for goals and ideals are not easily articulated. There are, however, areas of general agreement about the value of systematic and extensive reading.

Literature helps us grow, both personally and intellectually. It provides an objective base for knowledge and understanding. It links us with the cultural, philosophic, and religious world of which we are a part. It enables us to recognize human dreams and struggles in different places and times we otherwise would never know existed. It helps us develop mature sensibility and compassion for the condition of *all* living things—human, animal, and vegetable. It gives us the knowledge and perception to appreciate the beauty of order and arrangement, just as a well-structured song or a beautifully painted canvas can. It provides the comparative basis from which to see worthiness in the aims of all people, and it therefore helps us see beauty in the world around us. It exercises our emotions through interest, concern, tension, excitement, hope, fear, regret, laughter, and sympathy. It encourages us to assist creative and talented people who need recognition and support. Through our cumulative experience in reading, literature shapes our goals and values by clarifying our own identities—both positively, through acceptance of the admirable in human beings, and negatively, through rejection of the sinister. It enables us to develop a perspective on events occurring locally and globally, and thereby it gives us understanding and control. It is one of the shaping influences of life. It makes us human.

Types of Literature: The Genres

Literature may be classified into four categories or *genres:* 1– prose fiction, 2– poetry, 3– drama, and 4– nonfiction prose. Usually the first three are classed as **imaginative literature.**

The genres of imaginative literature have much in common, but they also have distinguishing characteristics. **Prose fiction,** or **narrative fiction,** includes **myths, parables, romances, novels,** and **short stories.** Originally, *fiction* meant anything made up, crafted, or shaped, but today the word refers to prose stories based in the author's imagination. The essence of fiction is **narration**—the relating or recounting of a sequence of events or actions. Works of fiction usually focus on one or a few major characters who change and grow (in ability to make decisions, awareness and insight, attitude toward others, sensitivity, and moral capacity) as a result of how they deal with other characters and how they attempt to solve their problems. While fiction, like all imaginative literature, may introduce true historical details, it is not real history. Its main purpose is not to create a precise historical record, but rather to interest, divert, stimulate, instruct, and exalt.

Poetry expresses a monologue or a conversation grounded in the most deeply felt experiences of human beings. It exists in many formal and informal shapes, from the brief **haiku** to the extensive **epic.** More economical than prose fiction in its use of words, poetry relies heavily on **imagery, figurative language,** and **sound.**

Drama is literature designed to be performed by actors for the benefit and delight of an audience. Like fiction, drama may focus on a single character or a small number of characters; and it enacts fictional events as if they were happening in the present. The audience therefore becomes a direct witness to the events as they occur, from start to finish. Although most modern plays use prose dialogue, on the principle that the language of drama should resemble the language of ordinary persons as much as possible, many plays from the past, such as those of ancient Greece and Renaissance England, are in poetic form.

Nonfiction prose consists of news reports, feature articles, essays, editorials, textbooks, historical and biographical works, and the like, all of which describe or interpret facts and present judgments and opinions. Major goals of nonfiction prose are to report truth and to draw logically sound conclusions. Whereas in imaginative literature the aim is to show truth in life and human nature, in nonfiction prose the goal is to reveal truth in the factual world of news, science, and history.

For the purpose of exploring techniques for reading, responding, and writing about literature, the following discussion will focus on the genre of fiction.

Elements of Fiction

Works of fiction share a number of common elements. For reference here, the more significant ones are **character**, **plot**, **structure**, and **idea** or **theme**.

Character

Stories, like plays, are about characters—characters who are *not* real people but who are nevertheless *like* real people. A **character** may be defined as a reasonable facsimile of a human being, with all the good and bad traits of being human. Most stories are concerned with a characters who are facing a major problem, which may involve interactions with other characters, with difficult situations, or with an idea or general circumstances that force action. The characters may win, lose, or tie. They may learn and be the better for the experience or may miss the point and be unchanged.

The range of characters in fiction is vast: A married couple struggling to repay an enormous debt, a woman meditating about her daughter's growth, a young man learning about sin and forgiveness, a young woman trying to overcome the bitter memory of early sexual abuse, a man regretting that he cannot admit a lie, a woman surrounded by her insensitive and self-seeking brothers, a man preserving love despite overwhelming odds, a woman learning to cope with her son's handicap—all these, and more, may be found in fiction just as they may also be found in all levels and conditions of life. Because as human beings all of us share the same capacities for concern, involvement, sympathy, happiness, sorrow, exhilaration, and disappointment, we are able to find endless interest in such characters and their ways of responding to their circumstances.

Plot

Fictional characters, who are drawn from life, go through a series of lifelike **actions** or **incidents**, which make up the story. In a well-done story, all the actions or incidents, speeches, thoughts, and observations are linked together to make up an entirety, sometimes called an **organic unity**. The essence of this unity is the development and resolution of a **conflict**—or conflicts—in which the **protagonist**, or central character, is engaged. The interactions of causes and effects as they develop **sequentially** or **chronologically** make up the story's **plot**. That is, a story's actions follow one another in time as the protagonist meets and tries to overcome opposing forces. Sometimes plot has been compared to a story's map, scheme, or blueprint.

Often the protagonist's struggle is directed against another character—an **antagonist**. Just as often, however, the struggle may occur between the protagonist and opposing groups, forces, ideas, and choices—all of which make up a collective antagonist. The conflict may be carried out wherever human beings spend their lives, such as a kitchen, a bedroom, a restaurant, a town square, a farm, an estate, a workshop, or a battlefield. The conflict may also take place internally, within the mind of the protagonist.

Structure

Structure refers to the way a story is assembled. Chronologically, all stories are similar because they move from beginning to end in accord with the time needed for *causes* to produce *effects*. But authors choose many different ways to put their stories together. Some stories are told in straightforward sequential order, and a description of the plot of such stories is identical to a description of the structure. Other stories, however, may get pieced together through out-of-sequence and widely separated episodes, speeches, second-hand reports, remembrances, dreams, nightmares, periods of delirium, fragments of letters, overheard conversations, and the like. In such stories, the plot and the structure diverge widely. Therefore, in dealing with the structure of stories, we emphasize not chronological order but the actual *arrangement* and *development* of the stories as they unfold, part by part. Usually we study an entire story, but we may also direct our attention toward a smaller aspect of arrangement such as an episode or passage of dialogue.

Idea or Theme

The word **idea** refers to the result or results of general and abstract thinking. In literary study the consideration of ideas relates to meaning, interpretation, explanation, and significance. Writers of fiction may deal with the triumphs and defeats of life, the admirable and the despicable, the humorous and the pathetic, but whatever their goal, they are always expressing ideas about human experience. We may therefore raise questions such as these as we look for ideas in fiction: *What does this mean? Why does the author include it? What idea or ideas does it show? Why is it significant?*

Fictional ideas may also be considered as major **themes** which tie individual works together. Often an author makes the theme obvious, as in the Aesop fable in which a man uses an ax to kill a fly on his son's forehead. The theme of this fable might loosely be expressed in a sentence like "the cure should not be worse than the disease." A major theme in Maupassant's "The Necklace" (see page 236) is that people may be destroyed or saved by unlucky and unforseeable events. The accidental loss of the borrowed necklace is just such an event, for this misfortune ruins the lives of both Mathilde and her husband.

The process of determining and describing the ideas or themes in stories is never complete. Thus in "The Necklace," one might note the additional themes that adversity brings out worth, that telling the truth is better than concealing it, that envy may produce ill fortune, and that we never fully appreciate the things we have until we lose them. Indeed, one of the ways in which we may judge stories is to determine the degree to which they embody valid and important ideas.

The Fiction Writer's Tools

Narration

Writers have a number of modes of presentation, or "tools," which they may use in writing their stories. The principal tool (and the heart of fiction) is **narration**, the reporting of actions in sequential order. The object of narration is to *render* the story, to make it clear and to bring it alive to the reader's imagination. The essence of narration is the movement of words and sentences in a continuous line through time, just as music involves the continuous rises and falls of musical notes (of varying lengths and intensities) through time. The writer of a fictional narrative creates a sequence of events leading from the initial details to the conclusion—from speech to speech, scene to scene, and action to action. As a result of this chronological movement, the reader's comprehension must necessarily also be chronological.

Style

The medium of fiction and of all literature is language, and the manipulation of language—the **style**—is a primary skill of the writer. A mark of a good style is *active verbs* and nouns that are **specific** and **concrete**. Even with the most active and graphic diction possible, writers can never render their incidents and scenes exactly, but you may judge them on how vividly they tell their stories.

Point of View

Point of view refers to the *voice* of the story, the speaker who does the narrating. It may be regarded as the story's *focus*, the *angle of vision* from which things are not only seen and reported but also judged. It is one of the most important ways in which writers knit their stories together, and it is also an essential means of attracting and engaging readers. By exerting their skill to create an effective point of view, writers make their stories seem authentic and real. Understanding point of view therefore requires close attention, for indeed, point of view may be one of the most subtle and difficult concepts in the study of fiction.

Basically, there are two kinds of points of view. In the first, the **first-person point of view**, a fictitious observer tells us what he or she saw, heard, concluded, and thought. This viewpoint is characterized by the use of the *I* pronoun as the speaker refers to his or her position as an observer or commentator. The **speaker,** or **narrator**—terms that are interchangeable—may sometimes seem to be the author speaking directly using an **authorial voice**, but more often the speaker is an independent character—a **persona** with characteristics that separate her or him from the author.

In common with all narrators, the first-person narrator establishes a clearly defined relationship to the story's events. Some narrators are deeply engaged in the action; others are only minor participants or observers; still others are not involved at all but are transmitting the reports of others more deeply involved. Sometimes the narrator uses the *we* pronoun if he or she is represented as part of a group that has witnessed the action or participated in it. Often, too, the narrator might use *we* when referring to ideas and interpretations shared with the reader or listener—the idea being to draw readers into the story as much as possible.

The second major point of view is the **third person** (*she, he, it, they, her, him, them,* etc.). The third-person point of view may be (1) **limited**, with the focus being on one particular character and what he or she does, says, hears, thinks, and otherwise experiences, (2) **omniscient**, with the possibility that the activities and thoughts of all the characters are open and fully known by the speaker, and (3) **dramatic,** or **objective,** in which the story is confined *only* to the reporting of actions and speeches, with no commentary and no revelation of the thoughts of any of the characters unless the characters themselves reveal their thoughts dramatically.

Everything we find in a story is the direct outcome of the point of view employed by the author. If we get a close-up and vivid account of various actions, the author has chosen to present things from a nearby or directly involved point of view. If there is a philosophical or moral cast to the events, we may conclude that the author has included such reflection or commentary as an aspect of the point of view. In full perspective, therefore, we may think of point of view as the *total position* from which elements of a story are viewed, understood, and presented.

Description

Together with narration, a vital aspect of fiction is **description,** which is intended to cause readers to imagine or re-create the scenes and actions of the story. Description can be both physical (places and persons) and psychological (an emotion or set of emotions). Excessive description sometimes interrupts or postpones a story's actions, so that many writers include only as much as is necessary to keep the action moving along.

Mood and **atmosphere** are important aspects of descriptive writing, and to the degree that descriptions are evocative, they may reach the level of **metaphor** and **symbolism.** These characteristics of fiction are a property of all literature, and you will also encounter them whenever you read poems and plays.

Dialogue

Another major tool of the writer of fiction is **dialogue.** By definition, dialogue is the conversation of two people, but more than two characters may also participate. It is of course the major medium of the playwright, and it is one of the means by which the fiction writer makes a story vivid and dramatic. Straight narration and description can do no more than make a secondhand ("hearsay") assertion that a character's thoughts and responses exist, but dialogue makes everything firsthand and real.

Dialogue is hence a means of *showing* rather than *reporting*. If characters feel pain or declare love, their own words may be taken as the expression of what is on their minds. Some dialogue may be terse and minimal; other dialogue may be expanded, depending on the situation, the personalities of the characters, and the author's intent. Dialogue may concern any topic, including personal feelings, reactions to the past, future plans, changing ideas, sudden realizations, and political, social, philosophic, or religious ideas.

Tone and Irony

In every story we may consider **tone**, that is, the ways in which authors convey attitudes toward readers and also toward the story material. **Irony**, one of the major components of tone, refers to language and situations that seem to reverse normal expectations. *Word choice* is the characteristic of **verbal irony**, in which what is meant is usually the opposite of what is said, as when we *mean* that people are doing badly even though we *say* that they are doing well. Broader forms of irony are *situational* and *dramatic*: **Situational irony** refers to circumstances in which bad things happen to good people, or in which rewards are not earned because forces beyond human comprehension seem to be in total control. In **dramatic irony** characters have only a nonexistent, partial, incorrect, or misguided understanding of what is happening to them, while both readers and other characters understand the situation more fully. Readers hence become concerned about the characters and hope that they will develop understanding quickly enough to avoid the problems bedeviling them and the pitfalls endangering them.

Symbolism and Allegory

In literature, even apparently ordinary things may acquire **symbolic** value; that is, everyday objects may be understood to have meanings that are beyond themselves, bigger than themselves. In fiction, many functional and essential incidents, objects, speeches, and characters may also be construed as symbols. Some symbols are widely recognized and therefore are considered as **cultural** or **universal**. Water, flowers, jewels, the sun, certain stars, the flag, altars, and minarets are examples of cultural symbols. Other symbols are **contextual**; that is, they take on symbolic meaning only in their individual works, as when in Maupassant's "The Necklace" Mathilde and her husband move into an attic flat to save money that they need to repay their enormous debt. These new quarters symbolize the hardship experienced by the poor.

When a complete story, in addition to maintaining its own narrative integrity, may be applied point-by-point to a parallel set of situations, it is an **allegory**. Many stories are not complete allegories, however, even though they may contain sections having allegorical parallels. Thus, the narrative of the Loisels' long servitude in Maupassant's "The Necklace" is similar to the lives and activities of many people who perform tasks for mistaken or meaningless reasons. "The Necklace" is therefore allegorical even though it is not an allegory.

The Elements Together

For analytical purposes, one or another of the fiction writer's major tools may be considered separately so that the artistic achievement of particular authors may be recognized. In fact, however, most authors use most of the tools simultaneously. Thus a story being told by a character who is a witness employs the *first-person point of view.* The story's major *character*, the *protagonist*, may go through a series of *actions* that fulfill the requirements of a carefully arranged *plot.* Because of this plot, together with the author's chosen method of *narration*, the story may follow a certain kind of arrangement, or *structure*, such as a straightforward *sequence* or a disjointed series of *episodes*. The *actions* and *descriptions* may demonstrate the story's *idea* or *theme*, and the writer's *style* may be manifested in *ironic* expressions. The major character's general circumstances may reveal *irony of situation*, while at the same time this situation may be made vivid through *dialogue* in which the character is a participant. Because the plight of the character is like the plight of many persons in the world, the story may be considered as an *allegory*, and the character herself or himself may be interpreted as a *symbol*.

Throughout the story, no matter what characteristics you are considering at the moment, it is most important to realize that a work of fiction, as the previous paragraph shows, is an entirety, a unity. Any reading of a story should be undertaken not to break things down into parts, but to understand and assimilate the work *as a whole*. The separate analysis of various topics is thus the means to that end, not the end itself. Finally, the study of fiction, like the study of all literature, is designed to foster growth and understanding and to encourage the improvement of life.

Reading a Story and Responding to It Actively

Regrettably, our first readings do not provide us with full understanding. After we complete a story, we may find it embarrassingly difficult to answer pointed questions or to say anything intelligent about it at all. But more active and thoughtful readings give us the understanding to develop well-considered answers. Obviously, we must first follow the story and understand its details; but just as importantly we must respond to the words, get at the ideas, and understand the implications of what is happening. We must apply our own experiences to verify the accuracy and truth of the situation and incidents, and we must articulate our own emotional responses to the characters and their problems.

To illustrate such active responding, the following story, "The Necklace" (1884), by the French writer Guy de Maupassant, (see box, below) is printed with marginal annotations like those that any reader might make during original and follow-up readings. Many observations, particularly at the beginning, are *assimilative*; that is, they do little more than record details about the action. But as the story progresses the comments reflect conclusions about the story's meaning. Toward the story's end, the comments are full rather than minimal; they result not only from first responses, but also from considered thought. Here, then, is Maupassant's "The Necklace."

GUY DE MAUPASSANT, an apostle of Gustave Flaubert, was one of the major nineteenth-century French naturalists. He was a meticulous writer, devoting great attention to reality and to economy of detail. His stories are focused on the difficulties and ironies of existence not only among the Parisian middle class, as in "The Necklace," but also among both peasants and higher society. Two of his better-known novels are *A Life* (1883) and *A Good Friend* (1885). Among his other famous stories are "The Rendezvous" and "The Umbrella." "The Necklace" is notable for its concluding ironic twist, and for this reason it is perhaps the best known of his stories.

Guy de Maupassant (1850-1893)

The Necklace   1884

Translated by Edgar V. Roberts

She was one of those pretty and charming women, born, as if by an error of destiny, into a family of clerks and copyists. She had no dowry, no prospects, no way of getting known, courted, loved, married by a rich and distinguished man. She finally settled for a marriage with a minor clerk in the Ministry of Education.

She was a simple person, without the money to dress well, but she was as unhappy as if she had gone through bankruptcy, for women have neither rank nor race. In place of high birth or important family connections, they can rely only on their beauty, their grace, and their charm. Their inborn finesse, their elegant taste, their engaging personalities, which are their only power, make working-class women the equals of the grandest ladies.

She suffered constantly, feeling herself destined for all delicacies and luxuries. She suffered because of her grim apartment with its drab walls, threadbare furniture, ugly curtains. All such things, which most other women in her situation would not even have noticed, tortured her and filled her with despair. The sight of the young country girl who did her simple housework awakened in her only a sense of desolation and lost hopes. She daydreamed of large, silent anterooms, decorated with oriental tapestries and lighted by high bronze floor lamps, with two elegant valets in short culottes dozing in large armchairs under the effects of forced-air heaters. She imagined large drawing rooms draped in the most expensive silks, with fine end tables on which were placed knickknacks of inestimable value. She dreamed of the perfume of dainty private rooms, which were designed only for intimate tête-à-têtes with the closest friends, who because of their achievements and fame would make her the envy of all other women.

"She" is pretty but poor. Apparently there is no other life for her than marriage. Without connections, she has no entry into high society, and marries an insignificant clerk.

She is unhappy.

A view of women that excludes the possibility of a career. In 1884, women had little else than their personalities to get ahead.

She suffers because of her cheap belongings, wanting expensive things. She dreams of wealth and of how other women would envy her if she had all these fine things. But these luxuries are unrealistic and unattainable for her.

When she sat down to dinner at her round little table covered with a cloth that had not been washed for three days, in front of her husband who opened the kettle while declaring ecstatically, "Ah, good old boiled beef! I don't know anything better," she dreamed of expensive banquets with shining placesettings, and wall hangings portraying ancient heroes and exotic birds in an enchanted forest. She imagined a gourmet-prepared main course carried on the most exquisite trays and served on the most beautiful dishes, with whispered gallantries which she would hear with a sphinxlike smile as she dined on the pink meat of a trout or the delicate wing of a quail.

> Her husband's taste is for plain things, while she dreams of expensive gourmet food. He has adjusted to his status. She has not.

5   She had no decent dresses, no jewels, nothing. And she loved nothing but these; she believed herself born only for these. She burned with the desire to please, to be envied, to be attractive and sought after.

> She lives for her unrealistic dreams, and these increase her frustration.

She had a rich friend, a comrade from convent days, whom she did not want to see anymore because she suffered so much when she returned home. She would weep for the entire day afterward with sorrow, regret, despair, and misery.

> She even thinks of giving up a rich friend because she is so depressed after visiting her.

Well, one evening, her husband came home glowing and carrying a large envelope.

"Here," he said, "this is something for you."

She quickly tore open the envelope and took out a card engraved with these words:

> A new section in the story.

> *The* CHANCELLOR OF EDUCATION *and* MRS. GEORGE RAMPONNEAU *request that* MR. AND MRS. LOISEL *do them the honor of coming to dinner at the Ministry of Education on the evening of January 8.*

> An invitation to dinner at the Ministry of Education. A big plum.

10   Instead of being delighted, as her husband had hoped, she threw the invitation spitefully on the table, muttering:

"What do you expect me to do with this?"

"But honey, I thought you'd be glad. You never get to go out, and this is a special occasion! I had a lot of trouble getting the invitation. Everyone wants one. The demand is high and not many clerks get invited. Everyone important will be there."

She looked at him angrily and stated impatiently: "What do you want me to wear to go there?"

15 He had not thought of that. He stammered:

"But your theater dress. That seems nice to me..."

He stopped, amazed and bewildered, as his wife began to cry. Large tears fell slowly from the corners of her eyes to her mouth. He said falteringly:

"What's wrong? What's the matter?"

But with a strong effort she had recovered, and she answered calmly as she wiped her damp cheeks:

20 "Nothing, except that I have nothing to wear and therefore can't go to the party. Give your invitation to someone else at the office whose wife will have nicer clothes than mine."

Distressed, he responded:

"Well, all right, Mathilde. How much would a new dress cost, something you could use at other times, but not anything fancy?"

She thought for a few moments, adding things up and thinking also of an amount that she could ask without getting an immediate refusal and a frightened outcry from the frugal clerk.

Finally she responded tentatively:

25 "I don't know exactly, but it seems to me that I could get by on four hundred francs."

He blanched slightly at this, because he had set aside just that amount to buy a shotgun for Sunday lark-hunts the next summer with a few friends in the Plain of Nanterre.

However, he said:

"All right, you've got four hundred francs, but make it a pretty dress."

As the day of the party drew near, Mrs. Loisel seemed sad, uneasy, anxious, even though her gown was all ready. One evening her husband said to her:

Margin notes:

It only upsets her.

She declares that she hasn't anything to wear.

He tries to persuade her that her theater dress might do for the occasion.

Her name is Mathilde.
He volunteers to pay for a new dress.

She is manipulating him.

The dress will cost him his next summer's vacation. (He doesn't seem to have included her in his plans.)

A new section, the third in the story. The day of the party is near.

"What's the matter? You've been acting funny for several days."

She answered:

"It's awful, but I don't have any jewels to wear, not a single gem, nothing to dress up my outfit. I'll look like a beggar. I'd almost rather not go to the party."

> Now she complains that she doesn't have any nice jewelry. She is manipulating him again.

He responded:

"You can wear a corsage of cut flowers. This year it's all the rage. For only ten francs you can get two or three gorgeous roses."

She was not convinced.

"No . . . there's nothing more humiliating than looking shabby in the company of rich women."

> She has a good point, but there seems to be no way out.

But her husband exclaimed:

"God, but you're silly! Go to your friend Mrs. Forrestier, and ask her to lend you some jewelry. You know her well enough to do that."

> He proposes a solution: borrow jewelry from Mrs. Forrestier, who is apparently the rich friend mentioned earlier.

She uttered a cry of joy:

"That's right. I hadn't thought of that."

The next day she went to her friend's house and described her problem.

Mrs. Forrestier went to her mirrored wardrobe, took out a large jewel box, opened it, and said to Mrs. Loisel:

"Choose, my dear."

> Mathilde will have her choice of jewels.

She saw bracelets, then a pearl necklace, then a Venetian cross of finely worked gold and gems. She tried on the jewelry in front of a mirror, and hesitated, unable to make up her mind about each one. She kept asking:

"Do you have anything else?"

"Certainly. Look to your heart's content. I don't know what you'd like best."

Suddenly she found a superb diamond necklace in a black satin box, and her heart throbbed with desire for it. Her hands shook as she picked it up. She fastened it around her neck, watched it gleam at her throat, and looked at herself ecstatically.

> A "superb" diamond necklace.

Then she asked, haltingly and anxiously:

"Could you lend me this, nothing but this?"

"Why yes, certainly."

> This is what she wants, just this.

She jumped up, hugged her friend joyfully, then hurried away with her treasure.

> She leaves with the "treasure."

The day of the party came. Mrs. Loisel was a success. She was prettier than anyone else, stylish, graceful, smiling and wild with joy. All the men saw her, asked her name, sought to be introduced. All the important administrators stood in line to waltz with her. The Chancellor himself eyed her.

She danced joyfully, passionately, intoxicated with pleasure, thinking of nothing but the moment, in the triumph of her beauty, in the glory of her success, on cloud nine with happiness made up of all the admiration, of all the aroused desire, of this victory so complete and so sweet to the heart of any woman.

She did not leave until four o'clock in the morning. Her husband, since midnight, had been sleeping in a little empty room with three other men whose wives had also been enjoying themselves.

55 He threw, over her shoulders, the shawl that he had brought for the trip home—a modest everyday wrap, the poverty of which contrasted sharply with the elegance of her evening gown. She felt it and hurried away to avoid being noticed by the other women who luxuriated in rich furs.

Loisel tried to hold her back:

"Wait a minute. You'll catch cold outdoors. I'll call a cab."

But she paid no attention and hurried down the stairs. When they reached the street they found no carriages. They began to look for one, shouting at cabmen passing by at a distance.

They walked toward the Seine, desperate, shivering. Finally, on a quay, they found one of those old night-going buggies that are seen in Paris only after dark, as if they were ashamed of their wretched appearance in daylight.

60 It took them to their door, on the Street of Martyrs, and they sadly climbed the stairs to their flat. For her, it was finished. As for him, he could think only that he had to begin work at the Ministry of Education at ten o'clock.

She took the shawl off her shoulders, in front of the mirror, to see herself once more in her glory. But

A new section.
The Party. Mathilde is a huge success.

Another judgment about women. Does the author mean that only women want to be admired? Don't men want admiration, too?

Loisel, with other husbands, is bored, while the wives are having a ball.

Ashamed of her shabby wrap, she rushes away to avoid being seen.

A comedown after the nice evening. They take a wretched-looking buggy home.

"Street of Martyrs." Is this name significant?

Loisel is down-to-earth.

suddenly she cried out. The necklace was no longer around her neck!

She has lost the necklace!

Her husband, already half undressed, asked:

"What's wrong?"

She turned toward him frantically:

5 "I . . . I . . . I no longer have Mrs. Forrestier's necklace."

He stood up, bewildered:

"What? . . . How? . . . It's not possible!"

And they looked in the folds of the gown, in the folds of the shawl, in the pockets, everywhere. They found nothing.

They can't find it.

He asked:

'0 "You're sure you still had it when you left the party?"

"Yes. I checked it in the vestibule of the Ministry."

"But if you'd lost it in the street, we would've heard it fall. It must be in the cab."

"Yes, probably. Did you notice the number?"

"No. Did you see it?"

'5 "No."

Overwhelmed, they looked at each other. Finally, Loisel got dressed again:

"I'm going out to retrace all our steps," he said, "to see if I can find the necklace that way."

And he went out. She stayed in her evening dress, without the energy to get ready for bed, stretched out in a chair, drained of strength and thought.

He goes out to search for the necklace.

Her husband came back at about seven o'clock. He had found nothing.

But is unsuccessful.

'0 He went to Police Headquarters and to the newspapers to announce a reward. He went to the small cab companies, and finally he followed up even the slightest hopeful lead.

He really tries. He's doing his best.

She waited the entire day, in the same enervated state, in the face of this frightful disaster.

Loisel came back in the evening, his face pale and haggard. He had found nothing.

"You'll have to write to your friend," he said, "that you broke a clasp on her necklace and that you're having it fixed. That'll give us time to look around."

Loisel's plan to explain delaying the return. He takes charge, is resourceful.

She wrote as he dictated.

85   By the end of the week they had lost all hope.   Things are hopeless.
And Loisel, looking five years older, declared:
"We'll have to see about replacing the jewels."

   The next day they took the case which had con-   They hunt for a
tained the necklace and went to the jeweler whose   replacement.
name was inside. He looked at his books:

   "I wasn't the one, Madam, who sold the necklace.
I only made the case."

90   Then they went from jeweler to jeweler, searching
for a necklace like the other one, racking their memories, both of them sick with worry and anguish.

   In a shop in the Palais-Royal, they found a neck-   A new diamond necklace of diamonds that seemed to them exactly like the   lace will cost 36,000
one they were looking for. It was priced at forty thou-   francs, a monumental
sand francs. They could buy it for thirty-six thousand.   amount.

   They got the jeweler to promise not to sell it for   They make a deal with
three days. And they made an agreement that he would   the jeweler. (Is Maupas-
buy it back for thirty-four thousand francs if the origi-   sant hinting that things
nal was recovered before the end of February.   might work out for them?)

   Loisel had saved eighteen thousand francs that his   It will take all of Loisel's
father had left him. He would have to borrow the rest.   inheritance plus another
                                                   18,000 francs that must
   He borrowed, asking a thousand francs from one,   be borrowed at enor-
five hundred from another, five louis° here, three louis   mous rates of interest.
there. He wrote promissory notes, undertook ruin-
ous obligations, did business with finance companies and the whole tribe of loan sharks. He compro-
mised himself for the remainder of his days, risked
his signature without knowing whether he would be
able to honor it, and, terrified by anguish over the
future, by the black misery that was about to de-
scend on him, by the prospect of all kinds of physical deprivations and moral tortures, he went to get
the new necklace, and put down thirty-six thousand
francs on the jeweler's counter.

95   Mrs. Loisel took the necklace back to Mrs. Forrestier, who said with an offended tone:

   "You should have brought it back sooner; I might   Mrs. Forrestier complains
have needed it."   about the delay.

   She did not open the case, as her friend feared she   Is this enough justifica-
might. If she had noticed the substitution, what would   tion for not telling the
                                                   truth? It seems to be for
                                                   the Loisels.

° *louis*: a gold coin worth twenty francs.

she have thought? What would she have said? Would she not have taken her for a thief?

Mrs. Loisel soon discovered the horrible life of the needy. She did her share, however, completely, heroically. That horrifying debt had to be paid. She would pay. They dismissed the maid; they changed their address; they rented an attic flat.

She learned to do the heavy housework, dirty kitchen jobs. She washed the dishes, wearing away her manicured fingernails on greasy pots and encrusted baking dishes. She handwashed dirty linen, shirts, and dish towels that she hung out on the line to dry. Each morning, she took the garbage down to the street, and she carried up water, stopping at each floor to catch her breath. And, dressed in cheap house dresses, she went to the fruit dealer, the grocer, the butchers, with her basket under her arms, haggling, insulting, defending her measly cash penny by penny.

They had to make installment payments every month, and, to buy more time, to refinance loans.

The husband worked evenings to make fair copies of tradesmen's accounts, and late into the night he made copies at five cents a page.

And this life lasted ten years.

At the end of ten years, they had paid back everything—everything—including the extra charges imposed by loan sharks and the accumulation of compound interest.

Mrs. Loisel looked old now. She had become the strong, hard, and rude woman of poor households. Her hair unkempt, with uneven skirts and rough, red hands, she spoke loudly, washed floors with large buckets of water. But sometimes, when her husband was at work, she sat down near the window, and she dreamed of that evening so long ago, of that party, where she had been so beautiful and so admired.

What would life have been like if she had not lost that necklace? Who knows? Who knows? Life is so peculiar, so uncertain. How little a thing it takes to destroy you or to save you!

Marginal notes:

A new section, the fifth.

They suffer to repay their debts. Loisel works late at night. Mathilde accepts a cheap attic flat, and does all the heavy housework herself to save on domestic help.

She pinches pennies, and haggles with the local tradesmen.

They struggle to meet payments.

Mr. Loisel moonlights to make extra money.

For ten years they struggle, but they endure.

The last section. They have finally paid back the entire debt.

Mrs. Loisel (how come the narrator does not say "Mathilde"?) is roughened and aged by the work. But she has behaved "heroically" (¶ 98), and has shown her mettle.

A moral? Our lives are shaped by small, uncertain things; we hang by a thread.

Well, one Sunday, when she had gone for a stroll along the Champs-Elysées to relax from the cares of the week, she suddenly noticed a woman walking with a child. It was Mrs. Forrestier, still youthful, still beautiful, still attractive.

Mrs. Loisel felt moved. Would she speak to her? Yes, certainly. And now that she had paid, she could tell all. Why not?

She walked closer.

"Hello, Jeanne."

110 The other gave no sign of recognition and was astonished to be addressed so familiarly by this working-class woman. She stammered:

"But . . . Madam! . . . I don't know. . . . You must have made a mistake."

"No. I'm Mathilde Loisel."

Her friend cried out:

"Oh! . . . My poor Mathilde, you've changed so much."

115 "Yes. I've had some tough times since I saw you last; in fact hardships . . . and all because of you! . . ."

"Of me . . . how so?"

"You remember the diamond necklace that you lent me to go to the party at the Ministry of Education?"

"Yes. What then?"

"Well, I lost it."

120 "How, since you gave it back to me?"

"I returned another exactly like it. And for ten years we've been paying for it. You understand this wasn't easy for us, who have nothing. . . . Finally it's over, and I'm damned glad."

Mrs. Forrestier stopped her.

"You say that you bought a diamond necklace to replace mine?"

"Yes, you didn't notice it, eh? It was exactly like yours."

125 And she smiled with proud and childish joy.

Mrs. Forrestier, deeply moved, took both her hands.

"Oh, my poor Mathilde! But mine was only costume jewelry. At most, it was worth only five hundred francs! . . ."

Sidenotes:

A scene on the Champs-Elysées. She sees Jeanne Forrestier, after ten years.

They seem to have lost contact with each other totally during the last ten years. Would this have happened in real life?

Jeanne notes Mathilde's changed appearance.

Mathilde tells Jeanne everything.

SURPRISE! The lost necklace was *not* real diamonds, and the Loisels slaved for no reason at all. But hard work and sacrifice probably brought out better qualities in Mathilde than she otherwise might have shown. Is this the moral of the story?

■ READING AND RESPONDING IN A JOURNAL

The marginal comments demonstrate the active reading-responding process you should apply with everything you read. Use the margins in your text to record your comments and questions, but also keep a **journal** for lengthier responses. Your journal, which may consist of a *notebook*, *notecards, separate sheets of paper*, or a *computer file*, will be immeasurably useful to you as you move from your initial impressions toward more carefully considered thought.

In keeping your journal, the objective is to learn assigned works inside and out and then to say perceptive things about them. To achieve this goal, you need to read the work more than once. You will need a good note-taking system so that as you read you can develop a "memory bank" of your own knowledge about a work. You can draw from this fund of ideas when you begin to write. As an aid in developing your own procedures for reading and "depositing" your ideas, you may wish to begin with the following "Guidelines for Reading" (next page). Of course, you will want to modify these suggestions, and add to them, as you become more experienced as a disciplined reader.

Responding to Literature: Likes and Dislikes

People read literature because they like it. Even if they don't like everything they read equally, they nevertheless enjoy reading itself, and usually pick out authors and types of literature that they think they might enjoy. It is therefore worth considering those qualities that at the simplest level produce responses of pleasure and also of displeasure. You either like or dislike a story, poem, or play. If you say no more than this, however, you have not said much. Analyzing and explaining your likes and dislikes requires you to describe the reasons for your responses. The goal should be to form your responses as judgments, which are usually *informed* and *informative*, rather than as simple reactions, which may be *uninformed* and *unexplained*.

Sometimes a reader's first responses are that a story is either "o.k." or "boring." These reactions usually mask an incomplete and superficial first reading. They are neither informative nor informed. As you study most stories, however, you will be drawn into them and become *interested* and *involved*. To be interested in a story is to be taken into it emotionally; to be involved suggests that your emotions become almost wrapped up in your story's characters, problems, and outcomes. Both "interest" and "in-

TEXT CONTINUES ON PAGE 248 ➤

Guidelines for Reading

1. OBSERVATIONS FOR BASIC UNDERSTANDING

a. EXPLAIN WORDS, SITUATIONS, AND CONCEPTS. Write down words that are new or not immediately clear. If you find a passage that you do not quickly understand, decide whether the problem arises from unknown words. Use your dictionary and record the relevant meanings in your journal, but be sure that these meanings clarify your understanding. Make note of special difficulties so that you may ask your instructor about them.

b. DETERMINE WHAT IS HAPPENING. What is the situation? Where do the actions take place? What do they show? Who is involved? Who is the major figure? Why is he or she major? What relationships do the characters have with each other? What concerns do the characters have? What do they do? Who says what to whom? How do the speeches advance the action and reveal the characters? Why does the story end as it does and where it does?

2. NOTES ON FIRST IMPRESSIONS

a. MAKE A RECORD OF YOUR REACTIONS AND RESPONSES, which you may derive from your marginal notations. What did you think was memorable, noteworthy, funny, or otherwise striking? Did you worry, get scared, laugh, smile, feel a thrill, learn a great deal, feel proud, find a lot to think about? In your journal, record these responses and explain them more fully.

b. DESCRIBE INTERESTING CHARACTERIZATIONS, EVENTS, TECHNIQUES, AND IDEAS. If you like a character or idea, explain what you like, and do the same for characters and ideas you don't like. Is there anything else in the work that you especially like or dislike? Are parts easy or difficult to understand? Why? Are there any surprises? What was your reaction to them? Be sure to use *your own* words when writing your explanations.

3. **DEVELOPMENT OF IDEAS AND ENLARGEMENT OF RESPONSES**

a. TRACE DEVELOPING PATTERNS. Make an outline or scheme: What conflicts appear? Do these conflicts exist between people, groups, or ideas? How does the author resolve them? Is one force, idea, or side the winner? Why? How do you respond to the winner, or loser?

b. WRITE EXPANDED NOTES ABOUT CHARACTERS, SITUATIONS, AND ACTIONS. What explanations need to be made about the characters? Which actions, scenes, and situations invite interpretation? What assumptions do the characters and speakers reveal about life and humanity generally, about themselves, the people around them, their families, their friends, and about work, the economy, religion, politics, philosophy, and the state of the world and the universe? What manners or customs do they exhibit? What sort of language do they use? What literary conventions and devices have you noticed, and what do these contribute to the action and ideas of the story?

c. WRITE A PARAGRAPH OR SEVERAL PARAGRAPHS DESCRIBING YOUR REACTIONS AND THOUGHTS. If you have an assignment, your paragraphs may be useful later because you might transfer them directly as early drafts. Even if you are making only a general preparation, however, always write down your thoughts.

d. MEMORIZE INTERESTING, WELL-WRITTEN, AND IMPORTANT PASSAGES. Use note cards to write them out in full, and keep them in your pocket or purse. When walking to class, riding public transportation, or otherwise not occupying your time, learn them by heart.

e. ALWAYS WRITE DOWN QUESTIONS THAT ARISE AS YOU READ. You may raise these in class, and they may also aid your own study.

volvement" describe genuine responses to reading. Once you get interested and involved, your reading ceases to be a task or assignment and grows into a pleasure.

Using Your Journal to Record Responses

No one can tell you what you should or should not like; liking is your own concern. While your experience of reading is still fresh, therefore, you should use your journal to record not only your observations about a work but also your responses. Be frank in your judgment. Write down what you like or dislike, and try to explain the reasons for your responses, even if these are brief and incomplete. If, after later thought and fuller understanding, you change or modify your first impressions, record these changes too. Here is a journal entry that explains a favorable response to Guy de Maupassant's "The Necklace":

> I like "The Necklace" because of the surprise ending. It isn't that I like Mathilde's bad luck, but I like the way Maupassant hides the most important fact in the story until the end. Mathilde does all that work and sacrifice for no reason at all, and the surprise ending makes this point strongly.

This paragraph is capable of expansion. It is a clear statement of liking, followed by references to likable things in the work. This response pattern, which can be simply phrased as "I like [dislike] this work *because...*," is a useful way to begin journal entries because it always requires that a response be followed with an explanation. If at first you cannot write any full sentences detailing the causes of your responses, at least make a brief list of the things you like or dislike. If you write nothing, you will probably forget your reactions. Recovering them later, either for discussion or writing, will be difficult.

Responding Favorably

Usually you can equate your interest in a work with liking it. You can be more specific about favorable responses by citing one or more of the following:

> ➤ You get involved with the characters. You like and admire them. When they are in danger you are concerned; when they succeed you are happy; when they speak you like what they say.

> ➤ You get so interested and involved in the outcome of the

action or ideas that you do not want to put the work down until you have finished it.

➤ When you read the last word in a story you are sorry to part with the characters and wish that there were more to read about them and their activities.

➤ You learn something new—something you had never known or thought before about human beings and their ways of handling their problems.

➤ You gain new insights into aspects of life that you thought you already understood.

➤ You learn about characters and customs of different places, times, and ways of life.

➤ You feel happy or thrilled because of reading the work.

➤ You are amused, and laugh often as you read.

➤ You like the author's ways of describing scenes and actions.

➤ You find that many of the ideas and expressions are beautiful and worth remembering.

Obviously, if you have none of these responses, or find a character or incident that is distasteful, you will not like the work.

Responding Unfavorably

Although so far we have dismissed *o.k.* and *boring* and stressed *interest, involvement,* and *liking,* it is important to know that disliking all or part of a work is normal and acceptable. You do not need to hide this response. Here, for example, are two short journal responses expressing dislike for Maupassant's "The Necklace":

1. I do not like "The Necklace" because Mathilde seems spoiled, and I don't think she is worth reading about.

2. "The Necklace" is not an adventure story, and I like reading only adventure stories.

These are both legitimate responses because they are based on a clear standard of judgment. The first stems from a distaste for one of the main character's unlikable traits; the second from a preference for rapidly moving stories that evoke interest in the dangers that main characters face and overcome.

As long as you include reasons for your dislike, as in these journal excerpts, you can use them again in considering the story more fully, when you will surely also expand thoughts, include new details, pick new topics for development as paragraphs, and otherwise modify your journal entry. You might even change your mind. However, even if you do not, it is better to record your original responses and reasons honestly than to force yourself to say you like a story that you do not like.

Putting Dislikes into a Larger Context

While it is important to be honest about disliking a work, it is more important to broaden your perspective and expand your taste. For example, a dislike based on the preference for only mystery or adventure stories, if generally applied, would cause a person to dislike most works of literature. This attitude seems unnecessarily self-limiting.

If negative responses are put in a larger context, it is possible to expand the capacity to like and appreciate good literature. For instance, some readers might be preoccupied with their own concerns and therefore be uninterested in remote or "irrelevant" literary figures. However, if by reading about literary characters they can gain insight into general problems of life, and therefore their own concerns, they can find something to like in just about any work. Other readers might like sports and therefore not read anything but the daily sports pages. What probably interests them about sports is *competition*, however, so if they can follow the competition or conflict in a literary work, they will have discovered something to like in that work. The principle is clear: *If a reason for liking a favorite work or type of work can be found in another work, then there is reason to like that new work.* A person who adapts to new reading in this open-minded way can redefine dislikes, no matter how slowly, and may consequently expand the ability to like and appreciate many kinds of literature.

■ WRITING ESSAYS ON LITERARY TOPICS

Writing is the sharpened, focused expression of thought and study. It begins with the search for something to say—an idea. Not all ideas are equal; some are better than others, and getting good ideas is an ability that you will develop the more you think and write. As you discover ideas and write them down, you will also improve your perceptions and increase your critical faculties.

In addition, because literature itself contains the subject material, though not in a systematic way, of philosophy, religion, psychology, sociology, and politics, learning to analyze literature and to write about it will also improve your capacity to deal with these and other disciplines.

At the outset, it is important to realize that **writing is a process which begins in uncertainty and hesitation, and which becomes certain and confident only as a result of diligent thought and considerable care.** When you read a complete, polished, well-formed piece of writing, you might believe at first that the writer wrote this perfect version in only one draft and never needed to make any changes and improvements in it at all. Nothing could be further from the truth.

If you could see the early drafts of writing you admire, you would be surprised and startled—and also encouraged—to see that good writers are also human, and that what they first write is often uncertain, vague, tangential, tentative, incomplete, and messy. Usually, they do not like these first drafts, but nevertheless they work with their efforts and build upon them: They discard some details, add others, chop paragraphs in half, reassemble the parts elsewhere, throw out much (and then maybe recover some of it), revise or completely rewrite sentences, change words, correct misspellings, and add new material to tie all the parts together and make them flow smoothly.

Three Major Stages of Thinking and Writing

For good and not-so-good writers alike, the writing task follows three basic stages. (1) The first—*discovering ideas*—shares many of the qualities of ordinary conversation. Usually, conversation is random and disorganized. It shifts from topic to topic, often without any apparent cause, and it is repetitive. In discovering ideas for writing, your process is much the same, for you jump from idea to idea, and do not necessarily identify the connections or bridges between them. (2) By the second step, however—*creating an early, rough draft of a critical paper*—your thought should be less like ordinary conversation and more like classroom discussion. Such discussions generally stick to a point, but they are also free and spontaneous, and digressions often occur. (3) At the third stage—*preparing a finished essay*—your thinking must be sharply focused, and your writing must be organized, definite, concise, and connected.

If you find that trying to write an essay gets you into difficulties like false starts, dead ends, total cessation of thought, digressions, despair, hopelessness, and other such frustrations, remember that *it is important just to start.* Just simply write anything at all—no matter how unacceptable your first efforts may seem—and force yourself to come to grips with the materials. Beginning to write does not commit you to your first ideas. They are not untouchable and holy just because they are on paper or on your computer screen. You may throw them out in favor of new ideas. You may also cross out words or move sections around, as you wish, but if you keep your first thoughts buried in your mind, you will have nothing to work with. It is essential to accept the uncertainties in the writing process and make them work *for* you rather than *against* you.

Discovering Ideas

You cannot know your own ideas fully until you write them down. Thus, the first thing to do in the writing process is to dig deeply into your mind and drag out all your responses and ideas about the story. Write anything and everything that occurs to you. Don't be embarrassed if things do not look great at first, but keep working toward improvement. If you have questions you can't answer, write them down and plan answering them later. In your attempts to discover ideas, use the following prewriting techniques.

Brainstorming or Freewriting

Brainstorming or **freewriting** is an informal way to describe your own written but private no-holds-barred conversation with yourself. It is your first step in writing. When you begin freewriting you do not know what is going to happen, so you let your mind play over all the possibilities you generate as you consider the work, or a particular element of the work, or your own early responses to it. In effect, you are talking to yourself and writing down all your thoughts, whether they fall into patterns or seem disjointed, unlikely, or even foolish. At this time, do not try to organize or criticize your thoughts. Later you can decide which ideas to keep and which to throw out. For now, *the goal is to get all your ideas on paper or on the computer screen.* As you are developing your essay later on, you may, *at any time*, return to the brainstorming or freewriting process to initiate and develop new ideas.

Focusing on Specific Topics

1. DEVELOPING SUBJECTS FROM BRAINSTORMING AND NOTE TAKING. Although the goal of brainstorming is to be totally free about the topics, you should recognize that you are trying to think creatively. You will therefore need to start directing your mind into specific channels. Once you start focusing on definite topics, your thinking, as we have

noted, is analogous to classroom discussion. Let us assume that in freewriting you produce a topic that you find especially interesting. You might then start to focus on this topic and write as much as you can about it. The following examples from early thoughts about Maupassant's "The Necklace" show how a writer may zero in on such a topic—in this case, "honor"—once the word comes up in freewriting:

> Mathilde could have gone to her friend and told her she lost the necklace. But she didn't. Was she overcome with shame? Would she have felt a loss of honor by confessing the loss of the necklace?
>
> What is honor? Doing what you think you should even if you don't want to, or if it's hard? Or is it pride? Was Mathilde too proud or too honorable to tell her friend? Does having honor mean going a harder way, when either would probably be okay? Do you have to suffer to be honorable? Does pride or honor produce a choice for suffering?
>
> Mathilde wants others to envy her, to find her attractive. Later she tells Loisel that she would feel humiliated at the party with rich women unless she wore jewelry. Maybe she is more concerned about being admired than about the necklace. Having a high self-esteem has something to do with honor, but more with pride.
>
> Duty. Is it the same as honor? Is Mathilde's duty to work so hard? Certainly her pride causes her to do her duty and behave honorably, and therefore pride is a step towards honor.
>
> Honor is a major part of life, I think. It seems bigger than any one life or person. Honor is just an idea or feeling—can an idea of honor be larger than a life, take over someone's life? Should it?

These paragraphs do not represent finished writing, but they do demonstrate how a writer may attempt to define a term and determine the degree to which it applies to a major character or circumstance in a story. Although the last paragraph departs from the story, this digression is perfectly acceptable because in the freewriting stage, writers treat ideas as they arise. If the ideas amount to something, they may be used in the developing essay; but if they don't, they may be discarded. The important principle in brainstorming is to record *all* ideas, with no initial concern about how they might seem to a reader. The results of freewriting are for the eyes of the writer only.

2. **BUILDING ON YOUR ORIGINAL NOTES.** An essential way to focus your mind is to use your journal notes as a mine for relevant topics. For example, let us assume that you have made an original note on "The Necklace" about the importance of the attic flat to which Mathilde and her husband move in order to save money. With this note as a start, you can develop a number of ideas, as in the following:

> The attic flat is important. Before, in her apartment, Mathilde was dreamier and less practical. She was delicate, but after losing the necklace, no way. She becomes a worker when in the flat. She can do a lot more now.

> M. gives up her servant, climbs stairs carrying buckets of water, washes greasy pots, throws water around to clean floors, does all the wash by hand.

> While she gets stronger, she also gets loud and frumpy—argues with shopkeepers to get the lowest prices. She stops caring for herself. A reversal here, from incapable and well groomed to coarse but capable. All this change happens in the attic flat.

Notice that no more than a brief original note can help you discover thoughts that you did not originally have. This act of stretching your mind leads you to put elements of the story together in ways that create support for ideas that you may use to build good essays. Even in an assertion as basic as "The attic flat is important," the process itself, which is a form of concentrated thought, leads you creatively forward.

3. **RAISING AND ANSWERING QUESTIONS.** Another major way to discover ideas about a work is to raise questions and then to try answering them. The "Guidelines for Reading" (p. 246) will help you formulate questions for development here. Of course you may raise other questions as you re-read the story, or you may be left with one or two major questions that you decide to pursue.

4. **USING THE PLUS-MINUS, PRO-CON, OR EITHER-OR METHOD.** A common method of discovering ideas is to develop a set of contrasts: Plus-Minus, Pro-Con, Either-Or. Let us suppose a Plus-Minus method of considering the character of Mathilde in "The Necklace": Should she be "admired" (plus) or "condemned" (minus)? [*See table, next page.*]

Once you begin putting contrasting ideas side by side, new discoveries will occur to you. Filling the columns almost demands that you list as many contrasting positions as you can and that you think about how the

PLUS: ADMIRED?	MINUS: CONDEMNED?
After she cries when they get the invitation, she recovers with a "strong effort"—maybe she doesn't want her husband to feel bad.	She only wants to be envied and admired for being attractive (end of first part), not for more important qualities.
She really scores a great victory at the dance. She does have the power to charm and captivate.	She wastes her time in daydreaming about things she can't have, and whines because she is unhappy.
Once she loses the necklace, she and her husband become impoverished. But she does "her share . . . completely, heroically" (paragraph 98) to make up for the loss.	She manipulates her husband into giving her a lot of money for a party dress, but they live poorly.
Even when she is poor, she still dreams about that marvelous, shining moment. She gets worse than she deserves.	She assumes that her friend would think she was a thief if she knew she was returning a different necklace. Shouldn't she have had more confidence in the friend?
At the end, she confesses the loss to her friend.	She gets loud and coarse, and haggles about pennies, thus undergoing a total cheapening of her character.

story material supports each position. It is in this way that true, genuine thinking takes place.

Your notes will therefore be useful regardless of how you finally organize your essay. You may develop either column in a full essay, or you might use the notes to support the idea that Mathilde is too complex to be wholly admired or condemned. You might even introduce an entirely new idea, such as that Mathilde should be pitied rather than condemned or admired. In short, arranging materials in the Plus-Minus pattern is a powerful way to discover ideas that can lead to ways of development that you might not otherwise find.

5. **TRACING DEVELOPING PATTERNS.** You can also discover ideas by making a list or scheme for the story or main idea. What conflicts appear? Do these conflicts exist between people, groups, or ideas? How does the author resolve them? Is one force, idea, or side the winner? Why? How do you respond to the winner, or loser?

> Using this method, you might make a list similar to this one: Beginning: M. is a fish out of water. She dreams of wealth, but her life is drab and her husband is ordinary.
>
> Fantasies—make her even more dissatisfied—punishes herself by thinking of a wealthy life.
>
> Her character relates to the places in the story: the Street of the Martyrs, the dinner party scene, the attic flat. Also the places she dreams of—she fills them with the most expensive things she can imagine.
>
> They get the dinner invitation—she pouts and whines. Her husband feels discomfort, but she doesn't really harm him. She manipulates him into buying her an expensive party dress, though.
>
> Her dream world hurts her real life when her desire for wealth causes her to borrow the necklace. Losing the necklace is just plain bad luck.
>
> The attic flat brings out her potential coarseness. But she also develops a spirit of sacrifice and cooperation. She loses, but she's really a winner.

These observations all focus on Mathilde's character; however, you might trace other patterns you find in the story. If you start planning an essay about one of these other patterns, be sure to account for all the actions and scenes that relate to your topic. Otherwise, you may miss a piece of evidence that can lead you to new conclusions.

Drafting Your Essay

As you use the brainstorming and focusing techniques for discovering ideas, you are also beginning to draft your essay. You will need to revise your ideas as connections among them become more clear, and as you re-examine the work for support for the ideas you are developing, but you already have many of the raw materials you need for developing your topic.

Writing by Hand, Typewriter, or Word Processor

It is important for you to realize that *writing is an inseparable part of thinking* and that unwritten *thought is incomplete thought.*

Because thinking and writing are so interdependent, it is essential to get ideas into a visible form so that you may develop them further. Make a regular practice of writing questions that occur to you, and also of writing explanations about your reactions and ideas. These questions and observations may lead you later to your most original and effective discoveries.

For many students, it is psychologically necessary to carry out this process by writing down ideas by hand or by typewriter. If you are one of these students, make your written or typed responses on *only one side* of your paper or notecards. This will enable you to spread your materials out and get an actual physical overview of them when you begin writing. Everything will be open to you; none of your ideas will be hidden on the back of the paper.

Today, word processing is thoroughly established as an indispensable tool for writers. The word processor can help you develop ideas, for it enables you to eliminate unworkable thoughts and replace them with others. You can move sentences and paragraphs tentatively into new contexts, test out how they look, and move them somewhere else if you choose.

In addition, with the rapid printers available today, you can print drafts even in the initial and tentative stages of writing. Using your printed draft, you can make additional notes, marginal corrections, and suggestions for further development. With the marked-up draft for guidance, you can go back to your word processor and fill in your changes and improvements, repeating this procedure as often as necessary. This facility makes the machine an additional incentive for improvement, right up to your final draft.

Word processing also helps you in the final preparation of your essays. Studies have shown that errors and awkward sentences are frequently found at the bottoms of pages prepared by hand or with a conventional typewriter. The reason is that writers hesitate to make improvements when they get near the end of a page be-

CONTINUED ON NEXT PAGE ➤

cause they shun the dreariness of starting the page over. Word processors eliminate this difficulty completely. Changes can be made anywhere in the draft, at any time, without damage to the appearance of the final draft.

Regardless of your writing method, it is important to realize that unwritten thought is incomplete thought. Even with the word processor's screen, you cannot lay everything out at once. You can see only a small part of what you are writing. Therefore, somewhere in your writing process, prepare a complete draft of what you have written. A clean, readable draft permits you to gather everything together and to make even more improvements through the act of revision.

Creating a Central Idea

By definition, an essay is *a fully developed and organized set of paragraphs that develop and enlarge a central idea.* All parts of an essay should contribute to the reader's understanding of the idea. To achieve unity and completeness, each paragraph refers to the central idea and demonstrates how selected details from the work relate to it and support it. The central idea will help you control and shape your essay, and it will provide guidance for your reader.

A successful essay about literature is a brief but thorough (not exhaustive) examination of a literary work in light of a particular element, such as *character, point of view,* or *symbolism.* Typical central ideas might be (1) that a character is strong and tenacious, or (2) that the point of view makes the action seem "distant and objective," or (3) that a major symbol governs the actions and thoughts of the major characters. In essays on these topics, all points must be tied to such central ideas. Thus, it is a fact that Mathilde Loisel in "The Necklace" endures ten years of slavish work and sacrifice. This fact is not relevant to an essay on her character, however, unless you connect it by showing how it demonstrates one of her major traits—in this case, her growing strength and perseverance.

Look through all of your ideas for one or two that catch your eye for development. If you have used more than one prewriting technique, the chances are that you have already discovered at least a few ideas that are more thought-provoking or important than the others.

Once you choose an idea that you think you can work with, write it as a complete sentence. A *complete sentence* is important: A simple phrase, such as "setting and character," does not focus thought the way a sentence does. A sentence moves the topic toward new exploration and discovery because it combines a topic with an outcome, such as "The setting of 'The Necklace' reflects Mathilde's character." You may choose to be even more specific: "Mathilde's strengths and weaknesses are reflected in the real and imaginary places in 'The Necklace.'"

With a single, central idea for your essay, you have a standard for accepting, rejecting, rearranging, and changing the ideas you have been developing. You may now draft a few paragraphs to see whether your idea seems valid, or you may decide that it would be more helpful to make an outline or list before you attempt to support your ideas in a rough draft. In either case, you need to use your notes for evidence to connect to your central idea. If you need more ideas, use any of the brainstorming-prewriting techniques to discover them. If you need to bolster your argument by including more details that are relevant, jot them down as you reread the work.

Using the central idea that *changes in the story's settings reflect Mathilde's character* might produce a paragraph like the following, which stresses her negative qualities:

> The original apartment in the Street of Martyrs and the dream world of wealthy places both show negative sides of Mathilde's character. The real-life apartment, though livable, is shabby. The furnishings all bring out her discontent. The shabbiness makes her think only of luxuriousness, and her one servant girl causes her to dream of having many servants. The luxury of her dream life heightens her unhappiness with what she actually has.

Even in such a discovery draft, however, where the purpose is to write initial thoughts about the central idea, many details from the story are used in support. In the final draft, this kind of support will be absolutely essential.

Creating a Thesis Sentence

With your central idea to guide you, you can now decide which of the earlier observations and ideas can be developed further. Your goal is to establish a number of major topics to support the central idea, and to express them in a **thesis sentence**—an organizing sentence that plans or forecasts the major topics you will treat in your essay. Suppose you choose three ideas from your discovery stage of development. If you put the central idea at the left and the list of topics at the right, you have the shape of the thesis sentence. Note that the first two topics have been taken from the discovery paragraph.

CENTRAL IDEA	TOPICS
The setting of "The Necklace" reflects Mathilde's character.	1. Real-life apartment
	2. Dream surroundings
	3. Attic flat

This arrangement leads to the following thesis sentence:

> Mathilde's character development is related to her first apartment, her dream-life mansion rooms, and her attic flat.

You can revise the thesis sentence at any stage of the writing process if you find you do not have enough evidence from the work to support it. Perhaps a new topic may occur to you, and you can include it, appropriately, as a part of your thesis sentence.

As we have seen, the central idea is the *glue* of the essay. The thesis sentence *lists the parts to be fastened together*—that is, the topics in which the central idea is to be demonstrated and argued. To alert the audience to the essay's structure, the thesis sentence is often placed at the end of the introductory paragraph, just before the body of the essay begins.

Writing a First Draft

To write a first draft, you support the points of your thesis sentence with your notes and discovery materials. You may alter, reject, and rearrange ideas and details as you wish, as long as you change the thesis sentence to account for the changes (a major reason why most writers write their introductions last). The thesis sentence shown earlier contains three topics (it could be two, or four, or more), to be used in forming the body of the essay.

YOUR TOPIC SENTENCE. Just as the organization of the entire essay is based on the thesis sentence, the form of each paragraph is based on its

Write with Your Readers in Mind

When you are writing, you must decide how much detail to discuss. Usually you base this decision on your judgment of your readers. For example, if you assume that they have not read the work you are writing about, you will need to include a short summary as background. Otherwise, they may not understand your argument.

Consider, too, whether your readers have any special interests or concerns. If they are particularly interested in politics, sociology, religion, or psychology, for example, you may need to select and develop your materials accordingly.

Your instructor will let you know who your audience is. Usually, it will be your instructor or the members of your class. They will be familiar with the work and will not expect you to retell the story. Rather they will look to you as an *explainer* or *interpreter*. Thus, you may omit details from the story that do not exemplify and support your central idea, even if the details are important parts of the story. What you write will always be based on your developing idea together with your assessment of your readers.

topic sentence. A topic sentence is an assertion about how a topic from the predicate of the thesis sentence supports the central idea. The third topic in our example is the relationship of Mathilde's character to the attic flat, and the resulting paragraph should emphasize this relationship. If you choose the coarsening of her character during the ten-year travail, you can then form a topic sentence by connecting the trait with the location, as follows:

The attic flat reflects the coarsening of Mathilde's character.

Beginning with this sentence, the paragraph can show how Mathide's rough, heavy housework has a direct effect on her behavior, appearance, and general outlook.

DEVELOP NO MORE THAN ONE TOPIC IN EACH PARAGRAPH. Usually you should treat each separate topic in a single paragraph. However, if a topic seems especially difficult, long, and heavily detailed, you may divide it into two or more subtopics, each receiving a separate paragraph of its own. Should you make this division, your topic then is really a section, and each paragraph in the section should have its own topic sentence.

UsING THE TOPIC SENTENCE TO DEVELOP A PARAGRAPH. Once you choose your thesis sentence, you can use the statement to focus your observations and conclusions. Let us see how our topic about the attic flat may be developed as a paragraph:

> The attic flat reflects the coarsening of Mathilde's character. Maupassant emphasizes the burdens she endures to save money, such as mopping floors, cleaning greasy and encrusted pots and pans, taking out the garbage, and handwashing clothes and dishes. This work makes her rough and coarse, an effect that is heightened by her giving up care of her hair and hands, wearing the cheapest dresses possible, and becoming loud and penny-pinching in haggling with the local shopkeepers. If at the beginning she is delicate and attractive, at the end she is unpleasant and coarse.

Notice that details from the story are introduced to provide support for the topic sentence. All the subjects—the hard work, the lack of personal care, the wearing of cheap dresses, and the haggling with the shopkeepers—are introduced not to retell the story but rather to exemplify the claim the writer is making about Mathilde's character.

Developing an Outline

So far we have been developing an *outline*—that is, a skeletal plan of organization for the essay. Some writers never use formal outlines at all, preferring to make informal lists of ideas, but others rely on them constantly. Still other writers insist that they cannot make an outline until they have finished their essays. Regardless of your preference, *your finished essay should have a tight structure*. Therefore, you should create a guiding outline to develop or to shape your essay.

The pattern we have been following here is the **analytical sentence outline**. This type is easier to create than it sounds. It consists of (1) an *introduction*, including the central idea and the thesis sentence, together with (2) *topic sentences* that are to be used in each paragraph of the body, followed by (3) a *conclusion*.

When applied to the subject we have been developing, such an outline looks like this:

Title: How Setting in "The Necklace" Is Related to the Character of Mathilde

1. **Introduction**

   a. *Central idea*: Maupassant uses his setting to show Mathilde's character.

   b. *Thesis sentence*: Her character development is related to her first apartment, her daydreams about elegant rooms in a mansion, and her attic flat.

2. **Body**: *Topic sentences* a, b, and c (and d, e, f, if necessary)

   a. Details about her first apartment explain her dissatisfaction and depression.

   b. Her daydreams about mansion rooms are like the apartment because they too make her unhappy.

   c. The attic flat reflects the coarsening of her character.

3. **Conclusion**

   Topic sentence: All details in the story, particularly the setting, are focused on the character of Mathilde.

The *conclusion* may be a summary of the body; it may evaluate the main idea; it may briefly suggest further points of discussion; or it may be a reflection on the details of the body.

Using the Outline

The two sample essays that follow are organized according to the principles of the analytical sentence outline. To emphasize the shaping effect of these outlines, all central ideas, thesis sentences, and topic sentences are underlined. In your own writing, you may underline these "skeletal" sentences as a check on your organization.

First Sample Essay, First Draft

The following sample essay is a first draft of the topic we have been developing. It follows the outline presented here, and includes details from the story in support of the various topics. It is by no means, however, as good a piece of writing as it can be. The draft omits a topic, some additional details, and some new insights that are included in the final draft (pp. 272–273). It therefore reveals the need to make improvements through additional brainstorming and discovery-prewriting techniques.

How Setting in "The Necklace" Is Related to the Character of Mathilde

[1]   In "The Necklace" Guy de Maupassant does not give much detail about the setting. He does not even describe the necklace itself, which is the central object in his plot, but he says only that it is "superb" (paragraph 47). Rather, he uses the setting to reflect the character of the central figure, Mathilde Loisel.* All Maupassant's details are presented to bring out her traits. Her character development is related to her first apartment, her daydreams about mansion rooms, and her attic flat.†

[2]   Details about her first apartment explain her dissatisfaction and depression. The walls are "drab," the furniture "threadbare," and the curtains "ugly" (paragraph 3). There is only a simple country girl to do the housework. The tablecloth is not changed daily, and the best dinner dish is boiled beef. Mathilde has no evening clothes, only a theater dress that she does not like. These details show her dissatisfaction with life with her low-salaried husband.

[3]   Her dream-life images of wealth are like the apartment because they too make her unhappy. In her daydreams about life in a mansion, the rooms are large, filled with expensive furniture and bric-a-brac, and draped in silk. She imagines private rooms for intimate talks, and big dinners with delicacies like trout and quail. With dreams of such a rich home, she feels even more despair about her modest apartment on the Street of Martyrs in Paris.

[4]   The attic flat reflects the coarsening of Mathilde's character. Maupassant emphasizes the burdens she endures to save money, such as mopping floors, cleaning greasy and encrusted pots and pans, taking out the garbage, and handwashing clothes and dishes. This work makes her rough and coarse, an effect that is heightened by her giving up care of her hair and hands, wearing the cheapest dresses possible, and becoming loud and penny-pinching in haggling with the local shopkeepers. If at the beginning she is delicate and attractive, at the end she is unpleasant and coarse.

[5]   In summary, Maupassant focuses everything in the story, including the setting, on the character of Mathilde. Anything extra is not needed, and he does not include it. Thus he says little about the big party scene except the necessary detail that Mathilde was a great "success" (paragraph 52). It is this detail that brings out some of her early attractiveness and charm (despite her more usual unhappiness). Thus, in "The Necklace," Maupassant uses setting as a means to his end—the story of Mathilde and her needless sacrifice.

---

* Central idea.
† Thesis sentence.

Developing and Strengthening Your Essay: Revision

After finishing a first draft like this one, you may wonder what more you can do. You have read the work several times, discovered ideas to write about through brainstorming techniques, made an outline of your ideas, and written a full draft. How can you do better?

The best way to begin is to observe that a major mistake writers make when writing about literature is to do no more than retell a story or re-word an idea. Retelling a story shows only that you have read it, not that you have thought about it. Writing a good essay requires you to arrange your thoughts into a pattern that can be followed by a perceptive reader.

Using Your Own Order of References

There are many ways to escape the trap of summarizing stories and to set up your own pattern of development. One is to stress *your own* order when referring to parts of a story. Do not treat details as they happen, but arrange them to suit your own thematic plans. Rarely, if ever, should you begin by talking about a work's opening; it is often better to talk first about the conclusion or middle. As you examine your first draft, if you find that you have followed the chronological order of the work instead of stressing your own order, you may use one of the prewriting techniques to figure out new ways to connect your materials. The principle is that you should introduce references to the work as a means of supporting the points—and only these points—that you wish to make.

Using Literary Material as Evidence

Whenever you write, your position is like that of a detective using clues as evidence for building a case, or of a lawyer using evidence as support for an **argument**. Your goal should be to convince your readers of your own knowledge and the reasonableness of your conclusions.

It is vital to use evidence convincingly so that your readers can follow your ideas. Let us look briefly at two drafts of a new example to see how writing may be improved by the pointed use of details. These are from drafts of a longer essay on the character of Mathilde. [*See next page.*]

A comparison of these paragraphs shows that the first has more words than the second (158 to 120), but that it is more appropriate for a rough than a final draft because the writer does little more than retell the story. The paragraph is cluttered with details that do not support any conclusions. If you examine it for what you might learn about Maupassant's ac-

1	2
The major extenuating detail about Mathilde is that she seems to be isolated, locked away from other people. She and her husband do not speak to each other much, except about external things. He speaks about his liking for boiled beef, and she states that she cannot accept the big invitation because she has no nice dresses. Once she gets the dress, she complains because she has no jewelry. Even when borrowing the necklace from Jeanne Forrestier, she does not say much. When she and her husband discover that the necklace is lost, they simply go over the details, and Loisel dictates a letter of explanation, which she writes in her own hand. Even when she meets Jeanne on the Champs-Elysées, she does not say a great deal about her life but only goes through enough details about the loss and replacement of the necklace to make Jeanne exclaim about the needlessness of the ten-year sacrifice.	The major flaw of Mathilde's character is that she is withdrawn and uncommunicative, apparently unwilling or unable to form an intimate relationship. For example, she and her husband do not speak to each other much, except about external things such as his taste for boiled beef and her lack of a party dress and jewelry. With such an uncommunicative marriage, one might suppose that she would be more open with her close friend, Jeanne Forrestier, but Mathilde does not say much even to her. This flaw hurts her greatly, because if she were more open she might have explained the loss and avoided the horrible sacrifice. This lack of openness, along with her self-indulgent dreaminess, is her biggest defect.

tual use of Mathilde's solitary traits in "The Necklace," you will find that it gives you little help. The writer needs to consider why these details should be shared, and to revise the paragraph according to the central idea.

On the other hand, the details in the right-hand paragraph all support the declared topic. Phrases such as "for example," "but even here," and "this lack" show that the writer of paragraph 2 has assumed that the audience knows the story and now wants help in interpretation. Paragraph 2 therefore guides readers *by connecting the details to the topic.* It uses these details *as evidence,* not as a retelling of actions. By contrast, paragraph 1 recounts a number of relevant actions but does not *connect* them to the topic. More details, of course, could have been added to the right-hand paragraph, but they are unnecessary because the paragraph demonstrates the point with the details used. There are many qualities that make good writing good, but one of the most important is shown in a comparison of the two paragraphs: *In good writing, no details are included unless they serve as evidence in an original pattern of thought.*

Keeping to Your Point

Whenever you write an essay about literature—or, for that matter, any essay about any subject—you must pay great attention to organization and to the correct use of references to the work assigned. As you write, you should constantly try to keep your material unified, for should you go off on a tangent you are no longer controlling but are being controlled. It is too easy to start with your point but then wander off and just retell the story. Once again, resist the tendency to be a narrator. Instead, be an interpreter, an explainer.

Checking Development and Organization

It bears repeating over and over again that one of the first requirements of a good essay is to stick to a point. Another major step toward excellence is to make your central idea expand and grow. The word *growth* is a metaphor describing the creation of new insights, the disclosure of ideas that were not at first noticeable, and the expression of new, fresh, and original interpretations.

BEING ORIGINAL. An argument against this idea might be that you cannot be original when you are writing about someone else's work. "The author has said everything," might go the argument, "and therefore I can do little more than follow the story." This claim presupposes that you have no choice in selecting material and no opportunity to make individual thoughts and original contributions.

But you do have choices and opportunities to be original. One obvious area of originality is *the development and formulation of your central idea.* For example, a natural first response to "The Necklace" is "The story is about a woman who loses a borrowed necklace and endures hardship to help pay for it." Because this response refers only to events in the story and not to any idea, an area of thought might be introduced if the hardship is called "needless." Just the use of this word alone demands that you explain the differences between *needed* and *unneeded* hardships, and your application of these differences to the heroine's plight would produce an original essay. Even better and more original insights could result if the topic of the budding essay were to connect the dreamy, withdrawn traits of the main character to her misfortunes and also to general misfortunes. A resulting central idea might be "People themselves create their own difficulties." Such an idea would require you to define not only the personal but also the representative nature of Mathilde's experiences, an avenue of exploration that could produce much in the way of a fresh, original essay about "The Necklace."

You can also develop your ability to treat your subject freshly and originally if you plan the body of the essay *to build up to what you think is your most important and incisive idea*. As examples of such planning, the following brief list of topics suggests how a central idea may be widened and expanded:

Subject: Mathilde as a growing character

1. Mathilde has normal daydreams about a better life.

2. She takes a risk, and loses, in trying to make her daydreams seem real.

3. She develops by facing her mistake and working hard to correct it.

The list shows how a subject may be enlarged if the exemplifying topic is treated in an increasing order of importance. In this case, the order moves from Mathilde's habit of daydreaming to the development of her character strength. The pattern shows how two primary standards of excellence in writing—organization and growth—can be met.

It should be clear that whenever you write you should always try to develop your central idea. Constantly adhere to your topic and constantly develop it. Nurture it and make it grow. Admittedly, in a short essay you will be able to move only a short distance with an idea, but you *should never be satisfied to leave the idea exactly where you found it*. To the degree that you can learn to develop your ideas, you will receive recognition for increasingly original writing.

Using Exact, Comprehensive, and Forceful Language

In addition to being organized and well developed, the best writing is expressed in *exact, comprehensive*, and *forceful* language. At any stage of the composition process, you should try to correct your earliest sentences and paragraphs, which usually need to be rethought, reworded, and rearranged.

First of all, ask yourself whether your sentences really *mean* what you intend, or whether you can make them more exact and therefore stronger. For example, consider these two sentences from essays about "The Necklace":

> It seems as though the main character's dreams of luxury cause her to respond as she does in the story.

> This incident, although it may seem trivial or unimportant, has substantial significance in the creation of the story; by this I mean the incident that occurred is essentially what the story is all about.

These sentences are inexact and vague and therefore unhelpful; neither of them goes anywhere. The first is satisfactory up to the verb "cause," but then it falls apart because the writer has lost sight of the meaning; just what, exactly, does "to respond as she does" mean? It is best to describe *what* that response is, rather than to be satisfied with nothing more than that there *is* a response. To make the sentence more exact, we may make the following revision:

> Mathilde's dreams of luxury make it impossible for her to accept her own possessions, and therefore she goes beyond her means to attend the party.

With this revision, the writer could consider the meaning of the story's early passages and contrast the ideas there with those in the latter part. Without the revision, it is not clear where the writer might go.

The second sentence is vague because again the writer has lost sight of the topic. If we adopt the principle of trying to be exact, however, we may bring the dead sentence to life:

> The accidental loss of the necklace, which is trivial though costly, supports the narrator's claim that major turns in life are produced not by earthshaking events, but rather by minor ones.

Second, in addition to exactness, it is vital to make sentences—all sentences, but particularly thesis and topic sentences—complete and comprehensive. As an example, consider the following sentence written in a student essay about "The Necklace":

> The idea in "The Necklace" is that Mathilde and her husband work hard to pay for the lost necklace.

This sentence does not offer us any ideas about the story. It needs additional rethinking and rephrasing to make it more comprehensive, as in the these two revisions:

> In "The Necklace" Maupassant shows that hard work and responsibility are basic and necessary in life.

> Maupassant's surprise ending of "The Necklace" symbolizes the need for always being truthful.

Both new sentences are connected to "Mathilde and her husband work hard to pay for the lost necklace," although they point toward differing treatments. The first concerns the virtue shown by the Loisels in their sacrifice. Because the second sentence includes the word *symbolizes*, an essay stemming from it would stress the Loisels' mistake in not confessing the loss. In dealing with the symbolic meaning of their failure, an essay developed along the lines of the sentence would focus on the negative aspects of their characters, and an essay developed from the first sentence would stress their positive aspects. Either of the revised sentences, therefore, is more comprehensive than the original sentence, and would help a writer get on the track toward an accurate and thoughtful essay.

Of course it is never easy to create fine sentences, but as a mode of improvement, you might create some self-testing mechanisms:

> ➤ *For treating story materials.* Always relate the materials to an idea or point. Do not say simply that "Mathilde works constantly for ten years to help pay off the debt." Instead, blend the material into a point, like this: "Mathilde's ten-year effort shows *the horror of indebtedness*," or "Mathilde's ten-year effort *demonstrates her ultimate strength of character*."

> ➤ *For responses and impressions.* Do not say simply, "The story's ending left me with a definite impression," but *state* what the impression is: "The story's ending *surprised me and also made me sympathetic to the major character*."

➤ *For ideas.* Try to make the idea clear and direct. Do not say, "Mathilde is living in a poor household," but rather get at an idea like this one: "The story of Mathilde *shows that poverty reduces quality of life.*"

➤ *For critical commentary.* Do not rest with a statement such as "I found 'The Necklace' interesting," but try to describe *what* was interesting and *why* it was interesting: "I found 'The Necklace' interesting *because it shows that unexpected or chance occurrences may either make or destroy people's lives.*"

Good writing begins with attempts, like these, to rephrase sentences to make them really say something. If you always name and pin down descriptions, responses, and judgments, no matter how difficult the task seems, your sentences can be strong because you will be making them exact.

First Sample Essay, Final Draft

If you refer again to the first draft (p. 264) of the essay about Maupassant's use of setting to illustrate Mathilde's character, you might notice that several parts of the draft need extensive reworking and revising. For example, paragraph 2 contains a series of short, unconnected comments, and the last sentence of that paragraph implies that Mathilde's dissatisfaction relates mainly to her husband rather than to her general circumstances. Paragraph 4 focuses too much on Mathilde's coarseness and not enough on her sacrifice and cooperation. The draft also ignores the fact that the story ends in another location, the Champs Elysées, where Maupassant continues to demonstrate the nature of Mathilde's character. Finally, there is not enough support in this draft for the contention (in paragraph 5) that *everything* in the story is related to the character of Mathilde.

To discover how these issues may be more fully considered, the following revision of the earlier draft creates more introductory detail, includes an additional paragraph, and reshapes each of the paragraphs to stress the relationship of central idea to topic. Within the limits of a short assignment, the essay illustrates all the principles of organization and unity we have been discussing here.

Maupassant's Use of Setting in "The Necklace" to Show the Character of Mathilde

[1]   In "The Necklace" Guy de Maupassant uses setting to reflect the strengths and weaknesses of the main character, Mathilde Loisel.[*] As a result, his setting is not particularly vivid or detailed. He does not even provide a description of the ill-fated necklace—the central object in the story—but states no more than that it is "superb" (paragraph 47). In fact, he includes descriptions of setting only if they illuminate qualities of Mathilde's character. Her changing character may be related to the first apartment, her daydreams about mansion rooms, the attic flat of the Loisels, and the public street.[†]

[2]   Details about the modest apartment of the Loisels on the Street of Martyrs indicate Mathilde's peevish lack of adjustment to life. Though everything is service-able, she is unhappy with the "drab" walls, "threadbare" furniture, and "ugly" curtains (paragraph 3). She has domestic help, but wants more servants than the simple country girl who does the household chores in the apartment. Her embarrassment and dissatisfaction are shown by details of her irregularly cleaned tablecloth and the plain and inelegant boiled beef that her husband adores. Even her best theater dress, which is appropriate for apartment life but which is inappropriate for more wealthy surroundings, makes her unhappy. All these details of the apartment establish that Mathilde's dominant character trait at the story's beginning is maladjustment. She therefore seems unpleasant and unsympathetic.

[3]   Like the real-life apartment, the impossibly expensive setting of her daydreams about living in a mansion strengthens her unhappiness and her avoidance of reality. All the rooms of her fantasies are large and expensive, draped in silk and filled with nothing but the best furniture and bric-a-brac. Maupassant gives us the following description of her dream world:

> She imagined a gourmet-prepared main course carried on the most exquisite trays and served on the most beautiful dishes, with whispered gallantries which she would hear with a sphinxlike smile as she dined on the pink meat of a trout or the delicate wing of a quail. (paragraph 4)

With impossible dreams like this one, her despair is complete. Ironically, this despair, together with her inability to live with reality, brings about her undoing. It makes her agree to borrow the necklace (which is just as unreal as her daydreams of wealth), and losing the necklace drives her into the reality of giving up her apartment and moving into the attic flat.

[4]   Also ironically, the attic flat is related to the coarsening of her character while at the same time it brings out her best qualities of cooperativeness and honesty. Maupassant emphasizes the drudgery of the work Mathilde endures to maintain the flat, such as walking up many stairs, washing floors with large buckets of water, cleaning greasy and encrusted pots and pans, taking out the garbage, handwashing

---

[*] Central idea.
[†] Thesis sentence.

clothes, and haggling loudly with local tradespeople. All this reflects her coarsening and loss of sensibility, also shown by her giving up hair and hand care, and wearing the cheapest dresses. The work she performs, however, makes her heroic (paragraph 98). As she cooperates to help her husband pay back the loans, her dreams of a mansion fade and all she has left is the memory of her triumphant appearance at the Minister of Education's party. Thus the attic flat brings out her physical change for the worse at the same time that it also brings out her psychological and moral change for the better.

[5]   Her walk on the Champs-Elysées illustrates another combination of traits—self-indulgence and frankness. The Champs-Elysées is the most fashionable street in Paris, and her walk to it is similar to her earlier indulgences in her daydreams of upper-class wealth. But it is on this street where she meets Jeanne, and it is Mathilde's frankness in confessing the loss and replacement to Jeanne that makes Mathilde, finally, completely honest. While the walk thus serves as the occasion for the story's concluding surprise and irony, Mathilde's being on the Champs-Elysées is totally in character, in keeping with her earlier reveries about luxury.

[6]   Other details in the story also have a similar bearing on Mathilde's character. For example, the story presents little detail about the party scene beyond the statement that Mathilde is a great "success" (paragraph 52)—a judgment that shows her ability to shine if given the chance. After she and Loisel accept the fact that the necklace cannot be found, Maupassant includes details about the Parisian streets, about the visits to loan sharks, and about the jewelry shops in order to bring out Mathilde's sense of honesty and pride as she "heroically" prepares to live her new life of poverty. Thus, in "The Necklace," Maupassant uses setting to highlight Mathilde's maladjustment, her needless misfortune, her loss of youth and beauty, and finally her growth as a responsible human being.

Several improvements to the first draft may be seen here. The language of paragraph 2 has been revised to show more clearly that Mathilde's dissatisfaction does not seem appropriate. In paragraph 3, the irony of the story is brought out, and the writer has connected the details to the central idea in a richer pattern of ideas, showing the effects of Mathilde's despair. A new paragraph, 5, includes additional details about how Mathilde's walk on the Champs-Elysées is related to her character. In paragraph 6, the fact that Mathilde "is able to shine" at the dinner party is interpreted according to the central idea. Finally, the conclusion is now much more specific, summarizing the change in Mathilde's character rather than saying simply that the setting reveals her "needless sacrifice." In short, the second draft reflects the complexity of "The Necklace" better than the first draft. Because the writer has revised the first-draft ideas about the story, the final essay is tightly structured, insightful, and forceful.

Summary

To sum up, follow these guidelines whenever you write about a story or any kind of literature:

> ➤ Never just retell the story. Use story materials only to support your central idea or argument.

> ➤ Throughout your essay, keep reminding your reader of your central idea.

> ➤ Within each paragraph, make sure that you stress your topic idea.

> ➤ Develop your topic. Make it bigger than it was when you began.

> ➤ Always make your statements exact, comprehensive, and forceful.

> ➤ Never just retell the story.

> ➤ **Never just retell the story.**

> ➤ *Never just retell the story.*

■ WRITING ABOUT RESPONSES: LIKES AND DISLIKES

Now that we have looked briefly at the processes of writing, with two drafts of the same essay for illustration, we are ready to apply the principles of development to another topic for writing—this one about likes and dislikes (already mentioned earlier, pp. 245–250). In writing about your responses, rely on your initial informed reactions. It is not easy to reconstruct your first responses after a lapse of time, so you will need your journal observations to guide you in prewriting. Develop your essay by stressing those characters, incidents, and ideas that interest (or do not interest) you.

As with many essays, you will be challenged to connect details from the work to your central idea. That is, once you have begun by stating that you like (or dislike) the story, you might forget to highlight this response as you enumerate details. Therefore you need to stress your involvement in the work as you bring out evidence from it. You can show your attitudes by indicating approval (or disapproval), by commenting favorably (or unfavorably) on the details, by indicating things that seem new (or shopworn) and particularly instructive (or wrong), and by giving assent to (or dissent from) ideas or expressions of feeling.

Organizing Your Essay About Likes and Dislikes

INTRODUCTION. Briefly describe the conditions that influence your responses. Your central idea should be why you like or dislike the work. Your thesis sentence should list the major causes of your response, which are to be developed in the body.

BODY. The most common approach is to consider specific details that you like or dislike. The list on pages 248–249 may help you articulate your responses. For example, you may have admired a particular character, or maybe you got so interested in the story that you could not put it down. Also, you may wish to develop a major idea, a fresh insight, or a particular outcome, as in the sample paragraph on page 248, which shows a surprise ending as the cause of a favorable response.

A second approach (see p. 250) is to explain any changes in your responses about the work (i.e., negative to positive and vice versa). This approach requires that you isolate the causes of the change, but it does *not* require you to retell the story from beginning to end.

1. One way to deal with such a change—the "bridge" method of transferring preference from one type of work to another—is shown in the following sample essay.

2. Another way is to explain a change in terms of a new awareness or understanding that you did not have on a first reading. Thus your first response to Maupassant's "The Necklace" might be unfavorable or neutral because the story concerns an unappealing character. Further consideration, however, might lead you to discover new insights that change your mind, such as the need to cooperate in the face of personal and family misfortunes. Your essay would then explain how these new insights have caused you to like the story.

CONCLUSION. Here you might summarize the reasons for your major response. You might also face any issues brought up by a change or modification of your first reactions. For example, if you have always held certain assumptions about your taste but like the work despite these assumptions, you may wish to talk about your own change or development. This topic is personal, but in an essay about likes or dislikes, discovery about yourself is legitimate and worthy.

Second Sample Essay

Some Reasons for Liking Maupassant's "The Necklace"

[1]   To me, the most likable kind of reading is adventure. There are many reasons for my preference, but an important one is that characters in adventure stories work hard to overcome obstacles. Because Guy de Maupassant's "The Necklace" is not adventure, I did not like it at first. But in one respect the story is <u>like</u> adventure: The major character, Mathilde, works hard with her husband, Loisel, for ten years to overcome a difficult obstacle. <u>Thus, because Mathilde does what adventure characters also do, the story is likable.</u>* <u>Mathilde's appeal results from her hard work, strong character, and sad fate, and also from the way our view of her changes.</u>†

[2]   <u>Mathilde's hard work makes her seem good.</u> Once she and her husband are faced with the huge debt of 18,000 francs, she works like a slave to help pay it back. She gives up her servant and moves to a cheaper place. She does the household drudgery, wears cheap clothes, and bargains with shopkeepers. Just like the characters in adventure stories who do hard and unpleasant things, she does what she has to, and this makes her admirable.

[3]   <u>Her strong character shows her endurance, a likable trait.</u> At first she is nagging and fussy, and she always dreams about wealth and tells lies, but she changes and gets better. She recognizes her blame in losing the necklace, and she has the toughness to help her husband redeem the debt. She sacrifices "heroically" (paragraph 98) by giving up her comfortable way of life, even though in the process she also loses her youth and beauty. Her jobs are not the exotic and glamorous ones of adventure stories, but her force of character makes her as likable as an adventure heroine.

[4]   <u>Her sad fate also makes her likable.</u> In adventure stories the characters often suffer as they do their jobs. Mathilde also suffers, but in a different way, because her suffering is permanent while the hardships of adventure characters are temporary. This fact makes her especially pitiable because all her sacrifices are not necessary. This unfairness invites the reader to take her side.

[5]   <u>The most important quality promoting admiration is the way in which Maupassant shifts our view of Mathilde.</u> As she goes deeper into her hard life, Maupassant stresses her work and not the innermost thoughts he reveals at the beginning. In other words, the view into her character at the start, when she dreams about wealth, invites dislike; but the focus at the end is on her achievements, with never a complaint—even though she still has golden memories, as the narrator tells us:

> But sometimes, when her husband was at work, she sat down near the window, and she dreamed of that evening so long ago, of that party, where she had been so beautiful and so admired. (paragraph 104)

A major quality of Maupassant's changed emphasis is that Mathilde's fond memories do not lead to anything unfortunate. His shift in focus, from Mathilde's dissatisfaction to her sharing of responsibility and sacrifice, encourages the reader to like her.

---

*Central idea.
†Thesis sentence.

[6]   "The Necklace" is not an adventure story, but Mathilde has some of the good qualities of adventure characters. Also, the surprise revelation that the lost necklace was false is an unforgettable twist, and this makes her more deserving than she seems at first. Maupassant has arranged the story so that the reader finally admires Mathilde. "The Necklace" is a skillful and likable story.

Commentary on the Essay

This essay demonstrates how a reader may develop appreciation by transferring a preference for one type of work to a work that does not belong to the type. In the essay, the "bridge" is an already established taste for adventure stories, and the grounds for liking "The Necklace" are that Mathilde, the main character, shares the admirable qualities of adventure heroes and heroines.

In paragraph 1, the introduction, the grounds for transferring preferences are established. Paragraph 2 deals with Mathilde's capacity to work hard, and paragraph 3 considers the equally admirable quality of endurance. The fourth paragraph describes how Mathilde's condition evokes sympathy and pity. These paragraphs hence explain the story's appeal by asserting that the main character is similar to admirable characters from works of adventure.

The fifth paragraph shows that Maupassant, as the story unfolds, alters the reader's perceptions of Mathilde from bad to good. For this reason paragraph 5 marks a new direction from paragraphs 2, 3, and 4: It moves away from the topic material itself—Mathide's character—to Maupassant's *technique* in handling the topic material.

Paragraph 6, the conclusion, restates the comparison and also introduces the surprise ending as an additional reason for liking "The Necklace." With the body and conclusion together, therefore, the essay establishes five separate reasons for approval. Three of these, derived directly from the main character, constitute the major grounds for liking the story, and two are related to Maupassant's techniques as an author.

Throughout the essay, the central idea is brought out in words and expressions such as "likable," "Mathilde's appeal," "strong character," "she does what she has to," "pitiable," and "take her side." Many of these expressions were first made in the writer's journal; and, mixed as they are with details from the story, they make for continuity. It is this thematic development, together with details from the story as supporting evidence, that shows how an essay on the responses of liking and disliking may be both informed and informative.

PART SIX

Workplace Writing

Linda Julian
Furman University

PART SIX

Workplace Writing: Teaching Writing Skills to Willing Learners

Even the most reluctant students of writing—those whose eyes have glazed over during important discussions of purpose, audience, organization, revision, and precise grammar—sharpen their pencils and look with renewed interest at the syllabus when teachers discuss business writing skills. These skills, usually the same ones students have unenthusiastically grappled with in writing essays, suddenly appeal because they are bathed in the golden glow of the marketplace. Students know that to get jobs and keep them, they must master the basic skills of writing for the workplace. Those writing skills which have previously been only marginally palatable take on the allure of "real life" when they are taught using documents from the world of business.

Many students have had part-time and summer jobs and know firsthand that employers expect competent writers on the job and often reward skillful writers with promotions and higher salaries. Students who had had little or no work experience are curious about the world of work and eagerly apply themselves to learning writing skills that may give them a head start in an increasingly competitive job market. Therefore, teachers who have been constantly battling apathy about writing suddenly discover that they have eager learners who will work diligently to craft a job application letter, a letter of demand for a replacement stereo speaker, or a proposal for a more equitable vacation plan.

On the other hand, students often have misconceptions about business writing which teachers should anticipate and deal with at the outset. Students sometimes think that workplace writing comes with a specialized vocabulary that smacks of governmentese and business lingo. Thus, they will labor to make simple and clear ideas sound "businesslike," usually by adding clichés and mixing phrases from the nineteenth-century ("pursuant to," "beg to acknowledge," "per your request," for example) with inflated diction ("first and foremost," "in view of the fact that," "make an evaluation of the processes currently being used," for example). This inflated diction often results from overuse of the passive voice, linking verbs, circumlocution, and tautology. We need to make clear from the beginning that business writing—like all good writing—relies on using language appropriate to the audience and purpose. Students may be surprised to learn that workplace writing is not the most formal kind of writing and therefore usually contains contractions and simple, direct words put together effectively. It also relies on dynamic verbs.

Students may also be surprised to learn that the brevity of many letters and other business documents and the speed with which some are produced do not mean that these documents are easy to write or that they should be taken lightly by the writer. On the contrary, students should realize that often the brief letters are the most challenging. They should also see that every letter is a public relations statement about the writer, a first-impression that can easily go wrong if the writer is careless and unconcerned about the impression created in business documents. In fact, a student who can write an excellent business letter is well on the way to excellence in all kinds of writing.

One major difference between business writing and other kinds of writing is the emphasis on efficiency and timeliness in workplace writing. Students probably have never stopped to consider the most important principle governing most business writing: Time is money. A discussion of this point may make a striking beginning for a unit on business writing. Students generally do not equate the writing they do with saving or wasting money, but teachers can show them that when messages are unclear and have to be questioned in follow-up letters and calls, busy workers are wasting time and effort that could be better spent in making money. They need to know that a letter costs about $20 for a company to write and mail. This substantial expense may have to be doubled or tripled when follow-up communications are required by inadequate messages.

They also need to know that business is lost sometimes on the basis of a poor first-impression made by a sloppy or poorly written document. Students can readily see that a letter is like an introduction to a stranger: appearance and substance and tact either make the person want to get to know the newcomer—or not.

Finally, a major misconception that we need to correct is students' major impression that secretaries will "fix" their writing once they have a job. As teachers, we need only ask students how secure they feel about their grammar and mechanics and general writing skills and then to imagine where and how a secretary, who may not have a college degree and the level of competence they have, could have acquired the necessary skills to make them look good on paper. They must understand that in this age of word processing, more and more executives do their own typing and editing at the computer, relying little on secretaries for editorial help.

General Characteristics of Workplace Writing

As in other kinds of writing, the most important decisions a business writer must make are the purpose of the document and the audience for it. Many business documents fail to achieve their goal because the writer tosses off a letter or report too quickly to plan the strategy appropriate to the audience and purpose. (See *The Simon & Schuster Handbook for Writers*, Chapter 1.)

Audience and purpose dictate major decisions about business documents: the choice of format, the organizational plan, the amount of background information necessary, the assumptions the writer can make about the reader, the level of language, the tone, and even the kinds of sentences appropriate for the task. Often students begin writing without knowing what they want to achieve with the piece of writing. For this reason, teachers may need to spend time having students analyze the purpose and audience for various types of business documents. In addition, many teachers require students to write a note, either on a cover sheet or in the upper-right hand corner of each assignment, identifying the intended audience and purpose. To emphasize the importance of audience and purpose, teachers may also want to have students write planning documents for each assignment, at least for the first few. Such a planning document might include answers to the following questions:

> ➤ Who is my audience?
> ➤ What do I know about my audience?
> ➤ What level of language will be appropriate for this reader?
> ➤ How much background information will I have to give this audience?
> ➤ On first glance, will the reader be receptive, neutral, or negative toward my message?
> ➤ What action do I want the reader to take?
> ➤ What strategies can I use to get the reader to take this action?
> ➤ What impression do I want this document to make on my reader?

In the business world, where time is money, students can also see that economical use of language is important. The most effective business documents avoid unnecessary passive voice, overuse of linking verbs, expletive constructions, tautological phrasing, and circumlocution. Students should also focus on the need for sentences that average fifteen to seventeen words so that documents may be read quickly, without the reader's having to reread in order to comprehend long, convoluted sentences. Also to engineer easy reading in business documents, teachers should point out the need for cumulative sentences as the dominant pattern rather than periodic sentences, which require readers to work harder at decoding the message.

Paragraphs, too, may be somewhat shorter in many business documents than they are in some kinds of essays. Students can see that shortening paragraphs and using topic sentences at the top of paragraphs aid in quick, efficient reading.

On the other hand, we must help students see that using the fewest number of words possible is not necessarily the best goal for a document. Economy does not mean brutally stripped-down language. Rather we need to emphasize that economy means using the fewest number of words to convey the tone and strategy of the message we are trying to send. Bluntness rarely wins friends and influences people—at least in a positive way.

Another point we need to make to our students is that many business documents are not read in their entirety. Some longer documents, especially proposals and reports, rely on headings and clear paragraph structure to enable overworked businesspeople to skim documents, reading only the parts they have immediate interest in.

Asked to identify the major differences between business writing and essay writing, students rarely think of these stylistic matters, beyond making documents "sound" like business documents by using "business" language, but students are quick to point out the differences in format. However, they underestimate how important adherence to conventional format is in workplace writing. As teachers, we can help them understand that although format is not the be-all and end-all of good business writing, deviating from acceptable formats is risky:

Why Care About Format?

➢ Business readers expect documents to look a certain way and may be distracted if they do not. Writers want to avoid doing anything that may distract a reader from processing the message.

> Writers who do not follow conventional formats may communicate that they do not think such things important, a message not likely to please a prospective employer or customer.

> Writers who do not follow conventional formats may suggest that they have not bothered to learn what the conventions of business are, a message that might not inspire confidence in the writer or his or her products or services.

Major Kinds of Workplace Writing

All students know that workplace writing includes letters and memos, but many do not know that letters communicate between companies or individuals at different addresses and that memos communicate within a company. They usually do not know about the many kinds of reports, proposals, and public relations documents that require research, planning, revision, editing, and proofing just as more familiar kinds of documents do.

A good way to begin a unit on workplace writing is to teach students how to write routine letters asking for information and then to have them write to companies or visit local companies requesting samples of some of the following kinds of documents:

Kinds of Business Documents

> Letter expressing favorable information

> Letter expressing neutral information

> Letter expressing negative information

> Letter ordering a product or service

> Letter acknowledging an order

> Job application package—cover letter and résumé

> A letter of recommendation

> A letter of congratulations

> A letter report

> A letter proposal

> A memo expressing favorable information

> A memo expressing neutral information

> A memo expressing negative information

- ➤ A memo explaining how to do something
- ➤ A memo analyzing how something works
- ➤ A feasibility report
- ➤ An informational report
- ➤ A proposal for changing a procedure or service
- ➤ A persuasive report
- ➤ A company brochure
- ➤ A news release
- ➤ An annual report

Students making such requests should ask the company to delete the names of the writer and addressee on letters and memos.

Some discussion about the kinds of skills involved in writing these varied documents should prove fruitful. Students need to see that knowing such organizational plans as comparison and contrast, narration, cause and effect, process analysis, and argument is critical. They will also recognize that in the samples, the problems with grammar and format are distracting and potentially destructive to the success of the message.

Letters and Memos

Letters and memos, the most common kinds of workplace writing, are often brief, though either letters or memos can be long and complex. For both, the language should be economical, the sentences should be easy to read, and the tone should be appropriate to the purpose and audience.

In general, however, workplace writers attempt to empathize with readers, putting words that refer to the reader (*you, your, yours*) in important positions and words that refer to the writer (*I, me, mine, myself, we, us, our, ours*) in less emphatic places. (Emphatic places include beginnings and endings of sentences, especially the first and last words in paragraphs.)

Usually, too, writers try to be as positive in their opening and closing as the situation warrants. These openings and closings, however, need to be briefer than many of the other paragraphs. In letters and memos first paragraphs that are longer than about four lines of type put the reader off, because they seem difficult to read and uninviting. The final paragraph is usually even briefer, two or three lines.

Letters go outside the company, and memos stay within the business. Otherwise, the major difference is in format.

Format of Letters

Letters are a kind of advertising for the individual writer and his or her company. Therefore, they must look professional and adhere to conventionally accepted format. Even the weight, texture, and color of the paper can send a message. For example, most people would be angry if the I.R.S. or a charity sent letters on expensive letterhead. We want letters from such groups to reflect a sense of thriftiness in their stationery.

In general, letters should be typed on professional weight white paper (sixteen to twenty-four pound range with some cotton rag) with a dark ribbon or fresh toner cartridge. They should appear neatly framed, with margins of at least an inch (up to two inches for a short letter). Letters should not, however, be centered on the page. They should be slightly top-heavy, and many professionals prefer that the right margin not be justified, because they find that readers are distracted by the extra spacing within lines. (See Troyka's Section 39a in *The Simon & Schuster Handbook for Writers*.)

Letter writers may choose from five formats, but two are most often used—the block style and the modified block style. Other forms are the traditional indented format, simplified style, and open punctuation.

In the block style, popular largely because it is easiest to type, each line in the letter begins at the left margin. Following the letterhead address of the company, the letter has at least a double space (three or four for a brief letter), the date, a double space, the inside address, a double space, a subject line or attention line, if required, a double space, a salutation, a double space, the body of the letter (single-spaced with double-spacing between paragraphs), a double space, the closing, four to five lines of space for the handwritten signature, a typed signature, a double space, the initials of the writer and typist, a double space, a distribution list (if necessary), and an enclosure notation (if needed).

If the letter is being written in block format from an individual who is not using letterhead, the letter should begin with the return address at the left margin about one and a half inches from the top of the page. It should *not* include the name of the writer but should include the full address followed by the date on the next line (no line between the address and date).

Whether or not the letter is on letterhead, the date should be written in traditional form (July 20, 1995), not military style (20 July 1995) or numerical style (7/20/95). Some people prefer not to abbreviate words like *avenue* and *road*, but if one prefers to abbreviate these words, he or she should use conventional abbreviations. In the inside address, many people prefer to use a courtesy title (*Mr.*, *Mrs.*, *Ms.*, *Miss* or *Dr.* or *The Reverend*), and such a title should appear in the salutation unless the writer knows the reader on a first-name basis. These days *Ms.* is the preferred form for women, though sometimes women sign their letters by indicating their preference in parentheses (*Mrs.* or *Miss*, perhaps) before the typed name of the writer.

Although writers usually want to find out the name of an individual to address when writing to a company or school or other group, occasionally they may not be able to and will need to use a salutation that is general. The old-fashioned version is "Dear Sir or Madam" or "Dear Sirs" or "Dear Ladies." These salutations are rarely used today. Instead, many writers prefer "Ladies and Gentlemen" (without the *dear*), although some consider this still a bit formal. Others use *Dear* with a job title or descriptive title: for example, "Dear Personnel Manager" or "Dear Mercedes Owner." Some people find these kinds of salutations too impersonal and simply leave out the salutation and complimentary closing, creating what is known as Simplified format.

In addition to the salutation, other parts of the format may be puzzling to students. Most students will not have written letters in which they used an attention line or a subject line, and they will be curious about these. By addressing a letter to a company and saluting the company but using an attention line, the writer is giving permission for anyone at the company to open the letter. Because they do not require courtesy titles, attention lines can also be used when the writer prefers to use courtesy titles but is unsure of the gender of the addressee based on his or her name—for example, "Lee Jamison" or "Cary Clark." Students should learn that if they want to use a courtesy title, they should call the company and find out whether or not the person is male or female, or they should use an attention line. In no case should they guess about gender when they have a name that could be either.

The subject line in a letter, which comes just after the inside address and before the salutation—with a double space before and after it—usually contains the word *Subject*, followed by a colon and a phrase which describes precisely what the letter is about. Such a line has several uses. It can speed the letter to the appropriate recipient in a company, it can prepare the way for the message by letting the reader know up front what it is about, and it can aid the recipient in filing.

Students also may be confused by the notations at the bottom of the letter, the initials of writer and typist, the enclosure notation, and the distribution list. In looking at sample letters, they may notice that the writer's initials may be separated from the typist's by either a colon or a virgule. They may find that the enclosure notation will say simply *enclosure, encl.*, or *attachments* or that it may say one of these followed by a colon and a description of the enclosure (for example, *encl.: check for $20.56*). The distribution list most often still uses the abbreviation *cc* for "carbon copy," even though few people have used carbon paper in the last thirty years. Occasionally one sees *xc*, which stands for "xerox copy" or *pc*, for "photo copy." Students may see some examples of documents with long distribution lists or even "blind" distribution lists (noted by *bcc*), lists of those to whom the letter is sent without the knowledge of the addressee.

There are two differences between the block format and the modified block format. The modified form centers the date and the signature block (closing, handwritten signature, and typed signature).

The traditional indented format is like the modified block format except that the paragraphs are indented. Many people like this form because they think that the time and expense necessary to set up all of the indentations makes the receiver of the letter feel special.

A newer form, the simplified format, omits parts required in more traditional formats. Simplified format omits the salutation and the complimentary closing. People who think that *Dear* in the salutation and such phrases as "Very truly yours" and "Sincerely yours" seem Victorian like the simplified format. Others think it is too impersonal.

The next two pages show examples of letters in the block format and the modified block format.

Heading for the Second Page of a Letter

When a letter requires more than a page, it also requires a heading on the second page. This heading includes the name of the receiver of the letter, the date, and either the number *2* or *page two*. These may be arranged across the top of the page or all beginning at the left margin:

| Ms. Consuelo Hernandez | 2 | April 19, 1995 |

or

Ms. Consuelo Hernandez
Page 2
April 19, 1995

Block Style (Letter Using Letterhead)

Henri's Italian Restaurant

III MEADOWLARK LANE
SAN FRANCISCO, CALIFORNIA 94111

April 23, 1995

Mr. George Littlejohn, Manager
Rudolph's Restaurant Supply
2235 Lake View Boulevard
Chicago, Illinois 60616

Dear Mr. Littlejohn:

Thank you for sending the recent shipment of pizza pans in response to our emergency order. Knowing you would have them here on time saved our peace of mind during this unexpected boom in business. However, I do have a question about the bill.

When we discussed the price of the pans, I thought it included the cost of shipping. The invoice, a copy of which I have enclosed, shows a charge of $63 for shipping them overnight express. Is this charge an error or did I misunderstand?

Once I've heard from you, I will pay the invoice immediately. Again, thanks for your prompt service with the much-needed pans.

Sincerely,

Louisa Melosi
Manager

LM/ny

Encl.: Invoice 1086

Modified Block Format
(Letter from an Individual Not Using Letterhead)

2316 Alfred Kind Highway
Augusta, Georgia 30906
April 23, 1995

Ms. Kelley Witherspoon
Assistant Manager
Read-A-Book-A-Day, Inc.
2300 North Avenue, N.W.
Atlanta, GA 30327

SUBJECT: Group order for a poetry reading

Dear Ms. Witherspoon:

Your expertise in locating books by little-known writers was mentioned to me by four booksellers in Atlanta, and I'm hoping you can help with ordering some books for an upcoming poetry reading.

My book group, the Eager Readers, will have at its next reading June 18 a relatively new poet, Angela Gatewood, who has published four books with small presses. We want to order 23 books for our members and a few extras for the public. Unfortunately, I have been unable to locate any books by her.

Would you be willing to try to find them and order them for us. If so, and if you can find them, please let me know the price and an estimate of the turn-around time for the order. We will certainly be happy to pay you a fee of $50 for locating any of the four books.

I look forward to hearing from you soon.

Sincerely,

Richard Radel

Format of Memos

Many students will believe that because memos do not go outside an organization, their format does not matter. Nevertheless, they need to learn that professionalism matters within an organization, too. Memos often represent a whole division or department of a company, and the impression that they make sends a message about the quality of that division or department. In addition, unexpected changes in format, even minor changes, can distract the reader from the message. Such distractions waste time and money.

Some firms print their own memo forms, and some now have templates that present the form on the computer so that the writer simply fills in the names of the sender and receiver, the date, and the subject. Some organizations have stationery for memos with only the word *Memorandum* or *Memo* preprinted. Some simply use blank sheets.

Memos usually have only five parts: the name(s) of the receivers (also known as the distribution list), the name of the writer, the date, the subject, and the message. Each of the first four of these includes a description word, usually typed in all caps, followed by a colon:

```
TO:
FROM:
DATE:
SUBJECT:
```

SUBJECT is sometimes RE, for "regarding," or CONCERNING. These four elements may be arranged in almost any order, although the TO notation usually goes first. They may be arranged in two columns, so that the DATE and SUBJECT notations appear on the same line as the TO and FROM notations. These elements are double spaced.

Following these elements are a triple space and the message, which usually is single-spaced with double-spacing between paragraphs, as in letters. If the memo is very short, it may be double-spaced.

Unlike letters, memos usually omit courtesy titles (Mr., Mrs., Ms.), and they lack salutations and complimentary closings. Although the memo may be signed at the bottom (preferred by some when the memo concerns money or confidential matters), more commonly the writer initials his or her typed name, which follows the FROM notation in the heading, or writes out the first name there. If the memo runs to a second page, it requires a page heading like that for a letter (see p. 000 above).

Examples of Memos

MEMORANDUM

TO: Paula Drake, Manager
              Human Resources

FROM: Jake Josselsohn, Manager
              Environmental Resources

DATE: June 24, 1995

SUBJECT: Vacation time during the week of July 4

     The new company policy about taking vacation time during the week of July 4 has caused some confusion in our department, and we would like clarification.

     Sixteen of our twenty-three employees in Environmental Resources have planned to take three or more days off that week, in contradiction to what I believe the new policy says. Does the policy mean that an employee may have three days but not more than three days during that busy time for us, or does it prohibit taking more than two days?

     The policy seemed clear when I first read it, but now that most of my employees have come in to question me about the number of allowable days, I find that the policy seems ambiguous.

     I look forward to receiving a written explanation by Friday if possible.

MEMORANDUM

TO: Harry Elsmore, Accounting   DATE: July 10, 1995

FROM: Jennifer Reid   SUBJECT: Little League
          Data Processing

     Congratulations on your Little League coaching! I read in today's paper that your team will now be competing in the state playoffs, and I wondered if you could use some help in chaperoning the team while you're in Little Rock.

     My husband and I would be happy to go along and help, and we'd be glad to drum up some additional help in the company. I know that Kenny has authorized some company T-shirts in support of the team, and I know our company is contributing to the cost of trophies. I know that in the past, the company has also hosted a banquet for players and parents. Would you be interested in my following up on that possibility for the team while they are in Little Rock?

     Please let me know what I can do, on behalf of the company, to help.

Strategies for Letters and Memos

Writing effective letters and memos requires that the writer have a strategy for the document before beginning to write. In addition to thinking about the audience and emphasizing the reader by using second-person pronouns more than first-person pronouns, the writer also needs to decide where in the message to put the most important information. In deciding on placement, the writer must consider whether the message is likely to be received favorably, neutrally, or unfavorably.

Favorable letters and memos open with the important information and then follow up with the details. For example, a memo saying that an employee's trip has been approved would begin with that information. People enjoy receiving positive information and will usually continue reading the letter or memo to find out the details once they have been given the good news.

Neutral messages, often routine documents like orders, responses to inquiries, or acknowledgments of orders or shipments, should be handled in much the same way. Writers should, however, make an effort to be as positive and empathetic to the reader as possible, especially in the opening and closing sentences.

Unfavorable news, sometimes called a "bad news message," requires a different approach—a much less direct beginning. Readers who read bad news in the first line of a letter or memo may not read the reasons for the bad news or notice the helpful alternatives, which an unskilled writer may have put after the bad news in the document. An effective bad news letter usually reverses this process, beginning with a positive tone and giving the reasons for the unfavorable news—and only then giving the bad news. The advantage of this arrangement is that the reader's disappointment or anger is more likely to be softened if he or she can see the reasoning explained in stages from the beginning. This kind of letter or memo can be even more effective when the writer can help the reader by suggesting other ways the reader might achieve the goal or solve the problem. (See next page for an example of a "Bad News" letter.)

Employment Documents

Students' keen interest in getting summer jobs as well as entry-level jobs at graduation motivates them to pay close attention to instruction about employment documents. Such interest is a boon to writing teachers, because it gives them the opportunity to emphasize points about

Example of a "Bad News" Letter

Fine Apparel for Women

1000 EAST BENNET STREET
MOBILE, ALABAMA 36608

January 6, 1995

Mrs. Adelaide Gresham
2310 Green Pond Road
Mobile, Alabama 36602

Dear Mrs. Gresham:

Thank you for your letter about your purchases during our New Year's sale. We are happy to know that the items you selected are exactly what you were looking for, but we are sorry that you are disappointed with the charges for alterations on the two suits you purchased.

As you may recall, our sale was advertised to only our preferred customers. Limiting the sale allowed us to cut our prices significantly as a way of thanking you for your patronage during the last five years. Normally, our sales do not offer the fifty-percent savings which we were able to offer in this case.

Cutting prices to this extent meant that we had to charge our customers a nominal fee for alterations, a policy stated in our newspaper ads and on the sale signs in the store. Although we, therefore, cannot refund the charges for your alterations, we are enclosing a schedule of two special sales during the next six weeks and our invitation to come in a day early for either sale so that you can have first choice of these special values.

Please accept this invitation with our special thanks for your patronage of Magnolia's.

Sincerely yours,

Alfred Dunnowitz,
Owner and Manager

AD/lj

Enclosure

writing in general that students may not have heeded in other units. Those students who have paid little attention to talk about audience and purpose and revision suddenly sit up a little straighter and make eye contact with the teacher.

Most students have at least heard of a résumé, though most do not know how to write an acceptable one. Few seem to understand that a job application package has two parts: the résumé and the job application letter, also known as a cover letter. They also need to know about additional kinds of letters that are involved in getting a job, such as thank you letters following interviews, inquiries about the status of an application, and letters accepting or rejecting a job.

One of the most difficult lessons to teach about employment documents is that they must be perfect and conventional. One of the best ways to make this point is to invite a human resources director or other executive to the class to discuss the number of résumés that are rejected simply because of sloppy appearance or a misspelling. Students need to hear that their résumés may not be read at all if the layout conveys a lack of attention to convention.

They need to know that for a college student, even a graduating senior, résumés are expected to be no longer than one page. Longer résumés risk not being read. Only employees who have been out of school for several years and, thus, have job experience should have multiple-page résumés.

Preparing to Write the Résumé

Before they even begin drafting a résumé or looking at sample résumés, students should be encouraged to spend time doing a thorough self-analysis. In particular they should list their previous or current jobs, activities, academic qualifications, and skills (especially experience with computers, foreign languages, money management, and travel). School activities can reveal leadership, experience with financial management, and organizational skills.

Some students are discouraged about beginning a résumé because they think they do not have anything to put on one. That empty-résumé feeling, however, is rarely the case. Students need help in seeing that their four years' work with a sorority or a service group has taught them much about planning, public relations, budgeting, and accountability. On the other hand, students must learn that employers are on the lookout for padded résumés, those which contain inflated—or even dishonest—descriptions of routine jobs or activities.

Writing the Résumé

Once students have done some brainstorming about their own achievements, they are ready to think about how résumés ought to look. At this point, teachers may find it useful to have the class critique both effective and ineffective résumés. Career Placement personnel at the school may be able to come to class to discuss the most recent trends in résumé writing.

The most common kind of arrangement for resumes of graduating or continuing students is the reverse-chronological résumé. Under its three or four main headings—Education, Employment Experience, Activities and Honors, and Personal—activities are cited from most recent to oldest. Because the educational block is generally the most important for students, it comes first. Often it will include a subheading for school-related activities. This section normally does not refer to high school activities or graduation unless they were extraordinary (attending high school abroad, for example), though students who are not graduating from college may wish to list their high school and graduation date.

As with employment history, this educational history needs to be accurate in terms of exact dates. If gaps of a year or more appear, these need to be explained in the cover letter.

Many job placement experts suggest that in the educational block, students should give their GPA (but only if it is above 3.0 on a 4.0 scale), note what percentage of their college expenses they have earned themselves, and list special courses *outside* the major that show additional expertise that might attract an employer's eye—for example, particular computer programs, foreign language proficiency, journalism courses, etc.).

As part of this block, often under a heading like *Educational Activities and Awards*, students should list their memberships and achievements. The most difficult part of this section is that many students have difficulty in making parallel the elements of such a list. They need to be reminded to clarify (in parenthesis) unclear, abbreviated, or Greek titles of organizations and to explain briefly what certain responsibilities might mean if an office has an unusual title. Although this section is commonly placed under the larger *Education* notation (which should be in larger type), it may also be a separate section after the Employment Experience section.

Similarly, in the Employment Experience section, students should succinctly describe the duties of a position they held, particularly if the job title is not descriptive. All jobs which involve managing money or being responsible for it should be listed. Students should list only the most recent jobs if their employment history goes back to their teens and includes numerous jobs. As in the education block, entries ought to be parallel in structure and specificity. (See the discussion in Section 39C of Troyka's *Simon & Schuster Handbook for Writers*.)

If the writer chooses to include a personal section, which many employers like to see, it may mention such items as hobbies and willingness to relocate. Employers like to know that candidates have interests other than career goals.

Job-seekers who have been out of school for a while or who are in specialized or creative fields may prefer to do an Emphatic Résumé, one which highlights special talents and achievements first, following these with *Education* and *Activities* sections.

Job placement experts disagree about two elements on résumés, and they seem evenly split in their vote. Some favor the use of a Job Objective at the beginning of the resume, but others argue that such an objective is a waste of space that could be better used for more specific details about the applicant. Those who do not favor their use argue that it is the cover letter that tailors the job application package to the job, not the résumé.

Similarly, these experts are divided about whether or not applicants should list reference on the résumé or simply state that they are available. Those who favor listing references on the résumé argue that doing so saves the company a step and may, in a time of urgency in hiring, expedite consideration of those résumés that have them listed. Those who argue against listing them say that references may change and that the list takes space better used to show the qualifications of the applicant.

Whether or not references appear on the résumé, students need to be reminded that listing someone as a reference is rude unless permission to do so has been arranged beforehand. Also students need to be told that family friends and ministers are not useful references. They should list two or three professors, one outside the major if possible, and one or two former employers. Reference lists should give professional titles and full names, professional addresses, and telephone numbers. These days, many employers prefer to check references by telephone, partly because doing so saves time and partly because it minimizes the fear of lawsuits that could result from unfavorable recommendations.

In addition, students need to be reminded that their name, not the word *résumé*, should go top and center. The résumé is a sales document for a person, and that person's name should be the first thing a reader sees.

Formatting the Résumé

The résumé, like the cover letter, should appear on business weight stationery, not photocopy paper. The paper should be white or off-white, and the printer cartridge should be fresh and dark.

A margin of an inch and a half effectively frames the résumé and keeps it from seeming too crowded on the page. The font should be 10 or 12 pitch, not smaller. Students need to work at spacing until they can uniformly space between major sections. They may need to cut or tighten up some descriptions or entries.

Examples of résumés are shown on the next two pages.

Cover Letters

Job application letters have one major purpose: to win a job interview for the writer. These letters, which usually accompany resumes, should be no longer than a page and should avoid overusing first-person pronouns such as *I* and *me*, even though the letter is about the writer. Such pronouns should be positioned within sentences and paragraphs rather than at the beginning, where they receive more emphasis.

In general, cover letters have three parts. The first paragraph should explain how the writer learned about the job. The applicant should say that the letter is in response to an ad in a particular newspaper or magazine, giving the date of the ad and the title of the position as it was listed in the ad. Or, if the applicant found out about the job through a contact, he or she should mention the person who made the job information available.

If the letter is a blanket letter, a job solicitation letter, which the applicant is sending to many firms in a particular geographic area or a specialization, the opening should make clear that the writer knows what kinds of positions are typically open so that he or she avoids a vague and negative opening like "I would like to apply for any entry-level job with your company" or "Please consider me for any new positions in management." Such statements usually result in the application's immediate rejection.

The second paragraph should highlight qualifications, though it should not simply list what is on the attached resume. This paragraph also provides an opportunity for the writer to explain potentially negative impressions such as gaps in dates on the resume, low grades, a major in a field different from the area in which the applicant is pursuing a job, the lack of extracurricular activities, or reasons why employment was brief or terminated at a particular company.

Example of a Reverse-Chronological Résumé

ALICIA K. ADAMS

Permanent Address   *Temporary Address*
3399 Whimscott Avenue   23 Gambrell Hall
Milwaukee, WI 52306   University of Georgia
414-682-4483   Athens, GA 30605
                                 706-233-4537

Career Goal
Entry-level sports reporting job on a weekly newspaper.

Education
University of Georgia—B.A. in Journalism anticipated in June 1995. GPA 3.97/4.0.
(Supporting courses in Political Science, Asian Studies, and Statistics).

Earned sixty percent of college expenses.

Fluency in Japanese and reading knowledge of Korean.

Georgia State University (1991–92)

Activities and Awards: Listed on Dean's List all twelve terms. Member of Phi Beta Kappa. President of Delta Gamma Sorority (1995). Recipient of Betty Littlejohn Creative Writing Award (1994). Member of Women's Golf Team (1994–95).

Employment Experience
• Sports reporter, *The Athens Herald*, twenty hours per week during the school year. Duties included covering men's and women's tennis and golf and doing football and basketball statistics.

• News intern, *The Atlanta Constitution*, summer 1994. Wrote features, assisted in editing wire copy, wrote cutlines for photographs, learned to do page layout on a Macintosh.

• Lifeguard, Three Trails Camp, Hendersonville, NC, summer 1993. Responsible for the water safety of fifty campers per week, Red Cross safety instruction for counselors, and swimming lessons for campers.

Personal
Willing to relocate to areas in the Northeast and Midwest.
Enjoys Japanese cooking, coaching Little League baseball, and camping.

References
Available upon request

Emphatic Résumé

ALEX L. MUELLER
20 Paris Boulevard
Tacoma, WA 98412
206-433-8857

The experience I gained from establishing and building my catering business have prepared me for an entry-level position as a food service manager.

Food Management Experience
   Began catering business in 1992. With one employee, marketed the service, did the shopping, prepared food, delivered and served receptions, parties, and small luncheons and dinners. Expanded in 1993 to a staff of seven, and in 1994, to twelve. Increased profits thirty percent between 1992 and August 1995, when business was sold.

Additional Business Experience
   Purchasing agent for Applejacks restaurants in Washington and Oregon (1990–92). Responsible for keeping thirty-six restaurants supplied with food and other supplies.

   Grill supervisor for Dante's on the Green in Seattle (1987–90). Duties included overseeing four cooks and sixteen servers for lunch and dinner shifts and managing special luncheons and dinners.

Education
   University of Arizona (1984–86)—B.S. in Hotel and Restaurant Management. (3.1/4.0 GPA)

   Special annual seminars in the summers of 1987, 1989, and 1992 at the Parisian Food Institute in Seattle.

Activities and Interests
   Past President of the Northwest Catering Association (1994) and member of the National Food Management Association. Hobbies include photography, tennis, and horseback riding.

The third paragraph, which, like the first, should be only four or five lines long, should request an interview. Career experts are divided on whether the applicant should offer to call the employer to set up the interview or whether the applicant should simply express willingness to have an interview at the employer's convenience, leaving it to the employer to make the initial contact.

Example of Job Application Letter for an Advertised Job

27 Albert Commons
Tempe, AZ 85281
July 20, 1995

Ms. Jane McMaster
Director of Personnel
Arizona State University
Tempe, AZ 85287

Dear Ms. McMaster:

The advertisement in Sunday's Tempe Sun for a public relations assistant at Arizona State attracted my attention. My education in journalism and my experience as a magazine writer have given me the qualifications to be a strong candidate for the position.

At the University of Missouri, where I earned a B.A. in magazine journalism, I took four courses in public relations. A three-term internship with the hospital in Columbia, Missouri, taught me the fine points of in-house public relations documents and gave me experience in writing news releases and dealing with the press. My enclosed resume will give you fuller details about my qualifications. Public relations work interests me because it offers great variety, and I would especially welcome the opportunity to serve Arizona State with my skills.

My schedule would permit me to be available after noon on weekdays to have an interview at your convenience. This job sounds like the perfect match for my qualifications.

Sincerely,

Andrew Wertheim

Other Employment Letters

Students should be aware that looking for jobs may require letters beyond job application letters. Among the kinds of letters they may need to write are letters requesting recommendations, letters requesting applications, letters thanking a prospective employer for an interview, letters inquiring about the status of an application, letters accepting or declining a job, and letters responding to a rejection letter from a company.

Job-seekers should telephone or write former teachers, current teachers, or former employers and request permission to list them as references on applications or resumes. Such a letter of request should be brief. If requesting that a letter be sent to a potential employer, the writer should give complete information to the person writing the recommendation: to whom it should be sent (complete name, title, and address) and the deadline for receipt of the recommendation. If some time has passed since the writer worked for or was the student of the person being asked for the recommendation, he or she should remind the recommender about the past job or courses when they knew one another. As a courtesy, the writer should say that he or she will let the reader know about the outcome of the application.

Letters requesting applications should specify the exact position for which the application is being requested and the deadline for returning it. Similarly, letters soliciting information about possible openings should make clear the exact kind of job the writer seeks.

Once job-seekers have had an interview, they should write promptly to thank the appropriate personnel for the interview. This brief letter reinforces the job candidate's interest in the job at the same time that it acknowledges the time and energy expended on the interview. It should mention some comments that were made in the interview or allude to something the candidate learned about as a result of the interview. Such a letter should be sent to the primary interviewer, though it should be sent also to anyone who spent a considerable amount of time with the job-seeker. [*The next page shows an example of this type of letter.*]

In some cases a person who has had an interview with a company may not hear immediately about the status of the application. If the applicant has several offers but has not heard about the status of the application at his or her top choice, the applicant should write a letter of inquiry. Such a follow-up letter gives the applicant a chance to share any additional information that might strengthen the application, and it gives the applicant an opportunity to express continued interest in the company.

Example of a Thank You Letter in Response to an Interview

```
                                          23 Melrose Street
                                          Detroit, MI 48215
                                          May 16, 1995

Mr. Joseph Siegel
Director of Public Relations
Greenway, Inc.
6668 Old Town Way
Buffalo, NY 14210

Dear Mr. Siegel:

    Thank you for the many kindnesses shown to me Thursday and Friday
during the interview at Greenway. I thoroughly enjoyed meeting everyone and
seeing the facilities. This close look at the company has intensified my interest
in the position.
    The process you showed me for revamping your news files is similar to one
I worked with as an intern in the PR department of Grice and Johns in Minne-
apolis. Although that system was less complex than the one you have developed,
I believe I could bring to the job some expertise in information retrieval.
    Greenway is a company whose philosophy I admire. I believe my qualifica-
tions make me a strong candidate for the position in Public Relations. If I may
provide additional information about my background or skills, I will be happy to
do so.

                                  Sincerely,


                                  Melissa Dwyer
```

A letter accepting a job should begin with the positive information of the acceptance, ask whatever practical questions may have arisen since the interview, and express enthusiasm about the opportunity. The writer should begin by thanking the firm for the confidence in him or her expressed in the offer. Like other "bad news" letters, a letter turning down a job should briefly give the reasons for declining the offer before it makes the statement of rejection.

When the applicant is turned down by a company—usually in a rejection letter—the applicant should respond. Occasionally, such responses, especially those which show appreciation for the interview process and continued interest in the company, may keep the applicant's file alive for future consideration.

Most students do not understand that companies expend much money and time in the process of hiring. Hiring is expensive. Applicants should always express their appreciation for interviews and for job offers, even those they decline.

Proposals and Reports

Two of the most common kinds of workplace documents are proposals and reports. These documents occur in many kinds of formats and serve many kinds of purposes in the workplace, everything from documenting travel expenses to studying the feasibility of installing a new air-conditioning system in a factory. Both kinds of documents may be extremely brief or extremely long, and they may be either formal or informal, depending on the purpose and audience.

Most students will have had only the most cursory acquaintance with many of these kinds of documents, though teachers can remind students that many of the documents students handle routinely are versions of these workplace documents. For example, students are familiar with agendas and minutes for meetings, and often they have sent school administrators requests for funding or arguments for changes in policies or facilities.

Students usually need to be told that some overlapping occurs with the terms *proposal* and *report*. Proposals are always persuasive: they always argue for some kind of change. Many documents which are called reports are, in fact, proposals. For example, feasibility reports always analyze the need for and potential success of change, but when they go so far as to argue for particular change based on the findings, they become proposals.

Reports may be informative or persuasive. Many routine business documents are informative reports: summaries of articles or speeches, travel reports, inspection reports, instructions, budget reports, procedural reports, and research reports, to name only a few.

Reports and proposals are often classified as formal or informal. These terms have nothing to do with length, and the terms *formal* and *informal* do not refer to the relative difficulty of the material, the tone, or the level of language. Both informal and formal proposals and reports may take the form of letters or memoranda. The major distinction is that a formal report usually is bound and usually contains subordinate documents of various kinds.

Formal Reports

Formal reports may be as brief as five to ten pages or as long as several hundred pages. The defining characteristics of formal reports are the numerous supplementary parts, many of which students will never have seen.

Parts of Formal Reports in the Order of Appearance in the Report

Title page—A page that gives the title of the report, the name of the company requesting the report, the date, the name of the writer of the report, and the company represented by the writer of the report.

Letter or **memo of transmittal**—A communication that accompanies the final report and is addressed to the person designated to receive the report. A letter is used when the report goes to someone outside the writer's firm; a memo is used when the report goes to someone within the firm.

Table of contents—a listing of the page on which each part of the report appears.

List of Figures—a list by title of graphs, charts, and other visual aids and the pages on which they are found.

Abstract or Executive Summary—A one-page summary of the main findings of the report. Abstracts are more technical and are meant for specialized readers; executive summaries are intended for more general managers.

Body—The text of the report, which may be single- or double-spaced.

Conclusions—The findings of the report, often summarized in a numbered list. In informative reports, this is the last part of the report before the appendices and bibliography.

Recommendations—In persuasive reports, this is a list, usually numbered, of actions that should be taken based on the conclusions drawn in the study.

Appendix—Usually titled and lettered consecutively (Appendix A), appendices are used for information which may be of interest to the reader but which would interrupt the focus if it were in the body of the report.

Bibliography—A listing of sources used in the report. These may be classified under such headings as *Primary Sources* and *Secondary Sources*, or they may be combined in a list alphabetized by last name of the author. Bibliographies in workplace writing may use any of the major style sheets but most often they use either the MLA style or the APA style for forms of documentation.

Unlike informal reports, these kinds of reports are often bound like books or have other kinds of special binding. Many companies generate formal reports internally for their own use, but many others hire consultants to analyze conditions or to study the feasibility of projects.

Informal Reports and Proposals

Like formal reports, informal reports may be brief or lengthy. Although they do not include the many parts of a formal report, they may include such parts as conclusions, recommendations, appendices, and a bibliography.

If the informal report or proposal is being sent within the company, it usually has a memorandum heading. If it is being sent outside the company, it may take the form of a letter, or it may have a letter as a cover document.

An informal proposal, like a formal one, has four special parts in the body. The introduction gives the background information necessary for the reader to understand the proposal. The second section is the proposal itself. The third section is the budget, and the fourth section is conclusions, which ties the parts of the document together and discusses negative and positive results of proceeding with the plan as it is discussed in the document.

Example of a Memorandum Proposal

MEMORANDUM

TO:	Letetia Majors, Manager
	Travel Coordinator
FROM:	Ernest Palenz, Director
	Human Resources
DATE:	January 16, 1995
SUBJECT:	Cost of using individual travel agents

During the last six months, my office has received a large number of complaints about the use of company funds for airline tickets at inflated prices. As a result, the vice president for finance asked me to study the problem and make recommendations to you for changing the system.

Background

I recall that last fall you did a study of the procedures now being used by employees to buy tickets for company travel and that you found some waste in the company's allowing individuals to use their personal travel agents to buy tickets for business trips. At the time, you recommended that a more detailed study be undertaken to determine how we might standardize the procedure and save money.

In conjunction with two members of your staff, Pam Williamson and Artie McKnight, I surveyed twenty travel agents in our area, asking about types of discounts available to firms, time restrictions in getting breaks on individual tickets, fees for canceled flights, policies about billing and payment, and special services.

Plan

Based on our study of the twenty travel agents, I propose that we process all airline tickets through your office and that we purchase all tickets through Linden Travel in Spartanburg, the firm which gave us the best rates and promised the most convenient services.

This proposal will necessitate several procedural changes:

1. Employees will need to fill out travel request forms at least six weeks ahead of scheduled travel, and these forms will need to be routed through your office as other travel expense reports are.

2. Employees will need to be flexible about airlines and scheduling, especially those who have short notice about trips.

3. Employees must be prepared to stay over Saturday nights at some destinations so that we can get the best rate on airline tickets (even with additional lodging and meals such tickets are often cheaper).

4. An additional staff position in your office will be needed for processing the requests, ordering tickets, and taking care of payment and other details.

Budget

Although the changes will require some start-up expenses, the program should save the company between 20% and 25%—including these costs—over the next three years. The initial costs include $31,000 for a staff assistant to process forms, $1,000 for the design and printing of 5,000 request forms, and $500 for six training sessions for employees.

Conclusions

Adopting this proposal will have several short-term and long-term implications:

1. Staff will likely resist the program initially, mainly because they are used to dealing with their own travel agents and because they dislike adding more paperwork to their jobs.

2. As we explain the long-term savings to the company that will result, we must let staff know that this savings will be passed on to them in tangible ways.

3. We will need to reevaluate the changes in twelve months, perhaps taking bids from the four or five travel agents we found the most cost effective in this study. As prices fluctuate and travel agents change policies, we may need to change agents.

Headings in Reports

Both formal and informal reports and proposals use headings for separate sections. The major reason for using headings it to make it possible for the reader easily to find the parts he or she wants or needs to read. Rarely is a report or proposal read in its entirety. A busy executive, for example, may read only the executive summary, the budget part of the body, and the conclusions and recommendations.

Students need to understand, however, that headings do not replace transition. They are in addition to all of the kinds of transitional devices good writers use in any kind of writing—repetition of key words, use of transitional words and phrases, use of pronouns, and use of parallelism. In a formal report, the headings may correspond to entries in the table of contents.

The placement and size of headings suggest the relative importance of the information introduced by them. Writers have five levels of headings from which to choose. These levels are similar to the levels in a traditional outline that uses Roman numerals, capital letters, Arabic numerals, small letters, and so on. Here are the kinds of headings, and information about their relative placement:

FIRST DEGREE HEADING

This level can be used for the title of the report and for major sections in a long report. It is all capitals and centered.

Second-Degree Heading

This level is used for major sections in a short report and major subdivisions in a long one. Only the first letters in words are capitalized, and the heading is underlined.

Third-Degree Heading

This kind of heading looks like a second-degree heading, but it begins at the left margin.

Fourth-degree heading. *This heading is on the same line as the sentence it precedes. Only the first word is capitalized, and the heading begins at the left margin.*

Fifth-degree headings *are part of the sentence which they introduce. They begin at the left margin, and only the first word is capitalized.*

Most students will have had little if any experience in using headings, and as a result, they will have some predictable problems. As with outlining, they need to be taught that if a section of a report cannot be divided into at least two sections, it cannot be divided: that is, any heading must always have at least one other at its level. Similarly, as writers work to achieve structural parallelism in topic outlines, they must also make subordinate headings in a given section parallel with one another. In addition, students need to be reminded that headings are not mixtures of sentences and phrases. Most headings in workplace writing are phrases.

Just as students generally dislike outlining, they also resist working to write precise, effective headings. This part of report writing is best left until students have done enough research and writing to have become interested in the project.

In addition to learning about headings, students may also be learning about visual aids, often referred to as graphics, in reports and proposals. Although visuals are used in most lengthy reports and proposals, they also figure prominently in other kinds of workplace writing, especially oral presentations.

Graphics

Graphics is a highly specialized field, and many companies hire large staffs of artists and designers to produce visuals for all kinds of publications and internal documents. In companies which do not have their own visual arts departments and in many which do, employees still need to understand the basic kinds of visuals and their uses for specific kinds of information. With today's computer technology, many writers create their own visuals as they produce documents.

In a speech or a report, visuals should occur just into the relevant discussion. Listeners or readers should have the visual earlier enough to help them understand the specifics being discussed. They are meaningless before the relevant section, and useless afterwards. Their usefulness is aided, of course, if they have precisely descriptive titles.

The four most common kinds of visuals are pie graphs, tables, bar graphs, and line graphs.

Pie graphs show the breakdown of a whole into relative proportions. The largest segment of the pie should begin at the center-top and move in a clockwise position, and the segments should get progressively smaller. Instead of having numerous tiny segments, a small wedge labeled "other" should be used, its components explained in a note.

Pie Graph

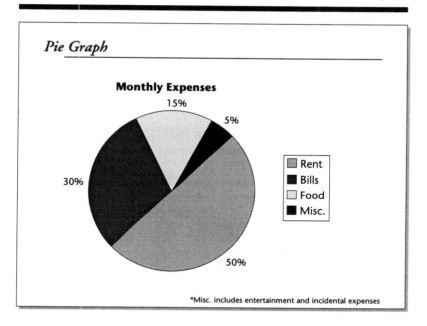

Monthly Expenses

15%

5%

30%

50%

Rent
Bills
Food
Misc.

*Misc. includes entertainment and incidental expenses

A second important kind of visual is a **table**. A grid, the table shows the intersection of two kinds of information, that labeled down the left column and that labeled across the top. It is particularly useful for showing numbers.

Table

Number of Male and Female Students in Each Class Who Have GPA's Over 3.5

Class	Female	Male
Freshmen	175	130
Sophomores	115	129
Juniors	192	187
Seniors	168	177

A **bar graph** is used to compare two or more (but not usually more than four) entities. It may be segmented to show complex similarities and differences.

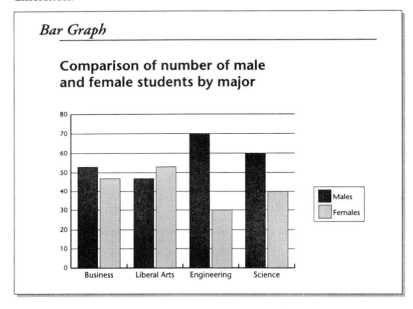

The fourth common kind of visual in workplace writing is a **line graph**. Such a graph shows change over time.

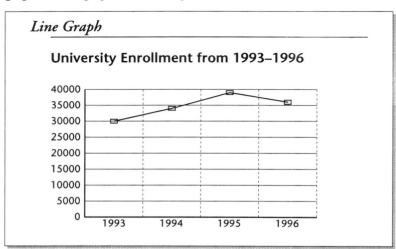

Students usually enjoy creating visuals, and their interest makes it easy for teachers to emphasize the professional appearance of documents and the precision needed to make them accurate and honest.

Activities for Teaching Workplace Writing

In addition to suggestions in other sections of this supplement, teachers may wish to try some of these activities for interesting students in the complexities of workplace writing and for furthering their understanding of it.

Letter-Writing Activities

1. Students enjoy role-playing, and teachers can increase students' enthusiasm for writing by assigning roles in small groups and having them solve problems by writing letters. For example, one student in a group might be a disgruntled parent writing to a teacher to complain about a class policy; another student might be the teacher, who must write both to the parent and to inform his or her principal; the student who takes the role of the principal may need to write to the school board about the continued harassment of teachers by parents, etc. Many such scenarios give effective opportunities for students to practice letter-writing.

2. The teacher might divide the class into groups and have each group represent an organization on the campus writing a persuasive letter for an increased budget to the student activities board which funds such groups.

3. Students can assume roles having to do with employment scenarios. They can practice writing all of the kinds of employment documents they may encounter in trying to find out about jobs, apply for a job, thank someone for an interview, check on the status of their application, etc.

4. They enjoy writing real letters of complaint to companies and organizations and sharing the responses with the class. The responses provide great texts for class discussion of strategy and tone.

Report-Writing Activities

1. To teach students about precision in language, have groups of them draft questionnaires all on the same subject, but a subject they could actually poll the student body at large about. Comparing the ways each group went about the questioning and the differences in tone and precision will teach students a lot about efficiency in language.

2. Ask students to sample a small group of students (twenty or so) about an issue and to analyze their findings. They might to this sampling with a written questionnaire or with an interview.

3. Ask students to request sample formal and informal reports from local companies. Then have them analyze the parts of each report and offer suggestions for improving it.

4. For an original experience with a formal report, ask students to come up with an issue at the school and to investigate it. For this they might use a questionnaire for students, interviews with several key people, primary documents at the school, and secondary reading. With a topic as simple as "The Reasons Students Transfer from State" or "The Campus Security Force: Overcharging for Parking Violations?," students have the opportunity to write everything from a letter of transmittal to conclusions and recommendations. You may wish to require a number of visual aids and an appendix or two.

5. Ask students to design a Public Relations campaign to inform all constituencies of the university that tuition will rise by six percent the following year. They can practice writing letters, proposals, reports, and other kinds of documents.

SUGGESTED READING

Bailey, Edward P., Jr. *The Plain English Approach to Business Writing.* New York: Oxford University Press, 1990.

Blackburn, Elizabeth, and Kelly Belanger. "You-Attitude and Positive Emphasis: Testing Received Wisdom in Business Communication." *The Bulletin of the Association for Business Communication* 56.2 June 1993): 1–9.

Boone, Louis E., David L. Kurtz, and Judy R. Block. *Contemporary Business Communication.* Englewood Cliffs, NJ: Prentice Hall, 1994.

Bracher, Peter. "Process, Pedagogy, and Business Writing." *Journal of Business Communication* 24.1 (Winter 1987): 43–50.

Brusaw, Charles T., Gerald J. Alred, and Walter E. Oliu. *The Business Writer's Handbook.* 4th ed. New York: St. Martin's, 1993.

Crow, Peter. "Plain English: What Counts Besides Readability?" *Journal of Business Communication* 25.1 (Winter 1988): 87–95.

Elliot, Norbert, Margaret Kilduff, and Robert Lynch. "The Assessment of Technical Writing: A Case Study." *Journal of Technical Writing and Communication* 24.2 (Winter 1994): 19–37.

Faigley, Lester, and Thomas P. Miller. "What We Learn From Writing on the Job." *College English* 44 (1982): 557–69.

Frailey, L. E. *Handbook of Business Letters.* 3rd ed. Englewood Cliffs, NJ: Prentice Hall, 1989.

Guffey, Mary Ellen. *Business Communication: Process and Product.* Belmont, CA: Wadsworth, 1994.

Half, Robert. *How to Get a Better Job in This Crazy World.* New York: Plume, 1990.

Hoffman, Marvin. "On Teaching Technical Writing: Creative Language in the Real World." *English Journal* 81.2 (Feb. 1992): 58–64.

Jackson, Tom. *The Perfect Resume.* New York: Doubleday, 1990.

Kennedy, Daniel S. *The Ultimate Sales Letter.* Holbrook, MA: Bob Adams, 1990.

Subramanian, Ram, Robert G. Insley, and Rodney D. Blackwell. "Performance and Readability: A Comparison of the Annual Reports of Profitable and Unprofitable Corporations." *Journal of Business Communication* 30.2 (1993): 49–61.

Tepper, Ron. *How to Write Winning Proposals for Your Company or Client.* New York: John Wiley, 1990.

PART SEVEN

Answer Key for the Simon & Schuster Handbook for Writers 4/e

Answer Key to the Simon & Schuster Handbook for Writers 4/e

■ CHAPTER ONE

Answers: Exercise 1–1

A. Dominant purpose is informative. It meets the criteria.

B. Dominant purpose is persuasive. It meets the criteria.

C. Dominant purpose is persuasive. It meets the criteria.

D. Dominant purpose is informative. It meets the criteria.

E. Dominant purpose is persuasive. It meets the criteria.

Answers: Exercise 1–2

A. Answers will vary. Samples have to come from a single issue of a newspaper. Editorials, essays, letters to the editor, and reviews can serve as examples of writing with the dominant purpose of being persuasive. News reports can serve as examples of informative writing.

B. Answers will vary, as for above.

Answers: Exercise 1–3

For each topic the student should write one paragraph (or more, according to how you have assigned the exercise) with an informative purpose and one paragraph with a persuasive purpose. The student should also be prepared to discuss (orally or in writing, according to your assignment) the differences in the two treatments of the same topic.

Answers: Exercise 1–4

A. (a) The tone is appropriate for academic writing.

(b) The material assumes a specialized reader who would be familiar with words such as *diabetes mellitus, acidosis,* and *bacilli.*

B. (a) The tone is informal and may be inappropriate for academic writing in some courses.

(b) The material does not assume a specialized reader.

C. (a) The tone is appropriate for academic writing.

(b) The material assumes a specialized reader who would be familiar with words such as *microbial, mucus, pedal,* and *gland.*

D. (a) The tone is appropriate for academic writing.

(b) The material assumes a small amount of specialized knowledge, though the gist of the message can be understood from the context. Specialized words include *outages, hot wire,* and *ground.*

    E.   (a) The tone is informal and may be inappropriate for academic writing in some courses.

          (b) The material does not assume a specialized reader.

■ CHAPTER TWO

Answers: Exercise 2–1

1.   The purpose is to inform. Because the assignment is for a biology class, the audience will likely be the instructor and perhaps other students in the class; these people are specialists. The assumption about an audience of specialists is further confirmed by the time limit of twenty minutes, which means that the student has to pack in many technical terms and processes in a short period of time. The special requirements include the twenty-minute time limit and, implied by the wording of the assignment, in-class writing.

2.   The purpose is to persuade. The audience is the general reading public (such as the class instructor and students in the class). The special requirements include a 500- to 700-word limit and a due date of one week.

3.   A student receiving this assignment has many decisions to make. The purpose can be either informative or persuasive, depending on the student's focus on the topic. The audience can be the general reading public or specialists, according to the student's judgment; if the political science course is advanced, chances are that the instructor expects the writing to be addressed to specialists. The only stated special requirement is a length of 1,000 words. The student should ask the instructor when the assignment is due and if the assignment calls for research. The student might also want to set a purpose and audience and check them with the instructor before proceeding, if time permits.

4.   The purpose is to persuade. The audience is readers of the college's student newspaper; they could be considered specialists in that they share the experience of attending the same college, but they are not specialists in technicalities concerning the functioning of college libraries. The special requirements include a 300-word limit, the need to draw on personal experience, and the need to interview a library staff member. The student should ask the instructor when the assignment is due.

5.   The purpose is to inform. Because the assignment is only one paragraph and is for an art class, chances are high that the audience is the course instructor and perhaps other students in the class. An assumption of some specialized knowledge is appropriate (unless the instructor says to write the material for people totally unfamiliar with the topic). The special requirements include the one-paragraph limit and, perhaps implied by the wording of the assignment, in-class writing.

Answers: Exercise 2–2

Answers will vary, but each topic should have an explanation of why it would be suitable for the writing situation described in the exercise.

Answers: Exercise 2–3

Answers will vary, but each topic should have an explanation of why it would be suitable for the writing situation described in the exercise.

Answers: Exercise 2–4

Class discussion will likely reveal disagreement about the main categories and the distribution of items. You can emphasize the role of the individual writer as decision maker. The list might be arranged in this way:

A. *Appeals of advertisement:* Celebrities (as salespeople), self-esteem (appeal to), sex appeal, suitability for readership, status symbols, level of sophistication.

B. *Use of color:* black and white vs. color, stimulates senses.

C. *Language:* amount of writing, connotations of words, intentional misuse of English, witty language, facts, slogans.

D. *Layout:* size of advertisement, placement of objects, product identification, grabs readers' attention, focal point, clarity of design.

NOTE: *Imagination* and *creativity* do not fit because they are part of all these and thus too general.

Answers: Exercise 2–5

Answers to this exercise will vary. The writer should be able to explain the principle that underlies each grouping.

Answers: Exercise 2–6

Each student will come up with a different response, but each one should be encouraged to write as detailed an answer as possible. Here is a sample response for item 2, *watching soap operas*:

who?—housewives, college students of both sexes, an increasing number of males of all ages, unsupervised young children; *what?*—watching soap operas regularly; *where?*—everywhere from office lounges in companies to college dorm rooms and nursing homes; *how?*—some for whole afternoons, some for selective viewing of only one or two shows, some openly, some secretly; *why?*—to escape reality, perhaps, or possibly simply to relax regularly or to keep up with peers' interests

Answers: Exercise 2–7

Answers will vary, but they should look somewhat like the model above Exercise 2–7.

Answers: Exercise 2–8

A. The fourth thesis statement succeeds because it states a main idea (about magazine advertisements' appeal to readers); it reflects a purpose (to persuade); it has a focus (that magazine advertisements must be skillfully done); and it briefly presents subdivisions (language, color, and design). The first and second thesis statements are too general, showing neither a purpose nor a focus. The third thesis statement shows a persuasive purpose but is still too general and has no focus ("must" is not explained).

B. The fourth thesis statement succeeds because it states a main idea (about playing tennis for fun and exercise); it reflects a purpose (to inform); it has a focus (what is required for playing tennis for fun and exercise); and it briefly presents subdivisions (agility, stamina, and strategy). The first statement is too general ("excellent" is a very broad term) and shows no purpose or focus. The second statement is also too vague ("fun" is a very broad term when used without a context) and shows no purpose or focus. The third statement reflects an informative purpose but lacks a focus ("various skills" is too vague).

C. The fourth statement succeeds because it states a main idea (characters in *Hamlet* seek revenge); it reflects a purpose (to inform); it has a focus (all three characters seek revenge); and it briefly states the major subdivisions (Hamlet, Fortinbras, and Laertes). The first statement is much too general, and though it suggests an informative intent, the statement lacks a focus. The second and third statements reflect an informative purpose but lacks a focus ("must" and "want" are vague words here).

D. The fourth statement succeeds because it states a main idea (strong friendships); it reflects a purpose (to persuade); it has a focus (what builds strong friendships); and it briefly states the major subdivisions (sensitivity and communication). The first statement uses vague language ("maintaining" and "work"), and it suggests neither a persuasive nor informative intent. The second statement reflects a persuasive purpose but depends on "good" used in a vague sense. The third statement reflects a persuasive purpose but "value" is too vague to provide a focus.

E. The fourth statement succeeds because it states a main idea (college students voting); it reflects a purpose (to inform); and it has a focus (how these students voted in state primaries and state elections this year compared with the last two years.). The first statement relies on too much vague language ("many," "people," "uninterested"), and it lacks a purpose or focus. The second statement suggests an informative purpose, but it relies on vague language ("dissatisfied" and "political process") and it lacks a focus. The third statement suggests an informative purpose but lacks a focus.

Answers: Exercise 2–9

1. The thesis is good because it reflects the purpose (to persuade), states a main idea, and focuses specifically on logical subdivisions of the topic.

2. The thesis suggests that the concert review will do what such reviews should do: evaluate in an attempt to persuade a reader. The words "was pleasing," however, are too vague; they need to be revised to be more specific. A brief indication of subdivisions might help the thesis communicates its message.

3. The thesis, though specific and focused, does not reflect a careful response to the assignment: the assignment requires an informative report, but this thesis reflects persuasive purpose.

4. This thesis is good because it states a main idea, reflects a purpose (to inform), and includes a focus.

5. This thesis does not address the assignment adequately because it deals only with liberal arts majors (not all of the seniors) and reflects an informative rather than a persuasive purpose, as was required by the assignment.

Answers: Exercise 2–10

Answer may vary from the following:

I. Sources of noise pollution
   A. Large cities
      1. Traffic
      2. Construction work
      3. Airplanes
   B. Workplace
      1. Factory machines
      2. Outdoor construction activities
   C. Leisure-time activities
      1. Stereo headphones
      2. Film soundtracks
      3. Disco music
II. Problems from noise pollution
   A. Damages hearing
   B. Alters moods
   C. Limits learning ability
III. How to reduce noise pollution
   A. Pressure from community groups
   B. Traffic regulations
   C. Pressure on management by workers
   D. Earplugs
   E. Reasonable sound levels

■ CHAPTER THREE

No answers for this chapter.

■ CHAPTER FOUR

Answers: Exercise 4–1

A. The topic sentence is the first sentence.

B. The topic sentence is the last sentence.

C. The topic sentence is the first sentence, and the second sentence is a limiting sentence.

D. The topic sentence is implied. The main idea is that peanuts, while nutritious, are also high in calories.

E. The topic sentence is the first sentence.

Answers: Exercise 4–2

A (paragraph 9). Reasons include learning current knowledge, keeping you learning through life, having a job, being a spouse, a parent, and a member of the community. Examples include job, spouse, parent, and member of the community. Number named is six.

B (paragraph 10). Names include oak, deer, fire fighters. Senses are invoked by sound of crashing oak, sight of flames, "fiery tomb," smoldering in ashes, deer family darting furiously, and the smell (implied) of burning trees.

C (paragraph 11). Examples include colonial Virginians using their cravats as handkerchiefs and people putting their knives in their mouths. Names include the French traveler, distinguished people, people in the theater. Numbers include the dates 1830 and the 19th century. Senses include the noise—chants, jeers, and shouts—made by the audience in the theater.

D (paragraph 12). Reasons include the fact that a package of peanuts provides half the daily protein requirement. Names include peanuts, package, and protein. Numbers include the 3.5-ounce package, 564 calories.

E (paragraph 13). Reasons include cities are the best places for women to find jobs, and the death rate is higher for young men in cities. Example named is the Bronx. Names used are the Bronx, New York State. Numbers include 79 percent, 85 percent, 95 percent, and 47 men for every 53 women.

Answers: Exercise 4–3

Obviously answers will vary considerably, but the main goal is to help students distinguish between generalities and good detail. Perhaps having each student share with the class what he or she considers the best detail in his or her paragraph would help make this point.

Answers: Exercise 4–4

A (paragraph 22). *Pronouns:* her, she. *Deliberate repetition:* Kathy, arms, hands opened, closed. *Parallel structures:* Many parallel clauses, starting with "Her shoulders raised"; open hands reaching out and closed hands bringing back.

B (paragraph 23). *Pronouns:* we, this. *Deliberate repetition:* we. *Parallel structures:* Once set in motion, must remain in motion; we must.

C (paragraph 24). *Pronouns:* they, their, we, our. *Deliberate repetition:* nose first. *Parallel structures:* come nose first, go first; probing, sniffing, exploring.

D (paragraph 25). *Pronouns:* them, they. *Deliberate repetition:* cloud, always, line, layer. *Parallel structures:* always shifting but always orderly, line after line, layer above layer.

E (paragraph 26). *Transitional expressions:* however, also. *Deliberate repetition:* brown bear, grizzlies. *Parallel structures:* Brownies tend to be, grizzlies tend to be.

Answers: Exercise 4–5

A (paragraph 9). *Transitional expressions:* after all, too. *Pronoun:* you. *Parallel structure:* historical, social, cultural; as a parent, as a member of the community.

B (paragraph 10). *Deliberate repetition:* destructive, destruction, destroy. *Parallel structure:* crashes, smolders, darts, lies.

C (paragraph 11). *Pronouns:* our, they. *Transitional expressions:* and, so. *Deliberate repetition:* people.

D (paragraph 12). *Transitional expressions:* but, that same. *Deliberate repetition:* peanuts, contains.

E (paragraph 13). *Transitional expressions:* first, but, second, for example. *Deliberate repetition:* men, women.

Answers: Exercise 4–6

Each paragraph will obviously differ in content, but this exercise should help students see that they need to support general statements with graphic details (developed through RENNS) that are smoothly linked by the techniques of coherence discussed in 4b: transitional expressions, pronouns, repetition, and parallelism.

Answers: Exercise 4–7

Answers to this exercise may vary; alternate versions that can be defended are acceptable.

A. In the original paragraph, the sentences appeared in this order: 3, 2, 4, 1.

B. In the original paragraph, the sentences appeared in this order: 3, 7, 6, 1, 5, 2, 4.

➤

C. In the original paragraph, the sentences appeared in this order: 4, 3, 1, 2.

Answers: Exercise 4–8

Students will likely see more than one arrangement in some of these paragraphs. **Note:** You might also ask students to analyze these paragraphs in light of what was previously discussed in this chapter: topic sentence, words in topic sentences that create focus and control (4a), development with RENNS (4c), and techniques of coherence (4d).

A **(paragraph 33).** Topic sentence last; specific to general.

B **(paragraph 34).** Topic sentence last; problem to solution (and perhaps time).

C **(paragraph 35).** Topic sentence first; general to specific (and perhaps least to most important).

D **(paragraph 36).** Topic sentence first; least to most important.

E **(paragraph 37).** Topic sentence first and repeated last; time (and perhaps general to specific).

Answers: Exercise 4–9

Answers will vary according to how each student conceives of each subject. Comparisons of the methods of arrangement can reveal the multiplicity of available choices.

Answers: Exercise 4–10

Some paragraphs can be interpreted to illustrate more than one pattern. This is a basic list only. **Note:** Exercise 4–13 asks students to analyze these paragraphs for many other features.

A **(paragraph 50).** comparison and contrast—point by point, example

B **(paragraph 51).** description, narration, analysis, example

C **(paragraph 52).** cause and effect, definition, analogy

D **(paragraph 53).** analysis, definition, example

E **(paragraph 54).** narration

F **(paragraph 55).** analogy

G **(paragraph 56).** example, classification

Answers: Exercise 4–11

Each student's paragraph will differ, but they all should have in common a clear use of RENNS and techniques of coherence.

Teaching Tip: Exercise 4–12

One way to help students succeed with this exercise is to talk the through these imaginary essays before they think about the beginnings and endings. A class discussion about what details might support the topics of each paragraph will strengthen students' understanding of the importance of evidence. At the same time, it will give students a fuller concept of the essay on which to base their introductory and concluding paragraphs. When the students write the introductions and conclusions, alert them to the lists of useful devices and of "what to avoid," explained in section 4e.

Answers: Exercise 4–13

1. Topic sentences
   A   (paragraph 50). first sentence
   B   (paragraph 51). first sentence
   C   (paragraph 52). second sentence
   D   (paragraph 53). first sentence
   E   (paragraph 54). last sentence
   F   (paragraph 55). first sentence
   G   (paragraph 56). first sentence

2. RENNS
   A   (paragraph 50). *Reasons:* Hanoi's main market has little to offer. Saigon has rows of "shop-houses." Hanoi has bicycles, while Saigon has motorcycles and a few private cars. *Examples:* The specific products in each market. *Names:* South Vietnam, Hanoi, Saigon, China, Mustangs. *Senses:* The sight of the frogs' legs being chopped off, the sight of dense bicycle traffic.

   B   (paragraph 51). *Examples:* upholstery, Renaissance dining room, figured silk hangings over stained-glass doors, velvet curtains, black pear wood. *Names:* Renaissance dining room, Papa's study, black pear wood. *Senses:* sight of red and black, sight of "dusty glooms," darkness, watching, touching.

   C   (paragraph 52). *Reasons:* felting causes wool to shrink, wool fibers stick together and cannot be pulled apart. *Names:* wool, fiver, yarn, fabric, garment. *Senses:* curly, rough surfaces.

   D   (paragraph 53). *Reasons:* not even grained, not apt to split, take polish well. *Examples:* fruitwoods, cherry, apple, pear, orange, oak, mahogany, walnut, birch, holly, maple. *Senses:* white of holly, almost black of walnut.

   E   (paragraph 54). *Names:* Liverpool public library, middle-aged white women, old car, faded housedress, shapeless cardigan sweater. *Numbers:* forty-five, five.

   F   (paragraph 55). *Reasons:* chopsticks are like the stick shift because they enhance and give ceremony to the act of eating, force the eater to focus on the act. *Names:* chopsticks, stick shift. *Senses:* tactile.

   G   (paragraph 56). *Reasons:* animals hoard because food is not available to them all year around. *Examples:* beavers, honeybees, desert rodents, burying beetles, etc. *Names:* ants, wolves, creatures, goodies, MacGregor's bowerbird, etc.

3. **Techniques of coherence.** In this order, if they appear: transitional expressions *(te)*, pronouns *(p)*, deliberate repetition *(dr)*, and parallel structures *(ps)*.

A **(paragraph 50).** *te:* still; *dr:* Hanoi, Saigon; *ps:* In Saigon there are/in Hanoi, there are.

B **(paragraph 51).** *p:* I; *dr:* red, black; *ps:* red, and black, and warm/ I watched, I touched, I took stock.

C **(paragraph 52).** *te:* but; *p:* their, they.

D **(paragraph 53).** *te:* too, therefore; *p:* they, other kinds; *dr:* hardwoods, apt; *ps:* all verbs in simple present, they are.

E **(paragraph 54).** *te:* by then, moreover; *p:* our, I, we, they, them, their, it; *ps:* I thought and I said.

F **(paragraph 55).** *te:* not to mention, therefore; *p:* they, it; *dr:* they.

G **(paragraph 56).** *te:* for example, still, so; *p:* their, they; *dr:* others; *ps:* creatures / others / still others.

4. **Paragraph arrangement**
   A **(paragraph 50).** general to specific
   B **(paragraph 51).** least to most important
   C **(paragraph 52).** general to specific
   D **(paragraph 53).** general to specific
   E **(paragraph 54).** time, least to most important
   F **(paragraph 55).** general to specific
   G **(paragraph 56).** general to specific

■ CHAPTER FIVE

Answers: Exercise 5–1

1. opinion
2. fact
3. opinion
4. fact
5. fact (it's a dictionary definition)
6. fact
7. fact
8. opinion
9. opinion
10. fact

Answers: Exercise 5–2

Answers may vary somewhat, but here is a fairly complete list of possibilities:

A. **Literal information**
   1. It is the first of February.
   2. "Everyone" (see implied information, below) is talking about starlings.
   3. Starlings came to this country on a passenger liner from Europe.

4. "This country" is the United States (Central Park and New York are mentioned).

5. One hundred starlings were deliberately released in Central Park.

6. From these one hundred are descended the countless millions of starlings today.

7. Edwin Way Teale said, "Their . . . Shakespeare."

8. Eugene Schieffelin was a wealthy New York drug manufacturer.

9. Schieffelin's hobby was introducing into America all the birds mentioned in Shakespeare.

10. The starlings adapted to their new country.

A. **Implied information**

1. "Everyone" is used for effect; the author does not mean each and every person.

2. By saying that the birds came "on a passenger liner" (rather than, for example, "in the cargo hold of a ship") the author begins to alert the reader to expect the unexpected (in this case, that someone wanted to introduce to America all the birds in Shakespeare).

3. Central Park is in New York City. (This is information the author assumes the reader has.)

4. "One man's fancy" are words that suggest that the man had somewhat unusual tastes.

5. The drugs that Schieffelin manufactured were legitimate, not illegal.

6. See item 2 in "Opinions" below.

A. **Opinions**

1. (In Teale's opinion) Schieffelin's hobby was somewhat strange ("curious").

2. (In Dillard's opinion) the starlings adapted too well ("splendidly"); here Dillard assumes that the reader knows that flocks of starlings can be a nuisance and even a danger (e.g., getting into airplane engines).

B. **Literal Information**

1. Gandhi envisaged a constitution and government for an independent India.

2. The constitution was spelled out at the forty-fifth convention of the All-India Congress.

3. The Congress began at Karachi on March 27, 1931.

4. The Congress was a political convention.

5. The Congress was attended by some 350 leaders.

6. The leaders were both men and women.

7. The leaders were just out of jail.

8. The leaders squatted in the heat under a tent in a semicircle at Gandhi's feet.

9. They all worked at spinning wheels.

10. They made up the so-called Subjects Committee, which was selected from the 5,000 delegates.

11. Gandhi wrote most of the resolutions and moved their adoption.

B.   Implied information

1. India was not independent before March 27, 1931.

2. Even though the Congress had met 45 times, India was still not independent.

3. The Congress took more than one day—it only "began" on March 27, 1931.

4. Most of the leaders likely were revolutionaries who had been political prisoners—because all were "just out of jail."

5. The leaders were very dedicated—they were willing to squat in the heat under a tent.

6. The ruling government did not provide the basic amenities for a convention: room in a building, decent ventilation, chairs, tables, and so forth.

7. The leaders' sitting at Gandhi's feet implied how they respected him.

8. Gandhi often worked at a spinning wheel as he spoke.

9. Everyone's spinning implied that they wanted to imitate Gandhi.

10. Five thousand people is too large a group to get policy matters decided.

11. Gandhi dominated the proceedings because everyone respected him so much.

B.   Opinions

1. The author had not seen before—or since—a political convention like this one in achievement and tone.

2. The revolutionary proclamations were "ringing."

3. The leaders were spinning away like children playing with toys as they talked.

4. Gandhi dominated the proceedings.

5. Gandhi wrote and spoke with his customary eloquence and surprising firmness.

Answers: Exercise 5–3

Answers will vary.

Answers: Exercise 5–4

Answers will vary.

Answers: Exercise 5–5

1. *Primary evidence:* The author is describing his own experiences in a first-person narrative. It can be assumed to be reliable since a reliable journal, *National Geographic,* published the account.

2. *Secondary evidence:* The assertions in this paragraph are carefully qualified and seem well substantiated by evidence. The material was published in a reliable science magazine.

3. *Both secondary and primary evidence:* The opening paragraph presents secondary evidence, but the quoted material that follows this paragraph serves to make Schlissel's observations reliable. The second paragraph presents primary evidence—a first-hand account from a diary by Mrs. John Kirkwood.

Answers: Exercise 5–6

1. Invalid. The shirt's being expensive does not mean that it shares other characteristics of faddish clothing.

2. Valid. The conclusion follows logically from the premises.

3. Invalid. Some outstanding literary works have not received a Pulitzer Prize.

4. Invalid. All states do send representatives, but that does not mean that all representatives come from a state.

5. Valid. The argument is valid, although some people may not agree that all risks are frightening.

6. Valid. The conclusion flows logically from the premises.

7. Invalid. The premises do not contain the conclusion. It is impossible to know whether this magazine is part of "most."

8. Invalid. The qualifying word "usually" in the first premise leaves open the possibility that there are science fiction novels that are not violent.

9. Valid. The conclusion is contained in the premises.

10. Invalid. The first premise does not stipulate that all great college basketball teams come from the Midwest (and Georgetown is among universities not in the Midwest that produce great basketball teams).

Answers: Exercise 5–7

1. *False authority.* A movie star is not an authority on the CIA.

2. *Red herring.* The social issue is introduced to divert attention from the real issue—whether or not money should have been spent to rescue the whales.

3. *Irrelevant argument,* or *non sequitur.* A person can be nervous about something and still be very good at it.

4. *Begging the question* or *circular argument.* "Dishonest" is merely a slightly different term for "deceitful."

5. *Argument to the person,* or *ad hominem.* These people are being at-

tacked for materialism, but they are perhaps excellent environ-
mentalists, whose cars and shoes are irrelevant to their environmental stance.

6. *Appeal to ignorance.* Just because no evidence exists for one side of
   the argument does not mean that the other side of the argument
   is valid.

7. *False cause,* or *post hoc ergo propter hoc.* The sequence of events does
   not prove any connection between them.

8. *False analogy.* Analogies are dangerous in argument because they
   equate things that are not the same. Riding a bicycle is much different from learning to run a company, and although the skills for
   riding a bicycle remain the same, those of running a company may
   change with the economy and other pressures so that one could
   "fall" if here or she did not adopt those skills.

9. *Self-contradiction.* Medicare cannot be free if it is paid for.

10. *Either-or.* Reading good literature is not the only way to appreciate
    culture.

■ CHAPTER SIX

Answers: Exercise 6–1

Assertions and thesis statements will vary for this exercise.

■ CHAPTER SEVEN

Answers: Exercise 7–1

1. Not only <u>humans</u>[N] use <u>them</u>.[P]

2. <u>Scientists</u>[N] conduct <u>experiments</u>[N] by placing <u>lobsters</u>[N] on <u>treadmills</u>.[N]

3. <u>Scientists</u>[N] can study (a) <u>lobster</u>[N] when <u>it</u>[P] is fitted with (a) small <u>mask</u>.[N]

4. The <u>lobster</u>[N] may reach <u>speeds</u>[N] up to (a) <u>kilometer</u>[N] (an) <u>hour</u>.[N]

5. Through (the) <u>mask</u>,[N] <u>researchers</u>[N] can monitor (the) <u>heartbeat</u>[N] of
    (the) <u>crustacean</u>[N] <u>that</u>[P] <u>they</u>[P] are studying.

Answers: Exercise 7–2

1. Clement C. Moore <u>wrote</u> the poem for his three daughters.

2. Moore <u>intended</u> it as a private gift, not for publication.

3. He <u>called</u> the poem "An account of a Visit from St. Nicholas."

4. Mysteriously and fortunately, the poem <u>was</u> <u>mailed</u> to a newspaper
    editor.

5. Today we <u>know</u> that poem as "The Night Before Christmas."

Answers: Exercise 7–3

Some students may also underline *a, an,* and *the* as limiting adjectives.

1. determined [adj]; successfully [adv]; three [adj]; very [adv]; old [adj]
2. Eventually [adv]; civic [adj]; closely [adv]; local [adj]; only [adv]; native [adj]; open [adj]
3. second [adj]; carefully [adv]; recycling [adj]; his [adj]; widely [adj]; unusual [adj]
4. New [adj]; gratefully [adv]; this [adj]; where [adv]; discarded [adj]; glass [adj]; aluminum [adj]; mandatory [adj]
5. third [adj]; so [adv]; passionately [adv]; beautiful[adj]; tall [adj]; her [adj]; Texas [adj]; those [adj]; grassy [adj]; popular [adj]

Answers: Exercise 7–4

1. noun [7a]
2. adjective [7e]
3. preposition [7g]
4. verb [7c]
5. preposition [7e]
6. verb [7c]
7. adjective [7e]
8. verbal [7d]
9. adverb [7f]
10. noun [7a]
11. adjective [7e]
12. coordinating conjunction [7h]
13. noun [7a]
14. preposition [7g]
15. verb [7c]
16. adjective [7e]
17. coordinating conjunction [7h]
18. conjunctive adverb [7f]
19. pronoun [7b]
20. noun [77a]
21. verb [7c]
22. subordinating conjunction [7h]
23. correlative conjunctions [7h]
24. adverb [7f]
25. adjective [7e]

Answers: Exercise 7–5

1. Mount Tambora, in present-day Indonesia, / erupted.
2. The eruption / exploded the top 4,000 feet of the mountain.
3. The blast / was heard over 900 miles away.
4. A thick cloud of volcanic ash / circled the globe and reached North America the following summer.
5. The sun / could not penetrate the cloud throughout the entire summer.

Answers: Exercise 7–6

1. Gory scenes on television give some <u>people</u> such a severe <u>fright</u> that they faint.
2. Others are injured when they try <u>ironing</u> or perhaps <u>painting</u> while they give the <u>television screen</u> their full <u>attention</u>.
3. Last month, the survey reports, one person threw a <u>glass</u> at the screen and sprained his <u>wrist</u>.

4. Another person gave her <u>knee</u> a bad <u>twist</u> while dancing along with a music video.

5. Also, an enthusiastic sports fan jumped for joy and banged his <u>head</u> on a chandelier.

Answers: Exercise 7–7

1. hominy [object complement]
2. whole dried corn kernels [subject complement]
3. inexpensive but time-consuming [subject complement]
4. breakfast treat [object complement]
5. delicious [subject complement]

Answers and Coverage: Exercise 7–8

Answers will vary. Here is one set of possibilities.

1. Juliette Low lived in England for a time *and learned* [verb phrase] about Boy Scouting from its founder, Sir Robert Baden-Powell.

2. His sister Agnes Baden-Powell had started a similar organization, *called Girl Guides* [verbal (participial) phrase], for girls.

3. Low returned to Savannah in 1912 *to start the first U.S. Girl Scout troop there* [infinitive phrase].

4. *"Scout" being more suitable to the adventuresome U.S. spirit than "Guide"* [absolute phrase], Low called her organization "Girl Scouts."

5. *The girls' hiking, camping, riding horses, and climbing trees* [noun phrase using gerunds] were activities not considered suitable for young ladies.

6. *Refusing to let anyone tell her that girls were not capable of vigorous activities* [verbal (participial) phrase], Low recruited volunteers and raised money so that the girls could have challenging experiences.

7. *A fact unknown to most of her friends* [prepositional phrase] was that Low had become partially deaf as a young woman.

8. Low made her hearing loss an asset *by asking for help* [prepositional phrase] for the girls but never hearing a refusal [for parallelism with *asking,* the second independent clause has been changed to a gerund phrase].

9. Most people found it impossible to turn her away, *her persistence being a significant factor in the early success of Girl Scouting* [absolute phrase].

10. *With members in the United States, the Virgin Islands, Guam, and Puerto Rico* [prepositional phrase], today Girl Scouts of the U.S.A. serves girls in more than three hundred councils.

Answers: Exercise 7–9

1. *Although Sao Miguel's Furnas volcano erupted thousands of years ago* [adv], the collapsed mountain top formed a lake bed *that is still hot* [adj].

2. The ground around Lake Furnas acts as a natural oven *because its temperature is more than 200° Fahrenheit* [adv].

3. To prepare the famous stew, *which is called* cozido [adj], cooks assemble chicken, beef, sausage, and vegetables in a pan.
4. *After the pan is tied in a cloth bag* [adv], it is buried in the hole.
5. The *cozido* simmers for about six hours, a cooking time *that brings it to tasty perfection* [adj].

Answers: Exercise 7–10

1. Most U.S. military personnel who overheard the unintelligible messages thought that they were some strange Japanese code. (One elliptical possibility is *Most U.S. military personnel who overheard the unintelligible messages thought them some strange Japanese code,* with *thought them* replacing *thought that they were.*)
2. When the Japanese were listening in, they could not understand the messages either. (One elliptical possibility is *The Japanese listening in could not understand the messages either.*)
3. A few members of the U.S. forces, Navajo speakers, understood what the messages said. (The elliptical phrase *Navajo speakers* omits *who were.*)
4. The overheard messages were in a code based on the Navajo language.
5. After Navajo Marines were specially recruited for this assignment, only they sent and received these messages. (One elliptical version is *Only Navajo Marines specially recruited for this assignment sent and received these messages.*)
6. Since the messages conveyed meaning by tone of voice as well as vocabulary, decoding techniques using only written words could not break the code.
7. If any Navajos were living in Japan, they never explained the mystery of the messages.
8. Because Navajo is an extraordinarily complex language, the Japanese were never able to break the code.
9. The Navajo code talkers conveyed important messages that affected the key battles of Saipan, Guadalcanal, and Iwo Jima.
10. Even though the Navajo were asked to avoid publicity after the war in case the code was needed again, ultimately, their achievement was widely recognized.

Answers: Exercise 7–11

1.	simple	
2.	compound	
3.	complex	
4.	compound-complex	
5.	complex	
6.	simple	
7.	compound	
8.	compound	
9.	complex	
10.	compound-complex	

■ CHAPTER EIGHT

Answers: Exercise 8–1

1. Green figures appear
2. This character represents
3. These fertility symbols take
4. any sign of spring triggers; a festival that emphasizes
5. people who have...are said; a green giant adorns

Answers: Exercise 8–2

1. contained
2. believed; occurred
3. feared; contributed
4. pointed; released; acted
5. absorbed; warmed

Answers: Exercise 8–3

1. rose; saw; crept
2. sprang; caught; ate
3. stole; stood
4. grew; bent; drank
5. laid; swam; lay
6. wore; grew; left; flew
7. saw; came; sat; took; did
8. found; caught; brought; fed
9. shrank; led; sought
10. broke; burst; fell; swept

Answers: Exercise 8–4

The following answers create the only possible set. Although both *can* and *will* would be correct in item 3, only *can* is correct in item 4. (Used in item 4, *will* creates a tense-sequence error.)

1. was
2. would
3. will
4. can
5. have

Answers: Exercise 8–5

This exercise has many possible sets of answers. Only item 4 is invariable and only by default. Its answer must be *do* because *do* cannot be used in any other item, Here is one set of answers.

1. will [*should* is acceptable, suggesting speculation; *will* is more definite]
2. must [*should* is acceptable, suggesting possibility; *can* is acceptable but less appropriate than *must* or *should*]
3. should [*will* is acceptable, suggesting certainty; *should* is acceptable, suggesting possibility; although both *can* and *must* are grammatically acceptable, they suggest a fervent stance that is less appropriate in tone than the other choices]
4. do [only item where *do* is correct]
5. can [*should* is acceptable, suggesting possibility; although *must* is gram-

matically correct, its suggestions of either demand or resignation are inappropriate in tone; *will* is grammatically correct but the singular subject is logically inappropriate for a predictive general statement—compare *Salespeople will expect...*]

Answers and Coverage: Exercise 8–6

1. laying [third person plural past progressive of *lay*]
2. lie [simple form of *lie* with modal auxiliary verb *could*]
3. lay [third person singular past tense of *lie*]
4. lying [third person singular past progressive of *lie*]
5. lay [third person plural past tense of *lie*]

Answers and Coverage: Exercise 8–7

1. discovered [past tense for completed action; 8g]
2. was emitting [past progressive for a continuing past action in the past concurrent with the time of *were astounded*; 8j]
3. use [simple present for regularly recurring action];
   stands for, means [simple present for general truth; 8h]
4. have found [present perfect for action complete and condition still prevailing; 8i]
5. agree [simple present for general truth];
   contradict [simple present for recurring action; 8h]
6. believes [simple present for current action];
   consist [simple present for general truth; 8h]
7. say; generates; release [simple present for regularly recurring actions; 8h]
8. assert; develop [simple present for regularly recurring actions; 8h];
   have predicted [present perfect for action completed but condition still in effect; 8i]
9. conduct; bring; occurs [simple present for regularly occurring general truths; 8h]
10. understood [simple present for general truth; 8h]; will not discover [simple future for condition not yet experienced; 8g]

Answers and Coverage: Exercise 8–8

1. was born [dependent clause past tense for completed action];
   live [independent clause present tense for happening now];
   tours [present tense for regularly occurring action]
2. will have been [independent clause future perfect tense for action completed by a specified time]
3. began [dependent clause past tense]
4. became [dependent clause simple past for completed action];
   plays [independent clause simple present for regularly occurring action]

5. continues [independent clause simple present];
   take [dependent clause simple present for same-time action]

6. know [dependent clause simple present for general truth];
   has made [independent clause present perfect for action
   completed but condition still in effect]

7. was traveling [independent clause in simple past for action
   completed in the past]; filmed [dependent clause in past
   progressive for ongoing action completed in the past]

8. became; studied [independent and dependent clauses in simple
   past for actions completed in the past]

9. fell asleep . . . was [dependent clause simple past for
   completed past action]

10. failed [dependent clause simple past for completed past action]

Answers: Exercise 8–9

1. As research studies *showed,* regular exercise *boosted* oxygen in the
   blood and *increased* physical endurance.

2. Another effect of exercise *is* that it *causes* the body to produce substances linked to feelings of well-being.

3. People who exercise regularly for several months sometimes find
   that exercise *can make* them more creative because it *helps* (or *can
   help*) them to think clearly and concentrate well.

4. After several months, exercisers also *will have* a better sense of their
   own capabilities and *will exhibit* signs of greater self-esteem.

5. Because effective exercise *requires* that a person make and observe
   a consistent routine, regular exercisers *become* efficient time managers.

Answers and Coverage: Exercise 8–10

1. were [8m–1]   4. be [8m–3]
2. were [8m–1]   5. continue [8m–3]; were [8m–2]
3. suspend [8m–3]; be [8m–4]

Answers and Coverage: Exercise 8–11

1. *Passive, change to active:* A farmer chose a coffin in the shape of a
   green onion.

2. *Active, change to passive:* A hunter was buried by his family in a
   wooden coffin shaped like a leopard.

3. *Passive, change to active:* The friends and relatives of a dead chief
   carried his body through his fishing village in a large, pink, wooden
   replica of a fish.

4. *Active, change to passive:* About ten coffins a year can be turned out
   by woodcarver Paa Joe.

5. *Passive, change to active:* Although museums display a few of these
   fantasy coffins, most of them end up buried in the ground.

■ CHAPTER NINE

Answers and Coverage: Exercise 9–1

1. we [subjective case]
2. Al and me [objective case after preposition *for*]
3. him and me [objective case after *for*]
4. We [subjective case]
5. me [objective case compound direct object]
6. him and me [objective case after preposition *between*]
7. we [subjective case]
8. us [objective case after preposition *to*]
9. I [subjective case, inverted word order]
10. him and me [objective case after *for*]
11. us [objective case after *between*]
12. me [objective case following *versus,* a preposition]

Answers and Coverage: Exercise 9–2

1. I [subjective case, 9a]
2. me [objective case, 9b]; we [subjective case, 9e]; you and her [objective case, 9b]
3. her [objective case, 9b]; me [objective case, 9b]
4. us [objective case, 9b]
5. she [subjective case, 9d]; me [objective case, 9b]

Answers and Coverage: Exercise 9–3

1. whoever [subjective case]
2. whoever [subjective case]
3. whomever [objective case]
4. who [subjective case]
5. whom [objective case]
6. who [subjective case]

Answers and Coverage: Exercise 9–4

1. he [subjective case in elliptical *as the careers that he and his friend Steve Jobs have had;* 9f]
2. their [possessive case before gerund; 9h]
3. them [objective case for object of infinitive *to get;* 9g]
4. they [subjective case as subject of elliptical clause *than they are;* 9f]
5. its [possessive case before gerund *creating;* 9h]
6. their [possessive case before gerund *leaving;* 9h]
7. them [objective case for object of infinitive *to interest;* 9g]
8. him [objective case for object of infinitive *to want;* 9g]
   [Note that in this sentence, *conceptualizing, designing,* and *engineering* are functioning as participial modifiers rather than as gerunds, see 9h]
9. its [possessive case before gerund *repeating;* 9h]

■ CHAPTER TEN

Answers: Exercise 10–1

Answers may vary somewhat. Some students may think that some of the pronouns replaced here with nouns are acceptable, but clarity is the issue—avoiding intervening information that distracts the reader, ambiguous references, and so on. Possible answers follow.

At the time Ludwig was crowned king, Wagner had gone into hiding to escape his many creditors. Ludwig sent his secretary to find Wagner and offer him the protection that only a royal patron could provide. The secretary delivered this message, telling Wagner to go at once to the royal court at Munich, where all his debts would be paid; moreover, Ludwig would provide him with everything he needed so that he could continue his composing free of material cares.

Thus began an intense friendship. Wagner enjoyed Ludwig's company, playing hard with him but also working hard. He spent Ludwig's money freely—too freely, many Bavarians believed. When he began to try to influence Bavarian politics, the people became restless.

Finally, Ludwig's advisors told him to choose between this friendship and his royal obligations. Regretfully, he chose to honor his responsibilities as king and told Wagner to leave the court. Ludwig's devotion continued, however, until Wagner's death. Ludwig himself met a bizarre end. Declared insane and force to give up the monarchy, he was found drowned. The mystery of his death—murder, suicide, accident—was never solved.

Answers: Exercise 10–2

Answers will vary somewhat. Here is one set of possibilities.

1. Scientific evidence supports lovers who claim that they feel swept away. [10c–1; revision changes referent for *they* from the possessive case, *lovers'*, to *lovers,* a noun in the objective case]

2. A person who falls in love is flooded with substances that the body manufactures. *Or:* When people fall in love, they are flooded with substances that their body manufactures. [10e; revision changes person from *you* not used for direct address to third person.]

3. Surprisingly, love owes its "natural high" to phenylethylamine (PEA), a chemical cousin to the amphetamines, as well as to emotion. [10c–4, 10d; revision eliminates overuse and imprecise use of *it* and *its.*]

4. As the body builds up a tolerance for PEA, more and more must be produced to create the euphoria of romantic love. [10c–3; revision eliminates two *its* with different referents.]

5. Although chocolate is high in PEA, gobbling it will not revive a wilting love affair. [10e; revision eliminates *your* not used for direct address.]

6. Infatuation based on PEA lasts no longer than four years. Most divorces take place after four years of marriage. [10c–3; revision eliminates imprecise use of *this.*]

7. Chemicals called endorphins are good news for romantics. Endorphins promote long-term intimate attachments. [10c–4; revision removes *they*, which seemed to refer to both *endorphins* and *romantics*.]

8. Endorphins' special effects on lovers allow these drugs to exert a soothing, not an exciting, influence. [10c–1; revision eliminates *they*, which referred to a passive noun.]

9. Oxytocin is called the "cuddle chemical" because it seems to encourage mothers to nuzzle their babies. [10d; revision eliminates second *it*; excessive use of *it*.]

10. Romantic love also owes a debt to oxytocin, for this drug promotes similar feelings in adult lovers. [10c–3; revision removes imprecise uses of *this* and *it*.]

Answers and Coverage: Exercise 10–3

Note: Reserving *that* for restrictive clauses and *which* for nonrestrictive clauses when the relative pronoun's referent is a thing (rather than a person) is a useful distinction. Because it is an often-ignored distinction, item 1 and the second part of item 4 show both *that* and *which* as acceptable. (Nonrestrictive relative clauses that have inanimate or nonhuman referents use *which*.)

1. that [restrictive reference to *power*, a thing; *which* is also acceptable]
2. which [nonrestrictive reference to *word lunatic*, a thing]
3. which [nonrestrictive reference to *moon*, a thing]
4. who [reference to *nurses*, people; restrictive];
   that [restrictive reference to *moon*; a thing; *which* is also acceptable]
5. which [nonrestrictive reference to *groups*, a thing];
   who [restrictive reference to *those*, which refers to *people*]

■ CHAPTER ELEVEN

Answers: Exercise 11–1

Answers will vary. Each set of sentences must use the subject once as a singular and once as a plural, and the verbs must agree accordingly.

Answers and Coverage: Exercise 11–2

1. are [expletive; 11f]
2. believe [not only . . . but also; 11e]
3. asks [either . . . or; 11e]
4. comes [inverted order; 11f]
5. is [expletive; 11f]

Answers and Coverage: Exercise 11–3

1. work [*one of . . . who;* 11j]
2. understands [*management*—collective noun meant as a single unit; 11h]
3. is [linking verb agrees with subject *part,* not with subject complement *hours;* 11i]
4. admire [*who* refers to collective noun *team* acting as individuals; 11j]; say [indefinite pronoun *some* meant as plural in context; 11g]
5. is [*All it takes to succeed at home* singular subject; 11g; also, verb agrees with singular subject, not with compound complement; 11i]

Answers and Coverage: Exercise 11–4

1. is [*one of the* construction; 11d]
2. was [singular subject; 11a]
3. are [words in inverted order; 11f];
   enter [agrees with antecedent of *whom publishers;* 11j]
4. is [singular verb with specific amount subject; 11k]
5. includes [singular subject in plural form; 11k]
6. seem [plural subject; 11b]
7. comes [singular verb with *each;* 11g]
8. are [inverted order; 11f]
9. believes [singular-context collective noun; 11h];
   cover [ignoring intervening words; 11c]
10. remains [agreeing with subject *bestseller,* not subject complement *cards;* 11f]

Answers and Coverage: Exercise 11–5

1. *it* seems [11m]; *its* bearers [11m]
2. to empower *himself or herself* [11g]
3. *they* must [11n]
4. . . . leader . . . into *his or her* [11q]
5. *He or she* inspires [11q]; *their* [11m] dream
6. Not all leaders . . . *their* [11m]
7. . . . leaders . . . *their* [11m]
8. . . . a number of major corporations offer *their* own [11m]
9. others that *their* [11m]; *he or she* is proposing
10. order to *their* [11m]; *his or her* life [11q]; perform *their* [11m]

■ CHAPTER TWELVE

Answers: Exercise 12-1

1.   A rapidly growing group
     (ADV ADJ)

    now takes television programming seriously
     (ADV   ADJ   ADV)

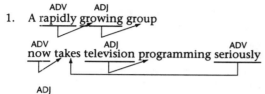

2.   These Investigators
     (ADJ)

    dramatically influences . . . our lives
     (ADV   ADJ)

    from political campaigns to breakfast foods
     (ADJ   ADJ)

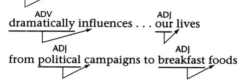

3.   Most Americans usually spend
     (ADJ   ADV)

    many years . . . printed language
     (ADJ   ADJ)

    practically no time
     (ADV ADJ)

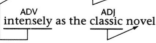

4.   Now college students can take
     (ADV ADJ)

    newly created courses in television studies.
     (ADV   ADJ   ADJ)

    analyze the situation comedy
     (ADJ)

    intensely as the classic novel
     (ADV   ADJ)

5.   better "texts"
     (ADJ)

    closely studying
     (ADV)

Answers and Coverage: Exercise 12–2

1. aggressive [12a, adjective modifies noun *bats*]; frequently [12b, adverb modifies verb *handle*]; extremely [12b, adverb modifies adjective *shy*]; gentle [12a, adjective modifies pronoun *them*]
2. bad [12d, adjective after linking verb *feel*]; ever [12c, avoid double negative with *don't*]
3. actually, greedily [adverbs modify verb *eat*]; good [12d, adjective after linking verb *feel*]
4. widely [12b, adverb modifies adjective *varying*]; terrifying [12a, adjective modifies noun *wingspan*]
5. bright [12d, adjective after linking verb *are*]

Answers: Exercise 12–3

Sentences called for in the second part of the instructions will vary. Here is the chart filled in.

Positive	Comparative	Superlative
little	littler	littlest
greedy	greedier	greediest
complete	more complete	most complete
gladly	more gladly	most gladly
few	fewer	fewest
thick	thicker	thickest
some	more	most

Answers and Coverage: Exercise 12–4

1. most likely [12e, correct superlatives]
2. many [12e, positive form; nothing is being compared]; ever [12c, avoid double negative]
3. fewer [12e, countable items use *fewer*, not *less*]
4. highly [12b, adverb used to modify adjective]; regularly [12b, adverb used to modify verb]
5. well [12d, adverb modifies verb *was paid*]; good [adjective modifies noun *time*]

■ CHAPTER THIRTEEN

Answers and Coverage: Exercise 13–1

Two pieces of information are given for each item: the reason for the sentence fragment and the number of the question in the "Test for Sentence Completeness" that explains what has caused each sentence fragment. (Exercise 13–3 asks students to correct the sentence fragments in this exercise.)

1. No verb (*unwrapping* is a verbal); question 1
2. Starts with the subordinating word *which;* questions 2 and 3
3. No subject; question 2
4. Complete sentence
5. Starts with a subordinating word and lacks independent clause to complete thought; question 3
6. No verb; question 2
7. No subject; question 2
8. Complete sentence
9. Starts with a subordinating word but lacks and independent clause to complete the thought; question 3
10. No subject; question 2

Answers and Coverage: Exercise 13–2

Answers will vary. Here is one set of possible responses.

1. Kwanzaa was created in 1966 by Maulana Karenga, an African American teacher who wanted to teach people about their African heritage. [dependent (relative) clause attached to independent clause]
2. The word *Kwanzaa* comes from the Swahili phrase *ya kwanza,* which means "first." [dependent (relative) clause attached to independent clause]
3. Kwanzaa allows African Americans to honor the history of black people. [subordinating conjunction dropped from dependent (adverb) clause]
4. Correct complete sentence
5. Although Christmas and Hanukkah are religious holidays, Kwanzaa is a cultural holiday. [subordinating phrase linked to independent clause]
6. The festival, which lasts seven days, celebrates seven principles that are called the *nguzo saba* in Swahili. [dependent (relative) clause attached to independent clause]
7. The seven principles are unity, self-determination, collective responsibility, cooperative economics, purpose, creativity, and faith. [relative pronoun dropped from dependent (relative) clause]

Answers and Coverage: Exercise 13–3

Answers will vary. Added or altered words are italicized. Here is one set of possibilities.

1. Researchers *unwrapped* [verbal changes to verb] the mummy containing the carefully preserved body of a woman in an ancient tomb.
2. *The body* [subordinating word *which* dropped, noun supplied] had been wound in twenty layers of silk.
3. *She* [pronoun supplied] turned out to be a Chinese aristocrat named Lady Dai.

4. *She* [subordinating conjunction *when* dropped] died around 168 B.C.
5. Correct complete sentence
6. & 7. combined to create correct complete sentence
8. Correct complete sentence
9. Jade was also believed to preserve bodies. [subordinating conjunction *because* dropped]
10. *Her body* [noun supplied] had decayed, unlike Lady Dai's.

Answers: Exercise 13–4

Answers will vary. Here is one possible revision.

The technological accomplishments of the first Americans are overlooked by modern textbooks on the history of science and have often been underestimated. One example is the great earthen mounds constructed by the Adena Mound Builders along the shores of the Mississippi River and its tributaries in the United States. More than 100,000 of such temple, burial, and dwelling sites are left today, as reflected in the names of such modern towns as Moundville, Missouri; Mound City, South Dakota; Mound Bayou, Mississippi, and Mound Valley, Kansas. In addition, as many as 30,000 people may have lived in Cahokia, an ancient urban complex of mounds and house sites located on the eastern bank of the Mississippi across from the present city of St. Louis. The average mound involved some three million hours of human labor to transport the same amount of earth as forty mile-long freight trains could carry. All this earth was moved without wheelbarrows, because the wheel was unknown to the early American cultures. The great mound at Cahokia is not as high as the pyramid of the Pharaoh Cheops in Egypt, but it is much larger at its base, representing a greater achievement than the Egyptian pyramid.

Coverage: Exercise 13–4

(1) correct complete sentence; (2) predicate with coordinating conjunction; (3) verbal phrase (present participle); (4) verbal phrase (past participle); (5) dependent clause with subordinating conjunction; (6) complete sentence; (7) prepositional phrase; (8) verbal phrase (present participle); (9) verbal phrase (infinitive); (10) predicate; (11) dependent clause with subordinating conjunction; (12) correct complete sentence; (13) verbal phrase (present participle)

Answers: Exercise 13–5

Answers will vary. Here is one set of possibilities.

Some of the most magnificent Easter eggs in the world were created by Peter Carl Fabergé, a master Russian goldsmith. In 1884, Czar Alexander III wanted a special Easter gift for his wife, the Czarina. Although Fabergé's first Imperial Easter egg appeared to be an ordinary hen's egg, the outer shell, made of gold, had been enameled to the off-white color of a hen's egg. It [or *The shell*] opened to reveal a yolk, also of gold, which contained a tiny chicken, elaborately crafted of several shades of gold. Hidden inside the chicken was a surprise, [or *:*] an intricate jeweled model of the imperial crown, which opened to reveal a tiny ruby egg. Because the Czar was so delighted, he commissioned Fabergé to create a new egg each Easter and gave the goldsmith one other instruction. The Czar told Fabergé to include a surprise in each egg, which, of course, Fabergé wisely did.

Coverage: Exercise 13–5

(1) phrase with no verb; (2) verbal phrase (past participle); (3) appositive; (4) verbal phrase (present participle); (5) dependent clause with subordinating conjunction; (6) verbal phrase (past participle); (7) verbal phrase (present participle); (8) complete sentence; (9) appositive; (10) dependent clause with relative pronoun; (11) dependent clause with subordinating conjunction; (12) complete sentence; (13) compound predicate; (14) appositive (infinitive phrase); (15) dependent clause with relative pronoun

Answers: Exercise 13–6

Answers will vary. Here is one set of possibilities.

Students looking for jobs need more than the "Help Wanted" section of a newspaper. One major tool is a carefully written résumé. A résumé should be written in a standard form (see Chapter 39) and proofread carefully to eliminate errors in spelling, punctuation, or grammar. For the content of the résumé students should analyze all types of experiences. A résumé can include not only paid jobs but also volunteer positions and extracurricular activities. Students have a better chance of getting a job if they have supervised other people, handled money, or taken on highly responsible tasks such as participating in political campaigns or chairing major committees at school. Many employers will consider student résumés, especially when the résumés include names of the students' supervisors.

Coverage: Exercise 13–6

(1) complete sentence; (2) appositive; (3) complete sentence; (4) second half of compound predicate with no subject; (5) prepositional phrase; (6) complete sentence; (7) dependent (noun) clause; (8) complete sentence; (9) dependent clause with subordinating conjunction; (10) dependent (adverb) clause; (11) complete sentence; (12) dependent (adverb) clause

■ CHAPTER FOURTEEN

Answers and Coverage: Exercise 14–1

The correction strategies will vary. Here is one set of possibilities:

1. Urban veterinarians report that summer in New York City can be hard on pets; however, [14c; comma splice corrected by using semicolon and comma (cause 2)] cats suffer less than other animals.

2. Many pets accidentally fall from open twenty-story windows. [14b; fused sentence corrected by using a period (cause 3)] Cats are the most common victims along with dogs, rabbits, iguanas, and turtles.

3. A research paper reports an amazing finding. [14b; comma splice caused by explanation corrected by using a period (cause 3)] Cats that fall five to nine stories suffer worse injuries than cats that fall much farther.

4. The average falling cat reaches maximum speed at five stories. [14c; fused sentence corrected by using a comma and a coordinating conjunction (cause 2)] Then after nine stories, the cat manages to get into a position that cushions the impact of landing.

5. A Manhattan cat has set a new record for surviving a high-rise fall. [14b; fused sentence corrected by using a period (cause 1)] It dropped forty-six stories from a midtown apartment balcony and landed unharmed in a café awning below.

Answers and Coverage: Exercise 14–2

(1) Correct complete sentence (2) The Internet connects thousands of on-line computer networks around the world, and [fused sentence caused by pronoun corrected by comma and coordinating conjunction *and*] it has created a new form of personal communication that requires new rules. (3) Correct complete sentence (4) Sometimes the faceless communication gives timid on-liners confidence to speak their minds. However, other times some users have less pleasant experiences. [comma splice corrected by a period] (5) A flame, for example, is an insulting message that is [fused sentence corrected by relative pronoun *that* to make final clause dependent] the on-line equivalent of a poison pen letter. (6) The quick response time of electronic mail encourages hasty people to react hastily, and [fused sentence corrected by adding coordinating conjunction *and*] instant anger can be thoughtlessly expressed. (7) Flamers cannot always be identified because [comma splice caused by explanation corrected by adding subordinating conjunction *because*] their real names are concealed by passwords. (8) Another prank is to impersonate another user by adopting his or her on-line name. As a result, [comma splice corrected by using a period] there is no way to identify the person sending a fake message. (9) Internet lurkers, who [fused sentence caused by pronoun corrected by adding relative pronoun *who*] read other people's messages in the public spaces but are too fearful of being flamed to send their own messages, are undesirable too.

Answers and Coverage: Exercise 14–3

1. Lovecraft wrote vividly of monsters from beyond space and time; however, [fused sentence: conjunctive adverb] he insisted that he did not believe in the supernatural.

2. "The Shadow over Innsmouth" is Lovecraft's famous tale about the strange inhabitants of a New England port; specifically, [comma splice: transitional expression] they are part fish and part human.

3. Correct complete sentence.

4. Many of Lovecraft's stories mention a sinister volume of secret lore called the *Necronomicon*; however, it [comma splice: conjunctive adverb] was entirely a product of his imagination.

5. No such book exists. [fused sentence: conjunctive adverb] Nevertheless, U.S. libraries still receive call slips for the *Necronomicon* filled out by gullible Lovecraft readers.

Answers and Coverage: Exercise 14–4

Answers will vary. Here is one set of revisions.

1. Ostriches are said to bury their heads in the sand so that their enemies will not notice them, but this, naturalists maintain, is a myth. [14c, fused sentence corrected with comma and coordinating conjunction]

2. A South African naturalist who examined eighty years of records from ostrich farms where over 200,000 of the birds were reared found that no one reported a single case of an ostrich burying its head, or even attempting to do so. [14d, comma splice corrected by creating dependent clause beginning with relative pronoun *who*]

3. Ostriches do listen intently for chirps, cries, and approaching footsteps with their heads near the ground; sometimes, they even lower their heads just to rest their neck muscles. [14b, fused sentence corrected with semicolon]

4. Correct complete sentence.

5. They never bury their heads in sand, and they would probably suffocate if they did. [14c, comma splice corrected with coordinating conjunction]

Answers: Exercise 14–5

Answers will vary. Here is one possible revision.

(1) During the nineteenth century, a number of fearless women traveled long distances from their homes. They visited places far more exotic than their native France or England. (2) Isabella Bird, for example, a British clergyman's daughter, began traveling and writing when she was in her forties; she often wrote by the light of a portable oil lamp and with a gun in her pocket. (3) In 1896, she celebrated her sixty-fourth birthday, and that same year she crossed northwest China hoping to reach Tibet. (4) While she was traveling, her guides collapsed with fever.

Then her rice supply grew dangerously low. (5) Only when tribal warfare broke out, however, and the bridges were torn down did she turn around. (6) Like Isabella Bird, Flora Transtan, a native of France, proved her adventurous spirit when she sailed from France to Peru, a trip that inspired her to write a book. (7) The book was published in 1838; however, its title, *Peregrinations of a Pariah*, meaning "travels of an outcast," suggests that not everyone admired its courageous author.

Coverage: Exercise 14–5

(1) comma splice with pronoun; (2) comma splice with pronoun; (3) fused sentence with pronoun; comma splice with pronoun; (4) comma splice with conjunctive adverb; (5) correct; (6) comma splice with pronoun; (7) comma splice with conjunctive adverb.

Answers and Coverage: Exercise 14–6

Answers will vary. Here is one possible revision.

(1) Archaeologists are studying modern Australia to learn how humans lived on this planet thousands of years ago because many customs of the Stone Age are still practiced by some Australian Aborigines today. [14d; fused sentence with second clause explaining first] (2) Correct complete sentence (3) Lorblanchet watched the Aboriginal painters work. These artists [14d; comma splice with second clause explaining first] create dramatic images by spitting red ocher paint on sandstone walls in caves. (4) The artists put a mixture of red ocher and water in their mouths; as a result [14e; comma splice with transitional expression] saliva becomes the third ingredient, which gives the paint the right consistency so that it adheres to the wall. (5) To create the mixture, they chew for several minutes, and [14c; fused sentence with second clause amplifying first] their lips and teeth turn brick-red. (6) Correct complete sentence (7) The imprint of an artist's hand is unique; indeed, [14e; fused sentence with transitional expression] it acts as an identifying marker. (8) Spit-painting is spiritually significant [14d; fused sentence with pronoun beginning second clause]; it is an act that unites painter and painting. (9) Spit, which [14d; comma splice with pronoun] is the product of human breath, is believed to imprint images of the artist's soul on the cave wall. (10) Similar hand prints were found in an 18,000-year-old cave painting in France; therefore, [14c, fused sentence with conjunctive adverb] Lorblanchet believes they were painted the same way.

■ CHAPTER FIFTEEN

Answers and Coverage: Exercise 15–1

Answers may vary somewhat because of the alternate ways to eliminate shifts in person and number.

(1) According to some experts, snobbery is measured by mental attitude, not extent of worldly goods [15a–1, reserve *you* for direct address]. (2) Because *they are* unsure of *their* social position, snobs are driven by what others think of them [15a–1, shift in number]. (3) *Snobs* tend to be too dependent on buying status symbols to define *their* place in the world, and *they* look down on others [15a–1, shift in person, shift in number]. (4) Correct sentence (5) When commoners were first admitted to Cambridge University in the 1700s, *all students* were required to identify *their* social position [15a–1, shift in number]. (6) The *commoners* had to use the Latin words *sine nobilitate*, meaning "without nobility" [15a–1, shift in number]. (7) Eventually, the students shortened this phrase to "s.nob," and the word came to signify *a person* aspiring to a higher social level [15a–1, shift in number, must agree with "*s.nob.*"].

Answers and Coverage: Exercise 15–2

Answers will vary. Here is one set of possibilities.

1. The Victorian male's custom of tipping his hat had serious drawbacks, though; for instance, if he was carrying parcels he would have to set them down first. [15a–1, shift in person]
2. In 1896, an inventor named James Boyle developed a self-tipping hat that solved the problem. [15a–3, shift in tense]
3. If a man nodded while wearing Boyle's invention, he activated a lifting mechanism concealed in the hat's crown. [15a–1, shift in number]
4. Boyle claimed that since the novelty of the moving hat would attract attention, it also could be used for advertising. [15a–2, shift in subject and voice]
5. He said that companies could place signs on the hats and that they would be able to advertise any product innovatively and inexpensively. [15a–4, indirect-direct discourse shift]

Answers: Exercise 15–3

(1) The robots of today can perform many more tasks than their earlier counterparts. (2) Twenty years ago, robots remained stationary and welded car bodies or lifted heavy steel bars. (3) Today's robots, on the other hand, perform work that includes cleaning offices, guarding hotel rooms, and inspecting automobiles. (4) At California's Memorial Medical Center of Long Beach, a doctor has performed brain surgery using a robot arm that allows her [or him] to drill into a person's skull and reach the brain more accurately. (5) A robot recently joined the police force in Dallas, and it forced a suspect into surrendering. (6) When the robot

broke a window, the suspect shouted "Help!" and asked, "What is that?" (7) Many people do not realize that service robots often prepare their fast food or sort the packages they bring to the post office. (8) In the near future, robots selling for about $20,000 will work without human assistance, and robots costing $50,000 will do household chores.

Coverage: Exercise 15–3

1. 15a–1, number
2. 15a–1, number between sentences 1 and 2;
   15a–1, number within the sentence
3. 15a–1, number between sentences 1 and 3; 15a–3, tense;
   15a–1, number within the sentence
4. 15a–1, number within the sentence; 15a–1, person
5. 15a–2, voice
6. 15a–4, indirect/direct discourse
7. 15a–1, person, 15a–3, tense
8. 15a–2, voice; 15a–1, number

Answers and Coverage: Exercise 15–4

Answers may vary somewhat. The final result must avoid all shifts.

1. *For many centuries*, the Ramah people of the Navajo nation had made this land their home [15b–3, interrupted verb phrase].
2. *Shortly after they arrived*, the Mormons established a small cemetery on a knoll surrounded by farms and ranchland [15b–2, wrong placement].
3. They were not the *only* ones to make use of this graveyard [15b–1, ambiguous placement].
4. *Even though their beliefs and practices differed strikingly from those of the Mormons*, the Navajo began burying their own dead there, too [15b–3, interruption of subject and verb].
5. Correct sentence
6. The Mormon graves, *grouped according to family relationships*, have headstones in a wide variety of folk art and commercially manufactured styles [15b–2, wrong placement (phrase modifies *graves*, not *headstones*].
7. *Painstakingly engraved* Mormon headstones display floral designs and representations of Mormon temples in Salt Lake City and elsewhere [15b–1, squinting modifier].
8. *In contrast*, the Navajo graves have simple metal markers and are not arranged by family relationship [15b–3, awkward placement].
9. *To speed the soul on its journey*, the Navajo bury valuable turquoise jewelry with their dead [15b–3, interruption of subject and verb].
10. *In all*, the little cemetery now contains about 71 Navajo graves and 209 Mormon graves [15b–3, awkward placement].

Answers and Coverage: Exercise 15–5

1. (a) To become / an entertainment lawyer, / the student / studied / corporate and copyright law / intensively.

   (b) The student / studied / corporate and copyright law / intensively / to become / an entertainment lawyer.

   (c) To become / an entertainment lawyer, / the student / intensively / studied / corporate and copyright law.

2. (a) The matchmaker / happily / introduced the / wrestler / to the / muscular artist.

   (b) The matchmaker / happily / introduced the / muscular artist / to the / wrestler.

   (c) Happily, / the matchmaker / introduced the / wrestler / to the / muscular artist.

   (d) Happily, / the matchmaker / introduced the / muscular artist / to the / wrestler.

   (e) The matchmaker / introduced the / wrestler / to the / muscular artist / happily.

   (f) The matchmaker / introduced the / muscular artist / to the / wrestler / happily.

3. (a) The computer hacker used / only / one simple password / to break into / the company files.

   (b) Only / the computer hacker used / one simple password / to break into / the company files.

   (c) To break into / the company files, / the computer hacker used / only / one simple password.

   (d) To break into / the company files, / only / the computer hacker used / one simple password.

4. (a) Not just / pediatricians/ know/ that / children/ need / love.

   (b) Pediatricians / know/ that / not just / children / need / love.

   (c) Pediatricians / know / that / children / need / not just / love.

   (d) Pediatricians / know / not just / that / children / need / love.

5. (a) As a rule, / bus drivers / have more patience / than the average citizen.

   (b) Bus drivers, / as a rule, / have more patience / than the average citizen.

   (c) Bus drivers / have more patience, / as a rule, / than the average citizen.

   (d) Bus drivers / have more patience / than the average citizen, / as a rule.

Answers and Coverage: Exercise 15–6

Answers may vary somewhat. Here is one set of possibilities.

1. To be successful, the student journalist must plan carefully. [dangling infinitive]
2. Being tense, an inexperienced journalist might begin on the wrong note. [dangling participle]
3. Until relaxed, the student journalist should mention only neutral topics. [unexpressed subject]
4. Correct
5. With a list of questions, the interviewer can make the process go more smoothly for everyone involved. [unexpressed subject]
6. A hostile interviewee sometimes answers factual questions incorrectly, although they are easy to answer. [unnecessary passive voice]
7. By being analytic and evaluative, an experienced journalist can learn a great deal from those mistakes. [dangling participle]
8. Knowing how to pace an interview, a journalist will more likely get honest answers to hard questions after he or she has caught the interviewee off guard. [unexpressed subject]
9. Correct
10. Essential information might be revealed when the journalist is leaving. [unexpressed subject]

Answers and Coverage: Exercise 15–7

Answers will vary. Here is one set of possibilities.

1. The Cold War between the United States and Russia motivated some 200,000 American families to construct backyard bomb shelters stocked with canned food, bottled water, batteries, and board games. [15d–1, mixed grammatical construction]
2. A frenzy of bomb shelter building took place because President John F. Kennedy warned people that they might need to make individual preparations against nuclear attack during the Berlin Wall crisis in 1961. [15d–2, faulty predication with *reason is . . . because*]
3. A few enterprising souls always make money during periods of panic, and shelter peddlers swarmed to cash in on fears of imminent mass destruction. [15d–2, faulty predication with *is where*]
4. Correct sentence
5. The purpose of a bomb shelter was to protect people underground for at least ninety days until, presumably, the air was free of radioactivity. [15d–2, faulty predication]
6. Spending their two-week honeymoon in a bomb shelter won nationwide publicity for a Miami couple. [15d–1, mixed construction]
7. The couple declared they had spent the entire two weeks playing cards, and suddenly the public lost interest. [15d–1, mixed construction]

8. One debate concerned whether a family safely locked in its bomb shelter could refuse to admit desperate neighbors. [15d–2, faulty predication]

9. In the late 1960s is when fear of the Cold War faded and bomb shelters were turned into wine cellars, mushroom gardens, or sites for teenage parties. [15d–2, faulty predication with *is when*]

10. A solid steel "shelter for four" was dug up in Fort Wayne, Indiana, and is now on exhibit at the Smithsonian National Museum of American History in Washington, D.C. [15d–1, mixed construction with *the fact that*]

Answers and Coverage: Exercise 15–8

Answers may vary somewhat. One set of possibilities is the following.

(1) Engineering students use innovative thinking to solve difficult problems as much as they use [15e–2, ambiguous comparison] theoretical knowledge. (2) One group of students at the University of California at Berkeley received a challenging assignment. [15e–3, small words omitted] (3) They had to create a package that would allow an egg to be dropped as much as, [15e–2, incomplete comparison] but not more than, eighty feet on to [15e–3, small word omitted] cement without breaking. (4) This complex problem was considered and possible solutions were [15e–1, incorrect elliptical] analyzed by fourth-year chemical engineering student Carla St. Laurent. (5) She gave so much thought to her professor's challenge that she came up with the winning solution. [15e–3, 15e–2, small word omitted, incomplete comparison] (6) She created a mother hen made of papier-maché that kept safe the egg dropped from a fourth-floor window. [15e–3, small words omitted]

Answers and Coverage: Exercise 15–ESL

1. In colleges and universities, where economists are common, they [15esl–1, missing pronoun subject] can teach and do research.

2. In government, there [15esl–2, missing expletive] are career opportunities as forecasters, statisticians, and even presidential advisors.

3. Harvard economist Jeffrey Sachs is an advisor to the new Russian government; he [15esl–1, missing pronoun subject] is advising on how to restructure the Russian economy.

4. Economists are applauded or ignored when the economy is strong; they [15esl–1, missing pronoun subject] are criticized when it [15esl–1, missing pronoun subject] is weak.

5. Businesses hire economics majors, too; there [15esl–2, missing expletive] is an up-to-date list of job opportunities for economists on file in the placement office.

■ CHAPTER SIXTEEN

Answers and Coverage: Exercise 16–1

Answers will vary. Here is one set of possibilities.

1. Evidence suggests that the only difference between creative people and the rest of us is that they are always poised to capture the new ideas we might not catch right away. [16a–1, unnecessary expletives; 16a–5, using pronouns]

2. Creative thinking involves seizing opportunities, staying alert, seeking challenges, and pushing boundaries. [16a–4, using stronger verbs]

3. Because the goal is to catch the idea first and evaluate it later, the alert person captures a fleeting thought by writing it down at once without worrying about its eventual value. [16a–2, unnecessary passive; 16a–5, using pronouns; 16a–3, reducing phrases]

4. An important part of creativity is daydreaming, which allows thoughts to bubble up spontaneously and surprise us with their freshness. [16a–1, unnecessary expletive; 16a–3, reducing clauses]

5. We can sometimes unlock our creativity by trying something different, such as turning pictures sideways or upside down to see them in new ways or molding clay while thinking about a difficult writing problem. [16a–2, unnecessary passive; 16a–3, reducing clauses to phrases and phrases to words; 16a–1, unnecessary expletive]

6. Robert Epstein stresses that many exciting advances in fields from astrophysics to car design to dance combine creative ideas from widely different sources. [16a–2, unnecessary passive; 16a–3, reducing clauses]

7. Epstein assigned his students the problem of retrieving a Ping-Pong ball at the sealed bottom of a vertical drainpipe. [16a–4, using strong verbs and avoiding nouns formed from verbs; 16a–3, reducing phrases to words and clauses to phrases]

8. Epstein gave the students tools that were too short to reach the ball or too wide to fit into the pipe. [16a–3, reducing phrases]

9. Stumped at first, the students tried unsuccessfully to capture the ball with the tools before stepping back from the immediate situation, seeing the big picture, and thinking creatively. [16a–3, reducing clauses to phrases and reducing phrases to words]

10. The students poured water down the drainpipe and the ball floated to the top, where they retrieved it. [16a–2, unnecessary passive; 16a–4, strong verbs; 16a–5, using pronouns]

Answers: Exercise 16–2

Answers will vary. Here is one set of possibilities.

(1) <u>As a matter of fact</u>, <u>it seems like</u> a great many folk beliefs that are popular are, <u>in a very real sense</u>, dead wrong. (2) For example, the Ameri-

can Academy of Ophthalmology <u>makes the statement that</u> reading in the dark will not <u>have the effect of</u> ruining a person's eyes. (3) <u>In the case of</u> spicy foods, specialists have proven that foods <u>of this sort</u> are not <u>necessarily</u> bad for the stomach, even for people who have been treated as ulcer patients. (4) What about our mothers' warning <u>that exists</u> about catching colds when we are <u>in the process of</u> becoming chilled?

(5) <u>It is certainly quite true</u> that more people <u>have a tendency</u> to get sick in winter than <u>people do</u> in summer. (6) <u>It seems that</u> lower temperatures are not <u>the blame factor,</u> however. (7) <u>In view of the fact</u> that cold weather often <u>has a tendency</u> to drive people indoors and to bring people together inside, <u>this factor has the appearance</u> of increasing our odds of infecting one another. (8) Finally, <u>there has been</u> a long-standing tradition <u>that states</u> that the full moon <u>has the effect on people</u> of making them crazy. (9) Investigations <u>that were made</u> by researchers <u>who were</u> tireless and careful <u>came to the ultimate conclusion</u> that <u>there is</u> no such relationship <u>in existence</u>.

Answers: Exercise 16–3

Answers will vary. Here is one set of possibilities.

(1) Now is the time to interview <u>and talk to each and every</u> family elder about the events <u>and happenings</u> of their lives. (2) <u>The reason for</u> the urgency <u>is because</u> the aging process of growing older can interrupt our dialogue with elderly relatives faster and more rapidly than we <u>could or should be able to</u> imagine. (3) <u>To give just one example,</u> in the 1980s, Ellen Miller, a woman in her forties, <u>started to begin</u> audiotaping her mother's <u>memories and reminiscences</u> of Berlin during <u>the era of</u> the early 1900s. (4) Before Miller <u>could have the chance</u> to videotape some sessions, however, Alzheimer's disease had robbed her mother of speech and memory. (5) <u>Upon her mother's death at the age of eighty-eight years,</u> Miller sat down, <u>listened again,</u> and heard once more the familiar gentle voice telling <u>stories and tales</u> of <u>far-off days on another continent</u> that vividly evoked those times. (6) <u>Then and there</u> Miller decided <u>on the spot</u> to make a film that would <u>bring together</u> these audiotapes combined with family photographs, her own narration, and her mother's favorite Beethoven piano sonata. (7) Ellen Miller advises those who want to <u>capture and preserve</u> their family history on tape to bring family heirlooms and photographs when the recording sessions <u>are being held</u>. (8) The interviewer should ask questions that are <u>specific and particular and not vague,</u> and <u>the interviewer</u> should keep his or her own comments to a minimum.

Answers and Coverage: Exercise 16–ESL

1. A car-repair shop in my neighborhood [*it* deleted] does good work.
2. I decided that was where I should go [*there* deleted] for an estimate.
3. The mechanic who looked at the damage [*he* deleted] asked how the accident had happened.

➤

4. The tires, which had almost no tread left, [*they* deleted] could not grip the icy pavement.

5. The car, which the mechanic said [*it* deleted] needed new tires as well as new doors, [*it* deleted] will be ready next week.

■ CHAPTER SEVENTEEN

Answers and Coverage: Exercise 17–1

Answers will vary somewhat. Here is one set of possibilities.

1. In 1994, a bill was signed by the California legislature that eliminated laws regulating elaborate hood ornaments for cars, dropped laws against horse and donkey mating, and repealed dozens of other ancient regulations. [17d–2, overused]

2. Some of the laws date back to Old West days, and one of these was the prohibition on dueling. [17d–1, illogical]

3. Correct

4. Another old law, dealing with the capture and possession of frogs used in jumping contests, was not repealed. Why then is it staying on the books? [17d–2, overused]

5. Calaveras County fair officials were upset and pleaded with state lawmakers to let the law stand, for in his story "The Celebrated Jumping Frog of Calaveras County," Mark Twain made the contest famous more than a century ago. The event still draws huge crowds every year. [17d–2, overused]

Answers: Exercise 17–2

Answers will vary somewhat. Students have to choose ideas best given to effective compounding. They are to choose which ideas seem to have equal weight and could therefore be contained in compound sentences. Their final version should have no more than two compound sentences—all other sentences should be left as they are.

Kudzu is the Asian vine that is choking out other vegetation in the Southern United States. It can grow a foot a day, <u>and</u> it can cover a car in a few weeks. Kudzu seems to have no redeeming qualities whatsoever, <u>but</u> a few clever people have come up with commercial uses. The following are some of their suggestions. The Kudzu Cafe in Atlanta serves Kudzu leaves in salads. A teacher at Georgia Tech University has his students make paper from Kudzu. Craftspeople make baskets and sculptures from the vine. Finally, when hamsters in laboratories are made chemically dependent on alcohol, Kudzu has been found to help control their addiction. Maybe what is good for hamsters will work for humans some day.

Answers: Exercise 17–3

Answers will vary. Here is one set of possibilities.

1a. Although sandals are worn primarily to protect the sole of the foot, they are also worn for comfort and style.

1b. Whereas they are also worn for comfort and style, sandals are worn primarily to protect the sole of the foot.

2a. After ornamentation was added to sandals worn by ancient peoples, footwear became a stylish article of clothing.

2b. When footwear became a stylish article of clothing, ornamentation was added to sandals worn by ancient people.

3a. Although sandalmakers were constrained by certain requirements in ancient Egyptian society, they had to cater to their clients' fashion whims.

3b. Because they had to cater to their clients' fashion whims, sandalmakers were constrained by certain requirements in ancient Egyptian society.

4a. For example, when the nobility demanded sandals with turned-up toes, peasants were expected to wear sandals with rounded or pointed toes.

4b. For example, whereas peasants were expected to wear sandals with rounded or pointed toes, the nobility demanded sandals with turned-up toes.

5a. As clothing had to be made from available materials, ancient Egyptian sandals were made of leather, woven palm leaves, or papyrus stalks.

5b. Clothing had to be made from available materials, so ancient Egyptian sandals were made of leather, woven palm leaves, or papyrus stalks.

Answers: Exercise 17–4

You may find that having students compare and discuss the differences in emphasis between the *a* and *b* answers to each item helps them clarify their understanding of the differences.

1a. Cornell was a textiles salesperson *who* explored the junk shops and secondhand bookstores of Manhattan between business appointments.

1b. Cornell, *who* was a textiles salesperson, explored the junk shops and secondhand bookstores of Manhattan between business appointments.

2a. Old books, records, prints, and bits of trash *that* became the raw material for his unique collages and boxes fascinated Cornell.

2b. Old books, records, prints, and bits of trash *that* fascinated Cornell became the raw material for his unique collages and boxes.

➤

3a. In 1931, a gallery owner named Julius Levy, *who* included Cornell's collages in an exhibition of surrealist art, encouraged Cornell to keep producing his art.

3b. In 1931, a gallery owner named Julius Levy, *who* encouraged Cornell to keep producing his art, included Cornell's collages in an exhibition of surrealist art.

4a. Cornell's boxes, *which* won international acclaim, often contained the same kinds of objects, such as brass rings and foreign postage stamps.

4b. Cornell's boxes, *which* often contained the same kinds of objects such as brass rings and foreign postage stamps, won international acclaim.

5a. Cornell, *who* rarely left his home in New York, and never ventured outside the United States, was deeply influenced by European art.

5b. Cornell, *who* was deeply influenced by European art, rarely left his home in New York and never ventured outside the United States.

Answers and Coverage: Exercise 17–5

Each sentence contains illogical and overused subordination. Answers will vary considerably. Here is one possibility.

Because too many young ape mothers in zoos were rejecting or abusing their infants, zoo keepers decided to stop their usual practice of separating mother and infant from the rest of the ape community. This practice was done so that the infant would supposedly be safe from harm from other apes. In the new arrangement, group settings were established that included older, experienced, loving ape mothers, as well as other infants and young mothers. The abusive mothers could learn from good role models how to love and care for their infants, and each mother would have childrearing support from the equivalent of aunts and cousins. The experiment was successful. When some pediatricians, who are doctors who specialize in child care, tried a similar program for abusive human mothers, it worked well even though the human mothers took far longer than the ape mothers to learn and use good mothering techniques.

Answers: Exercise 17–6

Answers will vary. Here is one set of possibilities.

1. Owl pellets are the latest teaching tool in biology classrooms around the country because they provide an alternative to dissecting frogs and other animals.

2. Inside the pellets are the remains of the owl's nightly meal, which include beautifully cleaned hummingbird skulls, rat skeletons, and lots of bird feathers.

3. The owl pellet market has been cornered by companies in New York, California, and Washington that distribute pellets to thousands of biology classrooms all over the world.
4. Company workers scour barns and the ground under trees where owls nest to pick up the pellets, which retail for $1 each.
5. The owl pellet business may have a short future because the rural areas of the United States are vanishing. Old barns are being bulldozed. When all the barns are torn down, the owls will be gone, too.

Answers: Exercise 17–7

Students use a topic of their own to imitate the styles of three different examples shown in this chapter. Imitation has a proud tradition as a learning tool. The classic rhetoricians said that versatility in style came from (1) a study of principles, (2) practice in writing, and (3) imitation of the practice of others. For a modern interpretation of classical rhetoric, see Edward P. J. Corbett. *Classical Rhetoric for the Modern Student* (New York: Oxford UP, 1971), especially pp. 416k and 496–538.

Answers: Exercise 17–8

Answers may vary. Here are two possibilities that students might enjoy comparing with their own.

1. Few people have ever seen a manatee because only about 2,000 of these seagoing mammals, known as dugongs in the South Pacific, are left in the world. Smaller than sea lions and bigger than seals, manatees bear an uncanny resemblance to humans, and they are thought to be the source of sailors' mermaid legends. Researchers are trying to preserve and protect the dying manatee population in every way they can. Divers at the Sea World amusement park in Florida rescued one manatee female they named Fathom. Severely injured, possibly from a boat's propeller, and unable to float or breathe properly, Fathom would have died in the wild. At Sea World, Fathom was given a tailor-made wet suit, and she recovered nicely.

2. Only about 2,000 manatees are left in the world, and few people have ever seen one of these seagoing mammals. Known as dugongs in the South Pacific, manatees are smaller than sea lions and bigger than seals. Because manatees bear an uncanny resemblance to humans, they are thought to be the source of sailors' mermaid legends. Researchers are trying to preserve and protect the dying manatee population in every way they can. When divers at the Sea World amusement park in Florida rescued one manatee female they named Fathom, she was severely injured, possibly from a boat's propeller. Unable to float or breathe properly, she would have died in the wild. Fathom was given a tailor-made wet suit at Sea World, where she recovered nicely.

■ CHAPTER EIGHTEEN

Answers: Exercise 18–1

Elements of parallelism in Parker's passage not shown in boldface are: *Repetitions:* you, me, I dirty (dirt), pity, onions, mattress(es), urine (privy, "accidents"), long, it, shovels. *Paired words:* with / with. *Imperatives (mild commands):* Listen, Put, hear. *Contrasts:* pity and understanding, with / without. *Words in a series:* my dirty, worn-out, ill-fitting shoes; smell of urine, sour milk, and spoiling food.

Answers: Exercise 18–2

Students use topics of their own to imitate the parallel style of three of the passages shown in this chapter: by Didion, Viorst, King, Kennedy, or Parker. Style imitation has a proud tradition as a learning tool. The classical rhetoricians said that versatility in style came from (1) a study of principles, (2) practice in writing, and (3) imitation of the practice of others. For a modern interpretation of classical rhetoric, see Edward P. J. Corbett. *Classical Rhetoric for the Modern Student* (New York: Oxford UP, 1971), especially pp. 416k and 496–538.

Answers and Coverage: Exercise 18–3

Answers will vary. Here is one set of possibilities.

1. According to psychologist Harry Levinson, the five main types of bad boss are *the workaholic, the bully, the bad communicator, the jellyfish,* and the *perfectionist.* [18b, words]

2. *To get ahead, to keep their self-respect, and simply to survive,* wise employees handle problem bosses with a variety of strategies. [18c, phrases]

3. To cope with a bad-tempered employer, workers can both *stand up for themselves* and *reason with a bullying boss.* [18d–2, correlative conjunctions]

4. Often bad bosses communicate poorly or fail to calculate the impact of their personality on others; *good bosses listen carefully and are sensitive to others' responses.* [18f, parallel sentence structures]

5. Employees *who take the trouble to understand what makes their boss tick, who engage in some self-analysis, and who stay flexible* [18e, repeating parallel function words] are better prepared to cope with a difficult job environment than employees *who suffer in silence.* [18d–3, parallel form with *than*]

Answers and Coverage: Exercise 18–4

1. A bulldog glares at pedestrians from the door of a fancy apartment building, *a pair of magnificent lions guards* the Fifth Avenue entrance to the New York Public Library, *and a couple of thoughtful pelicans*

perched high on a rooftop regard the passing parade of life. [18f, parallelism among sentences]

2. These architectural animals were made not only of stone, *but also of terra cotta, metal, and other more unusual materials.* [18d-2, parallelism with correlative conjunction *not only*]

3. A group of stone animal lovers is cataloguing New York City's stone zoo *that stretches across five boroughs and that includes* such rare specimens as quahogs, crocodiles, and vultures. [18e, repeating function words]

4. Once, the stone animals were thought to provide protection by warding off evil spirits; today, they provide decoration. [18f, balanced sentences]

5. Some of the New York City's stone animals are puzzling, such as a monkey holding a camera on one Victorian-style building, a *fish smiling on the front of a restaurant, and a squirrel chewing a nut on a doctor's office door.* [18c, clauses]

Answers and Coverage: Exercise 18-5

Reducing Traffic Fatalities

I. Passing stricter speed laws
   A. Making 50 m.p.h. top speed on any highway
   B. Raising fine for first-time speeding offenders
   C. Requiring jail sentences for repeat offenders

II. Legislating installation and use of safety devices
   A. Requiring all automobiles to have safety belts in front and back seats
   B. Making seat belt use mandatory for all drivers
   C. Forcing auto manufacturers to offer airbags as an option in all cars

Answers: Exercise 18-6

Answers will vary. See the answer to Exercise 18-2 for commentary on imitation as a learning device.

■ CHAPTER NINETEEN

Answers: Exercise 19-1

In this exercise, the first item has too many short sentences, the second too many compounds, the third long and complicated sentences. Students will revise in various ways. Here is one set of possibilities.

1. Secondhand jeans have become international status symbols as a new generation of teenagers embraces U. S. pop culture. The entrepreneurs are ready. West of the Mississippi River a thriving underground industry has emerged that buys, washes, and repairs

vintage Levi's. The jeans are resold in many countries, with Japan providing the largest market.

2. United States rock-and roll clothes from the 1960s are also popular throughout the world. So are used Air Jordan sneakers from the 1980s. However, the big winner is still blue jeans. The most popular brand is the Levi's 501, made by Levi Strauss & Company since 1873. The Levi's 501 button-fly style, which is no longer made, is the biggest winner of them all. Most used button-fly Levi's are found in the western U.S. People who lived in the eastern states with long, cold winters have always preferred the zipper fly that doesn't let in chilly air.

3. Even though the business is highly profitable, the cultural history of old clothes hooks most dealers. Some can tell fascinating tales of their collecting adventures. One dealer spent a week buying clothes of the Great Depression from a woman in Oklahoma whose mother had saved the family wardrobe. The clothes clearly showed the economic hardships they had endured. All the jeans were covered with patches; one pair alone had more than a hundred.

Answers: Exercise 19–2

Answers may vary. Ask students to explain their choices. Here is one set of possibilities.

1. Easy Jet, a multi-race winner, was sold for thirty million dollars. That is more than the average combined yearly income of a town of 2,000 people!

2. What might the popularity of horse racing suggest about the American national character? We may be a nation of gamblers. On the other hand, we simply may want financial independence.

3. Tradition holds that no race horse can have a name that contains more than eighteen letters. Apostrophes, hyphens, and spaces count in the total! Longer names would take up too much room on written records.

4. Lotteries have become as popular as horse racing. Many states run lotteries to raise money for basic services earlier provided from taxes. Did you know that in many states school books are purchased with funds gambled on lottery tickets?

5. Some television commercials for lotteries show winners riding in limousines. Most lottery ticket holders lose, though. That tempting chance to win a million dollars has odds worse than a million to one!

Answers and Coverage: Exercise 19–3

Students are to expand each sentence by adding (a) an adjective, (b) an adverb, (c) a prepositional phrase, (d) a participial phrase, (e) an absolute phrase, (f) an adverb clause, and (g) an adjective clause. They can refer for guidance to the expansion techniques shown in Chart 104. Here is a possible set of answers for item 1:

a. We went to the *county* fair.
b. We went *happily* to the fair.
c. We went to the fair *in the park*.
d. *Tired of studying*, we went to the fair, *looking for a good time*.
e. *Textbooks left open on our desks*, we went to the fair.
f. *After we finished studying*, we went to the fair.
g. We went to the fair, *which had just opened.*

Answers and Coverage: Exercise 19–4

1. *According to the 1771 edition of the Encyclopedia Britannica* [phrase], these early writing implements were made of boar bristles, the hair of camels, badgers, and squirrels, and the down feathers of swans.
2. Graphite, a form of the element carbon, was to become the *main* [word] component of pencil lead.
3. *In the late 1600s* [phrase], cabinetmakers were producing the first version of the modern pencil by encasing strips of graphite in wood.
4. *Following the sandwich-making principle,* [phrase] they sliced a strip of wood, cut a groove down the middle, glued the lead into the groove, then glued the two halves together.
5. At one time the ingredients of a fine pencil came from the geographically diverse areas of Siberia, *where the purest graphite was mined* [clause] and Florida, *where the best red cedar was grown.* [clause]
6. When an acute shortage of Southern red cedar developed in the United States during the early 1900s, *desperate* [word] pencil manu facturers bought old cedar fence posts.
7. The pencil makers had to substitute another kind of cedar, *so they dyed and perfumed it to match people's expectations of how a pencil should look and smell.* [clause]
8. Pencils have had some unlikely promoters, such as the naturalist and writer Henry David Thoreau, *who helped his father produce the highest-quality pencils in America during the 1840s.* [clause]
9. The inventor Thomas Edison engaged a pencil factory to produce specially made stubby pencils just for him *because he preferred short pencils.* [clause]
10. *Lacking a pencil,* [phrase] the Scottish poet Robert Burns once used his diamond ring to scratch verses on a windowpane.

Answers and Coverage: Exercise 19–5

Answers will vary. One possible revision is shown here.

One of civilization's great technological innovations, [19e, sentence converted into appositive to modify] the chimney represents a major step up from a hole in the roof or a slit in the wall. *In the warm climates of ancient Egypt and Mesopotamia* [19e–2, modifiers positioned for effect] the heating of houses was not an urgent problem. *So scholars believed* [19e–2, positioning modifiers for effect, with *this* changed to *so*] until a *4000-year-old palace that was peppered with chimneys* was uncovered during a recent excavation of the great lost city of Mari on the upper Euphrates River in ancient Persia. [19b–2, short sentences combined] Along came the Romans two thousand years later. [19f, inverting standard word order] The Romans, *who were* [19b–2, sentence converted into relative clause] engineering geniuses, developed elaborate chimneys as part of their heating systems. *After the Roman empire fell in the fourth century* A.D., *nobody* [19b–1, short sentences combined into one] from the former colonies knew how to make chimneys. For four centuries, western Europe had no chimneys. *How did chimneys finally get to western Europe?* [19c, revised to question] Nobody is quite sure. [19b–3, revised for short sentence] *A current theory holds that* around A.D. 800, chimneys were brought *by* Syrian and Egyptian traders from the East. [19b–3, short sentences combined into one long sentence for mix of sentence lengths]

Answers and Coverage: Exercise 19–6

Answers will vary. This is a summary exercise, so it should reflect many of the techniques of variety and emphasis discussed in this chapter. Here is one answer; many others are possible.

Born in 1809 [19e–1, participial phrase to modify] French educator Louis Braille became blind at three years of age [19b–1, combined two short sentences], and he was enrolled at the Institute for the Blind [19b–3, compound sentence to vary sentence lengths] in Paris [19e–1, prepositional phrase to modify] when he was ten [19e–1, adverb clause to modify]. Braille devised for blind people a writing system that consisted of raised dots on paper [19e–1, adjective clause to modify]. At the time of this accomplishment of enormous benefit to humanity, Braille was only twenty [19e–2, periodic sentence]. Braille's system used 43 configurations of raised dots to represent individual letters of the alphabet, some combinations of letters, and some punctuation marks [19b–1, revised string of too many short sentences]. A modified version is still used today [19b–3, no change because effective short sentence among long sentences]. Did you know that Louis Braille was also a distinguished musician [19c, a question to vary sentence structures]? So talented was he [19f, inverted word order] that as an adult he played the violoncello and the organ to great acclaim throughout Paris [19e–1, prepositional phrases to modify]. Sadly, Braille died when only 43 years of age [no change].

Answers: Exercise 19–7

Using their own topics, students imitate the variety and emphasis of two different passages shown in this chapter. They can choose from the Kohls, Dillard, Thomas, or Hughes. For a discussion of the technique of imitation, see the answer to Exercise 18–2.

■ CHAPTER TWENTY

Answers: Exercise 20–1

Answers will vary.

Answers and Coverage: Exercise 20–2

The response to this exercise is likely to elicit much debate, given that shades of connotative meaning are often fairly personal. The following are some possible answers.

1. *Positive:* exuberant, light-hearted, high-spirited, joyful; *Neutral:* carefree, animated; *Negative:* frivolous, rash, riotous, reckless

2. *Positive:* prudent, foresighted; *Neutral:* thrifty, economical, frugal, money-conscious; *Negative:* stingy, tight-fisted, penny-pinching

3. *Positive:* learned counsel, advocate; *Neutral:* lawyer, attorney, legal practitioner, public defender, prosecutor; *Negative:* shyster, ambulance chaser

4. *Positive:* fragrance, scent, perfume, incense; *Neutral:* smell, aroma, scent, whiff; *Negative:* odor, stink, stench, smoke

5. *Positive:* flexible, tolerant, adaptable; *Neutral:* yielding, undemanding;; *Negative:* wishy-washy, indulgent, weak, submissive, imitative

Answers: Exercise 20–3

Because of the many possibilities for re-wording posed by this exercise, the answers are likely to vary widely. Students may enjoy comparing the different choices they have made. The important principle for revision is that the new versions should have a high degree of specificity and concreteness. Here is one set of possibilities.

The used 1988 Buick was exactly what we were looking for. It was a maroon two-door model with a vinyl top, and it was priced at several hundred dollars less than we were expecting to pay. The seats were covered in black fabric that looked brand new. It had a tape player, air conditioning, and automatic transmission. We were especially pleased that it could get 28 miles per gallon on the highway. The dealer said we could drive it off the lot that very day. The only problem was that he would not take our 1956 Chevrolet with the cracked windshield and bent right fender as a trade-in.

Answers and Coverage: Exercise 20–4

1.	impossible [im-]	6.	semiconscious [semi-]
2.	reexamine [re-]	7.	misstated [mis-]
3.	malfunction [mal-]	8.	unbelievable [un-]
4.	interstate [inter-]	9.	preconceived [pre-]
5.	irreversible [ir-]	10.	hypersensitive [hyper-]

Answers and Coverage: Exercise 20–5

1. childless [-less, adjective]
2. objectify [-ify, verb]
3. beautify [-ify, verb]
4. harmonize [-ize, verb]
5. kinship [-ship, noun]
6. touchable [-able, adjective]
7. careless [-less, adjective]
8. merciful [-ful, adjective]
9. bachelorhood [-hood, noun]
10. compassionate [-ate, adjective]

■ CHAPTER TWENTY-ONE

Answers: Exercise 21–1

Answers will vary. Here are some possible nonsexist versions.

1. An individual's sense of space and distance is variable.
2. People establish their own "personal space" by what they can do, not what they can see, in a given area.
3. A parent is usually seen standing very close to his or her children. [*or* Parents are usually... to their children.]
4. Politicians, too, usually stand close to talk with one or two constituents but many feet away from large groups of people to whom they are talking.
5. The sizes of people's "bubbles" of personal space vary with their culture or ethnicity.
6. Germans will go to great lengths to preserve their "private sphere" at home and at work.
7. English businesspeople, however, are used to a common work space at the office.
8. For that reason, they are willing to exist close to their co-workers.
9. Some U. S. business executives use other people in the office to help protect their personal bubbles.
10. They have assistants [or *secretaries* or *receptionists*] announce all visitors and screen all phone calls.

Answers and Coverage: Exercise 21–2

1. mixed metaphor
2. simile
3. overstatement
4. irony
5. personification
6. simile
7. analogy
8. irony
9. overstatement
10. metaphor

Answers and Coverage: Exercise 21–3

Answers will vary. Here is one set of possibilities.

1. Carl either raises his grade point average or risks probation.
2. Carl's grandfather says that difficult problems inspire strong people to come up with solutions.

3. Carl makes up with energy what he lacks in intelligence.
4. Persistence is one of Carl's most notable traits.
5. The central question is: Will Carl pass or fail out of college?

Answers and Coverage: Exercise 21–4

Answers will vary. Here is one set of possibilities.

1. Socializing on the job is not allowed. [bureaucratic]
2. An index card posted on the bulletin board advertised a used bridal gown for sale. [doublespeak]
3. Shortly after Mrs. Harriman died, Mr. Harriman moved to Florida to be near his son, daughter-in-law, and their new baby. [euphemism]
4. I am worried about teaching myself to become a computer programmer. [pretentious]
5. My brother told a lie. [pretentious]
6. An individual's systems of thinking and feeling are at the center of his or her personality. [jargon]
7. He told the police officer that the car accident happened because he sneezed and couldn't see the other driver coming. [doublespeak]
8. When the negotiation is finished, we will be in a better position. [jargon]
9. The trash has piled up because the garbage men were on strike last month. [euphemism]
10. Full-time employees who have worked at the company for five years can participate in the savings program. [bureaucratic]

■ CHAPTER TWENTY-TWO

Answers: Exercise 22–1

1. Council	14. used to
2. than	15. their
3. council	16. accept
4. cites	17. assistance
5. to	18. patience
6. are	19. personal
7. their	20. morale
8. too	21. raise
9. weak	22. principle
10. may be	23. already
11. passed	24. know
12. no	25. respective
13. Formerly	

Answers: Exercise 22–2

1.	scarves	9.	phenomena
2.	species	10.	selves
3.	rodeos	11.	nachos
4.	moose	12.	fungi
5.	leeches	13.	loaves
6.	data	14.	push-ups
7.	logs	15.	theses
8.	brothers-in-law		

Answers: Exercise 22–3

1. (a) profitable
    (b) reproducible
    (c) controllable
    (d) coercible
    (e) recognizable
2. (a) luxuriance
    (b) prudence
    (c) deviance
    (d) resistance
    (e) independence
3. (a) truly
    (b) joking
    (c) fortunately
    (d) appeasing
    (e) appeasement
4. (a) happiness
    (b) pried
    (c) prying
    (d) dryly
    (e) beautifying
5. (a) committed
    (b) commitment
    (c) dropped
    (d) occurred
    (e) regretful
6. (a) relief
    (b) achieve
    (c) weird
    (d) niece
    (e) deceive

Answers: Exercise 22–4

1. all-powerful
2. Comparison-contrast; more agile
3. boldly striped; underbody
4. eleven feet; one-quarter; five hundred
5. self-confident
6. village destroyer; into
7. terror-stricken
8. spring-loaded; poisoned arrows
9. cattle killers
10. animal shows; pro-animal

Coverage: Exercise 22–4

1. *all-* prefixes hyphenated

2. hyphenated compound; open
3. -ly adverb as first word of compound; *under* prefixes spelled closed
4. not a double digit; fraction; not a double digit
5. *self-* prefixes hyphenated
6. open compound; closed compound
7. hyphenated compound
8. hyphenated compound; open compound
9. open compound
10. open compound; *pro-* prefix hyphenated before a vowel

Answers and Coverage: Exercise 22–5

	Incorrect	Correct	Section & Chart
1.	beautyful	beautiful	22c, Chart 101
2.	envelop	envelope	22c, Chart 101
3.	rite	right	22c, Chart 101
4.	recieve	receive	22c, Chart 101
5.	through	threw	22c, Chart 101
6.	tryed	tried	22c, Chart 101
7.	practiceing	practicing	22c, Chart 101
8.	freinds	friends	22c, Chart 101
9.	insure	ensure	22c, Chart 101
10.	publically	publicly	22c, Chart 101
11.	heart-ache	heartache	22d, Chart 103

■ CHAPTER TWENTY-THREE

Answers and Coverage: Exercise 23–1

1. After studying art in Crete, El Greco moved to Venice, Italy, probably before 1567 [23d, question mark deleted and *probably* added], apparently to study with the famous Venetian artist Titian.
2. Scholars wonder if Titian was referring to El Greco when Titian mentioned "a talented young pupil" in a letter to King Philip II. [23a, question mark deleted and replaced with period]
3. El Greco later moved to Rome with a letter of introduction (dated Nov. [period added] 19, 1570) to a rich, influential art patron, Cardinal Alessandro Farnese.
4. Cardinal Farnese introduced El Greco to the outstanding [23e, exclamation point deleted] people of the city.
5. By 1572, El Greco had moved to the city of Toledo in Spain, where he spent the rest of his life. [23e, exclamation point deleted and replaced with period]

➤

6. Toledo was a rich, cultured, and intellectual city where El Greco worked as a sculptor, painter, and architect. [23a, period added]

7. Toward the end of his life, El Greco suffered from a mysterious [23d, question mark deleted] illness that reduced his capacity for work. [23a, period added]

8. "Was El Greco's eyesight affected by the illness? [23c, question mark added]" is a question that has been asked for centuries. [23a, question mark deleted and replaced with period]

9. Visual problems might explain the elongated bodies in El Greco's portraits. [23a, question mark deleted and replaced with period]

10. From time to time, physicians write articles diagnosing [23d, question mark deleted] El Greco's illness based on this artist's paintings! [23e, acceptable exclamation point]

Answers: Exercise 23–2

During World War II, U.S. soldiers' mail was censored. Specially trained people read the mail. Many people wanted to know why this was necessary. The censors had to make sure that no military information was disclosed. Return addresses often read "Somewhere in the Pacific Area." to keep strategic positions secret. Have you ever heard the story about the soldier who could not write his sweetheart for many months but finally had time? He wrote her a long letter explaining the delay and telling her that he loved her very much. All the woman received, however, was a tiny slip of paper that read: "Your boyfriend is fine. He loves you. He also talks too much! Sincerely, The Censor."

■ CHAPTER TWENTY-FOUR

Answers: Exercise 24–1

Answers may vary slightly. Here is one set of possibilities.

1. Immigrants from Eastern Europe came to New York City, and they sold meat patties in stands all over the city to hungry passersby.

2. The patties were too messy to carry around, so some German sailors on shore leave asked that the meat patties be placed on soft roles of bread.

3. The combination of meat and bread came to be known as a hamburger, for the German sailors named the portable snack after their hometown of Hamburg.

4. The hamburger went national in 1903 at the United States Louisiana Purchase Exposition in St. Louis, and it was an instant success.

5. A patty served with no roll and on a plate is not a true hamburger, nor can a true hamburger be any shape but round.

6. Many burger lovers pile onions and pickles on their hamburgers and smother them with ketchup, yet others insist the only authentic hamburger is served plain.

7. Some cooks put a slice of cheese on their burger, or they place slices of bacon on top for a special treat.

8. Some people prefer not to eat red meat, but U.S. cooks used only beef until a decade ago.

9. People not willing to eat beef missed their burgers, so a variety of ingredients are now available for making different kinds of burgers.

10. Most supermarkets carry the ingredients for turkey burgers and pork burgers, and some also carry ground tofu for tofu burgers.

Answers: Exercise 24–2

1. snack, Kellogg's
2. sugar, it
3. after, his
4. market, the
5. correct
6. morning, the
7. 1800s, improved
8. time, perishable
9. orange
10. Consequently, today's

Answers and Coverage: Exercise 24–3

Answers may vary, but the following versions are possibilities.

1. Although it began as a flight of sheer fantasy, virtual reality is turning out to be one of the most versatile technological applications of this century. [adverb clause]

2. Now known as "virtual reality," computer-generated environments now have many important applications ranging from medicine and space exploration to entertainment. [participial phrase]

3. For example, surgeons can use virtual scalpels to practice difficult operations and predict their effects on the patient's total body system. [introductory words—transitional expression]

4. Recently, astronauts have been using virtual reality space walks to train themselves to function in the demanding zero-gravity environment of orbiting space satellites. [introductory word—transitional expression]

5. To enter the world of virtual reality for entertainment, you can use a glove and a specially-equipped helmet. [infinitive phrase]

6. By punching a few keys on the computer in a virtual reality room, the computer operator transports you into a colorful make-believe world. [prepositional phrase]

7. While two tiny television screens in the helmet's visor provide startlingly realistic three-dimensional vision, you can interact with objects in the virtual world by moving your glove. [verbal clause]

8. Looking up at the deep blue sky, you see a large prehistoric bird soaring above your head. [participial phrase]

9. Under your feet, the ground quakes and splits and becomes an ocean with a shark circling nearby. [prepositional phrase]

10. Fortunately, you can repel the shark with your virtual spear and you will not be hurt if he attacks. [introductory word—conjunctive adverb]

Answers: Exercise 24–4

1. Rabbits, squirrels, raccoons, and other small game; Shawnees, Cherokees, and European pioneers
2. weight, buffalo tracks . . . highways, and
3. the hunters, trappers, and scouts; vertical mountains, overgrown forests, and lush meadows
4. Virginia, North Carolina, Pennsylvania, and other . . .
5. Correct

Answers: Exercise 24–5

1. small, colorful
2. correct
3. small, sturdy; strong, curved
4. effortless, efficient
5. short, simple

Answers and Coverage: Exercise 24–6

1. Elena Piscopia, a resident of Venice, was the first woman to receive a doctoral degree. [nonrestrictive appositive]
2. Many university officials, reflective the beliefs of their time, opposed Elena's goal of higher education. [nonrestrictive participial phrase]
3. The doctoral examination of a woman, a unique phenomenon in 1678, drew crowds of curious spectators. [nonrestrictive appositive]
4. Elena Piscopia, who had prepared carefully for her questioners, completed the examination easily. [nonrestrictive relative clause]
5. Her replies, which were given entirely in Latin, amazed her examiners with their clarity and brilliance. [nonrestrictive relative clause]
6. Elena Piscopia's father, who was an exceptionally enlightened man for his time, supported and encouraged his daughter's education. [nonrestrictive relative clause]
7. None. [restrictive relative clause]
8. Christine de Pisane, widowed at twenty-five, turned to writing to support herself and her three children. [nonrestrictive participial phrase]
9. She found herself unprepared and taught herself a complete course of study, which included Latin, history, philosophy, and literature. [nonrestrictive relative clause]
10. She later wrote *The City of Ladies,* a book about women leading creative lives.

Answers and Coverage: Exercise 24–7

Answers may vary slightly. Here is one set of possibilities.
1. Inability to write, some say, [parenthetical expression] stems from lack of discipline and a tendency to procrastinate.
2. Therefore, [transitional word] according to this thinking, [parenthetical expression] the only way to overcome writer's block is to exert more willpower.

3. But writer's block can be a complex psychological event that happens to conscientious, hard-working people, not just the procrastinators. [expression of contrast]
4. Strange as it may seem, [parenthetical phrase] such people are often unconsciously rebelling against their own self-tyranny and rigid standards of perfection.
5. If I told you, my fellow writer, [direct address] that all it takes to start writing again is to quit pushing yourself, you would think I was crazy, wouldn't you? [tag sentence]

Answers: Exercise 24–8

1. "His father," replied the ambulance driver, "but he's unconscious."
2. "This boy looks like he needs surgery, but he is the son of the surgeon now on duty," said the clerk.
3. She explained in an agitated voice, "Surgeons do not operate on their own family members."
4. Correct
5. With a disgusted look, the clerk told the driver, "The surgeon is the boy's mother."

Coverage: Exercise 24–8

1. explanatory words in the middle of a quotation
2. explanatory words at the end of a quotation
3. explanatory words at the beginning of a quotation
4. Correct (no comma should follow the question mark)
5. explanatory words at the beginning of a quotation

Answers and Coverage: Exercise 24–9

1. Made by the noted German director Wim Wenders, *Paris, Texas* [comma after city in title] was set in an actual town in Lamar County, Texas, [comma after county and state] with a population of 24,699. [comma with numbers]
2. Correct
3. The custom of naming little towns in the United States after cosmopolitan urban centers in the Old World has resulted in such places as Athens, Georgia, and St. Petersburg, Florida. [comma after cities]
4. As of December 31, 1990 [comma with dates] the U.S. St. Petersburg had 238,629 [comma with numbers] and the U.S. Athens had 45,734. [comma with numbers]
5. By comparison, St. Petersburg, Russia, and Athens, Greece, [comma after cities] have populations of approximately four million and one million, respectively.

Answers: Exercise 24–10

1. Using specially prepared tape, recorders communicate hidden messages to listeners.
2. Some people who want to, learn supposedly without effort by listening to the tape.
3. To prevent shoplifting, twenty major department stores started using subliminal tapes.
4. Of the twenty, nine reported pilferage had decreased by about 37 percent.
5. Correct

Answers and Coverage: Exercise 24–11

1. In the 1920s, [keep: introductory phrase] the Harlem Renaissance [omit: do not separate subject from its verb, 24j–6] was not confined to New York City; Harlem was only one of several [omit: comma between noncoordinate adjectives or modifiers, 24j–3] African-American urban districts where the arts flourished during this decade.
2. Black urban singers began to attract a national audience, and [omit: comma after coordinating conjunction, 24j–1; position between independent clauses] Harlem surpassed Broadway in the originality of its musical revues, poetry, and fiction. [keep: commas to separate items]
3. One of the leading poets of the Harlem Renaissance [omit: do not separate subject from its verb, 24j–6] was Claude McKay, who [keep: nonrestrictive clause] arrived in the United States from Jamaica in 1912 at the age of twenty-three.
4. He studied briefly at Booker T. Washington's [omit: noncoordinating adjectives or modifiers] famous Tuskeegee Institute in Alabama.
5. In 1917, [keep: introductory phrase] he moved to Harlem. [keep: nonrestrictive clause, 14j–4] where he published his first poem.
6. McKay said that [omit: comma in indirect discourse, 24j–5] poetry was his vehicle of protest, and [keep: comma linking independent clauses, 24a] he wrote his 1919 poem "If We Must Die" in response to [omit: do not separate a preposition from its object, 24j–6] the race riots of that year.
7. In fact, [keep: introductory phrase] Harlem was a neighborhood seething in revolt [omit: coordinating conjunction joining two nouns, 24j–1] and racial pride.
8. Marcus Garvey [omit: coordinating conjunction joining two nouns, 24j–1] and his Universal Negro Improvement Association sought to transport blacks to [omit: do not separate a preposition from its object, 24j–6] a new and better life in Africa.
9. Garvey, who was born in Jamaica like Claude McKay, [keep: nonrestrictive clause] was one of the first people [omit: restrictive clause] who taught African Americans that black is beautiful.
10. The Harlem Renaissance continued through 1945, [keep: nonrestric-

tive clause] when writers from Langston Hughes and Richard Wright to Zora Neale Hurston and Margaret Walker launched their great literary careers.

■ CHAPTER TWENTY-FIVE

Answers and Coverage: Exercise 25–1

1. ... Conrad Gesner in 1559; he saw them... [25a, closely related independent clauses] person famous for growing exotic plants.

2. ... a favorite flower; in fact, the tulip's name... [25c, transitional expression connecting independent clauses] comes from a Turkish word for *turban*.

3. ... throughout Dutch society; it became a... [25a, closely related independent clauses] mark of good taste to have a garden full of them.

4. ... the rarest specimens; consequently, prices... [25c, conjunctive adverb connecting independent clauses]

5. Correct

6. ... to buy forty bulbs; but four tons... [25b, coordinating conjunction joining independent clauses]

7. ... following items: [25e, list introduced by a colon, not semicolon] 4,600 florins; an expensive, gilded carriage; and two gray horses, complete with harnesses, bridles, and bells [25d, between comma-containing items in a series]

8. ... on the stock exchanges; therefore, [25c, conjunctive adverb joining independent clauses] Dutch nobles, farmers, merchants, servants, [note that commas should be used between the items in the series here] and street-sweepers alike found themselves growing richer as prices rose.

9. made... a delivery; an hour later he found the messenger finishing lunch, which included the "onion" he had taken from the merchant's office [25a, closely related independent clauses containing one or more commas]

10. Although Holland's tulip madness has calmed down considerably today, growing tulips... [25e–1, use a comma, not a semicolon, to separate a dependent clause from an independent clause]

Answers: Exercise 25–2

1. The first roller coaster in the United States, installed in the late nineteenth century, was part of an amusement park in the Coney Island section of New York City: it was named the "Switchback Gravity Pleasure Railway."

2. The first roller coaster was extremely primitive; it was built of wood, had only two inclines, and reached a downhill speed of a mere six miles per hour.　➤

3. Riders got on at the top of the first incline and climbed out when the train reached the bottom; then the riders walked up the hill to the top of the second incline and climbed in for the ride to the bottom.

4. Soon a chain drive for roller coasters was developed to power the train on the uphill parts; therefore, higher inclines could be built to give riders a greater thrill.

5. Major breakthroughs in roller-coaster design occurred in the 1970s, when roller coaster designers drew on advanced knowledge from physics, mathematics, and human physiology; and the designers used computer simulations to check their work.

Additional Exercise (Exercise 25–2, continued)

1. Extraordinarily sophisticated scientific applications to roller coasters began to appear in the 1980s; in fact, some high school physics teachers were so impressed that they began to use examples of modern roller-coaster design to illustrate principles in physics.

2. A 360-degree circle cannot be used for a roller coaster loop because speed reduction at the top of a 360-degree circle could pull riders from their seats; in contrast, the tear-shaped clothoid loop has been found to permit roller-coaster riders to speed along safely upside down at 70 miles per hour.

3. The Shock Wave, opened in the late 1980s at an Illinois amusement park, has a height of 17 stories; a short downhill run of 70 miles per hour; rapidly reversing directions, patterned after a twisted pretzel; and a sequence of corkscrew spirals.

4. A recent visitor to New York's Coney Island amusement park reported that the 61-year-old wooden Cyclone was half-empty; and the new Double Loop, designed with the latest advances in roller-coaster engineering, drew huge crowds.

5. Many roller-coaster enthusiasts drive long distances to try out a new roller coaster; however, many other people are repelled by the thought of riding a roller coaster.

Answers and Coverage: Exercise 25–3

1. Some postcards offer colorful views of exotic places or reproduce famous paintings; others feature portraits of famous persons. [25a, between closely related independent clauses]

2. On postcard racks today you can find a wide variety of selections; you may find a classic scene from a Bogart film or a giant cactus wearing sunglasses. [25a, between closely related independent clauses]

3. Correct

4. Postcards have been popular for a long time; indeed, the "Golden Age of Postcards" lasted from the turn of the century to the Great Depression. [25c, between independent clauses joined by a transitional expression]

5. The first postcard was designed in 1859 by Emmanuel Hermenn; four years later the U.S. government began issuing specially designed "postal cards" with an illustration on one side and a space for an address and stamp on the other. [25a, between closely related independent clauses]

6. Some people try to collect postcards by category; for example, one man has 52 different postcards that have "Greetings from ... " and the name of one of the United States printed on them. [25c, between independent clauses joined by a transitional expression]

7. Correct

8. Today, postcards usually cost less than a dollar; therefore, they are an inexpensive alternative to a regular greeting card. [25c, between independent clauses joined by a conjunctive adverb]

9. Postcards are also a bargain in terms of postage; it costs less to mail a postcard than an envelope. [25a, between closely related independent clauses]

10. However, not all postcards are cheap; for instance, a rare postcard signed by the artist Alphonse Mucha recently sold for $3,000 at an auction. [25c, between independent clauses joined by a transitional expression]

■ CHAPTER TWENTY-SIX

Answers and Coverage: Exercise 26–1

1. craze: chocolate cake [26a, appositive]
2. Correct
3. both: chocolate [26a, list]
4. Unfortunately, lots [26a, not an independent clause]
5. *Ethics: Concepts* [26c, separate standard material]
6. words: "To [26a, quotation]
7. fame: Lee [26a, list]
8. such as astronauts [26a, not an independent clause]
9. Calling, "Max [26a, not an independent clause]
10. Cadets: [26c, formal salutation]
11. broken: Henry [26b, between two independent]
12. diseases: diphtheria [26a, list]
13. To: All; From: Management; Re: Vacation [26c, memo form]
14. pollution: "The [26a, quotation]
15. message: How [26b, between two independent clauses]

■ CHAPTER TWENTY-SEVEN

Answers: Exercise 27–1

1. Haydn's; music lovers'
2. composer's; children's
3. Haydn's; today's; orchestra's
4. musicians'
5. musicians'; women's; men's; concertgoers'; Brahms's; Beethoven's; Ives's; Strauss's
6. players'
7. singer-composer's
8. Esterhazy's; life's
9. patron's; London's
10. music-maker's; homeland's

Answers: Exercise 27–2

1. Athletic competition is encouraged in accordance with the participants' age and ability.
2. These athletes' training takes place in schools and other institutions.
3. Participants' handicaps do not prevent them from competing in sports from basketball to gymnastics and ice skating to wheelchair exercise.
4. The program's sponsor is the Joseph P. Kennedy, Jr., Foundation, which first sponsored the event in 1968.
5. The foundation's true beneficiary is American society, for a democracy's aim is equal opportunity and participation for all its members.

Coverage: Exercise 27–2

(1) plural possessive noun; (2) plural possessive noun; (3) plural possessive noun; (4) singular possessive noun; (5) singular possessive noun; singular possessive noun

Answers: Exercise 27–3

(1) One of Albert Einstein's biographers tells about the famous physicist's encounter with a little girl in his neighborhood. (2) The little girl stared at Einstein's soaking wet feet and said, "Mr. Einstein, you've come out without your boots again!" (3) Einstein laughed and, pulling up his trousers, replied, "Yes, and I've forgotten my socks, too." (4) Most people aren't as forgetful as Einstein, but sometimes our memories let all of us down. (5) We may not be able to remember if our first job started in '81 or '82; we may forget whether our employer's husband spells his name with two *t*'s or with one. (6) No one is absolutely sure how memory works. (7) Dr. Barbara Jones's study of memory suggests that personality

styles affect memory. (8) People with rigid personalities whose liveli-hoods depend on facts tend to have good memories. (9) Mr. Harry Lorayne's and Dr. Laird Cermak's studies of memory each provide a dif-ferent approach to improving that useful faculty. (10) Mr. Lorayne sug-gests relating what you want to remember to something verbal or vi-sual. (11) For instance, if you want to remember that your sister-in-law's name is Rose, you would picture her wearing a rose corsage. (12) Dr. Cermak's suggestions include consideration of psychological factors. (13) He notes that doctors are currently developing drugs that will pre-vent older people from losing the memories that are rightfully theirs.

Answers: Exercise 27–4

(1) Every summer Twinsburg, Ohio, comes to life when over one thou-sand pairs of twins gather for the town's annual festival. (2) The conver-sation at the gathering usually involves twins' stories about tricking people by exchanging identities, about knowing each other's thoughts, and about sharing secrets. (3) The stories are entertaining, but many psychologists find them informative as well. (4) Many studies have in-volved identical twins who were separated at birth. (5) Identical twins come from a single fertilized egg that splits soon after conception, re-sulting in two fetuses with identical genes. (6) Although identical twins may look like carbon copies of each other, they're like snowflakes: no pair is exactly alike.

■ CHAPTER TWENTY-EIGHT

Answers: Exercise 28–1

1. Canfield and Lebson write, "No one understands the sleeping hab-its of these sharks."

2. In the last two lines of the poem, Dickinson creates a powerful con-trast: "Parting is all we know of heaven. And all we need of hell."

3. "One can put up with 'Service with a Smile' if the smile is genuine and not mere compulsory toothbaring." wrote Cornelia Otis Skin-ner. She did not, on the other hand, advocate "Service with a Snarl."

4. "Promises," said Hannah Arendt, "are the uniquely human way of ordering the future."

5. According to Henry James, "Nothing . . . will ever take the place of the good old fashion of 'liking' a work of art or not liking it."

6. Pauline Kael, the movie critic, notes that "certain artists can, at moments in their lives, reach out and unify the audience" and in so doing give people the opportunity for "a shared response."

7. "Don't let anyone convince you that you can't fulfill your ambi-tions," warned the speaker, "or you surely won't."

8. "Why have women passion, intellect, moral activity—these three—

and a place in society where no one of the three can be exercised?" asked Florence Nightingale in the 1850s.

9. "In seven cases," the report continued, "outlets with the lowest prices had the highest percentages of defective merchandise."

10. Leslie Hanscom reports about the latest volume of the *Oxford English Dictionary*. "Most of the new words are originating in the USA."

Coverage: Exercise 28–1

(1) direct discourse; (2) short poetry quotation; (3) quotation within a quotation; short quotation; (4) direct discourse following an interruption; (5) quoted word within a quotation; (6) closing quotation marks needed; (7) interrupted direct discourse; (8) direct discourse; (9) interrupted short quotation; closing quotation marks needed; (10) short quotation

Answers and Coverage: Exercise 28–2

1. *Indirect discourse.* "What's the problem?" Charlie Chaplin asked him.

2. *Direct discourse.* MacArthur asked Chaplin how he could show a fat man slipping on a banana peel and still get a laugh.

3. · *Indirect discourse.* "Should I show the banana peel first, then the man approaching and slipping on it? Or should I show the fat man first, next the banana peel, and then the man slipping on it?" he wondered.

4. *Indirect discourse.* "Neither one," Chaplin said.

5. *Direct discourse.* Chaplin told him to show the fat man approaching, then the banana peel. Next he should show the fat man and the banana peel together. Then he should have the fat man step over the banana peel and disappear down a manhole.

Answers and Coverage: Exercise 28–3

1. Almost everyone who has had to make a difficult choice in life can relate to Robert Frost's poem "The Road Not Taken" [title of poem].

2. On a *Twilight Zone* episode called "Healer," the main character steals a magic artifact [television episode].

3. In her essay titled "In Search of Our Mothers' Gardens," Alice Walker says that she found her own garden because she was guided by a "heritage of a love of beauty and a respect for strength" [essay title; closing quotation marks needed].

4. Unable to get enough peace and quiet to write songs, such as his famous "Over There" and "You're a Grand Old Flag," George M. Cohan would sometimes hire a Pullman car drawing room on a train going far enough away to allow him to finish his work [song titles].

5. A snake gives Sherlock Holmes the clue he needs to solve a puzzling murder in the mystery story "The Speckled Band" [short story title].

Answers: Exercise 28–4

1. "Accept" and "except" sound enough alike to confuse many listeners (or *Accept* and *except* sound enough alike to confuse many listeners).
2. Mickey Mantle, Yogi Berra, and Whitey Ford helped make the Yankees champions in the 1950s.
3. Correct
4. An "antigen" is any substance from outside the body that activates the body's immune system. Today scientists are focusing intensive research on antigens.
5. *Valross,* "whale-horse," is the Norwegian word from which we get *walrus.*

Coverage: Exercise 28–4

(1) consistent treatment needed; (2) nicknames; (3) correct; (4) second use of a technical term; (5) translation of a term.

Answers: Exercise 28–5

1. One of the most famous passages in Shakespeare is Hamlet's soliloquy, which begins with the question "To be, or not to be?"
2. "Take this script," Rudyard Kipling said to the nurse who had cared for his first-born child, "and someday if you are in need of money you may be able to sell it at a handsome price."
3. Ernest Hemingway claimed this was the source of his famous phrase "a lost generation": in conversation with Papa Hemingway, a garage owner used the words to describe the young mechanics he employed.
4. After lulling the reader with a description of a beautiful dream palace in his poem "Kubla Khan," Coleridge changes the mood abruptly: "And 'mid this tumult Kubla heard from far / Ancestral voices prophesying war."
5. The words of Emma Lazarus, "Give me your tired, your poor, your huddled masses yearning to breathe free," open the inscription on the Statue of Liberty.

Coverage: Exercise 28–5

(1) quotation is a question; (2) commas always placed inside closing quotation marks; " (3) colon always placed outside closing quotation marks; (4) title of poem; quotation from poem; (5) commas always placed inside closing quotation marks

■ CHAPTER TWENTY-NINE

Answers and Coverage, Exercise 29–1

Answers will vary greatly. When checking them, note whether instructions were followed.

Answers and Coverage, Exercise 29–2

1. Railroad entrepreneur George Francis Train (his real name) dreamed of creating a chain of great cities across the country connected by his Union Pacific Railroad. [29b–1, interruptive aside]

2. Nowadays you can order almost anything (clothing, toys, greeting cards, and even meat) through mail-order catalogues. [29b–1, interruptive examples]

3. W. C. Fields offered two pieces of advice on job hunting: (1) never show up for an interview in bare feet, and (2) do not read your prospective employer's mail while he is questioning you about your qualifications. [29b–2, numbers of listed items]

4. Patients who pretend to have ailments are know to doctors as "Münchausens" after Baron Karl Friedrick Hieronymous von Münchausen. (He was a German army officer who had a reputation for wild and unbelievable tales.) [29b–1, interruptive explanation]

5. The questions raised by China's struggles to integrate capitalism with communism during the 1980s and 1990s (Will the country disintegrate into civil war? Can the present economic boom be sustained? What will emerge from the chaos?) cannot yet be clearly answered, even by those who follow the country's progress closely. [29b–1, interruptive examples; 29b–3, punctuation with parentheses]

Answers and Coverage, Exercise 29–3

Answers may vary somewhat, especially in usage of dashes and parentheses.

1. In 1994, Neil Yerman—a scribe and artist who writes with a turkey feather quill—[29a–1, dash for appositive] copied one letter at a time (304,805 of them, to be exact) to create a Torah scroll for Congregation Emanu-El in Manhattan. [29b–1, parentheses for an aside]

2. If we change our thoughts, we can change our moods: (1) Get up and go. When you most feel like moping, do something, anything. Try cleaning up a drawer. (2) Reach out. Make contact with people you care about. (3) Start smiling. Studies show that people send the same signals to their nervous system when they smile as the do then they are genuinely happy. [29b–2, parentheses for numbers of listed items]

3. A series of resolutions was passed 11–0 (with one council member abstaining) calling on the mayor and the district attorney to im-

prove safety conditions and step up law enforcement on city bus-
ses. [29b–1, parentheses for interruptive explanation]

4. Whatever it is you're doing—writing, painting or performing—art
   should not be hard to understand. Art is communication. [29a–1,
   dashed for interruptive example]

5. Thunder is caused when the flash of lightning heats the air around
   it to temperatures up to 30,000° F (16,649° C). [29b–2, numbers]

6. I love Ogden Nash's limericks about animals, especially his lines
   about the many limbs of a certain sea creature: "I marvel at thee,
   Octopus; / If I were thou, I'd call me Us." [29e–1, slash between lines
   of quoted poetry]

7. Correct

8. In his famous Letter from the Birmingham Jail on April 16, 1963,
   Martin Luther King, Jr., wrote: "You [the eight clergymen who had
   urged him not to hold a protest] deplore the demonstration taking place in Birmingham." [29c–1, brackets for words inserted into
   quotation]

9. The world's most expensive doll house (sold for $256,000 at a 1978
   London auction) [29b–1, interruptive explanation] contains sixteen
   rooms, a working chamber organ, and a silver clothes press—but
   no toilet. [29a–1, contrast]

10. Pillaging (excavating, removing, or trafficking [buying or selling])
    [brackets within parentheses for explanation within an explanation]
    artifacts from Federal or Indian land can be a felony punishable by
    up to five years' imprisonment and two hundred and fifty thou-
    sand dollars ($250,000) in fines under the Archaeological Resources
    Protection Act. [29b–2, repetition of a spelled-out number]

Answers and Coverage, Exercise 29–4

Answers will vary greatly. When checking them, note whether the directions were followed.

1. only three lines of the poem—with quotation marks and with slash
   marks between the first and second and between the second and
   third lines—in the sentence

2. parentheses to enclose a brief example in a sentence

3. dashes to set off the definition in the sentence

4. parentheses to enclose the numbers 1–4 that label the list within a
   sentence

5. ellipsis to indicate an omission from a quotation, with the meaning
   of the whole still clear

■ CHAPTER THIRTY

Answers, Exercise 30–1

A slash indicates no capital is needed. A capitalized italicized word indicates that a capital is needed.

1. President Abraham Lincoln's ̸Secretary, whose name was Kennedy, and President John F. Kennedy's ̸Secretary, whose name was Lincoln, advised these ill-fated presidents not to go out just before their assassinations.

2. The first child of *European* ̸Parents to be born in *North America* was Snorro, whose ̸Mother was the ̸Widow of Leif Erickson's ̸Brother.

3. The ̸Ancient *Egyptians,* the first to embalm their ̸Dead ̸Citizens, also embalmed their ̸Dead ̸Crocodiles.

4. In 1659 *Massachusetts* outlawed *Christmas* and fined anyone celebrating the ̸Holiday five ̸Shillings.

5. Mark Twain, the author of *"The Celebrated Jumping Frog of Calaveras County,"* once refused to invest in a friend's invention, calling it a "̸Wildcat speculation." The invention was the telephone!

6. An artificial hand invented in 1551 by a *Frenchman* (his name was Ambroise Tare) had ̸Fingers that moved by cogs and levers, thus enabling a handless member of the ̸Cavalry to grasp the reins of his horse.

7. "Take care, *O* traitor," roared the hero, "̸Or your ̸Villainy will do you in!"

8. Researchers at the *Institute* for *Policy Studies* of *Harvard University* discovered that the following jobs are considered most boring by those who hold them: (1) ̸Assembly line worker, (2) elevator operator, (3) pool typist, (4) ̸Bank ̸Guard, (5) ̸Housewife.

9. What is the most common item in a family medicine chest? Is it ̸Aspirin? *Adhesive* bandages? *A* thermometer? *An* antibacterial agent? [lower case for *adhesive, a,* and *an* also acceptable]

10. "I don't care what you do, my dear," the ̸Actress *Mrs.* Patrick Campbell is supposed to have said, "as long as you don't do it in the ̸Street and frighten the horses!"

11. The letter announcing that the company was closing its doors and everyone was losing their jobs ended with the words *"Have a happy day."*

12. The book that has sold the most copies of any book throughout the world is the *Bible.*

13. I registered for *Biology* 101 and *History* 121, but the courses I wanted in psychology and in art were filled by the time I got to registration.

14. The *Capitol* building is located in the nation's capital.

15. The sun does not shine for 186 days at the *North Pole.*

Answers: Exercise 30–2

1. The first rule in a old book about rules of etiquette reads, "Do not eat in mittens."
2. When he originated the role of Fonzie in the television series *Happy Days,* Henry Winkler earned about $750 per episode.
3. The *Monitor* and the *Merrimac* were the first iron-hulled ships to engage in battle.
4. Iowa's name comes from the Indian word *ayuhwa,* which means "sleepy ones."
5. The *New York Times* does not carry comic strips.
6. Judy Garland was the second lowest paid star in the film classic *The Wizard of Oz;* only the dog who portrayed Toto was paid less.
7. For distinguished accomplishments of people over age 70, we can look to Verdi, who wrote the song "Ave Maria" at age 85, and Tennyson, who wrote the short poem "Crossing the Bar" at age 80.
8. Handwriting experts say personality traits affect the way an individual dots an *i* and crosses a *t.*
9. The Italian word *ciao* is both a greeting and a farewell.
10. A sense of danger develops slowly in Shirley Jackson's short story "The Lottery."

Coverage: Exercise 30–2

(1) underlining not needed because title is not cited; (2) omit underlining with proper name; underline title of television show; (3) underline names of ships; (4) omit underlining with proper name; (5) underline title of a newspaper (does not include *the*); (6) underline movie title; underlining not needed for proper name; (7) do not underline title of short literary or musical works; (8) underline letters used as themselves; (9) omit underlining with proper name; underline foreign word; (10) use quotation marks for titles of short works

Answers: Exercise 30–3

1. In 1665, Harvard University graduated its first North American Indian, Caleb Cheeshateaumuck.
2. The first swim across the English Channel took twenty-one hours, forty-five minutes.
3. According to most doctors, the best places in the United States for allergy sufferers to live are in the deserts of Arizona.
4. When Sandra Day O'Connor was appointed to the Supreme Court by President Ronald Reagan in 1981, she became the first woman Supreme Court justice in American history.
5. Many college students today are required to take course in literature, social science, and language.

6. The energy crisis of 1973 prompted enforcement of a national speed limit of 55 mph.

7. It seems ironic that the paintings of Vincent van Gogh, who died penniless, now sell for millions of dollars.

8. The route of the Boston Marathon, run every April, covers twenty-six miles between Hopkinton, Massachusetts, and Boston, Massachusetts.

9. At fifty minutes before the scheduled liftoff, the Saturday launch was postponed.

10. The United Nations building in New York City has been a popular tourist attraction for years.

Answers, Exercise 30–4

1. The film *Quo Vadis* used 30,000 extras and 63 lions. [*or* thirty thousand extras and sixty-three lions]

2. The best time to use insecticides is 4:00 p.m. because that is when insects are most susceptible.

3. People in the United States spend $600 million a year on hot dogs. [Also correct are the spelled-out form, $600,000,000 and 600,000,000 dollars, but $600 million is most appropriate for academic writing.]

4. Four-fifths of everything alive on this earth is in the sea.

5. The earliest baseball game on record was played in 1846 on June 19 [*or* 19th] for a final score of 23 to 1 in four innings.

6. Aaron Montgomery Ward started the first mail order company in the United States in 1872 at 825 North Clark Street in Chicago.

7. The record for a human's broad jump is about 28 feet, one-quarter inch, and the record for a frog's broad jump is 13 feet, 5 inches.

8. Two hundred fifty words per minute is the reading speed of the typical reader. [*or:* The typical reader reads 250 words per minute.]

9. The yearly income of the average family in the United States in 1915 was $687. [Spelled-out form for money is also correct.]

10. Three out of four people who wear contact lenses are between 12 and 23 years of age.

11. Vine Deloria counts 315 Native American "tribes" in the United States today.

12. It will be about thirty degrees warmer in April.

13. Her date of birth may have been 26 B.C.E.

14. One teaspoon of baking soda will neutralize the acid in the 1 ½ cups of lemon juice.

15. They were born at 3:17 a.m. in 1900.

Coverage, Exercise 30–4

(1) numbers over 10 expressed in words and figures; (2) time; (3) money; (4) fraction; (5) date, words, and figures mixed in statistics; (6) address;

(7) statistics expressed with mixed figures and words; (8) sentence opened with figures; (9) date and money; (10) sentence opened with figures; (11) number over 10 expressed in words; (12) number over 10 expressed in words; (13) year expressed in words; (14) sentence opened with figures; measurement expressed in words; (15) time and date expressed in words

■ CHAPTER THIRTY-ONE

Answers: Exercise 31–1

A. *Analysis:* The quotation does not relate clearly to the sentence it follows. A transitional introduction to the quotation is needed. *Acceptable* (answers will vary): Many problems are caused when sensitive equipment overheats. Until now, researchers have failed to develop sensors that would warn of such overheating mainly because nearly all "microchips develop amnesia long before the temperature climbs to the boiling point of water" (Siwolop 111).

B. *Analysis.* The quotation omits several words but does not provide an ellipsis to indicate where material has been deleted. *Acceptable* (answers will vary): Many researchers believe that they would be able to "improve the efficiency of engines . . . if only they could supply them with electronic sensors" (Siwolop 111).

C. *Analysis.* The sentence is grammatically incorrect. The quotation does not fit with the rest of the sentence. Words need to be added so that the information flows smoothly. *Acceptable* (answers will vary): Several new developments have taken place at North Carolina State University in Raleigh where researchers "have successfully made microelectronic transistors that operate at temperatures of up to 1,200° F" (Siwolop 111).

D. *Analysis:* The tense of the verb in the quotation shifts from the tense of the verb in the previous sentence. Brackets can be used to change the tense of the verb in the quotation so that it agrees grammatically with the previous verb. *Acceptable* (answers will vary): In the past, there have been serious problems with sensors designed to detect heat. Until recently, "computer chips [couldn't] take the heat" (Siwolop 111) but now that problem may have been solved.

E. *Analysis:* The quotation is inaccurate; the word "long" is omitted while "up" is added. *Acceptable* (answers will vary): One of the problems in designing a heat sensor is that many "microchips develop amnesia long before the temperature climbs to the boiling point of water" (Siwolop 111).

Answers: Exercise 31–2

A. Answers will vary; here is one possibility:

Because genetic research is becoming increasingly important, scientists are seeking twins who are willing to participate in experiments either for pay or as volunteers. The Twins Foundation is confident that researchers will find the subjects they need because "there are approximately 4.5 million twin individuals in the United States alone, and about 70,000 more are born each year" (Begley 84).

B. Answers will vary; here is one possibility:

It is becoming increasingly difficult to assure that large-scale testing will be taken honestly. For example, in New York State, students stole copies of the Regents exam, and because of their actions "1,200 principals received instructions from the State Education Commissioner to look for *unusual scoring patterns* that would show that students had the answers beforehand" (Robbins 12).

C. Answers will vary.

Answers: Exercise 31–3

Analysis: This paraphrase is unacceptable because it uses many words and phrases from the original. Also, the first sentence uses the same sentence structures. *Acceptable paraphrase* (answers will vary considerably): When people want to create a sense of neighborhood where they live, they need to balance their interest in privacy with their desire for knowing their neighbors. Practically without being conscious of it, people manage the details of their lives to achieve the balance they need (Jacobs 141).

Answers: Exercise 31–4

A. Answers will vary; here is one acceptable paraphrase:

Women who live in underdeveloped or emerging countries frequently regard working with electronics as giving them higher status than other assembly line work. Most of these women are unaware that the electronics occupation may pose significant threats to their physical well-being. They have no way of knowing that NIOSH (National Institute on Occupational Safety and Health) has identified electronics plants in the United States as employing the largest amount of poison materials that may have a negative effect on workers' health in any industry. Certainly the dangers here in the United States are twice as threatening when they exist in Third World nations, which have no organization like NIOSH to act as watchdogs. In underdeveloped countries, the air in factories is often polluted with toxic vapors that arise from poisonous materials that are stored in uncovered vessels. The gas created by these chemicals and other substances is strong enough to make a worker lose consciousness (Ehrenreich and Fuentes 87).

Answers: Exercise 31–5

Analysis: This summary is unacceptable because it uses many words and phrases from the original. *Acceptable summary* (answers will vary considerably): When people respond badly to negative criticism, they are revealing poor self-esteem that usually results from childhood experience and that also indicates that they are afraid of success (Friedman 69).

Answers: Exercise 31–6

A. Answers will vary, but here is one possible summary:

A cloud hangs over testing programs because of an increase in cheating, as when students in New York State sold the state Regents examination in advance. This led to warnings that educators should watch for student scores that appear in unusual patterns (Robbins 12).

B. Answers will vary, but here is one possible summary:

Many women in underdeveloped countries regard electronics as a desirable career, but they are usually unaware that this industry has been identified by experts in the United States as posing serious threats to the health of workers (Ehrenreich and Fuentes 87).

C. Answers will vary.

■ CHAPTERS THIRTY-TWO THROUGH FORTY-ONE

No answers for these chapters.

■ CHAPTER FORTY-ONE

Answers and Coverage, Exercise 41–1

1. reasons [41c, plural object with *one of*]
   American [41c, singular for noun used as adjective]
2. United States [41c, *States* plural in *United States*]
   ten-foot [41c, singular for noun used as adjective]
3. rain, snow [41a, singular for noncount nouns]
4. much [41b, *much* the correct determiner with noncount noun *time*]
5. food, water [41a, noncount nouns always singular]

■ CHAPTER FORTY-TWO

Answers and Coverage, Exercise 42–1

1. *a* result [nonspecific use of singular count noun]; *the* first surgeon to cut into [singular count noun made specific by the word *first* and the phrase *to cut into . . .*, Rule 3 in Chart 177]; *the* human heart [representative use of singular count noun, Rule 2]
2. *the* middle of *the* twentieth century [widely understood meaning of singular count nouns, Rule 1]
3. *an* African American surgeon [first use of noun, *an* before vowel sound]

4. *An* injured young man, *a* Chicago hospital, *a* knife wound [first use of nouns, *an* or *a* depending on vowel or consonant sound]; *the* heart [wide comprehension of noun's meaning and the context make use specific, Rules 1 and 5]

5. *the* heart [wide comprehension, context, Rules 1 and 5]

▉ CHAPTER FORTY-THREE

Answers and Coverage, Exercise 43–1

1. The **beautiful antique glass** vase [Chart, 43b: adjective of judgment preceded adjective of age; adjective of age preceded adjective derived from noun]

2. her **mother's favorite jar** [Chart, 43b: determiner precedes descriptive adjective]

3. that **she almost** cried [43c, adverb of degree is positioned before word it modifies, *cried*]

4. "**Are you** all right?" [43a, inverted word order for questions, form of *be* precedes subject]

5. had **accidentally broken**, was **not extremely angry** [43c, adverbs of degree precede the word they modify]

▉ CHAPTER FORTY-FOUR

Answers, Exercise 44–1

Answers will vary.

▉ CHAPTER FORTY-FIVE

Answers and Coverage, Exercise 45–1

1. holding [45b, gerund after preposition]
2. do [45c, unmarked infinitive with *let*]
3. to replace [*replacing* also acceptable]
4. writing [45b, gerund after preposition]
5. training, typing [45a, gerunds as subjects]
6. to open [45c, infinitive following *hope*]
7. revive *or* to revive [45c, unmarked or marked infinitive with *help*]
8. buying [45b, gerund with *consider*];
   to look [45c, infinitive with *look at*]
9. putting, picking [45c, *putting* is gerund use after preposition; *picking* is same form for compound objects]
10. wishing [45b, gerund with *wish*]

Answers, Exercise 45–1

1. interesting [life conveys rather than experiences interest]
2. horrified [observers experience rather than convey horror]; injured [Kahlo experiences rather than causes injury]
3. disappointed [Kahlo experiences rather than causes disappointment]
4. disturbing [images cause rather than experience disturbance]
5. fascinating [works of art cause rather than experience fascination]; overwhelming [paintings overwhelm rather than experience being overwhelmed—*overwhelming* modifies the pronoun *them*, for which the reference is *paintings*]

■ CHAPTER FORTY-SIX

Answers and Coverage, Exercise 46–1

1. should have *or* ought to have [46a, past-tense form of auxiliary]
2. had to *or* needed to [46a, past-tense form of auxiliary]
3. could [46a, past-tense form of auxiliary]
4. may have, might have, could have, must have [46a, any of the past-tense forms for conveying possibility and making a guess are acceptable here]
5. should have *or* ought to have [46a, either past-tense form is acceptable here]; had to *or* needed to [46a, either past-tense form is acceptable]

Answers and Coverage, Exercise 46–2

1. should have been [46c, passive modal auxiliary verb with *Devi* receiving the action of the verb]
2. must have landed [46a, correct form for past-tense modal auxiliary verb expressing likelihood]
3. ought not to have [46a, correct form for modal auxiliary verb expressing advisability]
4. should not [46a, correct modal for expressing negative advisability rather than negative ability]
5. might not have [46c, correct form for active modal auxiliary verb expressing likelihood or possibility]